Appalachian Dance

Appalachian Dance

Creativity and Continuity in Six Communities

SUSAN EIKE SPALDING

University of Illinois Press
URBANA, CHICAGO, AND SPRINGFIELD

© 2014 by the Board of Trustees
of the University of Illinois
All rights reserved
Manufactured in the United States of America
1 2 3 4 5 C P 5 4 3 2 1
∞ This book is printed on acid-free paper.

Library of Congress Control Number: 2014946438
ISBN 978-0-252-03854-9 (hardcover)
ISBN 978-0-252-08015-9 (paperback)
ISBN 978-0-252-09645-7 (e-book)

To Elise, with thanks for the music.

Contents

Illustrations

Photographs

Maps

Preface

The first time I saw old time square dancing and flatfooting, I was traveling through the Appalachians in the early 1970s. I was instantly smitten, struck by something so compelling in the dancing that I could not stop thinking about it. I had grown up with one "foot" in modern dance and the other in folk dance. I was fortunate to have a modern dance teacher who emphasized improvisation and expressiveness, and fortunate to have Girl Scout leaders who valued folk dancing, both in its own right and as a means to develop interpersonal skills. But I had never experienced community-based dancing that grew out of and was passed down through local tradition, instead of being learned in a class. Something about the style of the movement and the sound of the music would not let me go.

Later, living in Southwest Virginia, I was able to experience these kinds of dancing for myself, in local venues. I wanted to know more and to share the dance with others. As a research fellow with the Center for Appalachian Studies and Services at East Tennessee State University, and with the help of Appalshop in Whitesburg, Kentucky, I began to document the dancing videographically. With folklorist Jane Harris Woodside, I also began to interview dancers, musicians, callers, and organizers in Southwest Virginia and Northeast Tennessee. I looked for written sources about old time dancing, yet discovered few. Most that I found were disturbingly general, talking about "the" dance of Appalachia as if it were one thing, as if clogging could be defined and described in one way, and as if square dance figures were the same everywhere in the region. I knew this to be false, because within an hour of my home in any direction, I saw that the dancing looked and felt different. I recorded the dancing at one location in Labanotation, a system that records movement in a score, detailing specific arm, leg, foot, hand, and head gestures in space and time. It became clear that this approach really did not capture the dancing completely, because even within one community's very clear aesthetic there was a great deal of individuality. As I continued the quest to understand the dancing, I was fortunate to receive support from the Virginia Foundation for the Humanities for video documentation and interviews and the production of an Appalshop documentary on dance in three Southwest Virginia communities, with commentary by folklorist Elizabeth Fine, sociologist Helen Lewis, and historian David Whisnant.

Supporting a continuing desire to highlight particular community traditions, the Center for Appalachian Studies and Services sponsored three conferences on Appalachian dance traditions. The first of these, in 1989, brought together scholars who had devoted their time to exactly this consideration, along with dancers representing local Native American, African American, and European American traditions. The result was an edited book of articles and interviews on square dance and footwork dance, mostly in the southeastern United States, incorporating some related traditions elsewhere. I was inspired, listening to and talking with all of these people, with their array of knowledge and experience. Believing that there were deeper and more thorough ways to think about dance, I became a midlife doctoral student at Temple University, where I was encouraged to craft a program that included dance, sociology, and anthropology, and to engage with the folklore program at the University of Pennsylvania. As a result of my work there, I began to look more closely at factors such as societal change and cultural interaction in the evolution of local tradition. I arrived in Kentucky as square dancing and footwork dancing traditions were on the wane, but I continued to seek out community dances. In 1999, a Berea College Undergraduate Research grant supported students Layla Thomas, LaVon Rice, and Dana Mason, who worked with me in documenting and interviewing Kentucky dancers; later documentation was undertaken in conjunction with the 2003 Smithsonian Festival of American Folklife, in which dancers from one Kentucky community participated. I became more and more aware of the interplay among popular dance, theatrical dance, and local dance customs, and came to see the importance of placing local traditions in a broader regional and national dance context.

I never imagined an eventual book, but the same impulse that inspired the first documentation, the desire to share what I have learned, has resulted in the present volume, encompassing documentation and interviews from the 1980s, 1990s, and the early years of the twenty-first century. In writing this book, I have tried to keep in mind many audiences: scholars in dance, American Studies, cultural studies, and Appalachian history, sociology, and culture, as well as graduate and undergraduate students in such classes, and casual readers with an interest in any of these subjects. As a result, I have, for example, included Appalachian history and culture content that may be new to the dance reader, and approaches in dance scholarship that may be unfamiliar to the Appalachian Studies reader.

Great numbers of individuals and institutions have helped me along the nearly three-decade journey to this book, beginning with the Center for Appalachian Studies and Services and then-director Richard Blaustein, who believed in my notions about the connection between traditional dance and local society, and who supported my first research and the Appalachian Dance conferences. Jane Harris Woodside, then-editor of *Now and Then Magazine*, was a wonderful colleague in these endeavors. Her background in folklore helped me immeasurably, along with her steady, practical partnership in organizing conferences and her clear editorial eye in preparing the book. Helen Lewis has been my mentor since the beginning, encouraging me, posing questions, and making observations that continually pushed my thinking. I learned a great deal from the artistry and cultural sensitivity of Appalshop videographer Anne Lewis Johnson and her tireless and detailed work with me in editing video footage into two documentaries. Odette Blum and Ilene Fox of the Dance Notation Bureau were each a great help in the early stages of the work. My Temple University mentors, Brenda Dixon-Gottschild, Sarah Hilsendager, and Magali Safarti-Larson, along with Roger Abrahams of the University of Pennsylvania, guided my thinking in new directions, helping me to focus on specifics that I might have missed. Among my mentors at the Laban Institute of Movement Studies were Jackie Hand-Vigario, Karen Kohn Bradley, and Janis Pforsich, each of whom advanced my use of Laban Movement Analysis in studying Appalachian dance.

Berea College has contributed to this work on many levels. Shannon Wilson and Harry Rice of the Hutchins Library Department of Special Collections and Archives have been more than helpful, with their intimate knowledge of Appalachian history and culture, and of the collections I needed to access. They collaborated with me in securing a transcription grant from the Kentucky Historical Society in order to make Peter Rogers's extensive interviews more accessible to me and to others. Interlibrary Loan Librarian Patty Tarter has been forever pleasant, diligent, and caring. The Kentucky Folklife Program has been another partner in my pursuit of local dance. I have enjoyed working with Bob Gates, Mark Brown, and Brent Bjorkman on Folklife Festivals and other projects. Beth Bingman and Rich Kirby of Appalshop have always been good friends, willing to connect me with resources and with other dancers.

The University of Illinois Press has been most helpful and encouraging. Editor Laurie Matheson has been patient with my lengthy process and has always been ready to answer questions, allay concerns, and provide guidance, as has Assistant Acquisitions Editor Dawn Durante. I am grateful to Jeff Place, archivist for the Smithsonian Center for Folklife and Cultural Heritage, for his ongoing interest. And equally grateful to T-Vaughn Webb, assistant director of the Blue

Ridge Institute and Museum of Ferrum College, for helping me to connect with the Martinsville community in 1992, whose dance was first documented by Kip Lornell in 1978. He also provided photos, as did Jonathan Jeffrey of the Western Kentucky University Archives; Jeanne Nicholson Siler, community historian with the Fayette Area Historical Initiative; Katharine Shearer, editor of Clinch Mountain Press; Brianne Wright, city archivist for the Kingsport Public Library and Archives; the Lexington Herald Leader; the Berea College Hutchins Library Department of Special Collections and Archives; Paula Allen Photography; Warren Case; Dale Johnson; Bev Futrell; and Joyce Whitaker. Photos have been prepared for submission through Sharon Ruble's professional care in digital photo imaging. It must be said that none of my work would have been possible without the unfailing support and encouragement of my family and friends. To each of them, I am deeply grateful.

Special thanks are due to individuals who share my passion for Appalachian dance. I have enjoyed dancing and talking with them and have learned from them for many years. Pat Napier brought the Kentucky square dancing of his youth to life for me and for generations of dancers through Christmas Country Dance School. Peter Rogers has taken me on literal and virtual tours of his childhood home area in Harlan and Letcher Counties in Kentucky, introduced me to the Carcassonne dance and to numbers of dancers there, and engaged me in many hours of enjoyable discussion about dancing and community life. I have had the joy of dancing to the old time music of Donna and Lewis Lamb, who have played for dances for decades. They have talked with me about their experiences, and they introduced me to dancing in Powell County, Kentucky. Ruby Caudill, Dale and Beverley Johnson, Jon and Loretta Henrickson, Richard Jett, Kirby Smith, Floyd Sloan, and Charlie and Joyce Whitaker have all enthusiastically carried on continuing conversations with me about their dancing. I am honored to have known each of these people, and I am grateful to them and to the many others who have given generously of their experience, memories, and information, dancing and talking with me over these nearly three decades. They are named in each chapter in the context of their communities. I offer this work to these individuals in all humility, in hopes that the stories I tell may in some measure reflect their experience.

1. Dynamic Traditions

Fiddles and banjos ring out in the evening air, and couples join hands together in a circle. At the sound of the caller's voice, the circle moves as one. At another call, sets of two couples form small "squares" and dance through sequences like "Cage the Bird" and "Take a Little Peek." Later, the music draws individuals to the dance floor to match their footwork to the sound of the band. This is old time Appalachian dancing, known in the region since the late nineteenth century.

Old time square dancing is a circle of any number of couples who divide into smaller groups of two couples to dance figures at the direction of a caller, beginning and ending the dance with figures for the whole group. Footwork dancing, known by any of its many names—flatfooting, clogging, hoedowning, and buck dancing, among others—is usually a solo improvisation to the rhythms of the music, though it may be danced in couples or in loosely connected groups. These dance forms exist within the framework of the specific culture and history of a given community, as well as within the broader culture and history of the region, and within the framework of a rich and varied regional dance heritage. Each community has its own versions of these dances. Six different dance communities are represented in this volume: three in Eastern Kentucky, one in Northeast Tennessee, and two in Southwest Virginia. Juxtaposed, the stories illustrate the diversity of Appalachian culture and experience, local and national influences that have contributed to each community's unique development, and the individual and group creativity that is manifested in the dance and the dance event in each place. Possibly the most prevalent forms in the region in the early twentieth century, old time square dancing and footwork dancing, have waxed and waned in popularity from decade to decade.

My initial goal in writing this book was to make clear the specificity of local tradition. Even though the same types of dance have occurred in many different communities, close observation reveals distinctions among the styles, forms, and context. Though the movement of the square dance of one community may appear almost identical to another's, it may mean something very different.[1] One dance may be an opportunity for couples to go out for an evening, dancing primarily with each other, and another may be an occasion for individuals and families to gather with lots of mixing. One group of dancers may be dance hobbyists who travel widely to dance at different venues, while another group dances always in the same location, using dance to strengthen bonds within an already close community. Though in each place the term "community" is important and a good description of the group of dancers, it is evident that each group defines itself in ways that are different from the others. The stories of these six communities demonstrate that Appalachian culture is neither homogeneous nor isolated.

Though at first I planned simply to describe the dancing and dance communities as seen through the eyes of the participants and as I experienced them, my attention was increasingly drawn to the dynamism of local traditions and the creativity involved in their evolution. Never static, dance traditions in each community constantly shift and change over the course of decades. Like all customs, they are characterized by "flexibility of substance" or continued evolution. Characteristics are retained, discarded, or altered according to adherence to precedents.[2] As cultural anthropologist Cynthia Novack (aka Cynthia Cohen Bull) observed in her book *Sharing the Dance*: "Culture is embodied. . . . Movement constitutes an ever-present reality in which we constantly participate. . . . In these actions, we participate in and reinforce culture, and we also create it."[3] Internal and external factors have influenced the dancing, dancers, and dance events in each community. Any change that has occurred is not mere passive reaction to events and trends but is an active response on the part of dancers, callers, musicians, and organizers. Any practice "is not only a collective sedimentation passed on through generations but an opportunity for individuality [and] agency" and results from an interplay of the two, according to psychological anthropologist Thomas Csordas.[4] Dance anthropologist Andree Grau acknowledges that a "tension [exists] between cultural norms and human creativity, between socio-historical constraints and human agency" as customs evolve.[5] Individuals and groups contribute to the evolution of cultural expression through a creative process by making choices from available repertoire based on expectations, experience, and local sensibility.[6] Dance in each community has changed over time as a result of such choices, both large and small, made by individuals—dancers, callers, musicians, leaders—based on their experiences and beliefs. These were grounded in a specific community and family history and were influenced by what they saw around them locally, by regional and national events, and sometimes by the intervention of institutions. A series of innovations adopted by the participants themselves in successive generations led to the movement, style, and structure of each locality's dancing as it appeared when I began documenting it. In the ensuing years, more such selections have changed the dance traditions further. Because of these creative decisions, differences abound among the communities. As a few examples, some communities promenade between figures and others do not; some begin or end their square dance with several figures for the whole group and others perform only one; people in some communities dance with an elongated vertical posture, and those in other communities prefer to use an angular bend to knees, hips, and elbows.

I have learned much from the work of scholars of dance traditions in other countries and our own.[7] In addition, in the last two decades a number of insightful books have analyzed dance forms similar to, and perhaps "cousins" of, Appalachian square dancing.[8] Some authors have documented Appalachian dance traditions in specific areas. LeeEllen Friedland interviewed dancers in Eastern Kentucky in 1979, Burt Feintuch discussed dancing and community in South Central Kentucky in 1981, Bob Dalsemer described dances in five West Virginia communities in 1982, and the traditional music periodical *The Old Time Herald* has for many years included descriptions of community dances by Phil Jamison and others. Perhaps the earliest extensive analysis of an Appalachian dance community was Gail Matthews's 1983 analysis of freestyle clogging in Haywood, North Carolina, in which she explored the relationship between style choices and values.[9] Recently, the Augusta Heritage Center in Elkins, West Virginia, has been conducting oral histories in connection with the Mountain Dance Trail. The present volume addresses two areas that remain almost entirely exclusive of one another: dance scholarship and Appalachian studies. Appalachian dance and culture are little represented at dance research conferences, and only a few sessions at Appalachian studies conferences include discussion of dance, though there seems to be considerable interest. I hope to bridge the gap between these two areas of study and to contribute to ongoing dialogues about the diversity of Appalachian culture, the embodiment of meaning in movement, and the dynamic nature of tradition.

In writing this book, I have tried to present each community on its own terms, to let people in each community tell their own stories, and to give the reader some regional and national context. Each community's account can stand alone, complete in itself, yet the stories have striking similarities and overlaps in some cases, and striking contrasts in others. I have enjoyed participating in the dancing whenever I could during the course of the last twenty-five years, and I have interviewed dancers, callers, musicians, and organizers during that time. Much of the material has been read by members of the communities over the years, and their suggestions and feedback have influenced my writing and research. This work is an attempt to express as genuinely as possible the experience of dancing as people have enjoyed it, or continue to enjoy it, in these six dance communities.

Though I have attempted to tell the stories of these communities with authenticity, it is not possible for me to be truly objective. As dance ethnographer Frank Hall points out, the researcher is not detached.[10] I was drawn to Appalachian old time dancing when I first saw it more than thirty years ago. The music made my heart happy then, and it continues to do so today. I enjoy doing this kind of dancing, and I enjoy seeing other people do it. My own predispositions, feelings, thoughts, and ideas affect my experience of the dance events, how I tell about the dancing, and how I choose which elements of context to foreground in each case. Dance ethnographer Theresa Buckland believes that "truth is a kaleidoscope of possibilities," depending on who is looking at the dance and where he or she chooses to focus.[11] There are many ways of telling the stories of these communities, and mine is only one.

Because the documentation and research have taken place over the course of more than two decades, I try to make clear in each chapter the period on which I focus, describing a particular dance evening that took place in a specific year. Each chapter casts back to previous decades, mostly as the consultants' narratives have led me, in order to comprehend more fully some of the many threads that contributed to each community's dancing as it appeared in the 1980s, 1990s, or early part of this century, whenever it was first documented.

Understanding Dance

Documenting dance either videographically or in a system of notation and analysis is an important first step in coming to understand it. My analytical grounding is in Laban Movement Analysis (LMA), an international system. LMA examines movement in terms of the qualities of space, time, weight, and flow, looking at the carriage of the whole body and the relationships of individual body parts, such as arms and legs. It also analyzes pairs and groups of people in terms of these qualities. The system contains no assessment as to good or bad; it simply serves as a tool for examining the detail of movement. For example, dancers in one community may swivel their legs in their footwork dancing, emphasizing a strong, quick upward and outward kick on the upbeat, while another may fluidly and resiliently bend and straighten their knees with each beat, keeping their feet close to the floor. In one community, several people may flatfoot in close proximity without touching or making eye contact, still linked with each other through mutual awareness. In another, the footwork dancing is always a partner dance with strong eye contact. A partner swing in one group may be exuberantly energetic, while in another it may be a casual walk-around. Using this system has helped me to appreciate the subtleties of the dancing as I watched it or participated in it. The movement of the dance does not exist in a vacuum, though, but is part of a dance event. The venue, the time of day, what else happens before, during, and after the dance, who participates, and even what they wear all communicate something about what the dance means to them, what place it holds in the community, and what values it expresses.

Participation in the dancing has allowed me to experience the style and the energy of it from the inside. In her book on samba, performance studies scholar Barbara Browning discussed the necessity of "thinking with your body" to understand dance.[12] It is easy to kinesthetically perceive one community's leisurely approach to dancing, and the sense of drive of another, the comfortable closeness of a partner hold in one, and the almost arm's length distance in another. One community's dancing focuses on connectedness, while another's centers on individual performance in the framework of a group, though the dance may appear similar. Still, each of us has our own movement vocabulary and our own cultural background. When I participate in dancing, my perceptions are filtered through my own background and my own imagination.[13] Acknowledging that, I have attempted to learn what the dance means to regular dancers in each place, using observation, participation, interview, and, where possible, participants' own writings. What they had to say about other aspects of their lives illuminated their dance experience as well. As some talked about their parents or grandparents, the school they attended, farming practices, wagon training, work in the North, or live radio shows, it was possible to piece together an idea of the ways that the history of the area, socially, politically, and economically, helped to shape the dance and what it expresses. As American studies scholar Jane Desmond points out, "Though we tend to think of dances . . . as distinctive aggregations of steps, every dance exists in a complex network of relationships to other dances and other nondance ways of using the body" and within the framework of the particular society and the many elements of its history.[14] Buckland believes that "when conceived as a repository of cultural meanings both past and present, the moving body may be a source to be observed and documented from the outside. Traces of the past may be discovered in the ways in which people execute particular movements and use their bodies."[15] The present book is about dance, and I believe that dance is important in and of itself. At the same time, dance provides a valuable way to reconsider the history and cultures of the Appalachian region.

Dance is more than recreation or entertainment. It is expressive of the dancer, of his or her relationship with the other dancers, of the group's aesthetic preferences, and of their cultural background. Dance grows out of a community and a culture, expresses what is important to it, helps to navigate through periods of change, and can sometimes contribute to change. It contains values important to the people who do it, and it helps to maintain or to modify those values. Dance ethnographer Andrew Ward believes, in fact, that we should "think about dance not just as an activity but as a way of being," a way of experiencing ourselves in relation to others and to our world. We choose styles and forms that support our understanding.[16] Dance is one aspect of a person's overall movement vocabulary that communicates how that person sees himself or herself in relation to people, situations, and social structures.

Because of this, movement and dance have relevance to many fields, among them sociology, anthropology, and political science. Desmond observed that "movement style is an important mode of distinction between social groups and is usually actively learned or passively absorbed in the home and community. So ubiquitous, so 'naturalized' as to be nearly unnoticed as a symbolic system, movement is a primary not secondary social 'text'—complex, . . . continuously changing, its articulation signals group affiliation and group differences, whether consciously performed or not."[17] Not only group affiliation, but larger social structures may be embodied in movement. Sociologist, anthropologist, and philosopher Pierre Bourdieu believed that "the unconscious braiding of movement practice and ideologies constrains people to perpetuate social structures at the level of the body."[18]

Underlying the demonstration of group affiliation and the perpetuation of social structures is the embodiment by dance and movement of "ideas about life's 'large questions': Where do I belong in the world? How do human beings behave? Where do I come from and with whom do I go through life? What do I value?" according to dance ethnographer and theorist Deidre Sklar.[19] Cynthia Cohen Bull's exploration of contrasting values inherent in the movement of classical ballet and Ghanaian traditional dance serves as an example. While ballet highlights the visual, concentrating on line and shape, Ghanaian dance is based in listening to the rhythms of the music. Ballet emphasizes "the body's precise placement and shaping in space" and clear group synchrony. Ghanaian dancers "appear unified, [but] they seldom produce an exact spatial unison because the emphasis of their movement lies in rhythmic, dynamic action." The spatial focus of ballet is carried into hierarchical distinctions between soloists and corps de ballet. The aural focus in Ghanaian dance "shifts attention to social relationships among dancers, musicians, and viewers . . . a sense of group participation prevails." Further, ballet expresses beliefs about gender roles. Though the movement of both male and female dancers requires great strength, the ballerina, lifted, supported, and turned by the danseur "convey[s] weightlessness, airiness. The danseur, by contrast, appears solid, stable."[20] Likewise, concepts and values are embedded in every dance form, classical, popular, or traditional. The dancing of each community presented here embodies its own set of values and concepts. Although community values and ideas are not the focus of this book, I have sought to identify them as they have emerged in relation to the dancing.

Even systems of thought are linked to movement patterns. Studying Jewish and Italian immigrant communities in New York, David Efron, a student of anthropologist Franz Boas, went so far as to say that not only were the "significant differences in gestural patterns . . . determined . . . by the interaction between learned traditions and social conditions" but also that "differences in gestural systems embody differences in the aesthetic structuring of thought."[21] Observing contrasts in movement style in the game of cricket as played in Britain and as played in the Trobriand Islands, dance ethnologist Sally Ann Ness hypothesized that the dissimilarities in phrasing and spatial organization "may well be the same differences that appear in such realms of activity as politics, economics, and religion."[22] If movement embodies values, perpetuates social structures, and is related to the structure of thought, one may consider how traditional dance not only reflects and expresses culture but also helps to shape it and to change it. Dance may have the potential to influence decision making, according to Grau. "Dance is a social fact, conveying meaning through human interactions; thus it reflects ideologies and world views. Yet dance can also be used to explore and manipulate the social reality, with the potential to influence decision-making in other social contexts and occasionally to prefigure political actions."[23] For example, it is perhaps no accident that among polite society in Europe and America, during the decades preceding the American and French Revolutions, the more democratic country dance for groups of people began to supplant the more hierarchical and performative minuet for couples. As a part of the fabric of other socially prescribed and meaningful ways of moving and embodying values, thought, and action, dance becomes a tool to navigate and negotiate social change, and perhaps to influence it. These community stories hint at that possibility.

Themes

A number of themes have presented themselves during the process of developing this book. Above, I described two overarching themes: the dynamic nature of tradition as it continuously evolves, and the individual and group creativity involved in shaping that evolution. Other themes have also emerged across several of the articles: the effect of cultural exchange in the evolution of tradition; the influence of national policies and trends; the consequences of industrialization; the role of an individual in creating or perpetuating a kind of dance; and the influence of institutions in supporting particular forms of dancing.

Cultural exchange has influenced the development of the dancing in each of the communities. Interaction among the three historically predominant ethnic groups in the region—European American, African American, and Native American—has been important in the evolution of old time dance. But rather than think only in terms of race, it is necessary to cast intercultural influences more broadly and more subtly, considering such interactions as urban/rural, popular/traditional, national/local, northern/southern. When one cultural group encounters the movement vocabulary of another, each person and each community make choices based on their own values, preferences, previous experience, and beliefs about what is appropriate and pleasing to do. Sometimes elements of the new are embraced and integrated into the existing form; sometimes the new form or style is seen as a threat, and efforts are made to suppress it, or to protect members of the community from it; sometimes it is enjoyed as a passing fad; and sometimes local traditions influence popular or elite culture.[24] During the jazz era, for instance, dance styles collided in almost all communities described in this volume, with markedly dissimilar outcomes.

Square dancing and footwork dancing are part of a rich tapestry of dance past and present in the region, as will be seen in chapter 2. They are also part of a larger fabric that includes social and philosophical trends and economic and political events. Each of the six communities has been influenced in its own way by national currents and has in turn contributed to their direction. The interface between popular culture and local tradition has been continuous since the early days of settlement of the region by those of European and African descent. The progressive ideals of the early twentieth century changed both the national and local disposition toward dance. Radio barn dance shows represented and redefined local traditions for a national audience and affected local people's attitudes toward regional dance and music. The work of folklorists as well as the folk revival of the mid-twentieth century drew attention to the local dancing and music and contributed to its evolution. While these trends served to sustain or promote these dance traditions in some communities, in others they contributed to its decline. Federal policies seemingly unrelated to dance produced changes in some local dancing. The end of racial segregation had unexpected consequences in an African American dance community, and the Office of Economic Opportunity contributed directly to the revival of another community's dance tradition. Perhaps most striking in their recurring appearance in old time dancers' accounts are the years of the Great Depression and of World War II. In almost every community, these two periods stood out in consultants' narratives—the former usually as a time of close community and self-sufficiency highlighted by dancing, and the latter as a time of rapid change and dispersal, when the dancing changed or even disappeared for a time.

The rapid industrialization of the region in the early twentieth century, along with increasing reliance on technology, had a marked effect on dancing, its look, and its place in the life of each community. The transition away from an agrarian economy in areas in the Great Valley of Virginia and Tennessee resulted in a new construct for community, helping to change the meaning of the dance. The migration of thousands of African American southerners to the coalfields had an effect on cultural expression there, as migrants brought new styles and forms of music and dance with them. Nostalgia for the past supported by new media technology and by popular culture caused square dancing and footwork dancing to wane and then to reemerge in new contexts with renewed vigor in some areas. Other communities responded by adhering strongly to existing traditions, still others by blending local tradition and popular culture to create new styles of dance.

In many of the communities presented here, one or more individuals stand out as motivating force, as organizer, as inspiration, or as tradition bearer. The particular goals and manner of leadership of key individuals guided the course of each community's dance. Organizers working for community development cast the dance in that light. Leaders who defined themselves as educators felt themselves to be working for the betterment of the participants through dancing. Those who saw themselves as tradition bearers hoped to keep tradition alive. Institutions such as state arts councils or parks and recreation departments, philanthropic societies, or networks like Council of the Southern Mountains nourished some of these dance communities. Parks and recreation departments and arts councils provided direct financial support and even venues. Philanthropic organizations like the Russell Sage Foundation provided both philosophical grounding and pragmatic application to create a powerful thrust that continues to the present, beyond the region more than within it. Smaller local institutions like a privately owned music center or sweet shop drew dancers in numbers and altered or even transformed traditions.

Organization of Chapters

Chapters 3 through 8 are the core of the book. I see these chapters as falling into either three pairs or two triads. As three pairs: chapters 3 and 4 describe two slowly evolving square dance communities, one black and one white, their divergent responses to social change, and the opposite effects of similar influences; chapters 5 and 6 represent reactions to the rapid social change of the early twentieth century, one a cultural blending to create a new style and the other a deliberate intervention with national effect; and chapters 7 and 8 describe contemporary dance communities that use dance for community development in contrasting ways. As two triads: chapters 3, 4, and 5 are geographically linked (Southwest Virginia and Northeast Tennessee) and demonstrate different kinds of cultural exchange in the evolution of old time dancing. They juxtapose the once-forgotten black fiddle and square dance traditions and the jazz era dancing more often associated with African American culture. These three chapters demonstrate three different responses to industrialization. In one, traditional dance returned after a hiatus, but in a different context; in another, the dance tradition was maintained almost unchanged for decades; and in the third, old time dancing was transformed. Chapters 6, 7, and 8 describe Kentucky communities. In chapter 6 the focus is on Pine Mountain Settlement School, because questions persisted about the relative merit and influence of settlement schools in relation to local dance traditions. The succeeding chapters describe two contemporary dance events whose leaders drew inspiration in part from their experience at settlement schools and carried forward some of the principles learned there. These three chapters illustrate some of the unexpected twists and turns that the evolution of tradition can take. Deliberate intervention had far-reaching results, and local tradition endured, adopting elements of the proffered replacement.

The reader will undoubtedly discover other themes that run through the chapters, and other similarities and differences among communities. I have become curious, for example, about the way musicians talk about music and dance. It would be interesting to compare the remarks of Leonard Bowles in chapter 3 with those of Lee Sexton in chapter 8. I hope that reading these stories will inspire further exploration in the worlds of American dance traditions in general and Appalachian dance traditions in particular, with an eye toward the ways dance embodies values and relates to other social structures.

2. Lively Dance Currents

The Myth of Isolation

When I mention my interest in regional dance traditions to people not acquainted with scholarship in Appalachian Studies, the first reactions often include comments about a pure Irish or English heritage here, or theories about the persistence of a very old dance tradition because of severe isolation and poverty. The truth is that the region was never as homogeneous, as poor, or as isolated as was once believed, and many kinds of social and theatrical dance were available to residents of the region as early as the 1790s.

Sociologist Wilma Dunaway believes that the "agrarian myth" of the noble self-sufficient subsistence farmer in Appalachia has roots in the Jeffersonian era.[1] The myth has been perpetuated and reborn as "a creature of the urban imagination."[2] In fact, travel across and through the mountains by rivers and trails predated the European and African descendants who traversed them in the eighteenth century. The region was already part of a "world system" of economy, as Dunaway points out, with Cherokee and Shawnee trading skins and furs to Europeans.[3] Geographer Gene Wilhelm documented trails and trade routes used by native peoples crossing the Blue Ridge for centuries. New settlers used the routes to move to the area and to travel back to the more settled areas to the east to sell produce and livestock.[4] By 1750, people living in Southwest Virginia drove herds of cattle and took wagonloads of farm goods across the state and to Baltimore, Philadelphia, and even New Orleans, interacting with local customs and gathering news along the way. A contemporary observer described "caravans" of "wagons . . . large and heavily laden with hides, beeswax, furs, feathers, ginseng, canes for fishing-rods, maple sugar, and other products of a mountains region."[5]

Map 1. Overview of the communities in Eastern Kentucky, Northeast Tennessee, and Southwest Virginia. Cartography by Dick Gilbreath, Director, Gyula Pauer Center for Cartography and GIS, University of Kentucky.

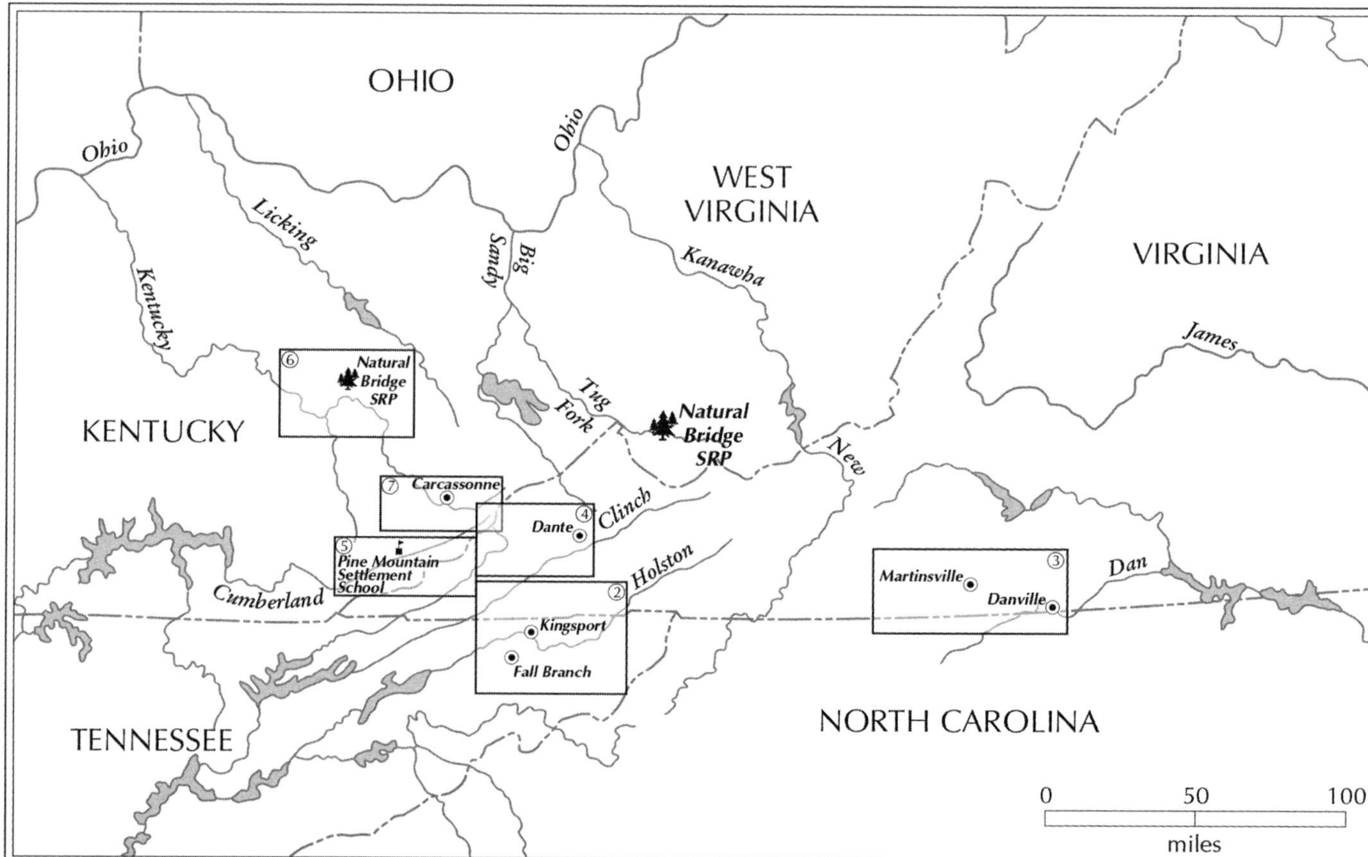

Several rivers flow outward from the mountains to the Ohio River and eventually to the Mississippi, with tributaries reaching far into remote counties, and travel on them likely predates eighteenth-century settlers. The Kentucky and Cumberland Rivers begin in the Eastern Kentucky hills, the Tennessee River has its sources in the mountains of Southwest Virginia, and the New River flows from Western North Carolina through Virginia's Blue Ridge, joining the Kanawha. All provided connections for trade and travel via the Ohio and Mississippi to New Orleans. If markets there were the destination, flatboat crews traveled back to Kentucky, Tennessee, and Virginia overland on the Natchez Trace. Otherwise, goods could be further carried by ocean vessel up the East Coast as far as New York. The Smith River empties ultimately into the coastal waters of North Carolina. It is the one river directly relevant to areas discussed in this book that flows east to the Atlantic Ocean, beginning in the Blue Ridge, flowing through Martinsville, and joining first the Dan River and then the Roanoke, providing easy transport of goods to eastern markets. Rafts, flatboats, keelboats, and eventually steamboats carried goods to market on these rivers from all over the region. In addition, manufactured goods, news, and professional people from the East regularly traveled the rivers and roads into the region throughout the nineteenth century. The Ohio River provided a standard tour route for professional performers beginning in 1820.[6]

Dunaway contends that the notion of the Appalachian region as predominantly subsistence farms was inaccurate, since at least 90 percent sold at least some products and relied on merchants for staples like coffee and sugar.[7] Exploring in the Appalachian region began in earnest in the 1730s.[8] Settlements were established within a few decades, and entrepreneurship followed immediately on its heels. Clay County, Kentucky, serves as an example. The first settlers arrived in the 1790s, and by 1804 a thriving salt manufacture was established, with the help of slave labor, on Goode Creek, a tributary of the Kentucky River.[9] A lively mercantile business grew up in the same area. In Southwest Virginia, "mountain agriculture was commercialized quite early and to a surprisingly high degree." Settlers had come with intentions of achieving economic independence.[10] Geographer Tyrel Moore found that the economy in the steep hills of the Cumberland Plateau of Eastern Kentucky in the nineteenth century was a blend of export, local exchange, and farming for family use. Ginseng, furs, deer hams, chestnuts, honey, and beeswax were exported to Ohio via waterways, and some products were traded among neighbors. Items such as butter, wool, and flax were produced on the family farms for their own use, or traded locally. Cattle, hogs, and grain were raised for food and for exchange. Most towns had grain mills, tanneries, salt works, and ironworks.[11] The romantic agrarian image is also belied by nineteenth century accounts. For example, an 1857 traveler on the recently constructed railroad to Bristol, Virginia/Tennessee stopped along the way in the "pleasant town" of Abingdon and in Saltville, the center of Southwest Virginia's thriving salt industry. Arriving in Bristol, a town newly established to accommodate the end of the railroad line, the visitor found a bustling place: "Trains of empty and loaded cars, engines puffing and fuming, vast piles of wood, machine-shops and taverns. . . . warehouses full of wheat and corn, great herds of grunting unambitious swine . . . crowds of busy men . . . speculators . . . insolent stage-drivers . . . babbling politicians."[12]

Studies have shown that during the nineteenth century, the Appalachian region was similar to other rural areas in terms of the heterogeneity of the population and accessibility. Roads increasingly connected the region internally and externally. According to historian Ronald Lewis, farmers carried produce and livestock out of the region to markets and returned with "goods, cash, and ideas. . . . lawyers, doctors, seasonal teachers, tax collectors, circuit preachers, peddlers, salesmen and mailmen traveled" the same routes in reverse, bringing news and popular culture to the communities in the mountains. "The high level of newspaper and periodical subscriptions, and later catalog circulation, in the mountains suggests an ongoing desire for knowledge of and goods from the broader world."[13] Appalachian farmers produced far more in terms of agricultural products for market than other southern farms and plantations, with the exception of cotton.[14] During the Civil War, the railroad became a link between Southwest Virginia and the southern states, and it became "a major Confederate breadbasket," supplying not only grain for bread, but also corn and vegetables. Southwest Virginia's lead mines were the only source of lead for Confederate ammunition, and the railroad transported it to the troops.[15]

Variations did come into being among residents of what was then the West, in terms of mobility and class. The earliest nonnative settlers of the region were all engaged in the business of establishing homes on the frontier and, as a result, were relatively equal. Quickly an elite emerged, related to market towns and to the adoption of slavery. Differences in connectedness to other settlements and to state governments developed among counties and even within the same county. For example, Greene County, Tennessee, in the fertile valley, had easy access to the Tennessee River and its tributaries and could transport goods to Knoxville using flatboats, unlike some of its neighboring counties. By 1830 there were, in effect, "two Appalachias," according to historian Van Beck Hall: the wealthier counties with market towns and the "back counties" farther from transportation.[16] Historian David Hsiung found that "[i]ndividuals linked to the road network developed an outward-looking view, but others who had more difficulty moving about the region were less geographically and emotionally connected and therefore developed a more inward-turning perspective."[17] While the larger towns connected easily with national markets, the more remote counties turned their attention to the needs of daily living. Though a few places, such as Tug Fork and Beech Creek, Kentucky, were inaccessible enough that they remained more or less self-contained until World War II, most areas had at least some connection to the larger towns and to popular culture and a broader economy. Even the "back counties" were not truly "backward," though their elite neighbors held that image of them. Analyzing voting patterns among settlers in Appalachian Virginia between 1790 and 1830, Hall found that they were "more diversified, less fearful of change, and more inclined to use government to accomplish development than were 'the more cosmopolitan, longer settled residents of Virginia counties east of the Blue Ridge.'" Both the wealthier counties and the "back counties" worked for such common goals as improved roads.[18] Even though popular culture was less available in the "back counties" during the nineteenth century, in most cases traveling minstrel and then medicine shows provided some contact with it.

Increasing railroad construction contributed both to the modernization of the region and to the distinctions between towns on travel corridors and those farther away. In the late 1800s, three major railroads were constructed into the Appalachian Mountains. The Chesapeake and Ohio connected Richmond, Virginia, with Huntington, West Virginia (1873); the Norfolk and Western linked southern West Virginia and southwest Virginia with the ports in Norfolk, Virginia (1883); and the Louisville and Nashville came to the edge of the Kentucky Cumberland Plateau in 1880, and finally into Letcher, Perry, and Harlan Counties in 1912. From the main lines, branch lines eventually were built to coal towns, with short lines leading up hollows facilitating travel within the region and beyond.[19] Southwest Virginia and Northeast Tennessee experienced similar railroad expansion during that time. Trains accelerated the export of natural resources such as timber and coal from the region, and the import of manufactured goods, furniture, farm supplies, catalogue orders, newspapers, and eventually telephones. As soon as railroad lines began to reach into the mountains in the mid-nineteenth century, professional performers took advantage of the opportunity to develop new audiences. The cash surrounding the railroad centers attracted more merchants to the towns, and the influx of residents required the construction of infrastructure, including roads, stores, hospitals, and churches. Often these were built by the company or corporation dominating the town, like the Kingsport Improvement Corporation in Northeast Tennessee and coal companies in the coal-rich areas of Southwest Virginia and Eastern Kentucky.[20] As the towns thrived, the contrasts between them and the rural areas increased. Industrialization and improved transport affected the larger towns in different ways. Though all were expanding rapidly, Kingsport, Tennessee, along with Martinsville, Virginia, and Harlan, Kentucky, each had its own experience and its own particular character as it grew. Other influences in surrounding counties and in their respective states contributed to distinct growth processes and results. Most burgeoning towns in the region in the late nineteenth century had one thing in common: the presence of an opera house or theater as a focal point. Both local performers and touring professionals graced the stages on a regular basis.

The advance of the timbering, coal, and textile industries facilitated by the railroads prompted population changes in both numbers and ethnicity. As workers came in for the new jobs, the populations of Eastern Kentucky and Northeast Tennessee more than doubled, and that of Southwest Virginia tripled during the period from 1880 to 1920. Included in this population explosion were African American southerners and new European immigrants. The African American population of central Appalachia grew dramatically from 14,360 in 1870 to 108,872 in 1930, with most living in the coalfields. Immigrants from many European countries (southern, central, and northern) were recruited to work in the coalfields until the outbreak of World War I. Lewis estimates that at the peak, these latter may have accounted for 25 percent of coal workers. These immigrants and African American southerners brought their own traditions and practiced them in the coalfields, contributing to the evolution of social dance and other forms of cultural expression.[21]

During this same period, local color writers, such as Mary Murfree and John Fox Jr., and academics, including Berea College President William Goodell Frost, promoted an image of the region as populated by "our contemporary ancestors" who had preserved intact a culture from the distant past. Appalachian people were described as either backward hillbillies or noble carriers of pure Anglo-Saxon culture. Neither image was accurate, but both helped to draw a group of people to the mountains who would also contribute to the evolution of the regional culture: settlement school workers. Grounded in progressive social and educational theory, they sought simultaneously to teach children contemporary middle-class practices, to draw them out of poverty, and to restore a hypothesized traditional culture. Olive Dame Campbell, the founder of John C. Campbell Settlement School in Brasstown, North Carolina, was one of a few who saw things differently. Writing in *Mountain Life and Work* in 1925, she said, "There is no fundamental reason for separating mountain people from lowland people, nor are mountain problems so different at bottom from those of other rural areas in the United States."[22] During the first half of the twentieth century, not only did people from other parts of the country and the world come to Appalachia, but also the region's residents left in large numbers to fight in World Wars I and II, and to find jobs in northern urban centers like Detroit and Chicago. Some returned home to the mountains, bringing new ideas and practices with them, and some stayed in the cities, contributing elements of their customs to the ones they found there. During the second half of the twentieth century, of course, transportation and communication systems were improving in the Appalachian region as in other predominantly rural areas, radio and then television were increasingly available, and cultural influences could mix and mingle at an ever-more-rapid pace. Now almost every kind of dance found anywhere in the United States can also be found somewhere in the region.

Centuries of Social and Theatrical Dance

Old time square dancing and footwork dancing are linked with the region in the popular imagination. People frequently associate Appalachian dance with clogging teams. But these are not the only forms of dance in the region. In fact, dance has a rich and varied history here, drawing on national and international trends, and including social dance, performance dance, some ceremonial dance, and dance education. The form and meaning of traditional Appalachian dance are "situated both in the context of other socially prescribed and socially meaningful ways of moving and in the context of the history of dance forms in specific societies" in the region.[23] The story of dance in the Appalachian region involves complex, multidimensional interplay between traditional and popular cultures, and among classes and ethnic groups. It reflects the diversity and fluidity of Appalachian society. The region's indigenous residents had dance traditions before the arrival of black and white settlers, and the newcomers brought with them their own traditions. During the nineteenth century, a wide assortment of dance forms and styles were introduced to the region by various means: through community social dancing, via the stage, in educational settings, and with the interchange of the growing number of cultural groups in the region.

Social Dance

Before settlers of European and African descent arrived in the Appalachian region, of course, Shawnee, Cherokee, and other native peoples had long-established dance traditions. In the mid-Atlantic colonies, English, French, Scots-Irish, and Germans of all classes enjoyed dances of the baroque period: minuets and country dancing to the phrases of melodic music. New dances and dance styles crossed the ocean to be taken into their repertoire.[24] Even under duress, African people from a variety of ethnic groups continued traditions of solo step dancing, circle dancing, and polyrhythmic music and movement. Very soon the European and African traditions began to influence each other, according to historian Mechal Sobel. By the eighteenth century, the large percentage of enslaved Africans in Virginia and the other southern states, up to 75 percent in the Tidewater area, contributed to the creation of a new culture that shared both European and African elements. Together they developed a worldview of shared "attitudes and their expression in social life: attitudes toward time, attitudes toward space, and understandings of causality and purpose."[25] When the first white and black settlers began to make their way into the mountains from the colonies, they brought this new and evolving culture with them. As they established homes and communities in the hills and interacted with native peoples, all three groups learned customs from each other, including dance. Since, as seen previously, settlers had a certain amount of mobility from the earliest days, and newcomers continued to arrive, contemporary dance styles were repeatedly available to them, and their dancing took on characteristics of the new styles in the ensuing decades. Dance forms and styles have continued to evolve to the present with influences from other traditions and from popular culture.

In the American colonies of the eighteenth century, country dances were popular, most often in longways formations with lines of two couples facing each other.[26] These dances came over the mountains and down the rivers with settlers, taking root along with the growth of towns like Lexington, Kentucky (1775); Abingdon, Virginia (1778); Jonesborough, Tennessee (1779); and Martinsville, Virginia (1808). By the turn of the nineteenth century, the towns enjoyed libraries, educational institutions, visiting theater troupes, and dancing and singing schools.[27] Dancing masters in these towns and others like them taught minuets, country dances, jigs, and reels to genteel youth and young men and women, along with discipline, manners, and deportment. For example, a dancing school was advertised in a 1789 Lexington, Kentucky, newspaper.[28] When four-couple cotillions became popular in the early 1800s, dancing masters were responsible for disseminating them. They also ventured to small towns and hamlets of the region, where travel was accessible by road or river. While dancing masters remained popular among the elite throughout the century, less moneyed rural residents learned the dances by observation and oral tradition.[29] According to accounts by his contemporaries, Davy Crockett, from East Tennessee, was a fine dancer and fiddler. J. S. French described Crockett, as a young man, doing country dances and solo footwork dances in 1803 or 1804.[30]

During the nineteenth century, social dance further evolved, and people in the central Appalachian region learned the new styles, with each community adapting them in different ways. Intercultural exchange continued to influence dance styles in the mountains as elsewhere. New European social dances were brought to the trans-Appalachian frontier, and African American musicians accompanied dance here as in the East. It is likely that the rhythms played by black fiddlers, even for European style dances, reflected their heritage.[31] Dance historian Phil Jamison has documented evidence that black fiddlers originated the practice of "calling" the figures of a dance, giving the dancers directions in rhyme. One might chant "Swing Mr. Adam and swing Miss Eve, / Swing old Adam before you leave." By the 1840s, "calling" set dances, in which one person directed or announced the figures, had become customary.[32] Numerous accounts between 1770 and 1853 in such places as Knoxville, Tennessee, and Lynchburg, Virginia, describe whites dancing to black music as well as blacks and whites observing and experimenting with each other's dances and music.[33] The Grand March became a popular way to begin a dance evening, with couples promenading in lines around the ballroom. Dancing master Henry Meyen's *The Ball Room Guide* of 1852 "noted that 'every well-arranged ball should commence with this graceful dance in a conversational character.' Meyen also suggested that the carriage of the dancer should be serious and grave and that the figures should go 'either in a circle, a straight, or serpentine line, either across or round the ballroom.' He warned that dancers should not participate in figures that might 'endanger the head dress of the ladies . . . and cause them to be offended, which must be by all means avoided.'"[34] Grand March figures are still danced today in some communities as a conclusion to an old time square dance, and calling figures is a regular part of every square dance.

A new form of cotillion, more like a party game or mixer, came on the scene in the mid-nineteenth century, as did a particular form called the "German cotillion." An 1885 news account of the celebrations surrounding the formation of Knott County in Eastern Kentucky describes local residents dancing a cotillion outdoors, though no description gives clues as to its features.[35] Play parties, singing games in which the words dictated the movement, were common in rural areas, including Appalachia, beginning in the mid-1800s. They have structural and movement similarities to country dances or square dances. Some play parties, such as "Weevilly Wheat" and "Johnny Brown," have been traced to European or African roots, respectively.[36] Couple dances emerged in the early to mid-nineteenth century, including the waltz (1820s) and the polka (1840s). Upon seeing the polka for the first time a prominent Kentucky lady expressed distaste at the intimacy and abandon of the whirling couples, but dancing masters continued to be in demand, teaching these new diversions and the accompanying social skills. An 1879 announcement for an event sponsored by the social "Dancing Club" in Paris, Kentucky, highly praised "the young gentlemen of our city [who] have acquired a widespread and very enviable reputation for the perfect manner in which they get up affairs of this kind."[37] All of these social dance customs had an effect on traditional community dancing as it appeared in the late twentieth century in the central Appalachian region. Square dances are almost always called, and their figures have similarities to country dance, cotillions, and play parties. Some communities have included waltzing among the dances in a typical evening, and the basic clogging step has a rhythm strikingly similar to polka.

By the late nineteenth century, the form known today as old time square dancing, in a circle with sets of two couples forming the squares, was taking shape in the southern mountains and in the southeastern United States, drawing upon the variety of sources described above, as well as others. Square dancing and footwork dancing became a primary form of recreation for rural Appalachian people in the late nineteenth and early twentieth century. It came to the attention of people beyond the region through the writing of British folk music collector Cecil Sharp. In 1917, he described what he called "The Kentucky Running Set," danced in sets of four or more couples. His careful descriptions were the first to document specific characteristics of Appalachian dance, though his interpretations were grounded in romanticized beliefs.[38] Every community had its own customs. Dancing could be simply a gathering of neighbors in someone's home on a Saturday night, or it could be the conclusion of a day of communal "working," shucking corn, shelling beans, or clearing land. In some communities these home-based dances moved to public spaces like lodge halls or school houses as early as the 1920s; in others they continued in the home until the mid-twentieth century. In one notable exception, a Henry County, Virginia, dance community continued dancing in the home until the 1970s. Often, dance evenings included other forms, such as waltz, two-step, or polka. Each new popular dance trend found its way into these dance events.

Cultural interaction continued in the twentieth century. Native American and African American Appalachians enjoyed square dancing. Walker Calhoun, committed to preserving Cherokee dance traditions, grew up square dancing in his Cherokee, North Carolina, home, and black residents of Virginia, Kentucky, and Tennessee describe square dancing in their homes as well.[39] During the decades surrounding the turn of the twentieth century, large numbers of central and southern European immigrants arrived to work in the timber, coal, and steel industries. Among these were Croatians, Hungarians, Bulgarians, Slavs, Germans, and Italians. They influenced dance and other customs. For example, Hungarians in the coal town of Dante, Virginia, held an annual autumn "Grape Arbor" celebration during the 1930s, and everyone in town came to enjoy the dancing and other festivities. As thousands of African American southerners migrated to the coalfields, they brought the Charleston and the lindy hop with them. From the 1920s to the 1960s, popular music greats such as Cab Calloway, Duke Ellington, and the Ink Spots brought swing music and rhythm and blues, along with the lindy, jitterbug, hucklebuck, and twist to small towns in and near the coalfields and industrial areas of Virginia, Tennessee, and Kentucky. Both black and white residents of Martinsville, Abingdon, Kingsport, Dante, Harlan, and Hazard danced to their music, either live or on records. Elements of many of these dances found their way into local dance traditions and were still reflected in them in the late twentieth century. Appalachian dance continues to evolve as people of Hispanic, Middle Eastern, and Asian descent establish homes and communities in the region. Annual Cinco de Mayo and Dieciseis de Septiembre celebrations take place in many towns, and salsa clubs are found in larger cities. Chinese New Year celebrations are open to all, traditional Middle Eastern dancing has a following among people of all ethnicities, and classical Indian dance is performed at special occasions.

In the twenty-first century, with the exception of a few community venues, there is little square dancing and traditional footwork dancing in the area that encompasses the six communities under discussion. In Eastern Kentucky, Northeast Tennessee, and Southwest Virginia these kinds of dancing occur primarily on special occasions and at festivals like Home Crafts Days in Wise, Virginia, and at folk dance weekends or weeklong workshops like Family Folk Week at Hindman Settlement School in Kentucky. Only a few communities square dance or clog/flatfoot/hoedown on a regular weekly or monthly basis, but people enjoy many other kinds of dance. Hip hop and rock dancing and music are popular among young people. Fraternities, schools, clubs, and churches sponsor step teams that express principles such as unity and group identity with their synchronized movement and confident personal presentation. An intergenerational contra dance network exists, and Argentine tango and salsa are thriving. Ballroom dancing, swing dance, and modern Western square dancing, round dancing, and line dancing have devoted followers. Local dancers in each form can connect to national networks. However in some other parts of the central Appalachian region, old time square dancing and footwork dancing enjoy an enthusiastic following. Western North Carolina is well known for traditional dancing, with a primary location being The Stompin' Ground in Maggie Valley. Floyd Country Store in Floyd, Virginia, not far from Roanoke and Blacksburg, Virginia, hosts the Friday Night Jamboree. Numerous square dance and clogging venues in West Virginia have been linked in the Mountain Dance Trail.

Theatrical Dance

Not only has dance been part of the social life of residents of the Appalachian region for more than two hundred years, but numerous opportunities have existed to enjoy dance as a performing art in a variety of contexts. Local audiences copied dance moves they observed on stage, taking them into local traditions, and the traveling dancers likely incorporated some local dance elements into their acts.

Theatrical performance was popular in the colonies and became part of frontier life as well. The first reported amateur performance west of the Alleghenies took place when officers performed for the troops at Fort Pitt (Pennsylvania) in 1790. Officers at forts in Tennessee, Kentucky, and Virginia may have done likewise. The first reference to an amateur performance in the young town of Lexington, Kentucky, appeared in 1799, and the first professional troupe was documented in 1810. By 1815 all the prominent towns of the Ohio valley hosted professional performances, and by 1820 a regular tour circuit was established, including Cincinnati, Louisville, Nashville, and St. Louis.[40] Tours continued on these routes throughout the nineteenth century and expanded their range with the proliferation of railroads midcentury. These performances were not simply plays. Dance historian Lynn Matluck Brooks describes dance touring groups in the late eighteenth century performing in theaters and fairs in the original colonies and offering interludes between acts of a play. Dance styles ranged from ballet and pantomimes to acrobatic dancing. Some of these dancers followed the innovations of John Durang, who in 1785 performed a dance that combined ballet steps with others taken from English, Irish, and American step dancing.[41] Once the new frontier opened, these performers followed the network of waterways and expanding roads into the Appalachian region. Circuses, so popular during the colonial period, also followed the new settlers. Though not dance as such, they were certainly a collection of movement arts, including gymnasts, acrobats, clowns, and equestrians. At first just demonstrations of horsemanship, they became increasingly spectacular. Documentation exists of a circus performance in at least one mountain town in eastern Tennessee in 1824, when circuses traveled as "wagon shows" on narrow country roads.[42]

European classical dance styles arrived west of the mountains just two years after they were first seen on the East Coast. In 1829, Celeste and Constance Keppler began to "introduce 'French dancing' to many a remote town." Among their programs were "Great National Dances," through which residents on the fringes of Appalachia first saw German, Italian, Irish, Turkish, and Russian dances, including the wildly popular "Russian Mazurka." When the Kepplers appeared in Cincinnati in 1829, newspaper accounts called their performance "Poetry in Motion," but local residents, apparently, were shocked. Their performances involved spectacle as well as dance, such as a depiction of Vesuvius erupting over Naples.[43] Other dancers followed, with frequent performances all along the tour route. The local taste for dance established, residents were enthralled with the expertise demonstrated by the incomparable Fanny Elssler when she toured from New Orleans to Cincinnati by river in 1840 with her famed *Cachuca*, also performing *Natalie* and *LaBayadere*. Beginning in 1846, American-born, French-trained ballerina Mary Ann Lee toured the West. In 1847 she "was cheered in Cincinnati where her American origin brought her an unusually warm reception."[44]

When minstrelsy was born in the 1820s, these blackface variety shows, drawing in part on and caricaturing music, dance, and customs of enslaved African Americans, followed a similar circuit. Though the famous ballerinas may not have strayed far from the river towns, their reputations—and "French dancing"—were spread by caricatures provided in these minstrel shows, in which blackface male performers donned ballet costumes, danced on their toes, and performed burlesques of the romantic ballets.[45] Medicine shows, usually caricaturing American Indians, developed soon thereafter, with a goal of selling patent medicines and tonics. Like minstrel shows, medicine shows were variety shows with a mix of song, patter, dance, and comedy. Almost every small town in the region was visited by these shows, which brought, among other things, new dance ideas that became part of local styles. They toured the mountains as well as the rest of the nation by wagon, riverboat, and rail from 1830 well into the early 1900s, both incorporating elements of local dance traditions they encountered and influencing their evolution.[46] The shows were remembered with a smile by older residents of Virginia, Tennessee, and Kentucky whom I interviewed.

Acrobatic teams like the Ravel family toured the United States during the nineteenth century, also following the river routes. The Ravels and their protégés presented a fast-paced program of acrobatics, *tableaus vivants* (academic poses based on Greek statues), contortionism, French vaudeville, pantomime, and comedy. They "romped into the hearts of Cincinnati theatre lovers in July, 1833," during the first tour of their decades-long presence in America.[47] Their signature pieces were rope dances, performed on long thick ropes suspended above the ground. Their protégées formed similar touring groups. A Cincinnati performance of such a group is detailed in a broadside:

> First night of the engagement of the wonderful Martinetti and Blondin Troupe, late Ravels. Great success! And last night of Raoul, or, The magic star! In twelve tableaux. Zoe Gilbert in a beautiful dance! P. Martinetti, as Courci! . . . After which, graceful groupings by the Martinetti family. After which, Divertisement! After which, the orchestra will execute a selection from Meyerbeer's grand opera, Robert the devil. The performance will conclude with the fairy pantomime of Raoul! or The magic star . . .[48]

This particular company performed almost nightly in towns skirting the Appalachian region in 1858–59, and among their divertissements were excerpts from ballets.

After the Civil War, the opera house became an important landmark in most Appalachian towns of three hundred or more. Historian William Faricy Condee has documented opera houses in almost every mining town between 1870 and 1930. They presented comic and dramatic plays, vaudeville, minstrel, or medicine variety shows that included dance, and sometimes Shakespeare plays, true operas, and classical dance. Various diversions, including music, songs, and dances, were presented between acts of the plays. Other opera house entertainment included acrobatics, fire eating, lectures, magic, Punch and Judy shows, pantomime, menageries, pie-eating contests, and Wild West shows, like the

Buffalo Bill show that appeared at the Maysville Opera in 1882.[49] It is likely that troupes such as Martinetti and Blondin were among the acts booked at opera houses, especially those near river towns. Among the many opera houses in the central Appalachian region were those in Abingdon, Virginia (mid-1800s); Danville, Virginia (1880); Pocohontas, Virginia (1890s); Winchester, Kentucky (1873); Long's Opera House, Harlan, Kentucky (1882); Harmeling Opera House, Bristol, Virginia (1889); and Jobe's Opera House, Johnson City, Tennessee (1884). Opera houses were usually built and operated by coal companies, fire companies, civic organizations such as the Knights of Pythias, or by private entrepreneurs. In 1922, the Harlan, Kentucky, *Enterprise* referred to the opera house as "the largest building in Harlan except for the courthouse." In Benham, Kentucky, a list of the "most important buildings" began with the theater. Even the store and the medical building fell further down the list.[50]

In small towns in Appalachia and elsewhere, the opera house was the center for entertainment for all classes, races, and ages, whereas in large cities each group had its own entertainment and social centers. In the early twentieth century, at least twenty nationalities resided in the Appalachian region, as did large numbers of African American southerners. All shared the opera house, though blacks were consigned to the balcony. The division between "high" and "low" culture did not exist as it does today. Rural folk with little schooling and the town's moneyed elite were equally likely to spend an evening at the opera house for a performance of Shakespeare or for a minstrel show. In fact, Shakespeare was regularly performed in nineteenth-century small towns in Appalachia and was very popular. The productions emphasized spectacle, including "Electrical Effects, Rich and Correct Costuming," touted in an advertisement, and incorporated other elements such as songs and dances. In the first decades of the twentieth century, other entertainments became popular, including films and plays by more recent playwrights. For example, in 1923 the New Harlan Theater (Opera House) advertised an evening of a movie with a coal mining theme followed by an Oscar Wilde play.In 1922 the opera house had presented a play based on John Fox Jr.'s *Little Shepherd of Kingdom Come*, "the Biggest Play of the Century . . . With All Live Folks Playing It! A PLAY NOT A PICTURE," according to the Harlan *Enterprise*. (Emphases from original playbill.)[51]

Local residents provided some of the entertainment at the opera houses, sometimes including dance. In Winchester, Kentucky, a 1911 news article reported that a Mrs. Reid's class performed to a packed audience. The recital included Delsarte dancing in flowing gowns, a violin trio, a Grecian drill, and "The Working Song," in which children acted out gender-appropriate tasks, with girls rocking dolls and boys sawing and hammering.[52] Besides such local presentations, Appalachian opera houses hosted well-known performers like singer Jennie Calef. It is likely that dancers of national repute performed here as well, once railroad travel became established in the region in the late nineteenth and early twentieth century. The Denishawn Dance Company was known to perform in Asheville and Charlotte, North Carolina, and Lynchburg, Virginia, in February 1923, so it is possible that they or others may have appeared in some of the many opera houses in other Appalachian towns.[53] In the mid-twentieth century, summer-stock theaters were established in various towns around the country, and the Appalachian region was no different. In summer-stock theaters, professional actors and dancers came from cities like New York and Chicago to perform plays and musical comedies. The Barter Theatre in Abingdon, Virginia, was among the first to offer summer-stock performances in the former opera house building. During the Depression, Abingdon native Robert Porterfield invited New York professionals to perform in exchange for food provided by the audience. The Mill Mountain Theater in Roanoke, Virginia (1964), and the Jenny Wiley Theater in Prestonsburg, Kentucky (1965), are two other examples of summer-stock theaters in the Appalachian region.

Performance opportunities for residents of the region have existed as well. Team clogging and square dancing had taken on performance aspects as a result of Bascom Lamar Lunsford's Mountain Dance and Folk Festival in Asheville, North Carolina, beginning in 1928. These types of performers gained national attention through the National Barn Dance and the Grand Ole Opry; as well, radio barn dances in small towns in Tennessee, Virginia, and Kentucky featured such teams as part of the entertainment for their live audiences in the 1930s. Other opportunities close to home allowed community members to demonstrate local dancing. Several communities established outdoor dramas based on local history, with roles portrayed by local actors, dancers, and musicians. *Wilderness Road* (1955) in Berea, Kentucky, and *Trail of the Lonesome Pine* (1964) in Big Stone Gap, Virginia, are two such outdoor dramas. The latter continues to the present.

Besides local dance styles, other forms of dance performance became available to local residents. Ballet schools were being established by the 1940s even in small towns in the Appalachian region. In Bristol, Virginia, Constance Hardinge founded the Bristol Ballet school in 1948, building the program with innovative approaches, including ballroom dance lessons for adults and cotillions, or formal dances, for youth.[54] In 1959 a performing company was established. Nationally known choreographers have set pieces on the company, and a number of Bristol Ballet dancers have gone on to professional dance careers. Other regional dance companies were established in the same area in the 1980s, including Mountain Movers, a modern dance company based in Johnson City, and the Kingsport Ballet. This kind of development is mirrored throughout the central Appalachian region, with the support of local and state arts councils and nonprofit organizations. Today the Appalachian region is home to two professional ballet companies with international reputations: the Pittsburgh Ballet Theatre and the

Alabama Ballet. Along with these two major companies, civic ballet companies throughout the region usually employ at least some professional dancers, produce a version of Marius Petipa's ballet *The Nutcracker* at Christmas, and conduct a regular season of classes and performances. Lexington, Kentucky, for example, has two such ballet companies with associated schools.

Dance Education

Social dance and theatrical dance have been taught in the region since the end of the eighteenth century, and dance for personal development has been taught since the late nineteenth century. Today, dance education in the Appalachian region encompasses all ages and many styles of dance. Professional dancers, college dance programs, private studios, and elementary and secondary schools all contribute to dance learning.

Dancing masters taught the latest trends in social dance to the moneyed classes for nearly a hundred years, as described earlier. Late in the nineteenth century, dance was included in the education of women at finishing schools and colleges. Eventually it became part of the training of those planning to be schoolteachers, and teachers coming into the region brought this knowledge with them. At the turn of the twentieth century, schoolchildren in the region might learn various systems of calisthenics, and young women from upper class families might study aesthetic dance or Delsarte's method.[55] The folk dance recreation movement that swept the nation beginning after 1910 had an effect here, too, especially among certain settlement schools, a number of which focused on English country dancing and Morris and sword dancing after it was introduced by Cecil Sharp in 1917 and promoted thereafter by the English Folk Dance and Song Society.[56] Folk dance and square dance became standard elements of teacher preparation midcentury, especially for teachers of physical education. Some colleges continued folk dance as a separate entity and established performing groups. The Bailey Mountain Cloggers of Mars Hill College in North Carolina have performed internationally since the 1970s. The Berea College Country Dancers in Kentucky grew from a novel social opportunity in the 1930s to become an international touring group. In 1963, they performed at the Kennedy White House, and they have toured to Japan, Denmark, El Salvador, and England.

Along with folk dance classes, colleges also initiated modern dance classes for women, based on the techniques of Isadora Duncan and Ruth St. Denis, and on the visionary dance education work at Teachers College, Columbia University, in New York City. Coursework later incorporated the theories and techniques of Martha Graham, Doris Humphrey, and others. Modern dance, developed in the early twentieth century, was emotionally expressive and built upon fundamental movements of the body rather than upon an academic technique like ballet. The University of Tennessee at Knoxville was one of the first colleges in the South to develop courses in modern dance. Teacher Dorothy Evelyn Koch worked tirelessly to promote modern dance on campus and in the Knoxville community. She and her dancers collaborated on a performance with a local African American high school choir, and in 1941 the Modern Dance Club presented "A Saga of East Tennessee," portraying important historical events of the region, such as the forced removal of the Cherokee to Oklahoma, pioneer settlement, the advent of industrial enterprise, and African American life. Her frequent concerts involved as many as one hundred students, drew favorable reviews from the press, and began building an enthusiastic audience for modern dance in the region.[57]

Women's colleges, especially, established modern dance programs. Lynchburg, Virginia, native Helen McGehee discovered modern dance when she entered Randolph-Macon Women's College in the late 1930s. She went on to become a leading dancer in the Martha Graham dance company, perhaps the preeminent modern company of the mid-twentieth century. Upon her retirement from the company, she returned to her hometown to establish a visiting artist program, bringing world-renowned dancers to the campus of her alma mater and providing professional dance opportunities for other young women of the region.[58] By the 1970s, dance was established in colleges throughout the region as it was in the nation, and every central Appalachian state had college major or minor programs in dance, some of which included modern dance, jazz, and ballet. In the 1980s, dance became part of elementary and high school education, either as part of the regular curriculum or with the assistance of guest artists; Kentucky and North Carolina were leaders in establishing curricular standards in dance for all students in the 1990s. A number of cities have elementary and high schools of performing arts elementary and high school dance programs.

Dance studios in towns large and small provide dance training in ballet, tap, jazz, hip hop, and other styles like Irish step dancing, clogging, East Indian classical dance, African dance, and Middle Eastern dancing. Local performing groups abound in many of these styles. Schools and community groups sponsor step teams as well, as a way of promoting personal pride, discipline, and group loyalty. Along with the many types of social dance and dance performance available in the region since the eighteenth century, such dance education forms a context for local dance traditions. Among people who have chosen old time square dancing and footwork dancing for recreation are those who have had experience learning other kinds of dance, or members of their families have done so. Traditional square dance and footwork dance are only two of the many forms that are performed, taught, and enjoyed recreationally in the central Appalachian region.

A Wealth of Dance Opportunities

Far from being isolated in terms of dance, people in the region have, for two hundred years, had rich resources to draw upon in terms of movement vocabulary and have made reciprocal contributions to dancing elsewhere. Residents of Appalachia have continually had access to a wide range of forms of social dance and theatrical dance. Rivers, railroads, roads, and finally airports have facilitated performers traveling across the region. Individual entrepreneurship followed by the support of industry and civic organization support made both amateur and professional performances available to growing audiences, increasing interest and demand. People in the region have learned social and theatrical dance in a variety of educational settings since 1800. Today an abundance of social dance forms and styles are available throughout the region, from hip hop to tango. Almost everyone in Appalachia lives within an hour's drive of opportunities to see local and regional dance groups and professional performers touring from New York and other theater and dance hubs. Towns of all sizes boast dance schools, and local dancers have performing outlets within the region and access to audition opportunities, should they choose to pursue a career. The kinds of dance discussed in the present volume, Appalachian square dancing and footwork dancing, have evolved over the course of the decades and centuries in the context of this rich and stimulating dance environment. Practitioners choose them from among other options and with an awareness of a range of dance opportunities. This rich dance heritage provides the context for these stories of six Appalachian dance communities.

3. Old Time Dancing in Northeast Tennessee

Traditional Values in an Industrial Region

On a hot Saturday night in August 1987, when I entered the Beechwood Family Music Center in Fall Branch, Tennessee, the dance floor was filled with people from toddlerhood to retirement age, relating first to one person and then another. Taps rattled on the concrete floor keeping time with sharp accented strokes to the music of the band Snake and the Grass. After the tune ended and the dancers began to drift to their seats, the leader of the band announced a square dance, and caller Veronia Miller stepped up on the low stage and took the microphone. "Get off your seat and on your feet. It's square dance time." The circle of twenty couples formed quickly as dancers ambled back onto the floor to choose a place. The band struck up a few introductory notes, and the dancers were off as Mrs. Miller called, "All join hands and circle right." Most kept a steady duple-time ostinato going with their feet throughout the ten-minute dance. Couples joined hands with other couples for four-person figures like "Cage the Bird," went through arches made by the upraised arms of the other dancers, and wound their long line into a spiral. At the end of the dance, Mrs. Miller called, "Promenade her to her seat and get her out of this awful heat." Couples danced toward the edges of the dance floor together with thanks for the dance and headed toward their own seats. But within moments another tune began, and the floor was full again, this time with two-stepping couples and a pair of two-year-olds who held hands and swayed with each other. These folks just couldn't stop dancing, and throughout the full three-hour evening, the dance floor was never empty, except during short breaks each hour.[1]

Beechwood was one of about a dozen places in the Northeast Tennessee–Southwest Virginia valley where old time dancing took place in the late 1980s and early 1990s. Other kinds of dancing were popular in the area as well, including ballroom, modern western club square dancing, line dancing, and, for

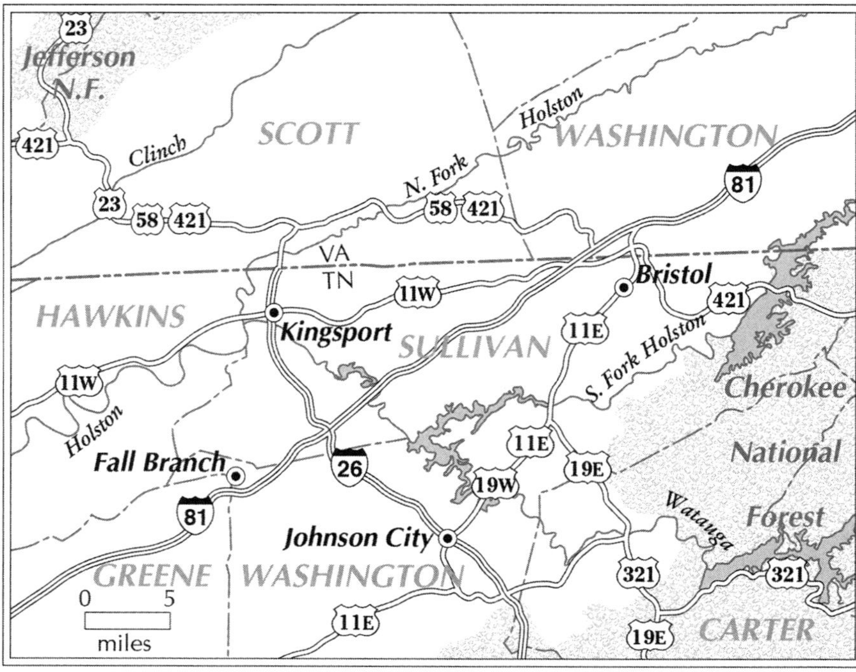

Map 2. Area surrounding Fall Branch, Tennessee: Northeast Tennessee and Southwest Virginia. Cartography by Dick Gilbreath, Director, Gyula Pauer Center for Cartography and GIS, University of Kentucky.

young people, hip hop. Dances similar to old time square dancing and footwork dancing were almost continuous threads in the culture of the Tri-Cities area of Northeast Tennessee, reaching back to the second half of the nineteenth century, according to the oldest consultants' accounts of their grandparents' stories. After a hiatus of a decade or two, these kinds of dancing once again became a popular recreation there during the 1970s and 1980s. This revival took place after the area had completed its evolution from predominantly rural to predominantly urban. I wondered why this particular social dance form resonated with some local people at this particular time. I danced at Beechwood during the late 1980s and enjoyed getting to know some of the people who went there regularly. I was so taken by the homey atmosphere, I produced a short video documentary about dancing at Beechwood, under the auspices of the Center for Appalachian Studies and Services at East Tennessee State University and with the help of Appalshop, in Whitesburg, Kentucky. Dancing there was, in part, the inspiration for three conferences on Appalachian dance traditions sponsored by the Center for Appalachian Studies and Services. In this discussion, I use Beechwood as a focal point for considering the ways social and economic shifts may have contributed to changes in dance traditions of Northeast Tennessee and Southwest Virginia in the twentieth century. I have been guided by what the dancers said about the dancing, and I have looked at the larger context. Many Beechwood dancers, almost all European Americans, came from several counties bordering the Tennessee-Virginia state line. Kingsport, Tennessee, is the city to which most of these dancers refer, and where they go for work, commerce, and entertainment. Other communities have different social and economic histories—and different styles and repertoires as a result.

Over the course of a century or more, the dancing in Northeast Tennessee underwent changes in venue, structure, style, and purpose or meaning. As the area moved ever more rapidly from an agrarian society to an industrial one, the dancing became more complex, with more variety and a certain level of hierarchy. Once danced almost exclusively in the home by groups of geographically close neighbors, it moved first to membership groups and then to public venues, and the construction of the dance community changed as a result. Whereas in the previous century dancing was a way for neighbors to socialize, it became entertainment for members of a group such as the Elks, and by 1987 it had become the recreational focus for people, otherwise unconnected, who built a community around it. Many of those who chose old time dancing were quick to place it in an older, rural setting and to express preferences for styles of music and dance that they associated with earlier times.

The area now known as the Standard Metropolitan Statistical Area of the Tri-Cities is composed of the valley counties of Sullivan, Greene, Washington, and Hawkins, in Tennessee, and Scott and Washington in Virginia.[2] This area is historically and culturally relatively cohesive because of its geography. Trade and travel were easier among these counties, and valley agriculture provided a good livelihood. Musicologist Charles Wolfe, in denoting the musical regions of Tennessee, identifies affinities between the music of Northeast Tennessee and Southwest Virginia, with some influence from Western North Carolina.[3] Beginning in the late nineteenth century, industrialization grew in the area, increasing more quickly with World War I and more quickly yet with World War

Figure 3.1. Right Hands Cross with three generations of dancers in the homey Beechwood atmosphere, 1987. Courtesy of Appalshop Archive, Appalshop Films Collection.

II. Historian Tom Lee says that "by the early twentieth century, the personal, informal relations of community life had largely succumbed to the hierarchical, regulated, impersonal, relations of the factory and the city," and "by 1950, farming had ceased to be a viable occupation for most rural folk."[4] Social and economic changes, from the beginnings as an agricultural area and a port in the late 1700s to the rapid industrialization in the twentieth century, seem to have influenced both changes of venue and changes in form and style. For those who chose old time square dancing and clogging as a recreational outlet in the late twentieth century, the dance event, style, and venue served both to maintain or re-create values from the more agrarian era, such as autonomy and cooperation, and to incorporate values associated with urbanization and industrialization, such as complexity, hierarchy, and specialization.

The Beechwood Family Music Center

The Beechwood Family Music Center, where these weekly dance evenings took place, still hosts weekly music performances in 2014, according to listings of the Kingsport, Tennessee, tourist attractions. In 1987, it had a rustic, homey feel, with wood-paneled walls covered with photos of those who had attended over the years. Theater-style seating allowed easy view of the dance floor and the band. Overlooking the dance floor, on one side of the room, a shingled roof sheltered the kitchen and dining area where founder Helen Baker and her grandchildren served hotdogs, popcorn, pop, and other refreshments. Her husband, Don Baker, sat toward the rear of the audience, monitoring the sound system. Most who came to dance on Friday nights were middle aged or retirement aged, and some brought their children and grandchildren. Few teens attended on their own, though Helen Baker had hoped to provide a recreational outlet that young people would enjoy. Hanging out at the mall or video arcade with groups of their own age seemed to call to them more than an evening with their elders. Many in attendance expressed gratitude that Mr. and Mrs. Baker established this place for dancing, saying it was the nicest place they knew of. New friends were made among the enthusiasts. Since the family-neighborhood unit no longer held the center of social life as it once did, these dancers, like other hobbyists, created a "family" out of a group with similar interests. Gifts of garden produce and jam were brought to each other at Beechwood, group photos were taken, successes were celebrated, and losses mourned. "We're all just one big family here at Beechwood" was a comment frequently echoed. Caller Veronia Miller said, "You meet so many nice people in square dancing. You know everybody and you know their children, and their children's children."[5]

Dancing was what everyone came for, and there were few who did not spend at least part of the evening on the dance floor. Helen Baker said that the few who only watched usually tried the dancing after a few visits. When people did sit out a tune, they watched, chatted with each other, listened to the music and applauded after each number. During the course of three hours on a Saturday night, there were usually three square dances of about ten minutes each, with the rest of the evening devoted to flatfooting and clogging, two-stepping, or waltzing. Bands would sometimes sing an occasional ballad or hymn. Many of the people who chose this kind of dancing as a regular recreation tended to live on or near their family homeplace and to socialize primarily with extended family, church, or civic organizations like the Masons. Among their other recreations, they listed flea marketing, sewing, or going to the Gray Fair, to tractor pulls or to country music shows. Most kept big gardens or small farms even as they held forty-hour-a-week jobs. Their dancing reflected an independent, live-and-let-live attitude, as people clogged or flatfooted in their own style for much of the evening. Dancing with them, I found them friendly, welcoming, and supportive people who would rarely judge another's dancing style.

A generation gap was evident at Beechwood. Three generations were present: retirement-age people, middle-age people, and children and teens. Those in the oldest generation were mostly lifelong dancers. Though some in the middle generation were the children or relatives of those in the older generation, many were not. Few of those in the middle generation had square danced before coming to Beechwood, and they had discovered on their own "what good fun this is." Both the middle and older generations brought grandchildren, and the middle generation brought their teenaged children. This same break appeared at other dance venues in the Tri-Cities area, raising the question of the causes of the break in continuity. Though the dancing appears to have continued in families and communities for decades, a break occurred in the 1950s. A combination of factors caused the break, and other factors seem to have drawn those in their middle years to a recreation they had not known in their youth.

Rural-Urban Connections

From its beginnings, Northeast Tennessee has drawn on many influences to create its particular kinds of cultural expression. European descendants began to establish homes and towns in this area by about 1770, along with free blacks and enslaved persons, and dancing was part of the social life, drawing on many influences, black, white, and indigenous, from the earliest days. The area became part of the state of Tennessee in 1796. Precolonial roads running northeast to southwest facilitated travel through the valley of Virginia and Tennessee, and on to Kentucky. The primary source of livelihood during the early decades was agriculture, but roads and rivers allowed the area to be connected to Western Tennessee, North and South Carolina, and the east coast.[6] During the early years, rivers were used in spring for distribution of local goods, such as the salt mined in Southwest Virginia, and other items such as grain, ginseng root, saltpeter, hams, beeswax, and gunpowder. When the water was high enough, flatboats traveled the river carrying goods and workers the 224 miles downriver to Knoxville. The boats were sold there, and the men traveled the 95 miles overland back to Northeast Tennessee on foot or, occasionally, by stagecoach.[7] During the nineteenth century, merchants in Northeast Tennessee offered items brought from Richmond, Baltimore, Philadelphia, Charleston, and New Orleans, and some imported from England. These ranged from the mundane, like muslin and stirrups, to the elegant, like black silk bonnets and Moroccan leather.[8] Also brought from these places were the popular social dances of the time—country dances, quadrilles, cotillions, jigs, reels, and longways dances—and by the mid-nineteenth century, couple dances like the waltz and polka.[9]

With the early growth of industry in the region, the conflict between the autonomy of the farm and relative regimentation of the factory and city became apparent. Railroads were built to transport coal and timber, beginning in the 1880s. By 1890 they connected Bristol, Tennessee-Virginia to Wise County, Virginia, and by 1907 to Eastern Kentucky. Building the railroads was dangerous work, accomplished largely by convicts, immigrants, and African Americans rather than local European Americans. This last group, while seeking nonfarm employment more and more, wanted the kind of work that would allow them to continue farming. They preferred jobs that let them "retain a modicum of independence from the regimentation of the time clock." From the point of view of industry, they "had to be transformed into reliable factory workers and to adapt to the complexities of the urban environment."[10] Though some traveled to work in the coalfields, many worked in textile, apparel, and furniture factories like those in Bristol, Johnson City, and Elizabethton, Tennessee.

By the late 1800s, the popular dances, such as cotillions, jigs, and reels, seem to have evolved into something resembling today's "old time square dancing," in a big circle, as one couple visited each other couple around the circle, dancing through a figure before moving on to the next couple at the direction of a caller. Once one couple had visited each of the others, the next couple would repeat the same figure and circuit. After all had had a turn "visiting" the others, a new figure would begin, so the dances would go on for a long time. People born in Northeast Tennessee at the turn of the twentieth century recalled square dancing and buck dancing or clogging in the years after 1910, and they recount stories from their grandparents' youth in the 1870s about large-group figured dancing similar to what we now call square dancing and the footwork dancing we now call flatfooting or clogging. Some report that their parents and grandparents also described enjoying newer popular dances like the waltz and polka, which had

Figure 3.2. Kingsport, Tennessee, 1928, surrounded by farmland. Courtesy of the Archives of the City of Kingsport, Tennessee.

found their way into the social life of Northeast Tennessee in the late nineteenth century as well.

Fiddle music was the usual accompaniment or stimulus for social dances in rural areas in Tennessee in the nineteenth century, although, based upon recordings of fiddlers who learned to play in the 1860s, the style was slower than it is today, with "careful, deliberate rhythms," probably matching the dance style. According to Charles Wolfe, East Tennessee had a distinctive fiddle style, using a short or "jiggy" bow and producing "choppy" music full of "short highly rhythmic passages," which foreshadowed today's playing and dancing. Fiddlers sometimes sang "jig" couplets as they played, "to relieve the monotony of the long dances." As with dancing, communities took varying views of fiddling. In some it was the "devil's box," while in others the fiddle was even taken to church or revival meetings.[11]

The string band music that accompanied dancing was associated with rural values at least a century prior to the time I danced at Beechwood. In the 1890s, people in Northeast Tennessee and elsewhere equated fiddle music and its associated dancing with an older time, as part of a "national nostalgia for simpler times and a simpler society" that occurred between 1880 and 1910.[12] But even then, the music included tunes made available by popular culture and the technology of the day, through printed songbooks and traveling minstrel shows, as well as older tunes like those played by Morristown fiddler Uncle Am Stewart, who learned to play soon after the Civil War. A recording of his playing includes tunes like Cumberland Gap, Sourwood Mountain, and Leather Breeches, all tunes that are still played today. In 1891, the *Knoxville Tribune* reported that each fiddler in a contest "played the sweet old tunes of by gone time with charmed bow string."[13] Tennessee candidate for governor Robert Love Taylor, from neighboring Carter County, used his fiddling to his campaign's advantage during the 1890s because it gave him the look of "a down to earth country boy." In the voters' eyes, "fiddling was associated with grass-roots values" and an "affirmation of heritage."[14]

Industrialization Arrives in a Rural Area

Rural values and industrial development met in early-twentieth-century Northeast Tennessee. Contemporary urban dance styles were also juxtaposed with rural ones. After 1910, business leaders began recruiting industry to the growing towns in the region, and one city was planned specifically to serve as an industrial town. George L. Carter chose a location on the Holston River in Sullivan County to establish the city of Kingsport, organized into industrial, residential, and commercial zones, with all utilities owned by the Kingsport Improvement Corporation, controlled by Carter himself. Kingsport grew rapidly, in part because of its production of high explosives for use in World War I. It was promoted as a "manifestation of the pioneer spirit and a haven for impoverished mountaineers," in order to attract new manufacturing companies. Its ordered plan insured that everyone would know their place in town as they did in the factory, in contrast to the more organically organized home- and community-centered agrarian society of the area. Men from farming families began to seek nonfarm employment to supplement agricultural income but maintained primary loyalty to home, family, and traditional values. In the event of labor unrest, it was an easy matter to return to the supportive rural family and community. Industrial leaders believed that mountaineers needed to develop "values and behavior . . . [for] . . . the discipline and regularity needed for factory work."[15]

With regular paychecks, sales of automobiles increased and women began to purchase stylish clothing. A shift was beginning in the area. Instead of factory wages supplementing farm income, the two complemented each other. During the Depression, in part because of the success of Tennessee Eastman, producer of organic chemicals and acetyls, and in part because of continuing farm income, Northeast Tennessee fared better than many other places. Those who lost jobs migrated readily back to rural areas, surviving long periods of unemployment. Farm subsidies initiated during the Depression helped to support farming, but not enough to make small farmers independent. Manufacturing income was becoming more important to farm families, as they relied increasingly on consumer goods. Still, though local inhabitants were sustained by industrial employment, they were "reticent to surrender the autonomy that was being lost" and continued farming in order to maintain it.[16]

Melvin Crawford, who danced at Beechwood in 1987 while in his mid-seventies, said that in his youth the area was "all farmers. No folk that worked. Tennessee Eastman came in here . . . trains hauled all the logs and the wood out. [Working at Eastman] was the only way you had to make a living, and farming."[17] Eastman began production of photographic film in 1929, along with acetate yarn and plastic. By the mid-1930s, the company had twenty-six manufacturing firms in Kingsport with four thousand workers. Though not the first manufacturing concern in Northeast Tennessee, it quickly became the largest.[18] Despite the growth of Tennessee Eastman and other factories, Northeast Tennessee life in the 1920s and 1930s still retained much of its rural and agricultural feel, with dirt roads and close-knit, almost autonomous communities. Bob Baines (b. 1913) described working on a large farm belonging to his neighbor: "He had three hundred acres. Twenty seven head of work horses. He put down a hundred acres of corn and then he'd put out a hundred acres of wheat, about six acres of Irish taters, about three or four acres of strawberries. We did that. I mean, stripping mountains of tobacco. They'd haul calves, gather up calves and go to Jonesborough in the wagon. The only way they had to take to Jonesborough. Used to drive turkeys from here to Jonesborough. It's about eight miles." At his blacksmith shop near the Baines' home, Mrs. Baines's grandfather "would shoe whole rows of horses, work on the equipment, make plows."

For fun, the boys played basketball and baseball, and girls played a game called three-girl station. Children had fun at Easter with egg-boilings, and whole families went fox hunting. "Back then, anybody going to church or anywhere, everybody walked. Road would be full of people walking," according to Mr. Baines. Most rural roads remained dirt roads cooperatively repaired by men of the immediate community until well through the 1930s, according to Nellie Baines, Bob Baines's wife. "The men took turn about working on the road. They had horses to haul rocks and fill up the gutters, where the wagons would cut in. And one man would take one month and the next man the next month, the farmers." Bob Baines said, "I was about fifteen years old before I ever saw Johnson City. Went then with my daddy with a load of tan bark on the wagon. I thought I never was going to get to Johnson City. It takes about fifteen minutes now to get there from here." The main roads were paved, but barely two cars wide, winding and bumpy. The Baines family and their neighbors lived approximately fifteen miles from Kingsport, and people in the area worked at Eastman and other factories, but they maintained their autonomy and independence in their rural community.[19]

The Jazz Age began in the early twentieth century, and the Charleston became as much a dance craze in Northeast Tennessee among both African Americans and European Americans as it was elsewhere in the country. People in Northeast Tennessee probably enjoyed popular animal dances such as the "buzzard lope" and learned the Charleston in dance halls and from moving pictures that were shown in the growing towns. It is likely that these were the kinds of dances enjoyed at Kingsport dance halls, and that some workers from rural areas danced there, enjoying the new styles. Dancer Nellie Baines's grandmother had loved to do the Charleston in the 1920s, and dancer Pauline Cassell could still demonstrate a Charleston step at Beechwood in 1987. Nineteenth-century ballroom dances like the waltz and polka were also popular among both rural and urban residents. Many rural Northeast Tennessee people at the time preferred what is now called "old time square dancing." Fern Simpson Warren, a retired elementary school teacher born in the first decade of the twentieth century, delighted in dancing in her childhood and youth.

In 1987, Mrs. Warren continued to raise beef cattle and to keep a big vegetable and flower garden at her white frame house near Fall Branch, and to dance regularly at Beechwood. She told about going as a girl in the 1910s and 1920s with her whole family on the weekends, especially during the summer, to have music and dancing at her grandparents' home in the small Sullivan County town of Harmony. Her father played the fiddle and her mother the piano, while the family and close neighbors danced a "big ring." One or another would call out actions for everyone to do, such as "swing your partner," "sashay," or "go in and out the windows," or "London Bridge," which was sometimes done as a separate dance to the song of the same name. Mrs. Warren remembered a singing game called "Weevilly Wheat." She did not use the term "play party." As she described the dance, a line of boys and men faced a line of women and girls, as in a longways set. Partners danced in from opposite corners, met in the center, swung, sashayed up and down the center, and "strutted like peacocks."[20] "Weevilly Wheat" is one name for the old play party sometimes known as "Charlie." It was mentioned as having taken place in Tennessee as early as 1803, in a brief biography of East Tennessee native Davy Crockett, and documented by local color writers in Tennessee in the mid- to late nineteenth century.[21] Mrs. Warren said that dancers sang along with the dancing, sometimes making up rhyming verses on the spot. A dancer might sing to a new sweetheart, or someone he or she wanted to tease. "After Weevilly Wheat, we'd all ring up and do another dance."

Besides the group dances, Mrs. Warren recalled everyone flatfooting, buck dancing, two-stepping, and doing the Charleston. Like Mrs. Warren, others reported their parents and grandparents doing dances similar to square dancing and flatfooting prior to the turn of the century. No one else I spoke with recalled doing singing games or play parties or other dances or games where dancers sang as they danced. No other accounts were given of longways dances in this area, except doing the Virginia reel in schools in the 1940s.

Because the roads were narrow and hard to travel, and cars were few, the close-knit rural "neighborhoods" continued to be the hubs of social activities. These "neighborhoods" had a radius of approximately three to five miles' walking distance, according to consultants. As a result, each neighborhood developed its own attitudes toward dancing and its own seasonal, monthly, or weekly pattern for having dances, and selected which dances would be the favorites. Some examples of these neighborhood dances from the first half of the twentieth century will give a sense of community variations.

Emmett and Pauline Cassell lived in Scott County, Virginia, which adjoins Sullivan County, Tennessee. Many Scott County residents now work for Tennessee Eastman or other plants in Kingsport, where they also go to shop. However, in earlier decades, the distance would have been too great to travel often for social occasions. The Cassells described relatives and neighbors gathering in various homes for music and dancing. Several men in the neighborhood called square dances and played fiddles or banjos. Emmett Cassell said, "There was always somebody there who could call. The caller would be in the head couple and do the calling. . . . They did practically the same dances all the time, it wasn't too complicated after you learned it." Mrs. Cassell told the familiar story of the host family piling all the furniture from one room onto the porch or in another room to clear a place to dance. Often, eight to sixteen couples would dance at one time. She said, "Several people didn't dance. They sat by the fire to socialize. People brought their children. All ages came." Mr. Cassell recalled going to dances before he could dance. In this community, these get-togethers were usually held in the winter because there was less farm work to do then. Dancing frequently lasted until the next morning, when families would walk the three or four miles back to their homes and put in a day's work on the farm. Emmett Cassell reminisced about the last all-night dance he recalled, in 1948. "You could dance all night then, and go home, work all day. Oh yea. Had to. I remember the last one of those all night dances we had, I guess it was at her home (Pauline's), and I had to leave about 5:30 in the morning to haul some cattle for one of our neighbors. And they were still dancing when I left."

On the other hand, Bob Baines reported that square dancing was a rare occurrence in the Washington County community of Locust Mount, though it was close enough to Fern Simpson Warren's childhood home that her father carried the Baines family's mail, and her family square danced regularly. Mr. Baines reported that occasionally in the 1920s and 1930s, Bethany School House, the Methodist school, would "have music," and people would square dance. But more regularly, the men who hosted an apple peeling or other working would take out their fiddles and banjos and play in the house, while other men buck danced alone or in small groups near them, with women watching and visiting. His whole family had danced and played music for generations. "They'd gather up you know, a whole bunch of them come down to my granddaddy's there, made music there for the night. It was just the working, you know. Have music of the night. Sometimes they'd all get together late of the evening. Mostly on Saturday nights, they'd make music."[22] In a Washington County, Virginia, community, both square dancing and flatfooting were enjoyed in the home, but as separate dances. In this community there were no singing games, but the London Bridge figure was used as the beginning or ending of a square dance. So one community chose mostly buck dancing for the men associated with workings, another chose mostly square dancing for couples, while still others did both. Because poor roads made travel difficult, dancing in the first third of the twentieth century usually took place within each community, rather than among several communities, and evolved to meet that community's needs and customs.

Marketing Local Music

In the 1920s, 1930s, and 1940s, dancing in the home was often accompanied by a solo fiddle or banjo or a combination. When two or more instruments were involved, they played the melody together repeatedly, multiplying the intensity of the sound. People reported dancing in the home to old time dance tunes like "Sally Ann" or "Old Joe Clark," just as they did at Beechwood decades later. However, popular culture was always an influence. Jazz bands and string bands, both white and black, toured the area with a variety of styles.[23] Mail-order instruments became common, along with instruction books. More dramatic changes were to come as a result of industry and technology, affecting dancing in Northeast Tennessee.

In the 1920s, Appalachian music, and southern music in general, experienced changes that both grew out of and supported the transformation of East Tennessee from primarily agrarian to urban centered, and paralleled the shifts in the dancing: local music was recorded for an enthusiastic audience, and radio "barn dance" shows became popular. In both cases, specific decisions were made by producers to shape the image of traditional music and to establish its link to the rural past and a simpler time and place.

The early commercial recordings of southern traditional music included many by string bands with fiddle, banjo, and guitar. According to Charles Wolfe, East Tennessee supplied a number of these because it was an "area rich in good mountain fiddlers." Since string band music evolved as accompaniment and impetus for dancing, one may infer that East Tennessee was also an area rich in dancing during the 1920s and 1930s. In 1924, Uncle Am Stuart, the champion fiddler from Morristown, Tennessee, recorded for Aeolian Vocalion, and not long thereafter Fiddlin' Dudley Vance from Bluff City, Tennessee, recorded.[24] Northeast Tennessee residents were able to hear their own neighbors on recordings, as well as hearing a variety of other kinds of music. However, recording companies soon made a decision to identify string band music with a particular image of rural life. Early recording artists dressed in their Sunday best and presented themselves with an air of dignity. They represented morality, stability, and home-centeredness. However, promoters, seeking a marketable image, encouraged a "hayseed" manner of dress and behavior, requiring musicians to wear overalls and to pose for publicity shots with dogs and moonshine jugs. They projected their own version of the rural life that was the source of the music.[25] The image they created had little to do with reality, but it helped to cement the connection of string band music and dance with rural life in the minds of listeners both locally and nationally.

A similar image was constructed for performers by producers of radio barn dance programs as they tried to establish a connection with the rural past in order to attract audiences. Radio barn dances appeared during the 1920s, when the South in general, and the Appalachian region in particular, was experiencing "a time of tremendous demographic, social and economic change." Whereas in 1890, only 10 percent of the southern population lived in cities, by 1930, almost one-third of the population did so. The National Radio Barn Dance was the first of its kind, opening in 1924 on WLS in Chicago. In 1925, George Hay established a similar program on Nashville's WSM, and it became instantly popular among listeners in the South. Two years later he dubbed it the Grand Ole Opry, to distinguish it from the classical music also heard on the station.[26] According to local journalist and historian Bob L. Cox, Northeast Tennessee had its own versions of the radio barn dance in the Saturday Night Jamboree on Bristol's WOPI, the Saturday Night Hayride on Kingsport's WKPT, and Barrel of Fun, the Saturday morning string band jam session broadcast from Johnson City's WJHL. These barn dances featured local performers like Fiddlin' Charlie Bowman from Gray Station, Tennessee, who played on WOPI in 1929–30. Beechwood dancers report attending these radio shows during the 1930s and 1940s.[27]

John Lair, founder of the National Barn Dance and the Renfro Valley Barn Dance, believed that he presented types of music that, along with rural ways of living, were in danger of becoming extinct, though he included not only traditional music but also Tin Pan Alley tunes that had been composed in the nineteenth century.[28] George Hay emphasized the "folk" aspect of the Grand Ole Opry, citing the audience "demand for the old folks and their tunes" and telling musicians not to play modern tunes or styles. Like the record producers, he soon began to emphasize the music's "rustic, hayseed quality," giving the performing groups names like Possum Hunters and Fruit Jar Drinkers, though many of them had urban experience, had traveled widely in vaudeville and minstrel shows, and had full-time nonfarm jobs other than music. According to historian Louis M. Kyriakoudes, the Grand Ole Opry spoke to its listeners' nostalgia for old ways and their anxieties about change, while at the same time promoting consumer products for them to purchase with their new nonfarm income.[29] As dance ethnographer Theresa Buckland observed, "Conceptions of the past are facts of the present . . . the content of such conceptions of the past . . . may well be largely or entirely the product of particular present interests."[30]

Recordings of local musicians and radio barn-dance shows like the Grand Ole Opry and the Saturday Night Hayride helped people in Northeast Tennessee to maintain a certain connection with regional cultural expression in the face of the many social and economic changes they were experiencing. They also provided local musicians with opportunities to hear other performers and to learn new ways of playing. The radio barn dances were performed for an audience in a theater, usually including square dancing by demonstration teams. Square dancing thus was presented as part and parcel of the comforting rural image produced by the barn dances and by recordings of "hillbilly" music, helping to keep square dancing in the constellation of traditional customs. The developing technology that made music and dance more widely available dovetailed with old time music and dance to establish a symbolic link between them and an older rural lifestyle in the popular imagination.

Mobility, Disposable Income, and a New Place to Dance

The industrial success of the Tri-Cities area, especially Kingsport, influenced who danced and where dances took place. Kingsport became a thriving industrial center in the 1940s, due largely to military contracts for World War II, but area residents clung to their traditional autonomy. Tennessee Eastman turned almost entirely to plastics, chemicals, and chemical-textile fibers for the war. The Kingsport Press produced manuals, hymnals, and Bibles for the armed forces, and the Holston Ordnance Works became the largest producer of military explosives in the world by 1944. More and more people commuted from all over Northeast Tennessee and from Scott and Washington Counties in Virginia in buses provided for each shift. The expanding plants used exclusively local labor, with the exception of engineers and management, so cash was in easy circulation. The size of farms decreased steadily and nonfarm jobs increased. By 1950, farming simply supplemented nonfarm wages, rather than the reverse.[31] While older residents tried to maintain their farms, a significant outmigration of young people took place in the 1950s. Statistics show that whereas 46 percent of the residents of Greene, Sullivan, and Washington Counties in Tennessee farmed for a living in 1940, by 1960, only 24 percent did so.[32] By 1970, though full-time agriculture had essentially come to an end in the Tri-Cities area, it was still common practice to have a big garden or small farm from which to harvest and preserve produce. People remained committed to their agrarian heritage and the independence it provided, but both dancing venues and dance participants began to change rapidly.

Square dancing moved out of the home in Northeast Tennessee in the 1950s, in part because of the rapid economic change. With the rise of nonfarm employment came increased mobility, leisure time, disposable income, and many more recreational opportunities. The walking-distance community of earlier decades became less relevant as mobility and prosperity increased. As more families owned cars, they could travel easily for recreation, and with more cash available for all kinds of consumer goods, they became less reliant on their neighbors. Dancer Elva Rowland hypothesized that the dancing moved out of the homes in part because people had disposable income to decorate their homes and didn't want big groups of people in them. "They got to fixing their houses up and got to putting carpet [linoleum] down. . . . We went over to dance at Meadowbrook [a community in Washington County, Tennessee] and you know they'd just waxed the carpet in the dining room and they gave us the dining room for dancing, you see. . . . I wish you'd seen the wax on the bottom of our feet . . . and I noticed I slowed down there and couldn't get my feet to go . . . and I looked and Lord they were black with wax. I bet we ruined that floor over there. And I'd say that's the reason. People got carpet in their house and then they got to putting rugs down." Pauline Cassell concurred. In talking about dancing in the home prior to 1950, she said, "We had hardwood floors. We didn't worry about the floors back then you know. We just had a good time."[33]

Occasionally a family would pull a horse-drawn wagon into the "hall" or "driveway" of the barn to provide a floor for dancing, and invite neighbors over to have music. But dancing mostly moved out of the homes to lodge halls, like Elks and Moose. This move may have contributed to the generation gap among the dancers at Beechwood. Older dancers tell that moving dancing out of the home removed it from the control of one or two individuals. The resultant problem of drinking and rowdiness eventually resulted in unsuitable environments for children, so that most of those coming of age between 1940 and 1970 did not experience dancing with their parents. The generation gap observed at Beechwood and elsewhere in the Tri-Cities was likely caused in part by this circumstance.

Besides lodges and clubs hosting square dances, towns and communities offered them in public places, and other forms of dance became readily available. Emmett and Pauline Cassell remember going to square dances in the early 1940s at the Kingsport Civic Auditorium (built in 1939), with a caller who hosted a show on WKPT. They even heard music by Victor recording artists The Johnson Brothers, a former vaudeville act from East Tennessee. Other cities had similar events. Johnson City, for example, had weekly Saturday night shows on the lawn of the city hall during the 1940s. The events had names referring to the rural past, like "The Railsplitters' Jamboree" and "The Smokey Mountain Jamboree."[34] Tobacco warehouses hosted square dances during the summer, the offseason for tobacco sales. Big band dances were also held at these public locations, offering jazz dancing to live music. The lindy, and later the jitterbug and rock 'n' roll dancing, became popular among teens and young adults. Men who joined the military learned other forms of dance from recreation specialists and chose to pursue them upon their return. This is also the generation of significant outmigration from the area, so they were distanced from community customs of socializing. Within a relatively few years, traditional square dancing and flatfooting had shifted from a home-based intergenerational recreation to paid entertainment primarily for adults in lodges or civic auditoriums and other public places. Different forms of dance became more readily available, and a generation of young people chose those forms rather than local traditions.

Modern Western Square Dance and the Cowboy Image

Modern western square dance had influenced Beechwood founders Don and Helen Baker, as well as some of the other dancers there. A number of people in Northeast Tennessee discovered modern western square dancing in the 1950s when they were young adults.[35] This kind of dancing exploded in popularity after World War II, when recreation specialists taught it to the armed forces and in community settings. Its complexity and challenge appealed to young adults, and it was one of the dance forms available instead of old time square dancing for people coming of age in the late 1940s and 1950s. It provided a ready-made network of dancers through the club system.

Its link with the cowboy image and music, another emblem of a rural past, was probably comforting in the period of "social dislocation" especially after World War II.[36] The cowboy had first emerged as a potent image for a rapidly changing America at the turn of the twentieth century, with the popular Wild West shows that appeared across the country, even in small Appalachian towns. Western movies followed in the 1930s, representing a simpler time in the face of uncertainty.[37] To many Americans, in Tennessee as elsewhere, the cowboy hero represented the pioneering spirit, independence, and ability to confront hardship alone, without institutional structures or restrictions. According to Bill

Malone, the cowboy represented a life "unrestrained by the confining regimens of city life, but bound by a code of proper behavior and loyalty to friends, symbolizing freedom and independence" to American people feeling increasingly constrained by urbanization and consumerism.[38] The image may have encapsulated some of the conflicts experienced by residents of Northeast Tennessee as the area became ever more industrialized and consumer oriented, and ever less rural and agricultural, making modern western square dancing, with its implicit references to the cowboy image, a good choice of recreation.

At the same time, because of its nationally standardized lesson structure, it served as a connection to mainstream America, becoming an easily accessible hobby during post–World War II prosperity. Though old time square dancing is much simpler, more informal, and less stratified than modern western square dancing, it shares some of the same characteristics of interaction between couples and even some of the same movement vocabulary. Don and Helen Baker, the owners of Beechwood, participated in western square dancing for years at the American Legion hall, as did some other Beechwood dancers, and Don even called the dances. However, Beechwood dancers in the 1980s often made the distinction between modern western and old-time square dancing, emphasizing the words "old time," and making comparisons that insured that the listener understood that old time square dancing, a local tradition, was preferable. At the same time, some sported western-style shirts or circular skirts reminiscent of the crinolined dresses worn by western square dancers, though most wore everyday clothing when they danced.

Wagon Training: Dancing and the Pioneer Spirit

Dancing at Beechwood had a connection to another recreation that both evoked the cowboy mystique and served to widen the territory of the dance community: wagon training. The first documented recreational wagon train in the United States was organized for a cause. In 1958, the Kiwanis Club in Tellico Plains, Tennessee (south of Knoxville), having spent years unsuccessfully lobbying for a road over the mountains to western North Carolina, hit upon the idea of using a wagon train to publicize the need for such a road. Member Sam Williams reportedly said, "Why don't we have a wagon train? We only have wagon roads!" To the organizers' surprise, sixty-seven "old, wood-spoke, steel-tire covered wagons" pulled by teams of horses and an additional three hundred twenty-five individual riders on horseback made the trip over the mountain. Only one person had wagon training experience—retired World War I cavalry officer Captain Frank Swan—so he served as wagonmaster. The wagon train was repeated annually, increasing in numbers, and resulting in the construction of the Cherohala Skyway. The organizers "sought prosperity and advancement for their rural communities," utilizing remnants of their agrarian past.[39] The 1958 wagon train was entirely primitive, with participants sleeping in bedrolls carried on their horses and all food and supplies carried in the wagons. Whole families participated, including adults, teens, small children, and dogs. As the years went on, motorized support vehicles joined the group. Photos show participants wearing indications of nineteenth-century clothing or overalls, and cowboy hats and shirts. String band music and square dancing and flatfooting were a regular part of the wagon train experience. A square dance in Tellico Plains at the wagon train's sendoff regularly attracted five thousand people, and a longtime participant referred to his "twenty five years of 'horses, saddles, roaring campfires, spur of the moment rodeos, and mountain hoedowns,'" deftly blending both cowboy and mountaineer references. A photo of the Tellico Plains square dance appeared in a 1959 issue of *Life* magazine, and in another photo, Estes Kefauver observed an on-the-trail square dance.[40]

Within a few years, wagon training became a popular recreation among families in the Tri-Cities area who, having once farmed exclusively, now had forty-hour-a-week jobs, farming or gardening on the side. Agriculture was becoming increasingly mechanized, and tractors replaced workhorses, but families still had their wagons, work horses, and even buggies. Wagon trains took place in several southwest Virginia and Northeast Tennessee counties, and in summer months during the 1980s it was not unusual to see a long line of wagons and horses wending their way down county roads. A number of Beechwood dancers were avid wagon train participants, according to dancer Bob Baines and caller Veronia Miller. Guy Barnes is credited with organizing the first wagon train in Gray Station, Tennessee, not far from Fall Branch. Soon thereafter, the Locust Mount Wagon Train, of which Bob Baines and Veronia Miller were members, started around 1962 and kept going into the mid-1970s. Members rode or transported their horses and wagons to a central meeting place, then traveled together on day trips or on camping trips for a weekend or a week. In the evenings, the participants would make music and square dance and flatfoot on a wooden floor brought along for the purpose. On these trips, western garb was worn and order was kept by the wagonmaster and his scouts. Baines was the wagonmaster for a big wagon train around 1970, which was more than a mile-and-a-half long, all horses, wagons, and buggies—covered wagons and open wagons, and horses "dressed up" with pretty harnesses. The wagonmaster rode in front, with helpers in the middle and at the end of the line, all equipped with walkie-talkies. "People would get out on the roads to look and they'd take pictures," exclaimed Nellie Baines.[41]

The members of the wagon train club established a cooperative group, reminiscent of earlier cooperative practices. They pooled their funds and held bingo games to purchase land and to construct a building near Harris's Tobacco Auction House in Locust Mount. The music and dancing, at first just part of the wagon training experience, became a regular event at the wagon train club. In the beginning it was very informal: a band was hired, and people brought covered dishes for a shared supper. In time, they held monthly or weekly get-togethers with music and dancing as activities completely separate from the wagon trains themselves. Many came for the music, not knowing the others who would come, and eventually became "one big family." Veronia Miller and her husband joined the club around 1974, and she served as secretary-treasurer. She said that by 1977, participation in the wagon trains dwindled, the land was sold, the money given to charity, and people began going to Slagle's Pasture to dance.[42]

The territory of the wagon train club was considerably larger than the old walking distance "neighborhoods" of the first half of the century. For example, another club, the Rich Valley Wagon Train Club, based in Benhams, Virginia, almost an hour's drive away, involved people from Northeast Tennessee and Southwest Virginia. Sometimes the Locust Mount wagon train club would take their horses and wagons an hour or more away to camp and ride trails, like the time Baines's and Miller's Locust Mount club went to Dungannon, Virginia. In addition, a connection was expressed, not with the former farming lifestyle in Northeast Tennessee but instead with the pioneers of the western frontier, who were so popular on the silver screen in the mid-twentieth century. The dancing was the local old time dancing, however, linking the social aspects with the regional past while expanding the dance community.

Folk Revival, Festivals, and New Venues

Wagon training emerged as a recreation in the mid-twentieth century, around the same time as the national folk revival, which aroused widespread interest in traditional music and dancing. The first focus of the folk revival was music of central Appalachia, and the attention drawn to the area by young musicians eager to learn old time tunes likely contributed to a rise in local participation. People from outside the region discovered traditional music through popularized folk performers like the Kingston Trio and wanted to search deeper for "authentic" music. Many came to the Appalachian region for fiddlers' conventions like the one at Union Grove, North Carolina. Revivalist bands like the New Lost City Ramblers, which included collectors Mike Seeger and John Cohen, formed to play the music themselves, taking it to a broader audience and creating growing interest.[43] Dancing was part of music festivals and fiddlers' conventions as well, and at least one revivalist dance group was formed in part as a result of their experience at the Union Grove, North Carolina, fiddlers' convention.[44] The youthful Green Grass Cloggers performed their exhilarating blend of traditional footwork and western square dance figures at local venues in Tennessee and Virginia and inspired the development of many a local clogging team, square dance team, or both. A team formed at the Carter Fold during the 1970s, and in the 1980s one formed at Beechwood, performing at area clubs and nursing homes and at the Tennessee Homecoming Celebration in 1986.

Music historian Bill Malone believed that the folk revival encouraged people to choose music, dance, and other forms of cultural expression that "reaffirm[ed] their identity, provide[d] bonding with people like themselves, or reestablish[ed] continuity with an older way of life."[45] Floyd Sloan, a regular dancer at Beechwood, is representative of this response. He had been enthralled by a flatfoot contest at a Fourth of July celebration in Kingsport in the 1930s, but his parents were opposed to dancing. However, as principal of tiny Rye Cove High School in Scott County, Virginia, he initiated a clogging team in 1971. Casting about for an act for his school to perform at the county 4-H talent show, he taught a clogging routine to a group of students. He said the audience was "aghast," and his group handily won the contest. The Rye Cove Cloggers grew and enjoyed more than a decade of disciplined practice and performance at local festivals and venues as renowned as the 1982 Knoxville World's Fair.[46]

In the 1960s, perhaps influenced by the folk revival, private establishments were opened expressly for the purpose of offering old time, bluegrass, and country music and dancing on Friday and Saturday nights. An example is the Slagle's Pasture annual bluegrass music festival, first held in 1968 on Clayton Slagle's farm, between Bluff City and Elizabethton, Tennessee. Slagle's Pasture featured big-name performers like Bill Monroe and Jim and Jesse McReynolds, and was widely known to string band musicians. Hundreds of people attended for the thirty-four years of its existence. Beginning in 1979, weekly dances were held there, with Hugh Miller, Veronia Miller's husband, calling the dances.[47] The Carter Fold is perhaps the most influential private venue for old time music and dance in Southwest Virginia and Northeast Tennessee. Founded in 1979 by Janette and Joe Carter, children of famed early country recording artists A. P. and Sara Carter, the building seats one thousand people. The Carters held music for the public at the old A. P. Carter's Store beginning in the mid-1970s, but attendance quickly outgrew the tiny space. Crowds—local residents and tourists alike—continue to the present to fill the theater every Saturday night, coming "as if on a mission to hear traditional music."[48] Janette Carter permitted no alcohol, allowed only acoustic instruments, limited the admission fee so that whole families could attend, and kept the focus squarely on old time music rather than bluegrass or country. She said she thought so many people came because

Figure 3.3. Don and Helen Baker, founders of Beechwood Family Music Center, Fall Branch, Tennessee, 1987. Courtesy of Appalshop Archive, Appalshop Films Collection.

"they just want to get next to something pure."[49] People clog and flatfoot every time a dance tune is played, but no waltzing, two-stepping, or square dancing was allowed. Establishments like these opened old time music and dancing to a wider audience, attracting visitors from elsewhere and area residents alike. The Carter Fold is probably responsible for many people returning to dancing after a hiatus, and for others taking their first clogging or flatfooting steps. Emmett and Pauline Cassell really did not dance much during the 1950s and 1960s, as they raised their family and other activities took precedence. It was the opening of the Fold that attracted them back to dancing.

The Carter Family Fold has been an inspiration to others to venture into the business. Beechwood Family Music Center was one such venue, established in 1982, and modeled after the Carter Fold. Helen and Don Baker loved to go to hear music at the Fold every Saturday night during the 1970s, and they often hosted informal music jams with dancing in their garage in Fall Branch, Tennessee. Driving home after an evening at the Fold, they joked about having such a place of their own. As Helen told it, "I came back into the den one day, and there he sat, with a piece of paper and a pencil. I said, 'What in the world are you drawing?' and he said, 'I'm drawing our building.' I said, 'What building?' and he said, 'Our music place.'"[50] And before long, Beechwood Family Music Center was born, based on principles similar to the Carter Fold. In 1987, their "building" was packed with dancers, and a community had formed around the weekend dances. Other places, like the Country Cabin of Josephine, organized by Anna Breeding in 1978 in Wise County, Virginia, to celebrate the musical heritage of her family and of the region, also drew inspiration from the Carter Fold. The growing interest encouraged nonprofit organizations like the Chilhowie, Virginia, Lions' Club to hold monthly old time dance events as fundraisers to support their projects. Because the folk revival sparked an interest in local dance, music, and crafts among area residents, things that once seemed simply old-fashioned became, to some people, more special. Evelyn Sturgill, a dancer from Chilhowie, Virginia, near the northern end of this old time dancing corridor, once said, "We have learned to appreciate all the things we were ashamed of. We get out our old quilts and things we used to make. We have had a revival of appreciation of our heritage."[51]

As a result of the move from home to membership group and finally to private venue, old time dancers expanded their dance territory during the twentieth century. Many of the dancers attending Beechwood in the 1980s were true dance hobbyists who readily traveled a few hours in any direction for a good dance. In the early 1990s, at least a dozen places within a sixty-mile corridor offered opportunities for square dancing or clogging. Some of the Beechwood dancers traveled an hour's drive northeast to dance at various Virginia venues: the Chilhowie Lions' Club, the Abingdon Tobacco Fairgrounds, the Marion Fireman's Jamboree, the Carter Fold, or to Steele Creek Park in Bristol, Tennessee. Dedicated dancers not only attended dances in that corridor, they also traveled to Western North Carolina to dance, making forays in couples or groups to The Stompin' Ground in Maggie Valley, long a destination for cloggers. People came from all these places to Beechwood as well. Numerous festivals were presented within easy driving distance. Jonesborough (Tennessee) Days always featured a flatfooting contest, often won by Bob Baines, and sometimes a square dance. Emmett and Pauline Cassell loved to go to Whitetop, Virginia, for festivals three or four times a year, like the Ramp Festival, the Syrup Festival, or the Molasses Festival. "If you want to hear good music, go up there," they said. Bluegrass festivals and fiddlers' conventions also provided opportunities for flatfooting, clogging, and buck dancing. The "neighborhood" had grown to a radius of sixty miles or more, and the community clustered around the dancing, rather than around a small town.

Modernization and Tradition at Beechwood, 1987: Dance Forms and Styles

In some ways, dancing at Beechwood re-created the experience of socializing in the early-twentieth-century walking-distance neighborhood, and in some ways it adapted to the faster-paced variety and increased mobility of the late twentieth century. Over the course of nearly a hundred years, old time dancing in Northeast Tennessee had evolved. Not only had the venue and dance

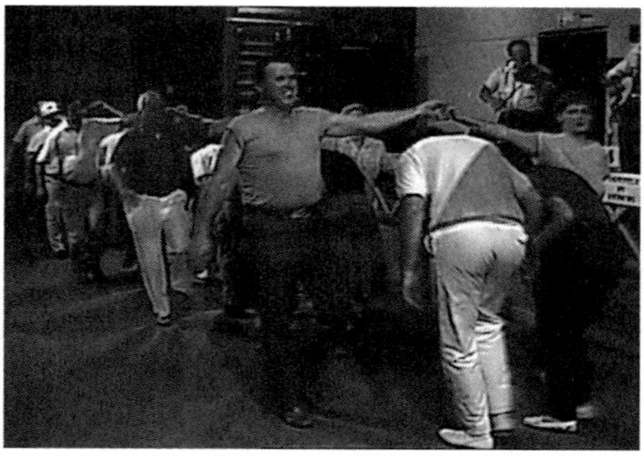

Figure 3.4. London Bridge, led by regular dance leader Hansel Dykes, 1987. Courtesy of Appalshop Archive, Appalshop Films Collection.

Figure 3.5. Two-stepping at Beechwood, 1989. Courtesy of the Archives of the City of Kingsport, Tennessee.

event changed, but so had the music, along with the dance forms and styles. Bits of the influences shaping the dancing were evident: home-based cooperative experiences, popular social dances, radio barn dances, modern western square dancing, wagon training, the folk revival, and influences from other areas and from other kinds of dancing. In the late 1980s and early 1990s, the choices made by Beechwood dancers reflected Beechwood's own history and urban characteristics such as variety, hierarchy, and division of roles as well as characteristics common to the agrarian past such as informality, cooperation, security, and contribution to the common good.

In 1987 more variety appeared both in the structure of the dance event and within each dance than had been portrayed at the beginning of the century. Whereas earlier, most communities chose only one or two kinds of dance, at Beechwood, several kinds of dances were done one after the other: square dancing, clogging, two-stepping, and waltzing.[52] Rather than being connected to a working or a dinner, the dancing itself was the focus of the evening. Dancers at Beechwood experienced a more complex dance than the kinds they and their parents had described doing fifty or sixty years earlier. By 1987, the simple "big ring" at the beginning of each dance, with everyone circling left and right, had evolved to include many permutations like promenading your partner, right and left chain, and gents dropping back to swing and promenade another lady, swinging her to his left and back to his right. Unlike in the 1930s, several circle fours, or "dances" as they were still known, were called in the course of each dance, including "bird in the cage," "right hands cross," and "butterfly twirl."[53] All couples danced at the same time, instead of one couple at a time visiting all the other couples in the circle, as had been the case earlier in the century. The big circle that ordinarily had concluded the square dance might lead into a London Bridge followed by the spiraling "wind the clock," ending again in a big circle. According to local dancers, many of these figures were danced in the first part of the twentieth century, but each was usually a separate dance.

Certain social customs continued to be reinforced by square dancing in the 1980s and 1990s. The male-female couple was the unit within the large group, but the couple itself was flexible, and the dance allowed interaction among all the dancers. Although in flatfooting it was not unusual for men to dance with men and women to dance with women, square dancing couples at Beechwood were always mixed. Any man or woman could invite anyone else of the opposite sex to dance, so that watching the dance floor, an outsider could rarely identify the married couples. Veronia Miller said that widows and single women did not hesitate to ask various men to dance, and the men were happy to oblige. During the course of one square dance, because of the way the movements were organized, every woman took hands at least briefly with each man, and each couple connected with each other couple. At Beechwood, finding a new couple to dance with was important, and the process was a random exchange to grab a pair near you, with no predetermined system of moving along. After each circle four, couples promenaded counterclockwise around the circle, and looked for a new couple when the next circle four was called. An even number of couples was not needed for a good dance. A circle four easily became a "circle six," in the case of an odd number of couples. While the variety and pace had increased, the sense of welcoming and mutual connectedness was reinforced by the form of the dance.

In the first half of the twentieth century, such partner exchanges provided opportunities for sanctioned flirtation. In the 1980s and 1990s, friendships were made and sealed on the dance floor, the community being built by ones, twos, fours, and the whole group. Caller Veronia Miller said as much in her synopsis of a square dance: "You start out in the circle, then you break them into 'Swing the Opposite,' and then they swing their partner, and then they promenade, and that gets them in twos going around. Then you can go to your 'Circle Fours,' then you can go back and have them 'All join hands in a circle,'" and do patterns involving the whole group. When you do the London Bridge, "you're with your partner, except you separate, the ladies go on one side and the gents go on the other. And then, when you do the Grapevine Swing, you're all in one big line."[54]

The square dance style at Beechwood reflected both traditional customs and modern innovations. Movements of hands and arms were purely functional, rather than decorative, and the point was not performance for an audience, but having a good time with friends. The arms were used only to take hands with other dancers to produce the circle fours or to swing the partner, as directed by the caller. They reached out only as far and as high as they must to accomplish this. The intent was not to make clear photographic pictures but to connect with new people in each new circle four. Motions were continuous. Although some teenaged dancers said that they liked people to watch them, in the square dance, interaction was the goal rather than producing an overall visual design for the viewer. In the late twentieth century as in the past, the focus of the square dancers was entirely upon each other within a closed circle. The step style, however, reflected modern influences. Instead of the simple bouncing walking step dancers recalled using for square dancing in past decades, a basic precision clogging rhythm was used by almost all dancers throughout the dance: RLR LRL (1&2 3&4).[55] Some dancers embellished the basic rhythm with extra beats on the toe or heel, but most kept their feet close to the floor. A few younger dancers added leg gestures learned in clogging classes or seen at competitions or talent contests. The unison sound seemed to underpin the figures, keeping everyone synchronized. The effect was heightened by the fact that most wore taps on their shoes or used special leather-soled shoes to dance. As dancers entered Beechwood, many carried small gym bags or bowling bags with a pair of shoes kept especially for dancing. As soon as they claimed seats, they routinely changed their shoes to get ready to dance. People said the taps made the shoes slicker so they could move more easily. They especially criticized rubber soled shoes like sneakers, because they would stick and cause accidents and awkwardness. Taps first appeared among dancers in Northeast Tennessee in the mid-1970s, probably as a result of seeing precision clogging teams. An eighteen-year-old dancer said his grandfather, who passed away in 1981, never had any, and Veronia Miller said she just purchased hers in 1986. She said that many bands opposed taps, because the dancers' different rhythms could affect their music, but she believed that bands enjoyed playing at Beechwood because the dancers had good rhythm.

Specialization

Something of a hierarchy in the dance event had developed by the 1980s. Unlike in the early 1900s, the caller, dance leader, and musicians fulfilled distinct roles for the square dances. At Beechwood, financial arrangements delineated the distinctions. Though not paid, caller Veronia Miller was allowed free admission, placing her in a position between the dancers, who paid to participate, and the band, which was given a percentage of the door. The caller's authority was limited, however. Although she controlled the choreography of the dance, she

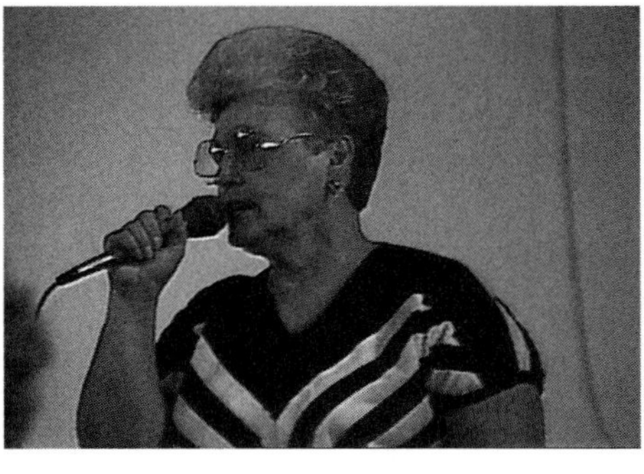

Figure 3.6. Caller Veronia Miller calls a square dance at Beechwood, 1987. Courtesy of Appalshop Archive, Appalshop Films Collection.

waited for a member of the audience or the band to request a square dance, in a way reflecting the earlier cooperative calling. She did not control the flow of the evening, only individual square dances. Late-twentieth-century specialization was tempered by communal values.

Though dancers traveled widely, enjoying dances in different locales, each community retained its distinctive repertoire and style, as they had sixty years before. For the dance to be pleasurable, the element of surprise had to be limited to a quick shift in a call rather than the introduction of a completely new movement or language vocabulary. A mutual trust and sense of security between caller and dancers was established. Veronia Miller often referred to the individuals who danced at Beechwood as "my people," as had her husband when he called at Slagle's Pasture, simultaneously reflecting familial attachment and choreographic concern.[56] Typically in the 1980s and 1990s, wherever there was square dancing, there was one regular caller from within that community. Etiquette dictated that anyone else led the dancing only at the invitation of the regular caller. Besides demonstrating respect for the authority of the local caller, this practice stemmed from practical considerations. Over the years, the regular dancers developed a rapport with a particular caller, becoming accustomed to that person's style and knowing the usual cues. Generally speaking, a visitor would accept an invitation to take the microphone only after watching the regular caller to determine if their styles were similar enough to suit the dancers. Mrs. Miller herself had called by invitation at the Abingdon Tobacco Warehouse and the Damascus Schoolhouse, but she would never have offered to do so, saying she believed that would be "too pushy." She told a story about a man who taught square dancing at a college in Kentucky, and whose calls, according to her, sounded like western square dance. He came to dance one night at Beechwood and insisted on calling a dance before she had. According to her, he used a singing style, and people that were used to dancing to "just plain old circle Appalachian square dance calls cannot get in there and pick up his calls and dance his dances. They tried. Everybody got up. They all got up there, and he started calling calls, and it was worded different to the way I call. And it was much faster. And they couldn't get it. And this couple would sit down, and that couple would sit down, and he wound up with four people on the floor. The man is good, but people here don't know how to dance to his way of calling."[57] At a square dance, the common good outweighed one individual's personal gratification, even the caller's, and though the caller controlled the action of the dance, the dancers had the ultimate control. A balance between security and variety was important.

Mrs. Miller acknowledged that changing times made it possible for her to call, though it was unusual for a woman to call old time square dances in Northeast Tennessee. She felt that most people accepted her as a caller because of evolving women's roles in society. In the past, "it just wasn't a woman's place to call a square dance . . . of course, we're getting women ministers now, but you know, used to be you never heard of a lady that was a minister. And I think it kind of follows the trends. . . . I feel like if there was a group of nothing but men calling, I'd get right up there and call with them," even though sometimes "you see eyebrows raised when a woman gets up to call a square dance." Veronia Miller had never been to a square dance before meeting her husband, Hugh Miller, who had grown up in a family of musicians and dancers in Bristol, Virginia. With him, she danced frequently at various locations around the Tri-Cities area, including the Marion, Virginia, Fireman's Jamboree and at Slagle's Pasture. Through him, she became involved in the wagon train club, with its monthly dances. When he called at Slagle's, she was the partner of dance leader Robert Dotson, a North Carolina Folk Heritage Award Winner. One night her husband had a Masonic meeting, so someone asked Mrs. Miller to call until he arrived. As she told it, she said, "I don't know how." They said, "Yes, you do." "Well, I figured if I can dance it, I ought to be able to call it as you dance it. And that's how I got started square dance calling."[58]

The place of the caller as a specialist outside the dance was, in this area, a development of the second half of the twentieth century, and it accompanied the move to more public venues. At home-based dances prior to 1950, any one of a number of men present in the home for music-making and dancing might call a square dance as he danced, though some were certainly more renowned and sought after than others. At Beechwood, Veronia Miller saw her role as keeping the interest of the dancers with some variety while also ensuring the successful progress of the dance, and she identified skills that supported these roles.[59] According to Mrs. Miller, a caller must have "a voice loud enough to come out over the music" and "has to speak very plain . . . go slow enough for the dancers to hear you." The caller must emphasize the important aspect of each sequence. For example, *Right* hand cross, How do you do, the *Left* one back, I'm fine, thank you." She guaranteed everyone's success by being attuned to the progress of the dancers as she called, waiting until everyone on the floor was nearing completion of one circle four before calling the next, but being careful not to hesitate so long as to let the dance lose momentum between calls. Mrs. Miller said she made a point of watching the slowest couple to be sure they were ready to go on. At the same time, she made the dance interesting by varying the ways she called the figures. Within the basic three-part structure, they might be called in any order. She made decisions based on the dancers' responses and her own sense of form, demonstrating an element of improvisation within strict limits, much like the dancers' solo flatfooting. She liked to change the order of the calls to keep the dancers alert. "I've noticed that if I say 'Right hands cross,' sometimes you'll see that left one come back, and when I see somebody doing that, I'll automatically say 'And both hands back' to get them off." Part of the fun of dancing at Beechwood was the surprise of not knowing exactly what would come next, coupled with the security of knowing that whatever was chosen would come from a shared repertoire.

As in the dances in the farming community, everyone was in the dance together to have a good time, and everyone supported each other for the common good. Confidence was established in the midst of ever-changing directions and ongoing flow. According to Veronia Miller, "That's the fun of Appalachian square dancing. You don't have to know what you're doing, just listen. The majority of the people in the square dance have square danced. And if you get with someone who has square danced, they can help you and show you." For the sake of contrast to this informal supportive atmosphere, Mrs. Miller mentioned modern western square dancing. In western, according to her, the participant needed to think too much, responding to over one hundred calls. She said that people did not seem happy because they were concentrating on doing it correctly. Whereas, "if you mess up in circle square dancing, someone gets you going right and everybody laughs about it and goes on" without breaking the rhythm.[60]

Almost as important as the caller was a good square dance leader. Though Veronia Miller had broken the gender barrier for callers, only a man, chosen by the caller, could lead the square dance. Usually it would be the most experienced man in the particular dance. Besides being familiar with the calls, Mrs. Miller said that the dance leader must have a good spring in his step, be "swift" and be able to "move on out," to keep the dancers moving at a good pace, particularly in portions of the dance where everyone follows in a line. Hansel Dykes, the usual leader at Beechwood at the time, was described as being a "proud dancer," reserved yet confident, capable of dancing with any woman regardless of her skill, and always clearly having a good time. The dancers "enjoy seeing someone out there putting that little extra into it." The square dance, though cooperative in feeling, by 1987 had a certain hierarchy. The caller directed the action, the leader kept it going at a good pace, and the dancers contributed their energy and skill. But all of it happened at the request of a dancer or musician, not because of the caller's decision.

Individuality

A less specialized or hierarchical structure occurred during most of the evening, when Beechwood dancers clogged or flatfooted alone, with one or more partners, or in a group, fluidly relating to the other dancers on the floor. This purely step dance allowed for even more individuation as long as the basic community style was maintained. One could see everything from Pauline Cassell's quietly elegant Charleston step, performed briefly for the camera, to eighteen-year-old Don Hensley's exuberant aerial heel clicks. In footwork dancing, groups or pairs of either gender would dance together, or individuals might drift from one "neighbor" on the dance floor to another. The feeling of being on the dance floor was conversational. An exchange between two people would open up as a third person joined in, and contributed his or her own rhythms or moves.

Some Beechwood dancers differentiated three styles: flatfooting, clogging, and buck dancing. Flatfooting and buck dancing were described as older forms. "In flatfooting, you're not supposed to raise your feet above two inches from the floor. Don't raise those feet but just enough to move them on the floor." In buck dancing, the knees were said to be lifted forward a little on each step, and the feet raised a little more off the floor. Clogging was identified as a newer form with much fancier footwork with feet coming high off the floor, with swinging and kicking leg gestures. During the 1980s people of all ages in Northeast Tennessee took clogging lessons and joined precision clogging teams. Middle-aged and older Beechwood participants placed a value on traditional ways of learning to dance, and one's dancing was believed to reflect an inner sensibility. Most people there demonstrated by their dancing that they preferred a close-to-the-floor step like old style flatfooting, some including beats of heels and toes. Veronia Miller believed that "dancing is your feet, not your other body movements. And when you get to put too much body English in with what's supposed to be the feet moving, it takes away from your ability to dance." Nellie Baines judged it indecorous for middle-aged people to "fling their legs around," and Elva Rowland commented, with a glance toward the dance floor, "You can tell every one of them down there that's had clogging lessons," and therefore did not do the older, more reserved style. Children liked to position themselves facing the audience to clog, with lots of up and down movement of arms and legs, in a manner very unlike the older, subtler dancers. Some elders said that as the youngsters grew older, they would develop more refinement in their dancing. Veronia Miller summarized their views: "I think that's a stage they go through when they're learning something, they like to show off. When you get more maturity, you don't do anything to attract attention."[61]

A young man from a dancing family agreed with the local aesthetic, though he would occasionally throw in a flashy move. He learned buck dancing from his father and grandfather, born in the 1940s and 1920s respectively. Going to the wagon trains at the Sullivan County community of Fairview was a regular family entertainment in his childhood during the 1970s. He based his analysis of good clogging on his father's opinion, and he criticized contemporary precision cloggers who played recorded music at a higher speed, so that they could dance faster. "I've seen people get up there and dance real fast, you know, just get up there and wear their shoes out. To me that is not clogging. They don't have rhythm. They're not paying attention. My dad said, 'You've got to get your rhythm. If you don't have your rhythm, you can't dance. Let your taps tell about the music. Let your feet do the talking.'" Bob Baines, recognized by many as an excellent dancer, agreed: "You've got to have music in you to do it." Veronia Miller identified a certain inner sense as the primary criterion for a good dancer: "You have to like to dance. It's what you feel within you."[62] Emphasizing the relationship to the music and the inner motivation for dancing demonstrated a preference for traditional conventions rather than modern styles and instruction methods.

Though drawing too much attention to oneself was considered unseemly, a challenge element appeared sometimes in the men's dancing, but never in the women's. Frequently, two men would dance in proximity with each other, challenging each other to try harder and harder things, and sometimes clowning around. Younger men like Hensley challenged each other by dancing faster, doing fancier steps, and pounding their feet harder into the floor, looking for all the world like roosters ready to fight. Older men like Kirby Smith, Fred Skeens, and Joe Carter, all widely recognized for their dancing ability, preferred other devices, like leg swings, jumps with heel clicks, and sideways scoots that challenged balance and equilibrium. Kirby Smith additionally inserted an occasional comical motion, like a quick hip-swivel, the humor of which lay in the fact that he and his observers all knew it was outside the flatfoot aesthetic. The idea seemed to be to show off by doing something a little improbable. These retired gentlemen challenged each other with finesse and risked dignity, and each challenge movement was accompanied by a sly grin.

Modernization and Tradition at Beechwood, 1987: Music

The dancers at Beechwood had definite ideas about what constituted good dance music. Their tastes in music reflected the same negotiation between variety and security, between leadership and collaboration, and between old and new as evidenced in the dancing. Older dancers, especially, looked for a specific kind of sound, keeping for reference the music from their youth. Middle-aged and younger dancers expressed opinions similar to their elders in preferring old time music.

The music at Beechwood during the 1980s and 1990s was performed by a string band of four to six members: fiddle, banjo, guitar, bass, sometimes mandolin or harmonica, and sometimes more than one guitar, banjo, or fiddle. Typically during a three-minute tune, individual instruments would take the lead for a verse or two, with the other instruments playing backup. Some Beechwood dancers were disgruntled with the switching about of the lead, preferring that the fiddler play for the entire eight to ten minutes of the square dance or the three minutes of the flatfoot number, as they remembered from their youth. "Without a fiddle you don't have dance music," commented one dancer. Emmett Cassell was especially articulate about dance music and summarized the expressed views of many Beechwood dancers: "To really flatfoot and clog, what you really need now is to get one of those old time bands and to just let the fiddler keep fiddling. Lot of the bluegrass bands'll start out pretty good with you, and then he'll quit and let the banjo picker pick a little bit and then the mandolin. That works up your dancing. They're pretty, but to really dance you want to just let that fiddler keep pulling it like, to get through. Listen to the bass for the rhythm, and the fiddle for the way you dance." Old-time musician Rich Kirby said that the "rhythms of old time music both mirror and inspire the flatfoot steps," and perhaps to some dancers the variety in musical leads disrupted their connection to the underlying rhythm.[63]

Most dancers at Beechwood analyzed the music this way: bluegrass was too fast for dancing, country rock could be good for two-stepping but nothing else, and country music was "no count for dancing." Robert Dotson said, "You've got to have the right kind of music to start with. Old-time music. You cannot dance to bluegrass. You can get out there and you can jump around, but you're not in time with it."[64] Veronia Miller believed people came to participate rather than to listen, so a good dance band with a variety of tempos was important. "Anytime you go and there's a group playing and there's no one on the floor dancing, then you know they're playing the wrong music." In fact, on different nights at Beechwood, the dance floor would be full or empty, depending upon the style of music played. I observed experienced dancers attempt to flatfoot to a band, determine the music was unacceptable, stop in their tracks, briefly face the band as if to communicate that opinion, and finally leave the floor. Variety was enjoyable, as long as it was cast within the framework of the preferred aesthetic. Snake and the Grass, the band that played at Beechwood on opening night, and one of the favorites there, consisted of six members: a fiddler, two banjoists, two guitarists, and a bass player. They did trade leads during the course of a dance, but they played mostly tunes from the standard old time repertoire, such as "Sally Ann." At one point during an evening, their version of "John Henry" filled the dance floor with enthusiastic cloggers.

The connection with days gone by was explicitly expressed when discussing the dance music. More than one dancer identified the Roan Mountain Hilltoppers as the quintessential old-time band and best for dancing. "Two old men about eighty-seven years old, and a younger man and his wife. For the bass, she's just got a tub and a stick with a string. You can't get much old timier than that. That old man that plays the fiddle [Joe Birchfield], he comes wobbling in there with his walking cane and he hangs that cane there in his hind pocket while he's fiddling. Stand up there and fiddle all night like there's nothing to it. Just float it across there like there ain't a thing in the world to it." The style of the music, combined with the age of the musicians and the homemade instrument contributed to the old time nature of this band's music. In a simultaneous reference both to the strong Appalachian work ethic and to home-based entertainment connected with workings, Emmett Cassell again voiced the views of other dancers. "The best music you're going to hear is not these big groups that travel around and do it for a living. It's the people that make a living at something else and play music because they enjoy it. Those are the best bands you get, as far as real good music."[65] As with the dancing, the music seemed more authentic coming from the joy of playing rather than from the desire to earn money. Not only was the old time sound and instrumentation important, but so was the sense of the music being home grown. Though old time music was preferred, most bands, even those identified as old time, reflected the influence of bluegrass, country, country-rock, or all three, bringing variety to their harmonies and rhythms, blending old and new.

Variety, Complexity, and Cooperation

Traditional Appalachian square dancing and clogging experienced a revival in Northeast Tennessee in the 1970s and 1980s. The revival came a few decades after the country, and this area in particular, had completed its evolution from predominantly rural to predominantly urban. Modern and traditional ways existed side by side in Northeast Tennessee in the 1980s. Dancing at Beechwood demonstrated both. The dance event and the dance itself appeared to have elements both of the rural, walking-distance community of the past and of the modern, industrialized society. I have come to believe that, for these dancers, old time square dancing served to navigate between rural and urban lifestyles and expectations, or to create a kind of blending of the two.

Mobility had produced a community of dancers who paid for their entertainment, replacing the geographical neighborhood where people walked to one another's homes to dance on Saturday nights. At Beechwood though, in the 1980s, people brought along garden produce to share, talked about their livestock and gardens, and helped out the members of their dance community when they could, reflecting an earlier rural experience. Modern society's increased pace and thirst for variety may have been reflected in the dancing. At the turn of the twentieth century, square dancing had been simple. One couple visited each of the other couples in the circle with only one figure, and then the next couple did the same. In the 1980s, everyone danced at once, and each square dance contained several figures for two couples and several for the whole group. Formerly, the figures for the whole group had been dances in themselves, rather than part of another dance. The caller deliberately learned new figures to introduce, instead of a community doing the same dance every week. Rather than local musicians gathering for their own fun, a different band was hired each week, providing variety for the participants. The tempo of the music and dance steps was considerably faster in the late twentieth century than reported from earlier decades, perhaps responding to the increased pace of life in general.

The planned, orderly structure of industrialized Kingsport may have had some influence on the dancing at Beechwood. A certain hierarchy and specialization had appeared. Instead of the caller and musicians being neighbors come to socialize, roles were established. The band was paid, though the caller was not. The band invited the caller to the stage with them when they felt it was time for a square dance, and she directed the dance from there, rather than dancing while calling, as once was the custom. Though Beechwood dancers stated their opposition to precision clogging, during the square dance most participants used a standardized footwork rhythm, unlike dancers in the less-industrialized areas of Western North Carolina and Eastern Kentucky. Still, as in former times, the couple was the basis of the dance community. Like the family in a rural community, they were not isolated: they related to each of the other couples in small squares of four, making sure not to miss anyone. Each individual related directly with each other individual at some point during the dance. The intent of the dance was relating to the other participants, like a cooperative rural community, rather than showing off individually. Even when clogging improvisationally, dancers usually interacted with others on the floor instead of performing for an audience. For the dancers, the dancing was egalitarian, supportive, and informal.

The role of old time square dancing and clogging had changed during the course of a century. Where once it was a primary form of entertainment in some communities, it had become one of many options from which to choose. Where it once was sometimes associated with workings and cooperative labor, it had come to serve purely as entertainment. In the first half of the twentieth century, it was home, family, and neighborhood based, while by the end of the century, square dancers were hobbyists who traveled an hour or two to participate in dancing at other venues, at fiddlers' conventions, or at music festivals, creating a broad geographic community centered around a common interest.

Every Friday and Saturday night at Beechwood, the dancers enacted their understanding of community as cooperative and secure, with everyone accepted and contributing to the common good, supportive of individuality and of friendships, and enjoying variety and small surprises within an established framework. Flatfooting with each other alone and in pairs or groups, two-stepping with a variety of partners, and going through the familiar array of patterns of the square dance, they reaffirmed connections with each of the other people on the dance floor in several ways. Couples separated, rejoined, connected with other couples, passed individually down the line of other oncoming dancers, wove among each other in a long line, and joined together to face inward in the circle. Drawing on elements from the rural past and from the industrial present, the dancers created a close-knit dance community. For its Beechwood enthusiasts, old time square dancing and flatfooting dovetailed a new, more complex, faster-paced lifestyle with its variety, specialization, hierarchy, and rapid change with the agrarian values of cooperation, community centeredness, and mutual trust and support. Perhaps, in some way, dancing at Beechwood stood in for the old walking-distance community and served as one way of adapting to the ever-more-rapid pace of change in Northeast Tennessee.

4. Blue Ridge Breakdown

Stability and Tradition in an African American Community

Square dancing and clogging and their accompanying string band music are not just European American art forms. Today, it is common knowledge that similar African American traditions flourished as well, but in the late twentieth century, few were aware of them. Ethnomusicologist Kip Lornell documented African American string band musicians in North Carolina and Virginia in the 1970s and helped to arouse interest in the traditions and bring new life to them. Charles Wolfe has written a number of articles about black string band music, and among his extensive writings on country music, he has frequently included discussion of African American influence. Cecelia Conway's groundbreaking book *African Banjo Echoes in Appalachia* opened the way for the growing awareness of these centuries-old traditions, and the annual Black Banjo Gathering she organizes has carried it further since it began in 2005.[1] Presently, black string band traditions are growing in popularity, with bands like the Ebony Hillbillies and the Carolina Chocolate Drops, the latter mentored by National Heritage Fellow fiddler and dance caller Joe Thompson. Such groups learn from African American musicians, either live or on record, who have played string band music since the 1920s, and they bring the traditions to a wider audience.

Less, perhaps, is known about African American square dancing traditions. Rarely is an African American set dance tradition mentioned in the media or in educational settings. When square dancing is taught in schools, if context is given at all, it is usually focused on European Americans, either mountaineers or cowboys. Widespread throughout the South since before the Civil War, this tradition essentially died away during the first few decades of the twentieth century. However, in Martinsville, Virginia, and its surrounding counties, it continued until about 1970, even during the postwar decades when white old time square dancing had fallen out of favor. It came to an end just at the mo-

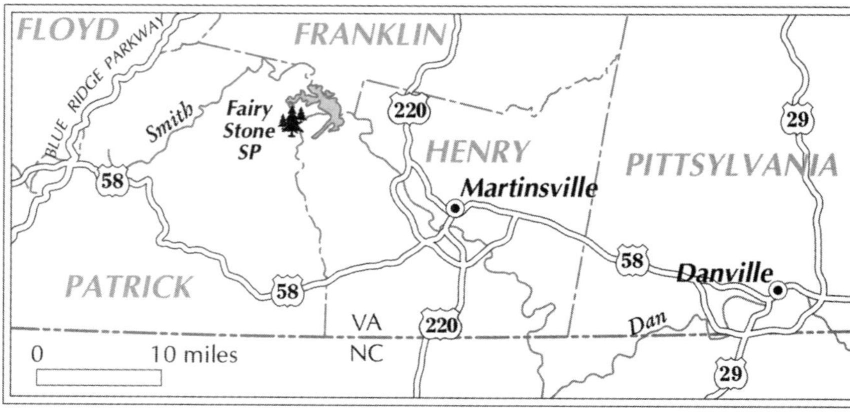

Map 3. Area surrounding Martinsville, Virginia. Cartography by Dick Gilbreath, Director, Gyula Pauer Center for Cartography and GIS, University of Kentucky.

ment that white communities began to revive their square dancing traditions. Its longevity was supported by a large and cohesive African American community that developed around Martinsville after the Civil War. The vibrant culture they established began to disperse with the end of segregation and the beginning of urban renewal in the late 1960s. The dance continued until that time, sustained by this community, by the dancers' identification with widespread rural and folk traditions, and by the values expressed in the dance itself. It lasted longer than similar dance traditions elsewhere, even in spite of its invisibility, attributable to the recording and radio industries, folk music and dance collectors, and the rise of exciting new dance and music styles.

African American people and Native American people throughout the Appalachian Mountains have enjoyed square dancing since the nineteenth century.[2] In fact, it is in all likelihood a creation developed from dance forms and styles of these cultural groups, together with European Americans. Historian Mechal Sobel asserts that, especially in the Piedmont to the east of the Blue Ridge, blacks and whites had established a shared culture through mutual influence in the decades prior to their migration to the mountains.[3] All forms of cultural expression were affected, including music and dancing, and the cross fertilization continued in the mountains. From many places in Southwest Virginia, Northeast Tennessee, North Carolina, and West Virginia come stories about square dancing in African American communities.[4]

This is the story of one African American dance community as seen primarily through the eyes of four people who were central to it through much of the twentieth century. Fiddler Leonard Bowles and his wife, dancer Naomi Bowles, and Leonard's first cousin, caller Ernest Brooks, and Brooks's wife had much to

Figure 4.1. Fiddler Leonard Bowles and caller Ernest Brooks during a Blue Ridge Institute videotaping of the Old Breakdown. Courtesy of the Blue Ridge Institute and Museum of Ferrum College.

say about the old Virginia breakdown, a dance similar to old time square dancing, in a black community in Martinsville, Henry County, Virginia. Through them, it is possible to understand a great deal about the form and style of their dance, why it was so important to them that it continued at least twenty years longer than it did in African American communities elsewhere, and the forces that supported or worked against the old breakdown in their community. Kip Lornell documented their dancing and music and interviewed Leonard Bowles between 1976 and 1978. In 1992 I enjoyed talking with the Bowles and Brooks families, discussing a videotape of their dancing, and dancing a little with them. Irvin Cook, Bowles's music partner, had passed away in 1987, and Bowles was keenly aware of his own role as a tradition bearer when I spoke with him.

African American Appalachian Old Time Dancing

Square dancing became very popular in the central Appalachian region in the late nineteenth and early twentieth centuries, according to the southern West Virginia consultants of Cortez Reece, ethnomusicologist and professor at Bluefield State College. As with many new dance forms, it was considered rather racy or risky compared with the somewhat tamer play parties that had been popular previously, and that reputation was part of its attraction for young people. Rural people of both African and European descent sang similar songs and danced similar dances, learning new fads as they came along.[5] Rosa Powell, born in 1905 in Abingdon, Virginia, said that square dancing occurred in her community during her childhood. Her mother-in-law told her about square dancing in the homes that had larger living rooms. "They would catch hands in a circle and then they'd form a line and couples would go underneath. About ten or twelve couples would come through, under kind of an arch." Mrs. Powell demonstrated raising her hand as if with a partner, to form an arch for other couples to go under, and described how two couples would get together to dance a figure. She remembered her mother-in-law laughing and telling her about a dance in a home that had windowsills at floor level. "They had the windows raised and going around and whoever it was she was dancing with was swinging partners and swung her out the window!"[6] Catherine Grubb of Ivanhoe, in the Virginia Blue Ridge, spoke energetically about her parents dancing in the 1920s and 1930s:

> A lot of black people wouldn't understand if I told them that my mom and dad, all they knew was country music. And that's what they danced off of. It's hard for them to believe that. I don't guess they knew anything much about rhythm and blues. They'd go to different houses, and they'd have barn dances. They'd have itinerant people that came around. I remember my dad talking about a man that used to come around that could play the fiddle. And my dad said they had this saying about him: he could put the fiddle up on the wall and play it! Another thing that they would talk about would be "playing the spoons." And my dad used to talk about doing this dance, buck and wings. They would do the square dancing. My mama—you'd have to just really get her in the mood—once in a while she'd show us how they would do.[7]

Several others gave accounts of square dancing in African American communities in Southwest Virginia and Northeast Tennessee. Joe Thompson of North Carolina described frolics being held by black families, especially in the 1920s and 1930s, saying that such events were opportunities "to dress up and 'show off.'" Howard Armstrong of Lafollette, Tennessee, played with his black string band all over East Tennessee and Southwest Virginia. Ellen Carter recalled seeing people square dancing in homes in Washington County, Virginia, as recently as the 1940s, the women wearing "long, pretty dresses." Iva Turk, from New Market, Tennessee, played the piano for square dancing in the home until the 1940s. Food would be served, and for the dancing everyone would take hands in a circle and then break into sets of two couples to dance. In Dante, Virginia, Bo Fain called square dances in his African American community into the 1940s.[8]

Ed Cabbell lived as a young child in Smyth County, in Southwest Virginia, on a farm that had been in his family since the end of the Civil War, and he subsequently spent many summers there. In the recreation program he attended in the 1950s, retired African American teachers taught square dancing as part of their heritage, saying, "This is the way our old people danced." It seems not to have been a regular recreation there by that time, but Cabbell's grandparents and great-grandparents, born in the 1890s and 1860s, respectively, had square danced in their homes until at least the 1930s, and they were happy to demonstrate it. Cabbell "grew up around blacks who played banjo, they clogged, they did all sorts of things which would be unusual to some blacks, but to me it was just everyday. All my life I've lived around blacks who have had all these things as a part of our culture. I wasn't raised up that these things were white." His grandmother was so expert at the footwork dancing that she could put a glass of water on her head while her feet flew, and never spill a drop. Buck dancing was common at fish fries in Cabbell's youth, and he did a dance that combined moves from buck and wing and the kind of holy dancing done in church. Hamboning, or patting rhythms on arms, legs, and torso, often accompanied buck dancing as recently as the 1950s and was especially popular as a feature of talent contests.[9]

In other places, like Dante and Pennington Gap, Virginia, and New Market, Tennessee, buck dancing and hamboning had mostly died out in African American communities by the 1940s. In Abingdon, Virginia, Rosa Powell last saw older boys buck dancing when she was a little girl (before 1920), accompanying their steps with the percussive sounds of bones. "They'd just do it on the porch, anywhere, just get out here on the porch and they used to have some kind of something that they said while they were doing it. There wasn't any music." Each African American community had its particular array of dance forms and styles, and each chose to continue or discontinue square dancing/breakdown and buck dancing at different times during the twentieth century.

The Blue Ridge area of Virginia is the center of a rich string band tradition, both black and white. The old breakdown was a popular entertainment in homes in African American communities in Martinsville and in Henry, Franklin, and Patrick Counties during the first half of the twentieth century, according to Kip Lornell. These communities were unusual in that the tradition was particularly vibrant and long lasting. Breakdowns were held regularly in Franklin County until 1967 and in Henry County until 1969. Musician John Lawson Tyree reported holding a square dance in Franklin County's Sontag section as recently as 1972.[10] The local black community was especially strong, both in numbers and in wage-earning ability, due to the number of plants and other businesses in the area and because there was an agricultural base in the rural area around the town. The strength of the community was fostered at least in part by Dana O. Baldwin, who contributed directly to the longevity of the string band and square dancing traditions.

Martinsville, Henry County, and "The Block"

Henry County is located in the eastern foothills of the Blue Ridge Mountains, near the North Carolina border. Its beautiful rolling hills and fields have a feeling of openness. Furniture and textile mills in Martinsville provided jobs for local people and attracted others to the area. As of the early 1990s, unemployment had never been perceived as a serious problem. The population remained relatively stable throughout the twentieth century, with a consistent African American presence. Some African American families can claim ownership of their land dating to before the Civil War. Since 1910, African Americans have continuously constituted approximately forty percent of Martinsville's population. Outside the city, in Henry County, the black population has varied from five percent to twenty percent, depending on the area.[11] The Bowles and Brooks families would likely agree with scholar and activist Ed Cabbell's remark: "There's something good about the mountains. There's solace here, and there's freedom here like nowhere else. I feel complete here."[12]

Founded by a plantation owner, Martinsville has been a manufacturing center since its early days, with plug tobacco its first main product, produced by local companies. By the twentieth century, Martinsville had become a center of furniture manufacturing, along with its nearby neighbor, High Point, North Carolina. In the 1920s, DuPont brought in chemical manufacturing, and other entrepreneurs established textile factories. Although few of the textile plants employed African Americans, the flourishing economy provided jobs in the tobacco and furniture industries, and Jobbers Pants Factory worked with black community leaders to open a plant staffed by African American women in 1933. A headline in the black

Figure 4.2. Dr. Dana Baldwin. Courtesy of Dr. John P. Bing.

Figure 4.3. "The Block," Martinsville, Virginia. Courtesy of the Fayette Area Historical Initiative.

Norfolk Journal and Guide newspaper in 1935 proclaimed: "No Unemployment in Martinsville, Where 1500 Negroes Work in Furniture Industry." Martinsville thrived because of these industries, and in the 1970s unemployment was only 1.9 percent. Though in 1992 the Bowles and Brooks families said jobs had always been plentiful, a decline had already begun. As manufacturing became more automated and less expensive labor was found overseas, unemployment increased dramatically in Martinsville and Henry County.[13]

Martinsville's black community thrived during the mid-twentieth century, fueled by a strong black business district. Dana O. Baldwin, the first African American physician in town, began development of the district in the 1920s. The following description of "Baldwin's Block," or simply "The Block," gives a sense of the atmosphere to be found there until the 1960s.

> The thumping beat of music from the jukebox at Edna's Café and Grill, a wave from the hand of an Albert Harris High School classmate standing by Reynolds's Barber Shop and Pool Room, the call of a friend from Bannister's Cab Stand, images dancing across the screen at the picture show at the Rex Theatre. Icons for those who remember, but history to those not familiar with Baldwin's block located on the corner of Barton and Fayette Streets in Martinsville, Virginia. . . . "The Block" stood as a gateway to the business, social, and cultural life of African Americans. Situated along Fayette Street beyond "The Block" were historic churches, schools, homes of African-American community leaders, and the popular Paradise Inn. One long-time resident declared, "You can't beat Fayette Street for living."[14]

Leonard Bowles recalled that "The Block" was "a blooming place like New York. They had beer joints, they had pool joints, everything you can mention. They had dances, we had dances." Baldwin and his brothers, entrepreneurs all, helped to establish a brick company, wood yard, pharmacy, hospital, movie theater, bowling alley, dance hall, swimming pool, ballpark, café, hotel, and a newspaper by and for African Americans. He organized the June German Ball, the Black Fiddlers' Convention, and numerous large social events each year. The first annual Martinsville Colored Fair was held in 1927; the fair eventually came to have "hot air balloons, live shows, nightly fireworks and high diving stunts in addition to the traditional midway rides, concessions and agricultural displays." Road shows came to town, such as the popular "Silas Green of New Orleans" tent show, with acrobats and chorus girls, which had toured the South for fifty years. Frequent large, public events were held, as evidenced by an announcement for a Count Basie engagement for "the last big dance of the season" in September 1941, before the tobacco warehouse opened for tobacco sales.[15]

The Black Fiddlers' Convention took place in the winter, usually February, from 1928 until well into the 1940s. It was held in the Rex movie theater or in the dance hall/gym, called the Gymtorium, that Baldwin had built to replace tobacco warehouses as locations for big social events. A 1939 notice announced that the Fiddlers' Convention and dance would be held at Baldwin-Rex Theater to benefit St. Mary's hospital, the local black hospital. "A free supper is included for all attending, with a 'breakdown' following at the Douglas Auditorium." Leonard Bowles said: "People from Danville, what we used to call far away—thirty, forty miles away—would come and stay all night . . . . Hundreds of people would come. Black people would look forward to the fiddlers' convention every year. They had harp players, piano players, the best buck timing, straight fiddle, and the best banjo. . . . They'd start around 8:30 or 9:00 in the evening and wouldn't stop until they finished around 2:00 or 3:00 in the morning."[16]

The string instrumentalists played only breakdowns, but the pianists played waltzes or popular tunes. Monetary prizes in each category were small, just one to five dollars, but coveted. The fifty-cent admission covered the cost of the prizes and helped to raise funds for the community hospital. No white people competed, but some did come to watch. The audience's applause judged the winners, and Mr. Bowles was proud of prizes he and his band had won. Once all categories had competed, everyone danced the old Virginia breakdown until the wee hours of the morning. Mr. Bowles did not know where Dana Baldwin got the idea for the convention, which started about seven years before the first Galax Old Fiddlers' Convention was held in 1935. Galax is just two hours west of Martinsville, but Mr. Bowles said that in his experience that contest did not have black people play, though in recent years they had included, on guitar and banjo, Marvin and Turner Foddrell of Patrick County, who played string band music, and others who played blues.[17] Dr. Baldwin was dedicated to the development of his community and undoubtedly saw the fiddlers' convention as an important effort in this regard. It is possible that his goals mirrored those of the first Galax convention: "Keeping alive the memories and sentiments of days gone by and making it possible for people of today to hear and enjoy the tunes of yesterday." Perhaps Dr. Baldwin established the fiddlers' convention to speak to the interests of rural black people and to draw them to town and to the black business district there. Its popularity surely "demonstrated the importance of stringband music for area blacks," as Kip Lornell believed. The convention was not the only place where this kind of music was celebrated. At the 1936 Colored Fair, J. H. Hundley of Irisburg presented a "unique exhibit . . . which included 20 or more stringed instruments which he produced by hand." Clearly there was an audience and a large pool of participants to keep the Black Fiddlers' Convention going for nearly two decades. It provided one of only a few public venues where the old breakdowns took place. Occasionally, they were held at lodge halls or at "beer joints," as Mr. Bowles called them, and sometimes at a big public "barn dance," like the one in August 1941 at the Douglas Auditorium.[18] Otherwise, in and around Martinsville they remained essentially home based.

The dynamic black community drew others from far and wide to join in its wide range of festivities over the course of five decades. Martinsville enjoyed other kinds of music and dance besides string band music and the old breakdown, sometimes as part of important social occasions. In 1927, Martinsville's Cotillion Club sponsored a June German Ball for the African American community. By 1938, it had become an official community event held at the Gymtorium. Musicians included stars like Cab Calloway, Jimmie Lunceford, Fats Waller, and later Fats Domino. The name "German" was derived from the popular cotillion or German cotillion that emerged around 1840. The dance at that time involved figures like those of the quadrille, and like party games similar to musical chairs, and was almost ubiquitous at balls during the second half of the nineteenth century. A formal dance event known as the June German had been held for whites only in large Virginia and North Carolina cities, and perhaps elsewhere, since at least the 1880s. A mid-twentieth-century photo of such a dance in North Carolina shows women in white formal gowns and men in tuxedos.[19] In 1918, the African American community in Rocky Mount, North Carolina, held its first June German. It grew to become the "South's largest dance" by the 1930s, reportedly drawing eight thousand participants. Martinsville organized its first June German Ball just nine years after Rocky Mount's first one. The ball was staged in one of the tobacco warehouses; the poster for the event listed an advance admission rate, an "at the door" rate, and a rate for white observers. A newspaper notice about the 1941 ball expressed excitement: "Buses are coming here with loads of beautiful ladies from West Virginia, North Carolina, and cities of Virginia to see and hear Andy Kirk and his Clouds of Joy playing at the Planters warehouse Friday June 6, all night long." This was a highlight of an otherwise busy social season. "Judging from the local newspaper's social write-ups, whether it was bridge or birthday parties, fiddler's contests or jitterbugging, revivals or parades—seven days a week and seven nights, too, Fayette Street had become a hopping place."[20]

Martinsville's black community was not just focused on entertainment, though entertainment helped to draw its members together and to strengthen its bonds. During its long and strong history, every member of the community worked for the betterment of the community as a whole and of the individuals within it. Five major black churches had been established beginning in 1870, and they developed clubs for both social and mutual-aid purposes. From these organizations sprang a large number of benevolent societies. Later, lodges like Elks and Masons were formed, followed by boy scout and girl scout troops and other youth organizations. When Dr. Baldwin arrived in 1910, he was the only black doctor for the large African American population of several counties. He looked for ways to invest in the advancement of his community, establishing the town's first black business district after he returned from World War I. In the ensuing years, The Block boasted thirty eating establishments, five hotels, several cab companies, insurance companies, and savings and loans, owned and operated by and for African Americans. Black citizens were among the 4,409 from Henry County who served in World War II, and a number of them were decorated heroes. Civic organizations worked for improved schools and increased pay for teachers, and large numbers of young people completed college degrees. In the late 1950s, Dr. Baldwin raised funds from the community to build a new hospital for the black community, in lieu of a proposed black wing at the Martinsville General Hospital.[21] Fayette Street's culture of business vitality and community cohesiveness extended well beyond the city limits, influencing Henry, Patrick, and Franklin Counties. Baldwin's philosophy encompassed goals both urban and rural; he believed that "the best way to promote the interests of the race is 'by advocating and working for better schools, better churches, better sanitation, by buying and working farms, by seeing to it that the children are instructed in civic duty in the schools and taught the importance and power of the ballot.'"[22]

Such vibrant black communities were commonplace in towns large and small in the Appalachian region prior to integration. Ivanhoe's black business section, for example, included a blacksmith shop, a dry cleaner, a meat market, and several other stores. Abingdon, Virginia, had a black shoemaker, restaurant, drugstore, pool hall, and a candy shop where people danced and congregated on Sundays, and a Mr. Moody owned a whole block of businesses. From the 1930s to the 1960s there, big bands and popular entertainers were brought in to perform at the tobacco warehouses. Among them were Count Basie and Glenn

Miller and, later, the Ink Spots. Similar stories come from other cities and towns in the region. All of these African American communities faded in the 1960s, as did Martinsville, with the coming of integration and urban renewal.[23]

The Old Breakdown and Rural Life

Group dances like square dancing seem to have been predominantly a rural, rather than urban, entertainment for both blacks and whites throughout the central Appalachian region in the first half of the twentieth century. Discussion of the old breakdown with the Bowles and Brooks couples, all born between 1919 and 1923, led naturally to descriptions of self-sufficient but cooperative farming communities around Martinsville during the first half of the twentieth century. It was a fondly remembered young adulthood, and the old breakdown was closely associated with the particular agrarian context. "We'd mostly raise gardens, raise chickens and eggs and carry them to town and sell them. Raised everything we ate, hogs and everything and take the flour of wheat and swap it for cornmeal. They'd sell all the hams and we children had to eat just the fatback meat," said Leonard Bowles. His family grew tobacco, but Ernest Brooks's family raised more cabbage, wheat, rye, and corn. Both men credit their youth on the farm, going to the fields as boys of eight or nine, with teaching them how to work and to succeed. According to Bowles, wage-paying jobs arrived in numbers with the timbering industry at the turn of the twentieth century, and sawmills, family-run or commercial, were an important part of the area's experience. Most labor in sawmills and factories was provided by local residents, though the managers came in from outside the area. Speaking of his early jobs in the 1930s, Bowles said, "I worked at the sawmill for five cents an hour . . . it was good money!" His uncles and other men traveled the 160 miles or more to West Virginia to work in the coal mines, coming home every nine days. To get there, they took the train to Roanoke and from there to Beckley, often "hobo-ing" on freight trains. Mrs. Brooks's mother's family all worked in the mines. For most of their careers, Mr. Brooks had worked as an assistant foreman for Bassett furniture and Mr. Bowles for the Lester Lumber Company until they both retired in the 1980s.[24]

Factory work provided most income in the early 1990s, though the identification continued to be with the farm. The Bowles family still lived in their home on what had been Naomi Bowles's homeplace. She said that she "stayed home [during the 1940s and 1950s] and canned until the kids got grown. We always had enough food to last the whole winter." She continued to garden and can fruits and vegetables when we spoke in 1992. They agreed that it was impossible to make a living by farming, but most people kept a large, producing garden in addition to having paying jobs. Caller Ernest Brooks echoed the sentiments of the others regarding the decades before 1950: "It was a tough time. I always said when I was coming up on a farm, if I get grown up, I never did want to work on a farm. Now I'm just crazy about my place . . . like to go out back and work in my garden." Rural recreations like hunting and fishing are popular pastimes, and Mr. Bowles described fishing trips to Smith Mountain Lake and other lakes in the area. The day after I first met with him, he and his sons left for a fishing trip at Virginia Beach. He often hunted around Ivanhoe and other areas in the Blue Ridge Mountains.[25]

During the first part of the twentieth century, as the Bowleses and Brookses described it, both black and white rural residents of the area preferred the dispersed settlement pattern described by geographers Karl Raitz and Richard Ulack. "Most families, they lived hollerin' distance, but they didn't live together. They really lived about a mile or two apart, but that was the neighborhood." Community groups were closely knit circles, consisting of families living within walking distance of one another.[26] The neighborhood grew larger with the arrival of the automobile, but people continued to associate within a close geographical area. Mr. Bowles in 1992, for example, identified his home as a certain supervisory district within his county. Though in his youth he lived just over the hill from his wife's community, they never met until they were in their twenties, and then it was an accidental encounter at a soda shop. This is not to promote the stereotypical notion of isolation. Rural residents took advantage of the numerous offerings on "The Block" in Martinsville that exposed them to modern trends. Numbers of men left the area for the service and for jobs, and families traveled and vacationed outside the area. Still, many people chose to live close to the place where they were born. All three of the Brookses' grown children lived in or near Martinsville, for example.

The rural, one-room schools like Green Pond that Mr. Brooks and Mr. and Mrs. Bowles attended were segregated until the late 1960s, but there are numerous accounts of interaction among blacks and whites in the Blue Ridge area of Virginia and North Carolina. Sample comments from Ivanhoe are: "Ivanhoe wasn't really segregated, just the schools. All the kids played together" and "My dad, his best friends were white." Though churches were segregated in Virginia's Wythe and Carroll Counties, "white people came [to the black church] for the revival." Appalachian scholar Cecelia Conway documented similar accounts of black and white families living in proximity in rural communities in the Blue Ridge Mountains of North Carolina.[27] Leonard Bowles grew up in such a mixed rural community. "We was the white and the black, in the same neighborhood," he said. They played ball together for recreation and had "all the corn shuckin's all together." Ernest Brooks adds: "Get up there and shuck corn, shuck corn, shuck corn and the person that got the red ear, shuck a red ear of corn, he'd get to drink. And the next family, he got his corn shuckin', and most time the women was in there quiltin' and we was up there shuckin' corn. And we had woodcuttings. And they put out some of the best dinners—vegetables, beef, chicken, pies and cakes and things." Although workings and the subsequent meals were apparently racially mixed, "the old breakdowns" were not. "They didn't go to what we had, and we didn't go to what they had," said Leonard Bowles, though he said that he did play for white square dances as did other black musicians like Joe Thompson, Uncle Homer Walker, and Howard Armstrong.[28]

Rural and urban cultures were distinct. Mrs. Brooks said she "was raised so much different," growing up on Fayette Street. She went to Albert Harris High School, a multiroom school with several teachers. She said she loved hearing stories about "the old days" in the country. Dancing in town was different too. Couples dances predominated at the June German Ball and the big band dances. Dance halls in town, like the one called Paradise, offered live music in their early days and then recorded music on the "piccolo" (juke box) in the 1930s. Dances like the Charleston, the two-step, and later the slow drag were popular. Naomi Bowles grew up a little closer to town than her husband and his cousin had, and her father was a teacher who farmed on the side. Mr. Bowles said that his wife thought she had "city living" where she was, while his family lived "way back in the mountain." In her youth in the late 1930s and early 1940s, Mrs. Bowles went to the "orchestra dances," as she called them, held at the tobacco auction houses and bringing in "all these jazzy people," big band performers. She said that both blacks and whites attended these dances. Mrs. Bowles said that when she and Mr. Bowles met, "He couldn't do my dance and I couldn't do his" because "people way back in the country didn't know anything about orchestras."

Even on "The Block" at one time there were places that sometimes held square dances. Leonard Bowles said, "A lot of people didn't like it because we were the country people. The city people couldn't do the dance we do. There was a difference there." He drew a distinction between dances: "A lot of people [did] that . . . yellow Cab Calloway stuff . . . they [didn't] like our black breakdown dances that we do. I guess it's too fast for them." He saw the old breakdown as black and rural, and the Charleston and couples dances as white-influenced, urban dances. Though she thought it old fashioned at first, once Naomi Bowles learned to do "the Virginia breakdown," she came to love it and to think of it as her own dance, "a pretty dance." She and other dancers came to incorporate Charleston steps at certain points in the breakdown.[29]

The Old Breakdown in the 1930s and 1940s

As in white communities, square dances or breakdowns flourished among black communities in Virginia, North Carolina, and Tennessee, and perhaps elsewhere, during the first half of the twentieth century, becoming less important as a recreation in each community at different times. In Abingdon, Virginia, square dancing seems to have ended among African Americans by the 1920s, once the big bands toured the area; in Alamance and Orange Counties in North Carolina, it began to "go out" in the late 1930s and early 1940s. In black schools in Smyth County, Virginia, in the 1950s, black teachers taught square dancing as a thing of the past. Martinsville and its surrounding counties seem to have been unusual among both black and white communities in that square dancing continued in the home until about 1970. Leonard Bowles asserted, "We were strong in this music" in the 1940s, and it was still "in full bloom" in the 1960s.[30]

The best descriptions to date of African American house parties in the 1930s and 1940s come from Martinsville and from Alamance and Orange Counties in North Carolina. The parties and the dances have similarities and differences as described by Leonard and Naomi Bowles and Ernest Brooks, and by Joe and Odell Thompson of North Carolina. North Carolina cousins Joe and Odell Thompson and Martinsville cousins Leonard Bowles and Ernest Brooks were all close to the same age, having been born between 1911 and 1923. They all became involved in dancing and music in their youth. Joe Thompson began playing sets at age 7 in 1925, and Leonard Bowles became involved at age 12 in 1931. Both learned to play music from their fathers and older male relatives. Joe and Odell Thompson said that their fathers, born in the 1880s and playing for square dances in the early 1900s, learned to play the music from white people, as they believed that others had learned the dancing by watching white people. Joe Thompson described dancing in his black community as basically the same as that of white people, except that "white people have a history for this stuff. Black people see the white folk doing it and they'd learn it."[31] However, scholars John Szwed and Morton Marks have documented the African American influence on European-based set dances as early as the beginning of the nineteenth century. In WPA ex-slave narratives, blacks and whites are reported listening to each other's music and playing for each other's dances during the plantation era; Cecelia Conway has observed direct mutual influence in the music in North Carolina in the twentieth century.[32] Joe and Odell Thompson's favorite breakdown tunes included "Old Corn Liquor," "Hook and Line," "Molly Put the Kettle On," "Soldiers Joy," "Black Annie," and "Donna's Got a Rambling Mind." Leonard Bowles named "Old Joe Clark," "John Henry," "Dog's Barking at the Moon," and the Grandpa Jones standard "My Uncle Bill has a Still on the Hill." Both Joe Thompson and Leonard Bowles said there were many black string players in the 1920s and 1930s, and that sometimes at a dance there might be two fiddles and two banjos, sometimes with a guitar playing a bass line.[33]

In both places, square dance/breakdown house parties were held every Saturday, all year round, one week in one family's home and the next in another, the same people attending every dance. In Martinsville, the dances would "start about dusk. We walked to people's houses," sometimes a few miles, and danced all night long. "They'd take the beds out of living room. Next morning, they'd cook breakfast and we'd help clean up and put it all back."[34] Ernest Brooks remembered that people in each neighborhood danced a little differently, so if someone attended a dance in a new place, it took awhile to get used to the particular dance customs. Otherwise, all the dancers had been "down on the sets." In Martinsville, according to Leonard Bowles, "Most of what they were giving a dance for was to try to survive. The people that owned the house sold an orange for a nickel, a piece of candy for something, chickens from their place. . . . They were trying to make a living and have some fun at the same time. . . . share and have fun too." At the end of each thirty-minute dance (or set, as it was called) the caller would say "Treat your partner," and each couple would dance to the kitchen where food and drink would be laid out for the men to buy for their partners. Like rent parties elsewhere, the breakdown served as a means of supplementing the family income. A break of fifteen or twenty minutes followed, allowing time for conversation and snacks before the beginning of the next breakdown.[35] Instead of selling "treats" during the breaks between square dances in North Carolina, a different band would play blues and rags for slow drags, two-steps, black bottom, breakaway, buck dances, and Charleston.

In North Carolina, these "frolics" also occurred at "box parties" at local schools, raising money through the sale of box suppers prepared by the single women. Such events were not mentioned in Martinsville, but the fiddlers' convention provided an annual public venue for the old breakdowns and helped to raise money for the black hospital. In both places the dances sometimes concluded a day of communal working. In both communities, as in European American Blue Ridge communities, dances were held in homes every night during Christmas. In Martinsville, the first one was on December 26, since Christmas Day was for staying home with family. Leonard Bowles said, "It never snowed too deep to have frolics!"[36]

According to both Ernest Brooks and Leonard Bowles, almost everyone in the community danced once they got old enough: aunts, uncles, cousins, and parents. Children were kept by someone who was not dancing on a given night, because some drinking occurred. Bowles and Brooks agreed that drunkenness was not common at the dances, though, because, as they said, "We knew how to have a little taste and have fun." Brooks learned to call sets even while banned from the dance as a child. When his family would have an old breakdown, the children would go up the steps to the room above the dance. The planks had spaces between them, and it was warm, with the heat from the fireplace rising to it. "We could lie down on the floor and look down there at them dancing, and I could look at the man calling the set." And so he watched and learned. "When I grew up they'd have the breakdowns about every Saturday night around

Figure 4.4. Irvin Cook, banjoist, Leonard Bowles, fiddler, and dancers beginning the dance, 1978. Courtesy of the Blue Ridge Institute and Museum of Ferrum College.

here, and I'd just listen at them and call it from there." Lots of callers were in the community, including Lance Holland, Bill Bowles, and Paul England, and "a whole lot of them. . . . Didn't but one call at the time, and he got tired the next one took over, because they'd last all night." Callers received no special treatment at the dances, but musicians were given food and drink.[37]

The old breakdowns faded later in Martinsville, Virginia, than in Alamance and Orange Counties, North Carolina, but some of the same forces were at work. Joe and Odell Thompson said that when people returned from the service after World War II, "[they] had all the music they wanted to hear" on the radio and television. Just prior to the war, "a little bit of dancing was going on, but it was breaking off sharply then. Back in those days, guitars got to coming out, then piccolos. And changing over to rock and roll, that's the biggest thing that stopped it all." Leonard Bowles said that at the Paradise Inn, people were doing a dance like "the boogie or hop or whatever it was. The people were in that, that's why they dropped it." These may not be the only reasons, and others will be discussed later. Regardless of the cause for the demise of the square dances, Leonard and Naomi Bowles, Ernest Brooks, and Irvin Cook, a banjoist who played with Bowles until his death in 1987, all repeatedly lamented the passing of the old breakdown and the lifestyle that accompanied it, in interviews from 1976 to 1992. Each frequently said that they "wish those days would come back."[38]

The Old Breakdown in 1978

In 1978 members of the families of Leonard Bowles and Ernest Brooks gathered together to perform a four-couple breakdown at the urging of Kip Lornell. During a 1976 interview, when Bowles mentioned that the community had done the old breakdown regularly until seven years before and would love to do it again, Lornell volunteered to have cameras present if they planned a dance. They rented the Elks Hall on Armistead Avenue in Martinsville, made costumes, and practiced together for several days prior to the videotaping. They performed a dance that they said accurately demonstrated their local breakdown. After the recording session, they continued to dance on occasion in the home. By 1992, they no longer danced in the community, but Naomi Bowles remarked that her children loved the old breakdown, and when they came home they encouraged her husband to take out his fiddle so they could dance. She said that her son, a teacher in New York, taught the old breakdown to his students in school. Mr. and Mrs. Bowles and I watched the videotape together, and their commentary and that of Ernest Brooks helped me to understand the dance.

For the videotaping, Leonard Bowles played fiddle and Irvin Cook played banjo and sang. The tune was "John Henry." Ernest Brooks called while he danced. Unlike many square dance communities, this Martinsville group incorporated three kinds of dances in one: a circle dance for the whole group, a couple dance in closed position, and a solo footwork dance. The group demonstrated its cohesiveness, its support for couple interaction, and its support for individual skill. Every person took a turn in each role, and each section had its own distinct dynamic expression. The "Change partners" movement was smooth and fluid, the "Choose your partner" solo was somewhat percussive, and the swing following each of these had an emphatic 4/4 rhythm. When the whole circle moved together, everyone stepped and swayed quietly and evenly.[39]

To begin the dance, Mr. Brooks and his partner led the line of couples dancing into the room to form a ring, circling right and then left. At the call "Bow to your opposite," each man turned to face the woman on his left with a balance step, finishing with a right elbow turn. With "Bow to your partner," each man turned to face his partner on his right, repeating the balance step and elbow turn. The whole group circled right and left, and when they returned to their original places, Mr. Brooks called "Press way back . . . First four cut out," then "Change partners." He and his partner and another couple moved to the center of the circle while the others stepped continuously side to side with a step-touch pattern, clapping all the while. The two couples in the center circled right and left, turned the neighbor with a right elbow turn, then the partner with a left elbow turn, and returned to swing or "hug" the neighbor, holding each other's upper arms, for about thirty-two counts of accented steps side to side. The sequence was repeated, first turning the partner, then the neighbor, then swinging the partner before returning to the ring of eight. The other two couples repeated this sequence while the first two couples did the swaying step pattern in place. Everyone circled right and left, and then, at the call "Choose your partner," one woman went to the center of the circle with several bars of fancy footwork. She concluded by bringing a man to the center to join her for the same kind of swing used in the "Change partners" move. They returned to the circle while another woman took the first woman's place in the center. Ordinarily, each man would have taken a turn in the center as well, but they did not for this particular session. The ring of dancers circled right and left, and at the call "Treat your partner," one couple went to the center for a long hugging swing that carried them out of the room. Each couple in turn moved to the center of the circle and then exited the room, with Ernest Brooks and his partner, the last to go, still moving to the center of the now imaginary circle before dancing out of the room.

Choosing and Changing Partners

When asked to compare their breakdown with white square dances he had seen, Leonard Bowles exclaimed that European Americans "dance *altogether* different. They use mostly swing your partner and all that, but one thing different they didn't make. Choose your partner. You get out there and you cut all kind of steps *by yourself* and get to choose who you want and dance with them." Though this was the only obvious formal difference, it was enough to make the dance emphatically "altogether different." It also served as the climax of the dance, the last section before the final swing out of the room. The emphasis on partner interaction was central to this particular community's dance, unlike some other communities, where couples connected repeatedly with other couples and with the whole group. The theme of partner relationship was built from beginning to end: from acknowledging your partner to changing partners, from choosing one particular partner with whom to dance to treating your partner to refreshments.

In "Choose your partner," each man and each woman took a turn with a solo in the center of the circle, showing off their dancing skill. Both this footwork and the side-to-side step were called "promenade," but the solo footwork was usually more intricate and percussive than the basic step used while marking time in the circle, with stronger accents and a more angular posture. Naomi Bowles liked to include some Charleston when she cut a step, and men who were particularly showy in days gone by were said to "do the buck." "[It's] one person's dance. Do all that kind of number and cluck your heels together. Like Ernest Holland, just dance and dance. Now he could jump up, straight up and cluck his heels twice before he hit the floor, and still not lose a step in the music."[40] When I asked Naomi Bowles if she had a special name for her footwork, she said, "Why, that's square dancing!" The footwork was as much a part of the dance for her as the figures. The purpose of the solo went beyond demonstrating skill, as illustrated by the call. The purpose is clarified by an exchange between Mr. Brooks and me. Mr. Brooks: "He promenades (footwork). If he runs and gets my partner, I can come out and go get his partner." SS: "The man promenades in the middle . . ." Mr. Brooks: "That's right, and chooses a partner." According to Mr. Bowles, "You always try to get the best looking one to dance with." But Mr. Brooks warned, "You do not choose someone else's real special girl." After the solo the chosen partner joined the soloist for a swing, which lasted a full thirty-two counts, almost as long as the solo. Some pairs clasped each other's upper arms as they faced each other directly, like a hug. The characteristic step pattern of the swing was fast step-together-step-rise (one-and-two-pause) to the man's left and back to his right. Joe Thompson referred to this as a "short dog" step, in describing North Carolina African American house dances.[41] A definite increase of energy intensity and percussive accents seemed to assert the importance of the interaction with the chosen partner as a climax of the dance. Upon completion of the swing, the man took the woman back to her place and "set her down," according to Mr. Bowles, taking their places to watch as the next man chose his partner.[42]

I have never experienced solo dancing in the center of the circle in European American square dances, though Old Dan Tucker, a solo for an odd man in the middle who then steals someone else's partner, has been performed historically as a dance in its own right or as the ending to a square dance. Evidence exists that this tradition of choosing a partner in a dance predates the Civil War. A former slave said, "Saturday night we played and danced, sometimes in the cabins and sometimes in the yards. . . . We would get in a ring and when the music started we would begin working our foots while we sung 'You steal my true love an' I'll steal your'en.'"[43] In his 1928 manual of "Negro Folk Dances," Hampton (Virginia) Institute professor Charles H. Williams described a dance he called "Plantation Days." It was "an arrangement of the old country dance or breakdown," a dance for four couples. It contained a similar move, but choreographed or "arranged." In it all the men stepped into the circle to face their partners and performed a prescribed step pattern followed by a right hand swing. They then moved on to each of the next women in the square with a new step pattern, until they returned home. The women repeated this same series of moves, once the men were home. Composer James P. Johnson recounted a similar figure danced by his mother, from Virginia. Dancer and caller Dot Kent depicted a dance called by Joe Thompson of North Carolina, in which each gent "faces his partner to 'cut the buck.' This is his chance to show off: buck dance, Charleston, 'jump up and down, he has to do something.' Then he promenades his own partner around the inside of the set." Each lady also took a turn.[44]

The concept of partner was important in an earlier section of the dance as well, with the call "Change partners." In this figure, much like "Georgia Rang-Tang" or "Georgia Alabam," as it is called in the Blue Ridge, each person would swing someone else's partner and then one's own. Two couples formed a small square in the center of the larger circle. The foursome circled right and then left. When Mr. Brooks shouted out, "Change partners," each man took right hands with the opposite woman, the other man's partner, and passed around her in a small circle to face his own partner. He reached out to take left hands with his own partner, passing around her in a small circle to join the opposite woman for a long swing. The sequence was repeated in reverse—partner, opposite, partner. Each swing lasted a full thirty-two counts like the "Choose your partner" swing, at least four times as long as the whole process of taking hands and passing around both women. Naomi Bowles described it this way: "You get in a square with four. Then you change partners and you hug them."[45] After the second swing, the two couples returned to the circle and the next two couples were directed to cut out and to change partners. Mrs. Brooks helped to emphasize the meaning of this move in a separate conversation when she discussed the differences between her city upbringing and their rural one. "At that time the city people didn't do those dances. Didn't know anything about changing partners. All I knew was couples dances. [In the breakdown] with all those couples you didn't have time to think about just one because they were all in one circle or changing partners." According to Leonard Bowles, the dance never changed or varied in figures or calls. When asked about other figures that may have been called, he was emphatic: "No no no no. That was not in the old-timey breakdown. Our dancing was called the breakdown. That wasn't the square dance, it was the *breakdown*." And the focus of the breakdown was primarily on partner relationships.[46]

The first movement of the dance after the entrance and opening circle left and right was unlike anything I have seen in old time square dancing elsewhere. Its appearance was very similar to "set to your partner" in English country dance but concluded with an elbow turn instead of a turn single. At the call "Bow to your opposite," men turned left and women turned right to face the person nearest to them who was not their partner. With arms relaxed by their sides, they faced each other and "promenaded," doing small steps to the right and left, one-and-two-pause to each side. A right elbow turn once around led into "Bow to your partner," and the same sequence was repeated with the partner. It served as an introduction to the partner interactions to come.

The dance culminated with a final focus on the partner. "Treat your partner" was tied both to the role of the dance in courtship and marriage and to the

Figure 4.5. The Old Breakdown, Martinsville, Virginia, 1978. Courtesy of the Blue Ridge Institute and Museum of Ferrum College.

importance of the dance as a means of sharing financial burdens. Besides being polite to buy your partner "treats" like fruit, it was a way to help your neighbor. At the call, one couple took the swing position and danced to the center of the circle with the swing step described above. "They dance and dance and they go and treat their partner," dancing into the kitchen where food was laid out. Once the first couple had danced out of the room, another entered the circle to swing and dance to the kitchen. Each couple did so in turn, with the caller and his partner leaving last. After the break, as Mr. Bowles said, "We start again [playing], here they come back again."[47]

A Communal Circle

The circle never lost its shape from the moment it was formed at the beginning of the dance. "Bow to your partner" took place on the periphery of the circle, and "Choose your partner" and "Change partners" were contained within the circle. Whether the circle was composed of four, six, eight, or more couples, up to twelve, according to Leonard Bowles and Ernest Brooks, the size and shape of the circle were important. Brooks emphasized this with his call "Press way back," so that the dancers stepped back holding hands in the circle at full arm's length in order to make the circle as big as it could possibly be. Mr. Bowles said this was to make enough room in the center of the circle for the dancing of each individual, each couple, and each foursome. Joe Thompson used the call "Great big eight" to accomplish the same purpose for his four-couple sets. Even at the end of the breakdown, the last couple went from their place on the periphery of the circle to the place where its center had been for their four or so measures of swing before dancing together out of the room. When the breakdowns were held in homes, observers surrounded the dancing circle and participated by their observation. "Anybody that isn't dancing's just pressed up against the walls around the room watching," said Leonard Bowles. The stable circle was maintained throughout the old breakdown in Martinsville, unlike in North Carolina, where Joe Thompson called several other figures for the whole group. The figures he called, including "Ladies back to back," a basket figure called "Feets in the basket," or a weaving figure called "Winding chain," had apparently not been used in Martinsville, at least in the memories of Mr. and Mrs. Bowles and Mr. Brooks.[48]

Continuous footwork was as important as the partner focus and the stability of the circle. Leonard Bowles insisted, "You've *got* to keep moving your feet, moving your feet!" When not in the center of the circle for the skillful footwork of "Choose your partner," or for the energetically rhythmic step of the swing, the dancers continuously stepped side to side, touching the ball of the opposite foot to the floor, step-touch, step-touch, each step and touch accompanied by a soft pat or clap, the action almost more important than the sound. National Heritage Fellow Bessie Jones emphasized similar continuous foot movement in African American dances and ring plays, saying that the ongoing step and clap kept the rhythm solid and each player ready to take his or her turn. The continuous stepping and clapping established a group rhythm for the breakdown and emphasized the cohesiveness of the group surrounding the individual, couple, or foursome dancing in the center. In response to a question about the difference between their footwork and that of neighboring European American communities, Mr. Bowles moved his hands from side to side. People elsewhere "don't move out like we do, they stay on *one spot* and don't move off of it." Naomi Bowles compared her community's dancing with that of some African American friends from North Carolina. Of her friends' dance community, she said, "They don't get down within their feet like we do. It's more up in here (gesturing to her torso)." The Martinsville dancers kept their feet very close to the floor, with just a little more lift in the feet during the "Choose your partner" solo. When I asked Mrs. Bowles if she listened to the sound of her feet, she said, "Oh, I can *feel* it in my feet." She went on to make both a historical comment and an aesthetic critique of clogging teams when she said, "It all came from what *we* do. They do all this clogging, throwing their legs way out . . . it's not *in* the square dancing like we square dance." Her tone reflected dislike for flamboyant arm and leg gestures, and she stressed her belief in their African American breakdown and footwork as historical sources of contemporary European American square dancing and clogging.[49]

The footwork may contribute to a deeper meaning of the dance. A three-way conversation among Mr. and Mrs. Brooks and Mr. Bowles centered on the view of organized religion toward dancing but led to an interesting conclusion. Mr. Bowles recounted a story about a time he was asked to play his fiddle for a program in the church. The preacher began tapping his feet, and Mrs. Bowles stood up and began moving as if to dance. Hearing the story, Mr. and Mrs. Brooks burst into laughter. I wondered aloud, "What would have happened if Mrs. Bowles had danced in church?" Mr. Bowles guessed, "Some of them would have called her crazy, and some of them, 'aren't you ashamed of yourself?' and some of them praising her." Mrs. Brooks explained to me in a serious tone, "You're not supposed to dance in church, you know." An emphatic exchange ensued between the two men. Mr. Bowles: "Well, shouting is the same thing as . . ." Mr. Brooks: "Shout! I see them in church. We use the quick step like they do!" Mr. Bowles, with a hint of sarcasm: "People don't dance in church!" Mrs. Brooks added, "People say that's holy dancing done in the church." Mr. Bowles concluded: "Well, it's holy dancing done in the sets!"[50] Besides the irony that similar movements are judged sacred or sinful depending on the context, he seemed to express the idea that the breakdown had a sustaining function within the community, almost as the church did.

When asked to identify good dancers, Mr. and Mrs. Bowles and Mr. Brooks almost invariably looked to their own elders, parents, grandparents, aunts, and uncles, talking about how skillfully and smoothly they danced. They identified the most important characteristic of a good dancer as awareness of the group and doing one's part to ensure everyone's enjoyment, but competition had a role too. Considering the question of good dancing, Ernest Brooks first identified a serious transgression, describing a man who sometimes "ran on too long" when cutting a step in the center of the circle, with no sense of the appropriate amount of showing off. He demonstrated the rest of the group promenading and patting without enthusiasm as the man danced on and on. Beyond that, he discussed the importance of the dancers and the set-caller working together to avoid "messing up." "If you mess up, you mess up everyone else" doing the dance. Each individual was responsible for the effectiveness and enjoyment of the whole circle. The set-caller served as a facilitator for the interactions but was not, strictly speaking, the authority figure. Mr. Brooks termed the set caller's most important ability as "*letting* them do like you tell them, and listen and do what you tell them" (emphasis added). Still, Mr. Brooks believed an attitude of competition is essential to good dancing. "Just go out there and do it. You're going to try to do better than him, and you'll probably come up to it."[51]

Music and Motion

Music and dance had an intimate interrelationship in this Martinsville community. Leonard Bowles perceived that "your steps and music work together. If you (a musician) see a good set-caller, and they're calling, don't you know you forget you're playing, you don't get tired or nothing, play and make music. . . . You're looking at their feet and you play with their feet. You get that step, see what kind of motion they've got and you're just going on. You never get tired." In years gone by, the heightened effect of two or more fiddles and banjos and perhaps a guitar must have energized the dancers as well. In the 1978 video recording, Leonard Bowles's fiddle and Irvin Cook's banjo had a definite drive that was hard to resist. Though each beat of their music had a little percussive accent, the dancers felt an even, underlying flow. Swaying his body side to side on each measure, Ernest Brooks said you must "*balance* with the music, *balance* with the music"; Naomi Bowles moved her hands side to side in a fluid undercurve arc, saying of the ongoing promenade step, "Get your feet going like that. Everybody in the same tune." She went on to say, "The music's got to get within your feet. You know when to stop and you know when to go on with it. Now if you don't have it in your feet, you're just going to mess the dance up."[52] As in other old time dance communities, the figures were called across the phrases of the music, rather than mirroring them as contra dance and English country dance do. Instead, the dancers' stepping feet and patting hands kept a steady ostinato on the beat, while the fiddle and banjo embroidered triplets around them. Soloists and couples tattooed little dance accents on top of that, or groups of four wove fluid curves through them all. Banjo player Irvin Cook sang a verse of the ballad of John Henry, played without singing for a while, then sang some more, and the set-caller shouted out directions as needed, between or on top of the singer's words.

A Long-Lived Tradition Wanes

The old breakdown continued as a house dance tradition in Henry County and neighboring counties decades longer than it seems to have lasted in other African American communities. It remained strong during the postwar years when old time square dancing faded in European American Appalachian communities, but it later declined in popularity at just the same time that square dancing was on the rise in those same white communities. In other areas, jazz dances had completely supplanted square dancing in African American communities by the 1940s.[53] But the Martinsville breakdown community continued their dance, reportedly unchanged, during at least six decades of new dances, from the Charleston to the jitterbug to the twist. In 1992, Naomi Bowles said that she danced both the breakdown and the electric slide at family gatherings. Despite the fact that hundreds in Martinsville were enthusiastically dancing to new beats and using new moves, this community adhered to their longstanding tradition.

A number of factors contributed both to the longevity of the old breakdown and to its decline. Among these were the major cultural shifts of the 1960s and 1970s, the rural associations of dances like the old breakdown, changes in musical tastes, decades of choices made by recording companies and folk music and dance collectors, and the folk revival. However, the dance continued through the upheaval of the 1960s. The continuing energy of the cohesive black community with the Baldwins at its center helped to sustain it. The identification of the dancers and musicians with broader rural and folk traditions and their belief in the values expressed in the dance carried the dance longer in this community than elsewhere. Between 1968 and 1973, school segregation came to an end in Martinsville, Dr. Dana O. Baldwin and his brother and business partner Samuel Baldwin passed away, and the buildings of "The Block" were razed in an urban renewal project. It was just at this time that the last breakdowns were held.

The events of the 1960s were preceded by a half-century of concerted effort by the flourishing black community of Martinsville to improve schools, to establish systems to care for each other, to achieve the right to vote, and to elect African American city officials. In 1940 the Parent Teachers Association and several civic organizations petitioned for equal pay for African American teachers, and in 1945 a branch of the NAACP was founded in town. Continual proposals to the school board resulted in new or improved schools, and a larger community hospital was completed. In the 1960s, picket lines demanded desegregation of eating establishments and more egalitarian hiring practices. Voter registration drives were led by local citizens, and in 1968, the first black city council member was elected. Discrimination and racial violence were not uncommon: black students had to walk to school while white students were provided with bus service; black people were passed over by store clerks in favor of white people behind them in line; and young black men accused of raping a white woman were executed. However, support came from beyond the community as "the black and white clergy united during the 1950s and 1960s to form the Ministerial Association of Martinsville and Henry County, which together with courageous members of the church community . . . worked together in order to prevent the more forceful elements . . . from destroying our community." An African American Martinsville lawyer whose father was active in civil rights said, "I don't get the impression that there was a real strong upheaval or wave or surge of people exercising their civil rights, sit-ins and certainly nothing like what we saw down in Greensboro. We had some things going on around us, and Martinsville was in the wake of all that."[54] The once self-contained African American community opened as its members achieved active participation in the political process once reserved for European Americans.

Integration had an unexpected consequence. The thriving black business sections in Martinsville, Ivanhoe, Abingdon, and elsewhere in the region became less strong as white businesses competed for black customers' business. Many black-owned businesses were unable to survive, and the community became more diffuse. The first mall opened on the outskirts of Martinsville in the mid-1960s, drawing people of all races away from downtown areas. Integrated schools changed the fabric of the community. Black schools had been an extension of home and family and, along with the churches, the centers of their communities. One resident said, "If we should act bad, grown-ups could correct you and they would tell your parents. And then your parents would discipline you. It was a well-knit group. . . . You knew when you did wrong that the neighbors were going to call, or send a message that you have misbehaved."[55] Teachers directly contacted the parents so that all adults worked together to guide children to become adults responsible to themselves, to each other, and to the whole community. Integrated schools did not serve this same function, and the community became less cohesive. African American scholar Henry Louis Gates wrote of this moment in his hometown in Piedmont, West Virginia: "Only later did I realize that for many of the colored people in Piedmont . . . integration was experienced as a loss. The warmth and nurturance of the womblike colored world was slowly and inevitably disappearing, in a process that really began on the day they closed the door for the last time at [the black] school."[56] The old breakdown, representative of this stable, self-contained, mutually supportive community, became less relevant as the community dispersed.

As some of the businesses in the Fayette Street area had closed, the dismantling of the buildings of The Block began in the 1960s with the first stages of urban renewal projects. The once "hopping" business district was no longer the hub of commerce and social life that it had been for Martinsville's black community. Perhaps the decisive events were the deaths of both Dr. Baldwin and his brother within four months in 1972–1973. The charismatic physician and entrepreneur had cared passionately for the community since his arrival in 1910 and had practiced medicine until his death at age 91. For sixty years he had served as an icon for the thriving and cohesive black community, as well as a force for change. His work and that of his brothers had affected people in both the city and its surrounding countryside. The loss "was not only a blow to their close families and friends, but to the area's business community." Soon thereafter, the demolition of The Block was completed, "leaving only some cracked sidewalks and curb cuts along Moss, Fayette, and Barton Streets as lonely reminders of the once vibrant and bustling black business area." A few establishments remained, such as the Paradise Inn, which stayed in business until the 1990s. Though it had been more than a quarter century since his last Black Fiddlers' Convention, the loss of Dr. Baldwin may have symbolized the finality of the passing of a way of life. The last breakdown Leonard Bowles recalled was in 1969 at the home of Frank Harris, but in Franklin County, ironically, the last one was held in 1972, the same year Dr. Baldwin died. The breakdown had outlived the June German Ball, which last occurred in 1965 or 1966. When I visited Martinsville in 1992 and asked how long it had been since the breakdowns were held regularly, Naomi Bowles said, "Ever since the world changed."[57] I did not pursue the question, but in retrospect, the impact of integration, destruction of The Block, and diffusion of the community—and perhaps the death of Dr. Baldwin, who had given credibility to the old breakdown and string band music through his Fiddlers' Conventions—may have been the dramatic shift to which she alluded.

The breakdown expressed the self-contained community that existed before integration and urban renewal. The large and cohesive African American community of Martinsville provided a fertile ground for the continuation of the breakdown tradition, and the fact that integration came relatively late to area schools may have contributed as well. During the upheaval of the 1960s, the dance continued to flourish in Martinsville, as it did in Henry, Franklin, and Patrick Counties. With its stable circle and ongoing footwork keeping everyone together in a group rhythm, the dance reflected the strong, self-reliant local black community. The circle was solid, safe, and reliable, containing the dancers with something like the nurturance described by Henry Louis Gates. The stability and the expression of continuity with a well-known past perhaps provided a sense of security in the rapidly changing world of the 1960s and helped this dance to continue when others had not.

The breakdown existed historically "to help families to survive" by selling treats between dances, just as the many civic organizations in town provided aid for families in need and supported community causes. Each person and family was dependent on the success of all others. The surrounding circle demonstrated this mutual support by stepping and patting while the solos, couples, and foursomes danced in the center. However, by the 1960s the actual need for sharing financial burdens through the dance no longer existed as it had in past decades. Jobs were plentiful in the area and families had established themselves. The focus on partner—changing partners and choosing partners—lost meaning as the participants became settled, middle-aged adults, and the solo and the long swing may have diminished in immediacy and excitement. The dance continued, but separated from its role in contributing to the welfare of family and community, it became purely a social event. With its driving purpose gone, less reason existed to hold dances after 1970, but the representation of mutual support had been clearly relevant during the upheaval of the 1960s.

Rural Aesthetics and Values

New music and dance styles, with their urban, modern flair and air of freedom and excitement, emerged alongside the old breakdown and its string band music. During the first four decades of the twentieth century, jazz dance styles based in African and African American culture became popular among both blacks and whites. Black people in the town of Martinsville and the surrounding counties had almost endless opportunities to enjoy these new sounds.

> By the 1950s, the jukeboxes—or piccolos—at the Paradise Inn, Nightingale's Lunch and the Baldwin Drug Store played a steady menu of doo-wop and early rock 'n roll, Fats Domino and Chuck Berry, all anticipating the summer arrival of the June German Ball. The big bands of Cab Calloway and Jimmie Lunceford who opened the original June German Balls gave way to the soulful sound of Ella Fitzgerald and Count Basie's jazz. They were eventually upstaged by the Inkspots, Motown, and by the 1960s—in keeping with the times—the louder, more urgent sounds of Little Richard and James Brown. . . . A steady string of singers made their way to Martinsville and Fayette Street, often on their way to the top of the charts as they made the round of Southern cities on what was sometimes called the "Chitlin' Circuit" until they achieved enough notoriety and acclaim to be invited to the Apollo in Harlem or signed by a major record label.[58]

Leonard Bowles attributed some of the decline in interest in the old breakdown to the new music and dance styles, but it may have been more than just a stylistic preference. Rosa Powell said that house parties ended in Abingdon when the big bands came in during the 1920s, but in Martinsville the breakdowns had existed side by side with the new jazz sound. They did not end when big bands began performing at the Planter's Warehouse. More than the styles themselves, the urban associations with music like jazz and Motown may have ultimately had an effect on the old breakdown. In the popular view in the 1960s, black culture came to be thought of as urban, and little recognition was given to a rural black way of life. Ed Cabbell articulated the conflict he felt, having grown up in the mountains of Virginia and West Virginia. He felt himself "a double minority," being a part of two separate cultures, the black minority and the Appalachian minority.[59] Leonard Bowles believed the rural background of the breakdown caused disdain among some people in the latter part of the twentieth century. He spoke of those who had moved to town, leaving behind their country homeplaces and customs: "Now that [they're] up in the city, [they] don't want to talk about nothing like that." Beyond the rural connections lay a painful past. In northeast Tennessee, where African Americans square danced regularly in the early twentieth century, the granddaughter of an avid dancer believed that her elders gave up square dancing because of its associations with slavery. Naomi Bowles said, "This generation, they don't want to go back and think about, you know, how we came along. Except *my* children!"[60] Whereas rural imagery and references supported the renewal of a square dance tradition in some white Appalachian communities as illustrated in chapter 3, such ruralism likely contributed to the eventual decline of square dance in some black communities. In Martinsville it may actually have sustained the dance longer.

In the 1970s, black musicians and dancers around Martinsville saw rural Appalachian traditions as their own, and not only for whites. They called the music they played and danced to "country" or "old time," a style which was recorded prior to the Depression and marketed as "hillbilly music," and they had grown up listening to both country and popular music on the radio.[61] This was not uncommon. For example, African American banjoist Carl Johnson, who regularly appears in the Black Banjo Gathering, grew up in Roanoke, Virginia, listening to the Grand Ole Opry and country radio. Naomi Bowles identified with contemporary representations of rural dance as we watched the 1978 video of her group. In it, the dancers all wore identical costumes they had made, though they would have ordinarily worn their usual clothing for the breakdown. The women wore white blouses and circular red gingham skirts with white ruffles at the hem, and the men wore dark trousers with white shirts and red ties. Watching the video, Mrs. Bowles remarked, "We wanted to look like the square dancers on TV." The old breakdown connected them with their own rural past and with a broader square dance tradition. The absence of black people from commercial representations of square dancing did not deter them from placing themselves in that context. Their enjoyment of old time music and dance, their continuation of rural customs like gardening, and their fond memories of days gone by overcame any negative associations with rural life. Perhaps their desire to keep old ways alive and the value they placed on rural family and community closeness helped to sustain the old breakdown, even without external reflection and support.

Unrecognized Traditions

The recording industry, folk music collectors, and folk festivals chose for the most part to ignore black string band music, resulting in the decline of the tradition. Similarly, folk dance collectors and the folk dance recreation movement ignored the old breakdown. Not seeing themselves reflected in radio and television programs and on records may have ultimately discouraged the old breakdown dancers and some of the many black fiddlers and banjo players who once participated in the Black Fiddlers' Convention. These once-vibrant music and dance traditions have a history stretching from the eighteenth century through the first half of the twentieth century. String band music, the usual accompaniment for square dances and breakdowns, has been documented among black musicians since at least 1774 and was popular among both black and white rural musicians in the nineteenth and early twentieth centuries.[62] Ex-slave narratives in WPA publications report wide use of fiddle and banjo, and a mapped analysis of the mention of these instruments shows a cluster around Henry and Patrick Counties. References to fiddles and banjos occur in the WPA accounts almost always in conjunction with slaves dancing on plantations. Former slaves born between 1840 and 1860 remembered contra dances and square dances most frequently, then cotillions, waltzes, and quadrilles. They also referred to some solo step dances, presumably derived at least partly from African origin, specifying "cutting the pigeon wing" most often, followed by "buck dancing," "knocking the back step," "jubas," "shuffles," and "jigs." These were usually "embellishments indulged in while square or contradancing," or sometimes performed in contests. Among tunes frequently named in these narratives are tunes found in the white string-band repertoire, like "Turkey in the Straw," "Arkansas Traveller," "Old Dan Tucker," and "Miss Liza Jane."[63]

Seeing their music as "rural" or "country," musicians around Martinsville "grew up in an era when the differences between black and white folk music were less clearly defined" than they later became, according to Kip Lornell. They played many of the same tunes as white musicians did, such as "Bile them Cabbage Down," "Leather Britches," and "Old Joe Clark," with only some stylistic differences distinguishing the black and white versions.[64] The recording industry had early on created an artificial separation between "hillbilly music" and "race music," deciding that there was no audience for black string bands. Few were recorded until John and Alan Lomax began recording for the Library of Congress in the 1930s. This distinction invisibilized a thriving early-twentieth-century tradition. In a 1975 interview with Charles Wolfe, black harmonica player and Grand Ole Opry star DeFord Bailey talked about "black hillbilly music." "Everybody around me grew up playin' that. Fiddles and banjos and guitars; they weren't playin' no blues then. It was black hillbilly music." In 1946 two of the few black "hoedown" musicians to be documented were recorded for the Library of Congress: James Cole and "the spectacular square dance band headed by fiddler John Lusk." The "Two Poor Boys" from Knoxville recorded a few sides, including "Sourwood Mountain" and "Old Hen Cackle." Black string players switched to blues in order to be recorded, helping to bring an end to the string band tradition. Recordings of black square dance callers are even fewer, though many recordings of white callers were made during the 1920s.[65] Likewise, the regional folk festivals that emerged during the 1920s and 1930s, including Southwest Virginia's Whitetop Festival, did not present black string bands or square dancers, though the black string players of Henry and Franklin

Counties lived nearby.[66] Radio barn dances adhered to similar stereotypes with a few exceptions, such as DeFord Bailey's performances on the early Grand Ole Opry. White musicians themselves took note of black string bands, however. Bluegrass founder Bill Monroe, guitarist Doc Watson, and others "point to [African American string band musicians] as influences, as models, as colleagues."[67]

Like the recording industry and folk music collectors, the folk dance recreation movement of the first half of the twentieth century largely ignored African American contributions, focusing almost exclusively on European American traditions. Folk dance manuals used in teacher training and recreation programs offered dances from England, other European countries, and New England. Some, like Helen Frost's 1924 *Clog and Character Dances*, included ostensibly black dances called "Mammy" and "Jockey," with photographic images of white people in blackface. The 1928 folk dance manual prepared by Charles Williams of Hampton Institute is a rare exception. Along with African American singing games is a description of the Charleston and the dance called "Plantation Days," described earlier. In contrast to majority representation, Dr. Baldwin's Black Fiddlers' Convention with its public breakdown, running annually into the late 1940s, gave support to old time music and dance in this community. The public nature of the event and the large attendance coming from miles around helped to increase visibility and gave practitioners a certain status. It also demonstrated their participation in a wider tradition in a way that was not reflected by the media. The old breakdown garnered almost no support from published materials or instruction manuals, as European American traditions did. Still, Martinsville dancers continued in their tradition even when similar ones had faded in European American communities.

Later, in the 1950s, 1960s, and 1970s, the square dance boom and the folk revival stimulated new energy and interest in old time square dancing in European American communities. But Martinsville's breakdown community did not benefit from this, though they saw their traditions as similar. The early focus of the folk revival of the 1960s and 1970s was European American Appalachian string band music and dance. Black string bands in the region were overlooked, while blues musicians were sought after.[68] Though Leonard Bowles and others in his area considered their music and dance to be in the same category as that which was being documented, they were passed over. This fact was not lost on him, and he pointed it out to me. He had earlier said, "Ain't nobody gonna listen, I ain't gonna play. I just play when guys get together at the clubhouse and go deer hunting."[69] Kip Lornell and the Blue Ridge Institute made efforts to rectify this situation in the late 1970s, with interviews and recordings like *Virginia Traditions: Non-Blues Secular Black Music*. Supported by the focus on local music and dance, some European American Appalachian communities returned to their old time square dances or started them anew. They established public venues for old time square dancing, sometimes using it as a popular fundraiser for schools, community needs, and nonprofit groups. Without the support of the folk revival, the Martinsville dancers did not make the move to public venues or market the dance to a wider circle, but they nevertheless continued to dance in the home with friends and family. Among themselves, however, they identified with the music and culture that was the focus of the folk revival, even though most revivalists and collectors did not share their perception.

The old breakdown was a private rather than a public event, taking place in people's homes, except for the Fiddlers' Convention and the occasional barn dances held on The Block. Though the house parties could be crowded with dancers and onlookers, everyone was known to each other, either coming from the neighborhood or invited by someone in the community. Like old time music, it was "social, domestic, and participatory," requiring an intimate setting.[70] Close-knit families were the sole retaining institutions for the old breakdown, and as elders passed on and youth moved away, the critical mass necessary for continuity diminished. In many European American communities, nonprofit groups, state parks, small businesses, and arts councils were among the institutions that brought new life to old time dancing during the 1970s and 1980s and beyond. No such institution or organization did the same for the old breakdown in Martinsville after the Fiddlers' Convention came to an end. The fact that it was still "in full bloom" in the 1960s speaks to the continuing strength of the community and the families who loved the dance, and to their committed identification with their traditions.

Looking Ahead

At the beginning of the twenty-first century, The Block was a big grassy area used for revivals, powwows, and community events. In 2005, cultural sharing activities took place there in relation to the first reenactment of the June German Ball. The Fayette Area Historical Initiative (FAHI), the sponsor of the reenactment, had established goals aimed at collecting and preserving local history and at long-term economic revitalization for the once-vibrant Fayette Street area. In 2011, according to the "Visit Martinsville" website, FAHI purchased the old Imperial Bank building on "The Block" to house an interactive museum and cultural center, created to "collect, preserve, and interpret African American experiences in Martinsville/Henry County."[71] Efforts were being made to use the former hub in new ways. By 1992, the old breakdown occurred only occasionally and spontaneously at Bowles family get-togethers, usually at the suggestion of a grown child come home to visit. As Naomi Bowles said, "My children can square dance. They can really get down." Though the old breakdown was no longer a regular recreation in the Martinsville African American community, at least one of the Bowles children carried the tradition forward in a new setting. The Bowles's oldest son taught school in New York at that time, and "he had his children square dancing. And that was the prettiest thing you've ever seen. They just danced that figure eight [Change partners]. Oh, they just turned around that figure. And he called the set and it was so pretty."[72] In 1976 and again in 1992, the desire was repeatedly expressed for the return of the dance and the times that it represented, with close family and community supporting each other. In 1976, Irvin Cook said, "I'm hoping it will come back. There always used to be a square dance somewhere!" Leonard Bowles was hopeful then too, seeing the growing folk revival interest in music and dance similar to his. "I think the world turns and it is coming back a little bit. It will be back."[73] With their international reputation, the Carolina Chocolate Drops and other musicians have inspired broad interest in black string band music in the twenty-first century. The context is of necessity different, because the cohesive community expressed by the old breakdown and the agrarian lifestyle in which it thrived are things of the past, but the music resonates with a growing audience.

5. Mr. Perry's Sweet Shop and a New Old Time Dance

On a summer Saturday afternoon in the 1940s in the coal town of Dante in Russell County, Virginia, the African American baseball team known as the Bearcats has just returned from a game in a neighboring community. In almost every house in Sawmill Hollow, the African American section of town, men and women are getting dressed up, preparing to go to Mr. Perry's Sweet Shop for an evening of dancing. Some couples bring their children and some aging parents go along to share in the fun. As they stroll up the street to "the Shop," other families sit on their porches and enjoy the procession of stylish people and the flirtatious interactions of the teens. Some white couples come over from Straight Hollow or down the road from Brushy Ridge, the still-agricultural hill above Sawmill Hollow, drawn by the music and the new styles of dancing. In 1992, African American dancer Eleanor Kincaid reminisced, "All ages (would come)—Grammaw, Grampaw, Momma, Daddy, uncles, sisters and brothers—everybody gathered." She laughed, "Children, those that weren't in bed, they were there. They would always look, they'd find somebody's porch to sit on." She gestured in the direction of the site up the hollow where the Sweet Shop once stood. "They'd just love to see the young folks, as they call them, dress up and go to the dance."[1] Mr. Perry's Sweet Shop has been gone for decades, but its influence lived on in the late twentieth century in the old time dancing in the coalfields surrounding Dante.

In 1984, the Dante Volunteer Fire Hall/Community Center began having country music each week to raise funds to buy fire trucks and rescue squad vehicles. The band, Pete Castle and the Phillips Brothers, donated their time and talents, and a group (including Betty, Pete Castle's wife and the daughter of the fire chief) organized the evenings, procuring refreshments to be sold and baking cakes for the cakewalk fundraiser. When I went to the Fire Hall in the

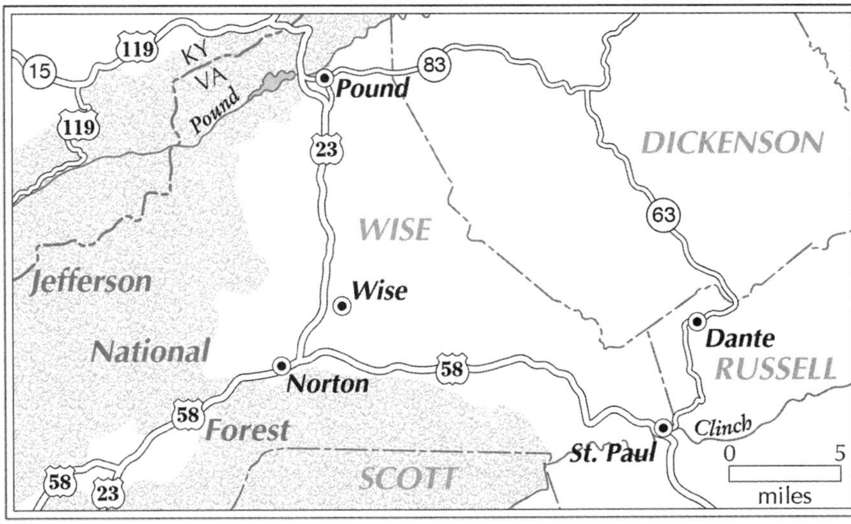

Map 4. Area surrounding Dante, Virginia. Cartography by Dick Gilbreath, Director, Gyula Pauer Center for Cartography and GIS, University of Kentucky.

late 1980s and early 1990s, couple dances predominated, associated with flirting. The floor was full of dancers, some dancing "solo," but with a group of friends, and most dancing with partners of the opposite sex. About one-third of the evening was spent in this kind of "dancing," as it was simply called, in the form and style identified as "old time" by dancers. Another third was spent dancing in a closed position, either two stepping or slow dancing with arms around each other, swaying easily in time with the music. Besides the cakewalks, the remainder of the evening was spent in visiting with neighbors and friends.[2]

When I first attended the dances at the Dante Fire Hall in the late 1980s, I was surprised to see a different form and style of dance among the predominantly European American crowd. The footwork dancing was similar in some ways to

Figure 5.1. Dancing at the Dante Fire Hall, 1989. Courtesy of Appalshop Archive, Appalshop Films Collection.

the kind I had experienced in other areas of Southwest Virginia and Northeast Tennessee, but here, instead of being a solo dance, it was almost always done in partners. The partners faced each other, moving toward and away from each other, all the while circling each other. It looked like a jitterbug in form, but the partners never held hands, and they kept up a stomping, swiveling step the whole time they danced. Every movement was angular, with elbows, knees, and heels punching the air on every beat. I was used to seeing different versions of square dancing and clogging in various regions of Southwest Virginia, but I had never seen this particular form and style of dance anywhere else. I was further intrigued because when I interviewed European American dancers in the area, they were quick to say that all old time dancing came from the Charleston. This puzzled me, because old time dancing had been defined elsewhere as square dancing and clogging, and had been closely associated with rural life in other communities. The Charleston had been an important part of popular urban culture in the 1920s, and in other areas in Southwest Virginia dancers remembered having done the Charleston, but they never identified it as the origin of old time dancing.

A few years later, I interviewed African American dancers in Southwest Virginia, asking about their experiences of old time dancing. Their common response was something like: "Ah! Old time dancing! Well, there was the Charleston and the Black Bottom and the Big Apple. Now everything changed in about 1946 with the jitterbug and the slow drag and the bebop and the camel walk and the shuffle. And then you had the bossa nova, that's just a variation on the jitterbug—you wore the flare bottom pants—and now there's the electric break."[3] The shared identification of the Charleston as the source of contemporary dancing interested me, as did the fact that the European American coalfield dancing exhibited characteristics like angularity, percussiveness, and downward emphasis, which scholars associate with African American dance. In these ways, coalfield old time dancers differed from those in the Blue Ridge or the Holston River Valley in Southwest Virginia and Northeast Tennessee.[4] I began to consider the history of the region, looking for clues. My hypothesis is that this distinctive, regional style evolved in part because of the rich intercultural exchange that took place in the coalfields during the first part of the twentieth century. Social and economic factors along with the values and beliefs embedded in the dancing likely also facilitated the development of a new form and style of expression.

The Cumberland Plateau from Farms to Coal

Until the late nineteenth century, the Cumberland Plateau was largely rural, dotted with small towns and communities, both black and white. Settlers began arriving in the area around Dante and St. Paul, Virginia, around 1790. Farming was hard in the area because only a thin layer of topsoil covered the rocky ground. To make a living, farmers continually opened new land for planting by clearing trees from the hillsides. What is now the town of Dante was originally called Turkey Foot because of the pattern of hollows made by the three forks of Lick Creek and a fourth small hollow like the spur on the foot. The Phillips family were the first documented settlers of Turkey Foot, arriving from North Carolina in the early 1800s, and Turkey Foot eventually became a small, rural community. The area was so remote that to acquire supplies not produced on the farms, such as coffee, sugar, and baking soda, it was necessary to take a wagon about forty miles to Abingdon, Virginia, the center of commerce for Southwest Virginia, a trip that could take two days each way. One person would make the trip three or four times a year, gathering orders from his neighbors before making the long and arduous journey.[5] As the nineteenth century went on, both African American and European American settlers established homeplaces in the rural areas and small communities. A 1917 photo shows John and Patsy Pierce Gose, an African American couple whose descendants still lived in the area in the 1990s, on their farm on Honey Branch, outside of Dante. Eleanor Kincaid grew up on a farm her family owned, on Pine Ridge near Castlewood, a few miles from Dante. Farther west, near Pennington Gap in Lee County, Virginia, Rachel Scott established a three-hundred-acre farm and a nineteen-room house, financed through her work as a barber for white people.[6] These are only a few illustrations of what was a common occurrence.

Agriculture was the primary means of support until the late 1800s, when the timber industry arrived, further denuding the mountains. Coal was known and used for heat by Native Americans and by the early settlers in the area, but it was not until the late nineteenth century that it claimed the attention of industrial developers. In the 1880s companies began to purchase mineral rights from landowners, allowing mining operations to access coal by any means necessary, and the first coal mining took place. The sale of timber and coal provided cash that had not been readily available in the area previously. The Norfolk and Western Railroad was completed to St. Paul in 1890, and timber and coal were hauled by wagon to St. Paul, then known as Estonoa, to be shipped to Norfolk, Virginia, or to Bluefield, West Virginia, and beyond. The whole area around Turkey Foot and Estonoa, owned by an Englishman since the Revolutionary War, was sold to coal companies in the late 1800s. In 1901 the company that purchased it organized the building of a railroad to Estonoa/St. Paul to facilitate the export of natural resources. Turkey Foot was renamed in honor of the company's vice president, William Joseph Dante, in 1903, and by that time it had already begun its rapid growth. It boasted a hotel, railroad station, company store, steam heat for the company offices and executives' homes, and some housing for miners.[7] Dante became a thriving coal camp, with rows of nearly identical clapboard houses wedged between the hills in each of the hollows. Each hollow was designated by name and by race. Sawmill Hollow on the left fork of Lick Creek was for black families; Straight Hollow, on the middle fork, was mixed; Bear Wallow, on the right fork, was for white families. In Dante proper was the business district, and the "spur" was known as Hospital Hollow.

The economy changed quickly from a rural agrarian economy to an industrial one, and people responded with dramatic changes in cultural expression. In his study of company towns, historian David Corbin notes, "The company town quickly and ruthlessly destroyed old cultures and stimulated the development of a new one."[8] African Americans and European Americans from the region left their rural homes and communities to move to the new camps for jobs. European immigrants arrived from Italy, Hungary, and Yugoslavia, along with African American southerners, to provide the labor for the mines. The rapid changes and the many newcomers with their varied customs created an atmosphere ripe for the creation of new social forms. Sociologist Ann Swidler refers to periods like these as times of "unsettled lives," when people "establish new styles or strategies of meaning." Historian Eric Hobsbawm likewise believes the invention of new forms to be associated with periods of rapid transformation of society and social patterns, unsuited to the former ways of doing things.[9]

Square dancing and rhythmic footwork dancing were described among both black and white residents of Southwest Virginia since the late 1800s, and as recently as the mid-1900s.[10] These were reportedly the principal forms of dance in the rural culture of the Cumberland Plateau of Virginia among both groups, and they continued, with diminishing importance, after the establishment of coal camps in the early twentieth century. African American musicians Howard Armstrong from Northeast Tennessee and Carl Martin from Wise County, Virginia, toured nationally with their bands from the 1920s to the 1950s, playing all kinds of music to suit various audiences' tastes: old time fiddle tunes for square dancing, blues, swing, and the popular tunes of the day. Armstrong toured extensively in the coalfields of the Cumberland Plateau, playing for both black and white square dances. "If we played for the (white) country people, the common class, well, we'd play square dance music like 'Old Joe Clark' and 'Ida Red.' . . . Now the regular Black people you could play blues for . . . they'd also have square dances, and you'd be surprised to know how close they were to the white square dances." The African American community in and around Dante enjoyed square dances called by Bo Fain.[11]

Old time dancing among both African Americans and European Americans around Dante tended to be family centered, prior to the arrival of the coal industry. As in the Valley and the Blue Ridge, "neighborhoods" at the turn of the century were walking-distance clusters with a diameter of up to five miles. Neighbors gathered in each other's homes about once a month, especially in winter, to "have a hoedown," with old time square dancing and the footwork dancing known as flatfooting or buck dancing. Often whole families came together, though sometimes only the younger people danced and sometimes only the elders, but all participated in the dancing or socializing or both. The story is often told of families of either ethnicity hosting a dance in conjunction with a cornshucking, molasses stiroff, or other "working." They danced at weddings, Christmas holidays, and sometimes for no special occasion. European American dancer Nova Deel recalled, "My Daddy owned a farm and my uncle would call the hoedown dances. People would move all their furniture out and turn their home over for a dance. We would walk for miles to get there." Describing a visiting couple structure, in which one couple danced a figure with each other couple, she said, "My uncle would call the Four-handed Reel for sixteen people in the circle. 'First couple out' and they'd dance with all the other couples. Then the next couple would go." The circle danced to the accompaniment of fiddle or banjo, with one of the men calling the figures. Others ringed the room, watching and visiting.[12] Old time dancing was a way of solidifying the walking-distance community and the bonds between families.

Solo footwork dancing was common among both black and white coalfields dancers from the mid-1800s until the mid-1900s, and similarities and differences among styles can be identified. Buck dancing, and sometimes "Hambone," were the names given to this kind of dancing among African American people in this area. According to local consultants, groups of men and women gathered spontaneously and danced, making sounds with their feet, clapping, and patting their hands on arms, legs, and torso, and rhythmically beating assorted instruments such as washboard and spoons, and sometimes playing banjos, guitars, and fiddles. Eleanor Kincaid's husband, Earl Kincaid, described making music with spoons, jingling pop lids nailed to a board, and beating a bass drum made from a washtub. African American consultant Shirley Taylor, from Lee County, Virginia, described buck dancing: "We'd just be out in the street somewhere, just wherever you got happy and wanted to start dancing, people said, 'Let's have a little dance.' Lots of times on the weekends they'd all gather down in town around the depot and somebody'd have a drum or they'd just get two sticks and they'd start beating on anything and they'd just start [buck] dancing. Mostly they'd be outside, or sometimes in the living room they'd have hardwood floors and they'd just dance."[13] When viewing a videotape of John "Dee" Holman and Quentin "Fris" Holloway's old time buck dancing demonstration,[14] Earl Kincaid exclaimed, "My Uncle Roy used to do that!" and immediately went to the kitchen to get a bread pan to demonstrate his own patting and buck dancing. His demonstration, like that of others in the area, emphasized elbows angled out to the sides at shoulder height, heels kicking to the sides as his legs swiveled in, feet digging into the floor, and a downward gaze as he listened to the rhythms he made on the bread pan. Mr. Kincaid remembered his family buck dancing in the home, making music and telling tales by the fire, and "barn dances in the country. A bunch of guys would sit around and talk and buck dance on Saturday nights."[15]

Flatfooting, as the rural footwork dance was called by European Americans in the area, could likewise take place anywhere, but it seems not to have involved patting arms, legs, or torso to make rhythms. Often it was a spontaneous expression after a working or whenever people gathered, a fiddler or banjo player striking up a tune, and men, especially, getting up to flatfoot. Just as often, flatfooting occurred in the home during an evening of square dancing. European American dancer Nova Deel said, "Everybody would flatfoot, and the main dance was the backstep. It was sort of like the buck and wing. You weren't a good dancer if you couldn't do the backstep." She demonstrated, placing one foot directly behind the other, letting the front foot slip out and arc around to step behind the first foot. Eleanor Kincaid compared flatfooting with the sand dancing that she and her friends did in their youth. "We carried sand in our pockets. When that record started playing, we'd put sand down on the floor and [here she made a swishing sound, moving her hands back and forth]. It was the same as flatfooting."[16]

An element of competition sometimes characterized the footwork dancing of both black and white dancers. Eleanor Kincaid described men buck dancing in Sawmill Hollow, challenging each other: "There was always somebody jumping up in the middle of the road, clapping their heels together, showing how old they were and how young they were [by how many times they could click their heels together before landing]. Jump up in the air, clap their heels together and come back down. One man said, bet you can't do this. I'm older than you and I can *still* do that!" Similar stories were told of European American men trying to outdance each other with faster and fancier footwork.

A Time of Change

New arrivals to the coalfields brought their own traditions with them, beginning in about 1906, and square dancing and footwork dancing continued to be enjoyed as recreations during the early twentieth century. European immigrants, especially Hungarians, Italians, and Poles, were recruited to work in the Appalachian coalfields upon their arrival to the United States from that time until the beginning of World War I. According to coalfields attorney Frank Kilgore, there were two primary reasons for seeking immigrants: they had special trades or skills, like stone masonry or bridge and tunnel building, that local workers did not have; and the pool of local workers was not large enough to meet the growing demand for coal leading up to World War I. Katharine Shearer, coordinator of the Dante History Project, learned that "local folks would work [in the coal mines] in the cold weather, and then when it was time to plant a crop, they would leave . . . they would go back to the farm and they would take care of their farming responsibilities." Rural workers were so committed to their homeplaces that many walked miles to work in the coal mines, worked shifts ranging from ten to sixteen hours of drilling or loading coal, and made the long walk home afterward. The coal operators brought in immigrants and black sharecroppers in order to have a year-round workforce and to offset the impact of strikes organized by the newly forming labor unions. These new arrivals were easier to control because they did not own land to which they could return and which would have provided them with a certain amount of financial independence.[17]

Though at first local residents were hostile toward the newcomers, they eventually established friendships with them, especially during the second generation. The immigrants became strong union supporters and good neighbors, and some of them married local residents. Eleanor Kincaid remembered a Hungarian gentleman who sent treats home for her in her father's lunch bucket. She said, "There was no language barrier. It wasn't like we couldn't communicate," even though they spoke different tongues. The Hungarians had an annual Grape Harvest Dance each October in the Hungarian boardinghouse. Bunches of grapes, purchased because not enough were grown in Dante, adorned the room, and food was served in abundance. People danced the polka, waltz, and chowbash, a Hungarian dance "sort of like the foxtrot." People remember it as "the festivity of the year," attended by coal company executives as well as workers and "carried out in style." European American dancer Nova Deel recalled attending the "Grape Arbor," as she knew it, along with other Dante residents. Other coalfield towns like Stonega and Lynch, Kentucky, and Pocohontas, West Virginia, had similar festivals. Frank Kilgore asserted that the Appalachian coalfields were the largest melting pot in the United States outside of New York City. By the early years of the current century, there were still numerous ethnic surnames in the area surrounding Dante.[18]

African American southerners, primarily from Alabama, Georgia, and North Carolina, made up the largest group to come to the Southwest Virginia coalfields during the boom. Columbus Avery of Williamson, West Virginia, was one of the people sent to recruit, and he recalled bringing a total of at least two thousand black men from the South to Eastern Kentucky and Southwest Virginia over the course of two years in the early 1920s.[19] Whole communities of young men were brought in on "the transportation," passenger and freight trains sent specifically to round up labor, first for the construction industry and then for the coal mines. With them they brought new music and dances. African culture scholar Robert Farris Thompson suggests that most enslaved southerners had come from cohesive West African cultures, which they were able to maintain and further unify within the institutions of slavery and peonage. Thompson cited

Figure 5.2. Downtown Dante, 1920. The Dante Hotel is in the center. Courtesy of Thomas Boyd.

jazz, "the most sophisticated and important popular North American music," as a product of the powerful influence of this group, along with the dances associated with it, like the Charleston and the lindy hop.[20] Arriving by the hundreds in the unsettled environment of the coalfields, they were positioned to influence the dance traditions of the region. The Eastern European influences in jazz music likely also contributed to its popularity in the melting-pot environment of the coalfields.

Dante grew rapidly. It was the second coal town established in Southwest Virginia, Pocohontas being the first, and it quickly became the largest. At its peak in the 1920s, approximately four thousand people lived in the once tiny town. Clinchfield Coal Company provided a hospital, post office, commissary, theater, pharmacy, barbershop, and service station, and built schools and churches in each hollow. Everything was available to the workers, who were paid in scrip that could only be used in the company businesses, usually resulting in permanent indebtedness for the miners. In order to maintain control of the workers, the company discouraged private enterprise and prevented the establishment of a town council. As Katharine Shearer, coordinator for the Dante History Project, reported, "Clinchfield provided everything, and in return they wanted complete loyalty." Dante became the largest town in Russell County, and its "economic engine." After World War I, the demand for coal continued for a while, as required for the rebuilding of Europe, but by the mid-1920s, it had diminished. Clinchfield, unlike some other companies, kept the mines running on a much-reduced schedule so that workers could manage to pay their house rent and have a place to live. Another coal boom ensued with World War II, but after the war, mechanization and the decreased worldwide demand for coal resulted in the loss of scores of mining jobs. In 1959, the mines in Dante closed completely, resulting in a "great exodus from the region." It is estimated that one-third of the population left the area to find jobs, many moving to the Great Lakes region for manufacturing jobs. Anyone who chose to stay had to commute to jobs elsewhere or to work in one of the small stores in town. With the shrinking population, these shops lost business; eventually, most closed. The job insecurity caused by the cycle of coal boom and bust added to the unsettled atmosphere in the coalfields.[21]

Dante was one of the better coal towns in terms of the housing and services provided.[22] Even so, the oppressive working conditions and the constant danger had a leveling effect among ethnic groups, though racial disparities existed in education, housing, and recreation. Neighbors and co-workers supported each other in hard times, and some African Americans had supervisory mine jobs and union leadership positions. The houses were built and owned by the coal company, whose contract did "not create the relationship of landlord and tenant, but only of master and servant," regardless of ethnicity.[23] Both blacks and whites in some coal company towns compared the situation to slavery. Former slave George Echols said it felt the same, and some said the coal camps were worse, with not enough to eat and no freedom to gather or to go anywhere.[24] Still, the 1920s, 1930s, and 1940s are remembered by Dante residents as exciting times, with strong communities and lots of entertainment options. Boys played baseball, sometimes ten or twelve games a day; whole families had all-day sledding parties followed by bonfires and hot chocolate; children and young adults went with friends to movies and attended carnivals when they came to town. In Wise County coal towns, reports are similar. Everybody in the neighborhood spent time together evenings and weekends, parents and children shooting marbles and jumping rope together. Everyone listened to the Grand Ole Opry, and dancing was a major social outlet.[25]

Almost everyone in Dante has said that there never were problems related to race, but segregation was nevertheless institutionalized. Not only were schools separate, black children had school in a little church for many years before their own Arty Lee School was built. Housing was assigned according to race. The homes for black families were either in Sawmill Hollow, which was a flood plain, or near the mouth of the No. 2 mine at the end of Straight Hollow, where the noise and dust were constant, especially if three shifts a day were running. Baseball was a primary outlet for workers in the coalfields, and the towns of Dante and Clinchco had a thriving rivalry. The company supported the white team, providing uniforms and arranging games. The Bearcats, the black team, had to support themselves financially, "traveled far and wide to get games," and invited black teams from other towns to come to Dante to play. Though they used the same field, they always played at separate times. The movie theater, which offered films every night of the week, maintained separate sections for

Figure 5.3. Earl and Eleanor Kincaid on their front porch, 1990s. Photo by Paula Allen.

black and white patrons, which was sometimes a source of discontent. Emogene Kincaid, Earl Kincaid's sister-in-law, grew up in Straight Hollow, with white families living nearby. She said they all played together, going to each other's houses to play with dollhouses or to play ball. They went to the movies on Thursday or Saturday, and often the black and white children sat together, despite the official policies. Sometimes, however, the white children would sit in their own section while the black children went to theirs, and "it was a hurtful thing," even though they walked home together and socialized afterward.[26]

Despite inequities, people of all ethnic groups "stuck together if anybody needed anything and we survived," according to Earl Kincaid. His brother Matthew Kincaid said, "Your neighbors would never let you go to bed hungry."[27] Telling of close friendly relations among the races, a woman from another coal camp described taking food to each other and said, "Our young people had great times together. They would play and dance together. We helped each other out like good neighbors."[28] Shirley Taylor, who grew up in Pennington Gap, Virginia, a multiethnic coal mining area about seventy miles west of Dante, expressed a similar experience. She said she had never known of a fight related to race issues, "because everybody just seems to be close in this community."[29] Emogene Kincaid described the day racial integration went into effect in Dante. White people could always eat at the town drugstore, but black people had never been allowed to do so. On that special day, she dressed her children up and took them to the drugstore and sat down to eat. She said they "didn't have any trouble at all because, like I said, everybody knew everybody."[30]

New ways were developed through the interaction among local residents, African American southerners, and European immigrants. Some of the forms of cultural expression that had evolved among rural Appalachian African Americans and European Americans seemed no longer expressive of their experience. New forms were created using elements of the many available in the fertile cultural mix.

Figure 5.4. Sawmill Hollow, 1990s, seen from the site of the ball field. Photo by Paula Allen.

Mr. Perry's Sweet Shop

The exchange of dance ideas took place most thoroughly in gathering places in the black sections of the coal camps. Dance venues like Mr. Perry's Sweet Shop in Dante's Sawmill Hollow, Frank White's Blue Room in Trammel, and Club Shorty George in Norton were social hubs for the African American communities. Such establishments were to be found in many places in the Appalachian region. Other examples are the Tea Room in Marion, Virginia, the Rabbit Box in New Market, Tennessee, and the Moroccan Grill in Bristol, Virginia. These places sold food, drinks, or ice cream, and some offered opportunities to dance, having musicians or jukeboxes. African American pianist, singer, and dancer Earl Gilmore from Clinchco, Virginia, said, "Dancing was about the top thing that drew people together. When Friday came we knew we had three days of celebration—Dancing, dancing, dancing." Among other dance venues for African American coalfields residents were fundraisers for churches and civic organizations, sometimes known as "chitlin' struts." Food would be sold, including such things as fish, chitlins, cornbread, slaw, and sweet potatoes. After dancing a while, everyone would stop and buy something to eat and then go back to dancing. The pattern would go on sometimes until four or five in the morning. Sometimes a special ball would be held as a fundraiser, like the Eldora Ball held in Kingsport, Tennessee, until into the 1990s.[31]

Mr. Perry's Sweet Shop in Dante was a social center for whole families. In its first version, it was small, about the size of a home in Sawmill Hollow, with a coin-operated piccolo-record machine (jukebox). The shop was a restaurant offering sandwiches and cold drinks, and it had a pool room and a store. Booths lined the walls, and tables were moved aside for the dancing. Every Friday and Saturday night there were "socials" for which everyone got dressed up and went dancing. Mr. Perry apparently was an entrepreneur and a community leader of sorts, managing the baseball team, and intervening to help youngsters get jobs. Earl Kincaid's first job was due to Perry's assistance, and he went on to work in the mines for forty-two years, to serve as church superintendent for forty years, and to lead several Boy Scout troops in Dante. In the years following Perry's first small shop, he opened a second, larger one in Sawmill in a two-story, cinderblock building. He needed the larger space to make room for the many people who came, sometimes three hundred or four hundred in an evening. In this newer building, the upstairs was used for recreation and the downstairs for the store and restaurant. In this larger establishment, he brought in bands. Sometimes there would be a special ball, announced by posters, following a big baseball game or other special occasion. At some point he opened another restaurant and dance hall in Kingsport, Tennessee. Mr. Perry passed away in 1990 at age 90, having seen nearly a century of change in and around Dante.[32]

Eleanor Kincaid described how her father took her to dance halls when she was a child in the 1930s: "There weren't any old people back then! They were young at heart. They liked young things, they liked young people. You have young people around old people, they stay young. You don't have young people around old people, they get old." The presence of the adults also had an effect on discipline, according to Earl Kincaid. "They kept the younger people straight. When they'd go out and catch one doing the wrong thing, buddy he'd had it! Buddy I mean you had to respect the older people!" The participation of the older and younger generations together was pleasurable for the elders and linked them with their own youth while providing a means of enforcing standards of behavior. Just as in the dances in the rural homeplaces, the event included the entire family of several generations, and consisted of watching as well as dancing. The parents and grandparents participated in their children's courtship by their presence at the weekend dances at Mr. Perry's, as relatives and neighbors had at the square dances in the homes. Both European Americans and African Americans in rural Appalachian settings had experienced the "communal life," as described by folklorist and anthropologist Zora Neale Hurston, and it continued at the Sweet Shop.

At the coal town dance halls, what Hurston called "an all permeating drama" was also evidenced. As she said, "An audience is a necessary part of any drama."[33] The drama at the Sweet Shop was provided by the young dancers themselves and their personal presentation and interaction. Eleanor Kincaid said everyone in Sawmill Hollow loved to watch the young folks dress up and go to the dance. She described the young men at Mr. Perry's in the late 1930s and 1940s, who emulated the Cab Calloway style in favor at Harlem's Savoy Ballroom: "They had the zoot suit and the Big Apple hats. Everybody had one, and the big jivin' chain and it had to go all the way down and touch your shoe and come up the other side. It would be hooked on the pocket and they would unsnap it when they would meet a girl and they would catch up so much (of the chain) and swing it around their finger and talk. *That* was cool. If you saw him in his zoot suit and his jivin' chain—Yeeaahh!" Her husband Earl added, "You're jivin' that girl you see." Bessie Jones, who documented African American dance and games, would identify this as "play," or "small life dramas . . . ceremonials testifying to the ongoingness of life."[34] Young people at Mr. Perry's Sweet Shop enacted the life drama of courtship, witnessed by their families.

According to cultural historian Katrina Hazzard-Gordon, dance venues like these "saw the first large-scale cross fertilization of dances."[35] The dancing at Mr. Perry's Sweet Shop was a powerful magnet, drawing not only the African American residents of Dante and other towns across the coalfields, but also European American residents of Dante and its environs, who came to Mr. Perry's from Straight Hollow and Bear Wallow, as well as from rural areas surrounding Dante, like Brushy Ridge, the hill rising above Sawmill Hollow, making the easy walk past the ball field to arrive at Mr. Perry's. The pattern of whites going to black dance venues mirrored the phenomenon at the Savoy Ballroom and at the tobacco warehouses in the Blue Ridge and the Holston River Valley of Southwest Virginia. White dancers frequented the African American dance halls across the coalfields, watching and learning the movements of the Charleston and lindy hop firsthand. At Frank White's Blue Room in Trammel, for example, the counter was in the middle of the room. African Americans filled one side, European Americans the other. The white patrons would watch the black patrons dancing and practice the moves they saw. Apparently white dancers were welcome at the black dance venues. African American dancer Earl Kincaid mused on dancing at Mr. Perry's, "We weren't studying about race."[36]

Other opportunities existed for the exchange of dance ideas in the region, in addition to the sweet shops and tea rooms. Shirley Taylor's father, Spike Carson, was a band director who played throughout the coalfields and beyond with his group, "The Black and White Band," even taking them to Mardi Gras on occasion. His jazz band, composed of musicians of both races, played at both black and white events and clubs, and was broadcast every Saturday on the Virgil Q. Wax show. Fundraising events offered other chances for trading dance styles. Shirley Taylor remembered that at black fundraising dances "all the whites would show up to support us." I imagine that the exciting new dances drew white patrons to these events as much as the desire to support their black neighbors. Blacks typically never attended white events, though. "We never did care anything about it," Mrs. Taylor insisted. Institutionalized segregation resulted in the mixing working only one way: European Americans attending African American events. Here, as in the Valley and the Blue Ridge, performances of big name bands like Cab Calloway, Count Basie, Glenn Miller, Fats Domino, Little Richard, Nat King Cole, and the Ink Spots provided occasions for large-scale exchanges of movement forms and styles. From the 1920s into the 1950s, such performers toured the region, playing at tobacco warehouses, armories, or civic auditoriums. Often bands would be booked for two nights, one night for blacks and one night for whites. On the night scheduled for African Americans, European Americans could pay admission to watch the dancing, though the reverse seems not to have been true. Sometimes a velvet rope would divide the dance floor, separating the white viewers from the black dancers. In at least one place, the time came when the white audience was so taken up with the dancing that they broke over the dividing line and joined in. Besides attending dances with their black neighbors, white coalfield residents learned these popular dances through the media. European American dancer Nova Deel perfected her Charleston technique in the late 1920s by watching the Saturday afternoon newsreels at the Dante movie theater and then going home to practice with her friends. Each week she would add new steps to her repertoire, incorporating them into her own flatfooting style. All her rehearsing was rewarded when she earned a prize of a silver half-dollar in a contest in town.[37]

Jazz-era dancing transcended race. Emerging from African American communities, it soon became everyone's style, from the big cities to Appalachian towns and coal camps. People flocked to the sweet shops, tea rooms, and clubs for the exciting dance and music. Early on, the Charleston was the favorite dance, with its angled knees and elbows and swiveling legs. African American southerners in all likelihood brought the Charleston with them when they came to the coalfields on the transportation in the early twentieth century. This nationally popular dance was named for Charleston, South Carolina, where it was said to have evolved from earlier forms of dance. Jazz historians Marshall and Jean Stearns document its widespread popularity in the early 1920s and note references to it in 1903. Zora Neal Hurston places the origins of the Charleston, as a popular dance, in the 1890s, Roger Abrahams traces it to slavery times, and Robert Farris Thompson and Beverly J. Robinson propose possible African origins.[38] By the 1920s the Charleston was already evolving into another dance called the "hop" and later the lindy hop, an improvisational partner dance to swing music that originated in Harlem. A partner dance with certain basic steps, the lindy's most notable characteristic was the "breakaway," in which partners improvised moves together or individually. Famed lindy hopper Shorty Snowden told of the origins of the breakaway, saying he and others began making up their own steps, like his signature "Shorty George." He said, "I was always looking for someone dancing in the street or just walking or doing anything that suggests a step. If I could see it, I could do it."

In the late 1930s, aerial steps were introduced in the breakaway, like "the Hip to Hip, the Side Flip, and Over the Back (phrases describing the trajectory of the girl in the air)."[39] These new dances differed from square dancing and flatfooting in their focus on the partner rather than the group, in their improvisational structure, and in their drama and excitement. Describing the dancing at Mr. Perry's, Eleanor Kincaid said, "Everything was a partner dance." Shirley Taylor described the acrobatics of the lindy at the dance halls in the coal towns, saying, "He'd pick you up and flip you over with the real wide skirts on, and you'd just come back up on your feet." Besides the lindy, dancers did a partner dance called the "slow drag." "You just hold onto each other and sort of slide your feet around. You'd dance smooth . . . you'd have a slight dip to the side, slight rock or something. It all flowed with the music. Whatever it was, was in your bones." Sometimes people danced alone to the faster music, just as they had when buck dancing in the home or on the street. "If you got up by yourself, you'd be soloing . . . and sometimes they would have dances they would do in a group . . . you had your partner there, but everybody was dancing, but there wasn't anybody touching. Everybody'd be just dancing."[40] As Katrina Hazzard-Gordon observed of jazz-era dancing, "The partnering relationship . . . still had some communal ties to group dancing."[41] This was similar to rural practices at the same time. European American dancer Nova Deel referred to the practice of dancing alone but in a group in the home: "You'd mostly flatfoot by yourselves, but you could have a partner." Though primarily different, the new dances introduced at Mr. Perry's had some similarities to local dancing, and the two probably reinforced and built upon each other, contributing to the style I saw at the Dante Fire Hall.

A Network Across the Coalfields

In the early part of the twentieth century, when the Cumberland Plateau was predominantly rural, dancing served to bring people together and to reinforce intergenerational ties. Prior to the arrival of the jazz dances, square dancing and flatfooting or buck dancing strengthened the close-knit neighborhood in a narrow geographical area for both groups. When the large numbers of African American southerners began to arrive, living in the coal towns, their bonds were not so much with a local community as with the many friends from their homes in Alabama and elsewhere. These friends were spread across the coalfields, and they did not hesitate to travel in order to socialize or to share important occasions. The geographically broad African American coalfields community,

Figure 5.5. American Legion square dance at the Dante Hall, about 1936. Caller F. L. Thompson is at left. Courtesy of Nancy Ring.

regional rather than local, was reinforced by dance, baseball, service organizations, schools, and perhaps other institutions or practices. The dynamic and cohesive network strengthened the impact of the new dance forms, and the dancing energized it in return.

By the 1930s, square dancing began to move from the home to public halls in Dante as elsewhere in the region. A photo shows European American caller F. L. Thompson at the microphone during an American Legion square dance at Dante Hall in Bear Wallow Hollow, the European American section of town, in the late 1930s.[42] Earl and Eleanor Kincaid remembered African American square dance caller Bo Fain leading square dances to the music of a band at one of the black schools into the 1940s. In a video made from home movies of Dante in 1939, Fain appeared, striding in jodhpurs and knee boots and fitted jacket. Whether he was dressed for horseback riding or making a stylistic statement cannot be said, but the Stearns describe a "king" dancer at the Savoy wearing similar attire after his appearance in the 1937 film *A Day at the Races*.[43] Square dances appear not to have been mixed-race events, unlike the dancing at the sweet shops and tea rooms, though both black and white musicians are known to have played for square dances of both groups. Some white dancers returned to their rural homeplaces for square dancing, even when square dances were held in town. For them, the place that the generations came together, the center of their intergenerational community, was primarily in the country, at the homeplace where parents and grandparents still lived. For both groups, square dancing and footwork dancing maintained a rural association, as opposed to the Charleston and the lindy popular in town.

The coal camp offered everything from a movie theater and ball fields to "a commissary with groceries, a confectionery, a men's department, a ladies department, a drugstore and a druggist, a Doctor's office. You didn't have to leave for anything except to pay taxes in Clintwood (the county seat)."[44] But, according to several consultants, dance halls like Mr. Perry's Sweet Shop drew people from all over the coalfields, supporting a network among African American communities. They listed dance halls they frequented across the coalfields and beyond, at distances of thirty to fifty miles. Black people from every town went to each of the other towns to dance and socialize. Before the 1950s, roads were few, narrow, and unpaved, so drives of this distance could easily take two or three hours. Not everyone owned a car, so whole groups would pile into any car that was going to one of these weekly dances. James Mabry reported that he bought his first car "for the community" to help others, as well as himself, to travel in order to connect with friends in other towns.[45] European American square dance caller Kirby Smith told of climbing into the back of his brother's truck with many of his brothers and cousins to make the more-than-two-hour trek from their home in Russell County, in the coalfields, to Abingdon, Virginia, in the 1940s for a square dance at the tobacco warehouse. They were attracted by "some big professional caller calling . . oh yeah, that was big stuff . . . ," but this seems to have been a rare event, unlike the weekly excursions described by African Americans who lived in the coal towns at the time.[46]

Segregated education also helped to establish connections among African American communities in the coalfields. African American children came from Clinchco in the 1930s to attend Arty Lee School in Sawmill Hollow. African American service clubs and fraternal organizations that sponsored elegant charity balls, like Kingsport's Eldora Ball, further linked people across the region.[47] The network was still in existence in the early 1990s.

Echoes of an Era

The new dances of the jazz era were exciting diversions in the coalfields during the first half of the twentieth century. By the end of the century, the African American sweet shops and tea rooms did not exist as they had decades earlier, but the influence of the dance styles that flourished there could still be seen in the dancing at the Dante Fire Hall. Comparisons with dance styles in other areas of Southwest Virginia contribute to this understanding. European American old time dancing in the coalfields of Virginia's Cumberland Plateau in the 1980s and 1990s reflected similarities with jazz-era dancing in the particular partner relationship, and it reflected similarities with old style Charleston and buck dancing in the use of the body, angularity, step style, and accented movement. This dancing contrasted with old time dancing farther east. In the Blue Ridge, two hours away, square dancing occupied most of the evening, with a circle of as many as three hundred participants surrounding a school cafeteria, and flatfooting took place as a solo in a group, introspective and responsive to the phrases of the music. Musician Rich Kirby has noted similar distinctions between the music of the two regions. According to him, Blue Ridge music is usually more fluid and melodic, and the fiddle is more often the lead instrument. Coalfields music emphasizes rhythm with percussive accents, and the banjo tends to predominate.[48] Couple dances were rare in the Blue Ridge, with the exception of an occasional waltz. In the Holston River Valley on the eastern edge of the coalfields, the European American clogging style had some of the angularity and percussiveness found in Dante, and occasionally partners danced together with "swing dance" moves as they clogged. Two or three square dances during each dance evening attracted large numbers to the dance floor. One can imagine that dance customs in the coalfields had had some influence on the valley style but seemingly almost none on the Blue Ridge style. Old time dancing evolved within different sets of circumstances in the two most distant areas of Southwest Virginia. The Blue Ridge area did not experience either the upheaval of the coalfields or the influx of thousands of African American southerners and European immigrants. Instead, it remained a relatively stable agrarian area, with both black and white people traveling to the coalfields of West Virginia or to the furniture factories of North Carolina for work, returning home on weekends.

In the late 1980s and early 1990s, the main "dancing" at the Dante Fire Hall took a distinct form, similar to jazz-era couple dances like the lindy hop or jitterbug, but without the "breakaway." Dancers walked to the floor in pairs, faced their partners directly and looked into their eyes, established a mutual rhythm with a slight downward bounce and perhaps a nod of the head, and began dancing. The image was like preparing to "jump in" in a game of jump rope. Their movements while dancing did not necessarily mirror each other, but their rhythmic synchronicity was apparent as they repeatedly advanced toward and retreated away from each other, all the while moving in a small circle around each other. The form was remarkably like the description given by African American educator Mabel Hardison Parker Smith of Big Stone Gap, who was born in 1905. Gracefully demonstrating lindy hop basics, holding hands with an imaginary partner, she said, "You'd go forward and back with your partner, and around."[49] The Fire Hall dancers strutted toward each other and glided away from each other, all the while doing a specific pattern of footwork. One foot hit the floor percussively on each beat, and the other foot kicked sharply outward to the side as the leg swiveled inward. The dancers propelled themselves around each other in small, counterclockwise circles. They used the forward-back-around pattern of the lindy hop and jitterbug, but instead of holding hands, they simply faced each other. They used a swivel step designed after the Charleston, dancing to bluegrass or country music.

African American coalfield residents who had been youth or young adults in the 1930s and 1940s briefly demonstrated the Charleston and buck dancing, with angular knees and elbows, syncopated rhythms, and percussive impact as they swiveled their legs in and out and punched the floor with their heels.

The similarity to the dancing at the Dante Fire Hall was unmistakable, where the movement was marked by a striking angularity of posture and gesture, sharp downward movement on each beat, punctuated by digging the heels into the floor. Fire hall regular Nova Deel cautioned about the importance of controlling the downward movement: "A dancer who *falls* and hits the floor real hard can't dance." European American coalfields dancers involved their whole bodies in their dancing, in ways that old time dancers in other parts of Southwest Virginia did not. The spine was fluid, bent elbows pumped sideways with the beat of the music, and shoulders rotated or tilted slightly with each beat, reminiscent of the African American Charleston and buck dance demonstrations I saw. Nova Deel said, "Your whole body has to move your feet," but "don't move your body too much. It throws you off 'til you can't keep the step. You've got to have control of your body to keep your feet going like you want 'em." Each movement of the Fire Hall dancers, like traditional African American Charleston and buck dancers, had its own little accent, and the side-out, Charleston-style leg gestures had stronger accents, heightened in apparent intensity because they occurred on the weaker "two" count. The direction of the leg gestures was up, so they defied both time and gravity with sudden bursts of force. By contrast, Blue Ridge dancing in both black and white communities tended to be more easily resilient, with a more elongated posture. The torso and arms were relatively still but were allowed to move naturally in response to the action of the feet. At the dance in Fancy Gap, Virginia, for example, three-minute tunes were interspersed between the square dances, and thirty or so people would take the opportunity to flatfoot. As they arrived on the dance floor, they would cast their gaze downward and continually turn slightly to the left and right as if to take in all the other dancers while they did their own individual footwork. They appeared to be all dancing together, rather than dancing with one other person. Footwork lightly patted the floor, rather than being strongly accented. The step had a slight downward emphasis, and the footwork responded to the music. As one Fancy Gap dancer said, "You just pat a tune with your feet, tick-tap-tap hitting the tune right along."[50]

The circular form of the square dance, with its divisions into sets of two couples, seemed not to have been retained as a feature of coalfields social dancing by the late 1980s. At the Dante Fire Hall, the one place the form of the circle existed was in the cakewalk. Locally, a cakewalk is a raffle in which participants buy a chance to win a cake, with proceeds benefiting a local cause. Several times during each dance evening at the fire hall, a homemade cake would be brought from the kitchen, and most of those in attendance would line up to pay twenty-five cents for a chance on the cake. The cakes were contributed by women of the community and proceeds from their sales were a primary source of funds for the community center. As the band played a tune, people walked counterclockwise around the periphery of the room, stepping on the numbers painted permanently on the floor. The line of people of all ages, some with babies in arms, completely encircled the dance floor and all the tables, passing next to the fire and rescue squad vehicles the funds had purchased. Couples talked, some youngsters flatfooted as they traveled around the room, and a few people danced in the center of the dance floor, scurrying to stand on a number when the music ended. When the music stopped, a number was drawn. The person standing on the corresponding number became the happy winner of a homemade cake.

In the cakewalk, people demonstrated their commitment to the community's welfare. Dancer Nova Deel was firm in her belief that people who didn't go to the dances didn't care about their community. The dances here actually originated as cakewalks, and one night someone stepped out of the line and started dancing. Thereafter, the Saturday night events always involved dancing. The cakewalks and the dances that sprang from them resulted from the generosity of local citizens with the leadership of Pete and Betty Castle. Guitarist Pete Castle devoted his musical talents to the betterment of his community for decades. He and his brother and other musicians had a band that entertained at Dante Elementary School fall and spring festivals, raising money for the school. Then, he said, "We took our band and played cakewalks and sessions for the fire department and rescue squad to help raise money, before the county ever give any monies to rescue squads of the Dante Volunteer Fire Department, which we started in 1969." The band that played at the Fire Hall in 1989, Pete Castle and the Phillips Brothers, was quite well known regionally, performing at Ralph Stanley's festivals and on sessions with Bill Monroe. Also a songwriter, Castle further contributed to his community by penning songs in honor of fallen coal miners.[51] His wife, Betty Castle, was one of the organizers of the dance, baking cakes and overseeing the finances.

Some similarities among the fire-hall dances, Saturday nights at Mr. Perry's, and home-centered square dances are easy enough to observe, despite the obvious differences in the events. Both were intergenerational gatherings in which

Figure 5.6. Dante Fire Hall dance, 1989. Whole families came together to the dance to raise funds to support the fire department and rescue squad. Courtesy of Appalshop Archive, Appalshop Films Collection.

communities witnessed the interaction of couples. At the Fire Hall, tables were aligned parallel to the dance floor, and most people sat at the tables in such a way as to be able to see the dancing and the band. The arrangement of the tables and the family clusters gathered at them called up the image of the porches in Sawmill Hollow, where the courtship drama was played out at Mr. Perry's in the presence of families. The setting also brought to mind the gathering of rural families and neighbors surrounding the square dancing circle in the home after a corn shucking. Historically, among both groups, dancing took place within the kinship group, and the interaction was witnessed by parents, grandparents, aunts, uncles, cousins, and neighbors. The similarities in customs, perhaps, helped to solidify the dance traditions of the late twentieth century. Sociologist Helen Lewis observed, in watching footage of the dancing, that all over the coalfields families attended dances together, the grounding in the social group giving them the freedom to move beyond it.[52] At the Dante Fire Hall in the 1980s and 1990s, whole families attended together in several generations, the parents and grandparents watching as the young adults danced in flirting couples before them. Older adults and young children also danced. It was not unusual to see a three-year-old toddling onto the dance floor, arms upraised, to be quickly scooped into the arms of an adult who continued to dance with his or her partner.

Community and Cultural Shift

Concepts and values are embedded in movement, and people choose dance forms and styles that resonate with their experience and their beliefs.[53] Though jazz-era dances were popular throughout Southwest Virginia, the distinctive dance form and style that gained prominence in the coalfields did not do so in other areas. Part of the cause lies in the significant African American presence in the coalfields and in economic and industrial factors. The transformation may also have been due, at least in part, to the values embedded in the movement of the old and new dances and to people's beliefs about community, change, and the individual's relationship to it. Square dancing had been associated with rural communities. The form of square dancing is an inward facing circle, in which every couple visits each of the other couples around the ring. In sets of two couples, they form "stars" and "clovers" and interact in a variety of ways, taking hands or dancing around each other at the direction of a caller. This had been a recreation reinforcing an already tightly knit community of families. This sort of community did not exist in the coal camp, where long-time Russell County residents lived in assigned housing next door to people from Alabama and Hungary, and worked alongside them in the mines. Nor was it the only type of community in the increasingly mobile industrial American society. Square dancing did not fit the contemporary social structure.

In square dancing, the community was expressed as a consistent spatial formation, the circle, systematically broken into smaller circles in which each couple interacted with each other couple. In jazz partner dances like the lindy hop, the community was expressed as a gathering of discrete couples, and within each couple, each individual was personally expressive and responsive to the partner. The lindy hop involved moment-to-moment improvisation and required the ability to respond instantly to a shift of weight or a movement of the arm, matching perhaps the need to react quickly to the rapidly changing social and economic environment of the first half of the twentieth century in which it flourished. A correlation may be drawn between the established formation and verse-chorus choreographic structure of the square dance and the stability of an agrarian way of life. Each person had a place in the community circle and contributed to its success through cooperation. Each individual was responsible for carrying out the caller's directions in order to keep the whole group functioning well together. Buck dancing, the Charleston, and the lindy hop and jitterbug that evolved from them are not patterned dances like square dancing. Bess Lomax Hawes, in recording African American dances taught by Bessie Jones, noted that Jones described each dance in terms of its steps and movements without placing the dancers in spatial relationship to the room or to each other, as would be required by square dances. She perceived dancing as a body art rather than as a spatial art. This was true of the Charleston and lindy hop, in which partners responded spontaneously to each other's movement cues.[54] Particularly in the flamboyant 1930s and 1940s version, with flips, kicks, and high jumps, the lindy was about risk taking and about weight sharing, literal mutual support, both key elements in survival in the oppressive and dangerous coal-camp environment. Square dancing was about taking hands, weaving patterns, and linking the group into a unified whole, perhaps more suitable to a stable rural community. In the solo dances from both traditions, buck dancing and flatfooting, the individual had the freedom to express himself or herself within the communal relationship. This similar value, along with related stylistic characteristics, such as a downward pulse on each step, may have provided one bridge between the dancing of the two groups, and toward the evolution of the dancing as it appeared at the Dante Fire Hall.

The young white folks who went dancing at Mr. Perry's, though, were not thinking about values or beliefs. Like youngsters of every generation, they were enthralled by the new kind of dancing, which contrasted so sharply with the old "country" entertainment of their parents. White youngsters everywhere in the country were drawn to this kind of dancing, and they went wherever they could to find it. In Virginia valley towns like Abingdon and in Blue Ridge towns like Independence, European American young people thronged to big-band concerts and went to African American gathering places like the Tea Room in Marion,

Virginia. Though many people there remember doing the Charleston as teens and young adults in the 1920s and 1930s, the style of the jazz-era dances seems not to have had the same lasting effect on old time dance style in those regions.

The emphasis on partner dances at Mr. Perry's, as elsewhere in the coalfields, was part of a national trend.[55] However, the economic realities of the coalfields perhaps contributed to the rise of this kind of dancing and the waning of community-based square dancing. In the coal mines, married men worked harder and longer in the piece-rate system because they had families who relied on their earnings. Company managers preferred married workers for this reason, and during slack periods, they first laid off single men of all ethnicities. On the other hand, married men were also usually strong supporters of the union because they saw the coalfields as a permanent home for their families and so had more to gain by improving working conditions. Not only did they fight hard for the union, the support of their wives enabled them to hold out for longer periods during the strikes. Women, black and white, joined together as a powerful organizing force.[56] Marriage, then, was highly valued in the coalfields because it contributed to economic survival, insuring job security and helping to achieve more equitable working conditions. In this atmosphere, couple dances and the "drama" of courtship became predominant. Though the basic unit of the square dance is also the couple, it is the couple in relation to a stable community structure rather than as a stand-alone unit in itself. Square dances, reinforcing an entire community as an interdependent entity, may have become less relevant to the needs of the residents of the coal towns than were couple dances that embodied reaction to ever-changing circumstances and involved the pair's functioning independently from the rest of the group. Parallels may be drawn with the rise of couple dances such as the waltz during the nineteenth century, as the single-family unit became more important with the rise of the middle class. The emphasis on the couple continued in the dances at the Dante Fire Hall, more so than at old time dance venues in other Southwest Virginia regions. I was told that here, dance partners were chosen as prospective dates rather than simply for the moments of dancing fun. This was rarely the case in the Blue Ridge or the Holston River Valley of Southwest Virginia.

The atmosphere of confrontation with the coal companies may have contributed to the persistence of the dance style. The footwork and patting dances from which the Charleston and its successors evolved were instruments of communication in times of slavery and peonage. Enslaved African Americans used the rhythmic sounds to signal the presence of "patty-rollers," the night patrollers who roamed southern communities to ensure that slaves —and, later, sharecroppers—were not away from their homes or inciting trouble.[57] The history of resistance which imbued these dances helped perhaps to bolster the miners and their families as they withstood hardships and battled the coal companies.

Resistance contributed to the significance of old time dancing and music in the coalfields into the late twentieth century. Though many European American coalfield residents had looked upon clogging or flatfooting as old fashioned, the 1989 strike against Pittston Coal Company inspired spontaneous dancing on the picket lines. One European American dancer said that though his father danced, he himself never did until the day the union went out on strike. He said, "[I felt] I'd just as well get into something, and I did. I started dancing," as a protest and to support the United Mine Workers. He stated that he danced to demonstrate the talents of the people of the area to the mine bosses and to television viewers. When he danced on the picket line, he exclaimed that he thought about "getting hold of those scabs [non-union workers] and stomping on them."[58] His rhythmic footwork and hand-patting attracted attention to the cause of the pickets, and it also directed energy against those who undermined the effect of the strike by taking the jobs of the striking miners.

Reflecting the Past

In the 1950s the last big coal boom dwindled, and outmigration began in earnest for all ethnicities. Outmigration among African Americans exceeded that for European Americans, so that by 1980 the black population in Southwest Virginia was only 2 percent, whereas it had been 15 percent since the early nineteenth century, and as much as 25 percent in some counties.[59] Still, a number of European Americans and African Americans alike have strong connections to the region and have chosen to stay. Both black and white high schools have biennial reunions attended by 250 or more, including some who moved out of state and intend to return to the region to retire.[60]

Besides being defined differently, old time dancing seemed to have a different place in the sense of history and tradition among the African American and European American coalfields dancers with whom I spoke, representing something different to dancers of each ethnic group. European American dancers looked upon "old time dancing" as square dancing and footwork dancing, and associated them with their rural history and customs. These consultants saw square dancing and flatfooting or clogging as traditional art forms distinct from other dances and perceived them as connections to an earlier way of life and set of values. In the twenty-first century, square dancing and clogging continue to be regular features of events and festivals like Home Craft Days at Mountain Empire Community College in Big Stone Gap, along with string band music and demonstrations of traditional crafts such as quilting, grist milling, basketry, and making apple butter. Square dancing seems not to take place on a regular basis anywhere in the coalfields of Southwest Virginia.

African American consultants identified the Charleston both as old time dancing and as the source of contemporary dances. They listed a long series of the dance's descendants, including sand dancing, the lindy hop, the jitterbug, the hucklebuck, the bop, disco, and hip hop, saying that all these dances are "the same thing." African American dancer Shirley Taylor described her grandson's winning a dance contest doing "the Hammer," dance moves named for 1980s rap/hip hop innovator M. C. Hammer, and then being phoned to come into town to perform at a street dance. "In our days we would call it jitterbug, but today they would call it rap," she remarked. Eleanor Kincaid agreed, but added her belief that clogging was also a descendant of the Charleston: "If you get the names of them and follow through with the feet, you can see the similarity of them." They saw the dancing as proceeding in an unbroken line, each dance harking back to the one before and presaging the next. What the dances had in common was the footwork, along with display, angularity, and percussiveness of style, and solo or couple form. Katrina Hazzard-Gordon expressed the same idea in a 1992 lecture, saying that the steps and movements to old African American dances are recycled repeatedly, becoming new dances with new names.[61] These consultants perceived tradition as a process, moving ever forward. Dance to them was what Hurston would call a "verbal noun," something in action, in perpetual process, rather than something fixed and structurally established. It is "not historical reenactment . . . but a memory retrieved."[62] For the coalfields European American dancers with whom I spoke, tradition cast back to a previous time, recapturing elements of it, while for the African American dancers I talked with, tradition ran in a continuous thread from the past to the present, and perhaps into the future.

In each case, young people were crucial to the continuation of the tradition as defined by the community, and because of the economy, there were fewer and fewer young people. As Shirley Taylor observed, "There's nothing here [jobs] for black or white either one to do, and they're still leaving as soon as they get out of school, because there's no kind of work here for you to do." Young people from Dante who were interviewed by Ferrum College professor Peter Crow expressed conflicting views about the region. "I'm really proud to be from here, but at the same time I don't see my future here," said one young woman. But a young man said, "I feel like I have just as many advantages as anyone else does," and spoke of the benefits of raising a family in the region.[63] Both African American and European American consultants expressed regret that there were few regular social outlets that included the extended family and the community as dancing had previously. In the 1980s the traditions by both definitions lived on in the region in overlapping threads, not as community or family expressions, but as peer group manifestations for youth. Working in schools in the region at the time, I observed African American and European American youngsters, as well as Latino and Asian children, practicing hip hop dancing and clogging at every opportunity, in bus lines, during gym class, in the halls. These were their dances, regardless of racial or ethnic background, and the heritage they expressed was of less concern to these young people than the immediate fun of dancing. Today, clogging teams, practiced in the moves taught by the National Clogging Organization, perform at local festivals, and high school dance teams entertain at basketball game halftimes, using hip hop moves just as students do nationally. Just as in the Holston River Valley, regular dancers at the Country Cabin at Josephine, in Wise County, seem to prefer two-stepping to clogging. A particular regional style may no longer exist here.

In the late twentieth century, however, old time dancing in Dante carried within it bits of the history of its surrounding area. In the coalfields, more than in other regions of Southwest Virginia, a style of old time dancing evolved that incorporated elements of flatfooting and the lindy hop as well as characteristics associated with both European and African aesthetics. Throughout Southwest Virginia, jazz-era dances were available to both black and white people at big-band dances and at local establishments. It may be that the new style emerged in the coalfields rather than elsewhere because of the particular intercultural exchange that took place, with thousands of African American southerners and hundreds of European immigrants arriving all at once. They made the dance styles immediately and continually available in ways that the media and occasional large-scale events did not elsewhere. They introduced exciting new forms into a region where sudden economic changes, reconfigured living situations, and strained rural neighborhood ties created social upheaval in which old customs were disrupted. Though square dancing was sponsored in Dante by local groups of both ethnicities into the 1940s, its form and style did not have the same relevance to the experiences and expectations of either African American or European American residents of the town. In response to the many changes, dancers drew on elements of both jazz-era dancing and the rural footwork dancing to create a new style that endured until the late twentieth century.

6. Dance at Pine Mountain Settlement School

Ideals and Institutions

Pine Mountain Settlement School was an important promoter of folk dance during its long existence as a school. Its founders supported students and community members in their enjoyment of local traditional dances, and the school eventually became known as a center for English country dance. For the leaders, dance was a way of meeting educational goals as well as developing good citizens and promoting good health. It also provided a link to the heritage, both real and imagined, of the people they served, providing a way to draw on the past to prepare students for the future. For many years, the Pine Mountain leaders used dance as an emblem in promoting the school. The dance repertoire established there continued in the repertoire of the Berea College Country Dancers and in the regional Mountain Folk Festival, both founded in the 1930s and active in

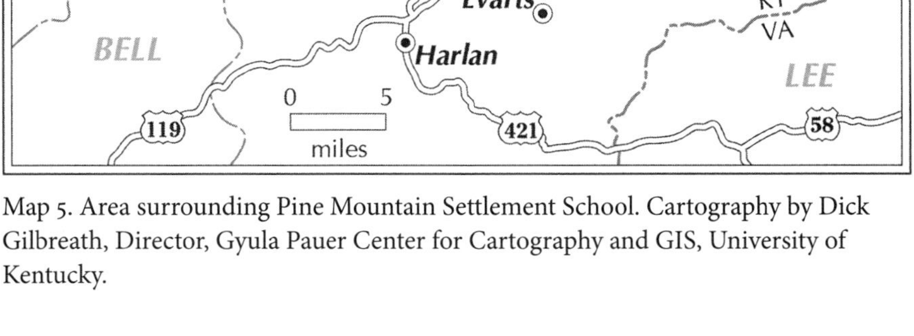

Map 5. Area surrounding Pine Mountain Settlement School. Cartography by Dick Gilbreath, Director, Gyula Pauer Center for Cartography and GIS, University of Kentucky.

the twenty-first century. The instruction offered at Pine Mountain and at other Kentucky settlement schools influenced dancing today at two important Kentucky dance venues, the Carcassonne Community Center and Hoedown Island at Natural Bridge State Resort Park, and helped to establish English country dance nationally as a living tradition.

In 1913, when Pine Mountain came into being, its founders had had considerable practice in developing such schools in Eastern Kentucky. Katherine Pettit had first visited the mountains in 1895, and during the summers of 1899, 1900, and 1901 she had established summer sessions based in ribbon-bedecked tents in various Eastern Kentucky communities. In 1902, she and May Stone founded Hindman Settlement School, the success of which led to the establishment of Pine Mountain Settlement School. Pettit's writings and those of her colleagues demonstrate an evolution in thinking about the role of dance in these endeavors. In her summer-session reports, Pettit decried the drinking and shooting that she saw accompanying dancing in the area, and in 1901 she began to offer social occasions in her own tent at which people could sing and play games instead. By 1913 her views had changed. Reports from Pine Mountain tell of boys and girls "running sets" at the school, the teachers offering occasions for dancing at which guns and alcohol were forbidden. The intervening years saw a blossoming of theory and practice in education, recreation, health, folklore, and social reform nationally and internationally and the development of institutions such

Figure 6.1. Katherine Pettit in Eastern Kentucky in 1899. Courtesy of Berea College Southern Appalachian Archives.

as the Russell Sage Foundation, the Conference of Southern Mountain Workers, and the English Folk Dance Society of America that helped to transform the thinking of the directors at Pine Mountain, resulting in their leadership in the promotion of dance in the region.

Katherine Pettit in Her Time

Katherine Pettit was born in 1868 near Lexington, Kentucky, the daughter of a prosperous farmer. She attended Sayre Female Academy for two years. Instilled at an early age with an interest in the hardships of people in Eastern Kentucky, Pettit became active in her twenties in the Women's Christian Temperance Union and in the rural library service of the State Federation of Women's Clubs. Like many middle- and upper-class women coming of age at the cusp between the Victorian and Progressive Eras, Pettit began to define a role outside the home and to consider ways to contribute to society. She focused on the well-being of children and women, as did progressive women in Europe and America. Progressive education principles were taught in women's colleges, including the importance of manual training and domestic education, in order to improve the lot of working-class people.[1] Pettit surely absorbed these principles during her time at Sayre, and many of her settlement-school colleagues were graduates of women's colleges in the East and Midwest. The importance of good hygiene and social practices was not only taught in women's colleges but explained in women's magazines readily available in Lexington, as in most towns. In addition, America was at a crossroads. As thousands of immigrants came into the country and brought their own customs, people in the United States began to wonder what a true American culture might be and to look for examples. Settlement houses in large urban areas, like Hull House, founded in Chicago in 1889 by Jane Addams, provided ways to integrate these newcomers into mainstream American society while attempting to help them maintain their own traditions in some ways. In the search for an American identity, folklorists collected American songs and stories, local color writers romanticized the Appalachian region, and, along with Berea College President William Goodell Frost, they pointed the way to the region's residents as being "true Americans" and presumably of pure Anglo-Saxon stock.[2] Efforts were made to revive Appalachian handcrafts such as weaving and quilting, which had almost died out, in an effort to keep this culture alive, and nationally the Arts and Crafts movement highlighted handmade beauty and craftsman's skill. Katherine Pettit began her work among these many influences: increasing independence of women, developing progressive education ideals, emerging social work practice, the quest for American identity, and a return to an ideal of handcrafted beauty. Her writings reflect all of these factors.

Progressive Ideals Meet Eastern Kentucky

Katherine Pettit first visited the mountains of Harlan and Perry Counties in 1895. According to Lucy Furman's obituary of Pettit, written in 1936, Pettit wanted to stay in the region and begin a "Home Industrial." Unable to do that, she returned in following summers as a member of the rural library service of the State Federation of Women's Clubs, delivering reading material and distributing packets of flower seeds to every household, signaling her parallel commitments to education and aesthetics. In 1899, 1900, and 1901 Pettit spent periods of several weeks living and teaching in each of three different areas in Eastern Kentucky.[3]

Dance is not mentioned in Pettit's reports from the 1899 Summer Program at Camp Cedar Grove or the 1900 Summer Program at Camp Industrial near Hindman, but her views of and goals for her work were revealed with increasing clarity, and the elements surrounding the later inclusion of dance at Pine Mountain Settlement School can be seen to be taking shape in an emphasis on beauty, order, propriety, good health, social activity, and ancestry. The Kindergarten movement influenced her colleagues in teaching singing games, telling stories, and making pinwheels with children in the homes they visited, and hygiene education was evident in her frequent references to dirty and airless cabins and dirty hands.[4] At the same time, traditional middle- and upper-class customs predominated in the way the workers decorated their tents by spreading rugs on the wooden floors, and hanging pictures, and placing potted ferns in the interior. In her report, Pettit expressed satisfaction when some local people emulated them, and she decried the lack of decoration in most people's homes. Her search for America's heritage included collecting what she called "old English ballads" and encouraging women to once again take up the dying arts of spinning, weaving, and basketry. However, a funeral at which traditional hymns were lined out appeared to her to include "much shouting with something almost like a savage religious dance," apparently not within the realm of the supposed English ancestry or of her middle-class cultural expectations. Early in her Eastern Kentucky career, she began making choices as to which traditions to encourage and which to ignore. Because of her participation in the WCTU, she frequently asked men and boys to sign the Temperance Pledge not to drink or to smoke, and she and her colleagues taught children temperance songs to sing at public events. Only later did her writings begin to make the connection between drinking and dancing, and to decry dancing as a result. At the end of her 1900 report, Pettit declared her belief that the settlement plan is the "best way of reaching and helping these people" and proclaimed her hopes for a "permanent Social Settlement and Industrial School." She stated as her goals to live in a model home, to set an example of "cleanliness, neatness, order," and pure language, to provide literary and industrial study, and to lead pure Christian lives "if we wish to elevate and uplift them."[5] Later, when she welcomed dance into the Pine Mountain world, it was within this framework of belief.

Music and dance were of greater interest when Pettit returned to Eastern Kentucky with May Stone and others in the summer of 1901 for a ten-week camp at Sassafras. Their view of the former was positive, and of the latter, negative. The singing and music they offered were so popular among the people in the area, especially with the organ at the camp, that they began holding regular singing classes and teaching songs to the children, who, they claimed, "really know no songs." One questions the truth of this observation because of mentions of ballad singing. For example, when area residents went to the camp for a candy pulling, "they sang old ballads in their own peculiar way."[6] Perhaps these ballads did not fit the workers' expectations of "songs." Still, Pettit began collecting the ballads and published them in the *Journal of American Folklore* in 1907. Dancing, on the other hand, was always mentioned in the context of drinking and fighting, horrifying to these workers invested in the ideals of the temperance movement. For example, Pettit and Stone wrote that "every Saturday night all the 'bad uns' around here 'hev a gathering' where they pick the banjo, dance, drink moonshine, swear and fight. They stay all night and go home Sunday morning drunk and shooting down the road."[7] On two different occasions, the teachers told about young people spending Sunday "picking the banjo, dancing, singing, drinking, quarreling, and shooting" in the school house, beginning as early as 7 A.M.. On one of these occasions, Pettit, scheduled to teach Sunday school that afternoon, went ahead with the lesson and found these same young people very attentive. Pettit and Stone learned that here, even Christmas ("new" Christmas on December 25) was not a time for the religious ceremony and family celebration to which they were accustomed; instead, young people had "frolics," with "no giving of presents or any religious celebration, but drinking of moonshine, fighting, and a general carousing," which likely included dancing.

The population around Sassafras, at the juncture of Perry, Leslie, and Knott Counties, was more dense than in the previous two places they had set up camp, so this may have resulted in more "frolics" and carousing than Pettit had seen previously. Midway during the summer of 1901, Stone, Pettit, and their colleagues began "wondering what we can do to show them how the young people can meet in a social way and have a good time without doing the dreadful things they do," echoing similar questions at Hull House and other urban settlements. As a result, they held a social at the camp, playing games and singing until 9 P.M., and reported that the young people enjoyed it.[8] These socials became a standard offering of the camp and of its successor schools at Hindman and Pine Mountain. Rather than simply teaching about the evils of alcohol, they offered what they saw as a positive social alternative, but, prior to Pine Mountain, it did not include dancing.

As they left Sassafras in the fall of 1901, Stone and Pettit reflected on their experiences. Preparing to establish Hindman Settlement School under the auspices of the WCTU the following year, they simultaneously stated their goal for intervention and their belief in the potential of the mountain people for revitalizing American culture: "We look back on the sad and lonely lives of those with whom and for whom we have lived the past three months and feel that the most important question for us is how to bring the strong, wealthy and learned Kentuckians into healthful touch with the poorest, most ignorant and humblest mountaineer and at the same time make the one appreciate the vitalizing, strengthening influence of the other. . . . How can we make the people of the Blue Grass feel and see the need of the people in the lowliest cabin on the mountain sides?"[9] By the early years of Pine Mountain, dance became one way to make this connection.

Pine Mountain Settlement School Ideals

During the decade between the conclusion of the Sassafras Camp and the establishment of Pine Mountain Settlement School, theory and practice in education, recreation, and dance had burgeoned nationally, along with an interest in preservation of American heritage, an effort to develop the working class as productive citizens, and other social reform movements. The founders of Pine Mountain, well-read and well-connected women as they were, undoubtedly kept abreast of these developments. Their board of directors, almost all from large urban centers, would have made sure they used the best in contemporary practice. New teachers, well-traveled graduates of women's colleges, certainly brought these ideas with them. When Katherine Pettit and Ethel deLong established Pine Mountain Settlement School in 1913 on land donated by "Uncle" William Creech, it embodied these ideals and practices. Recreation was believed to promote good health, to provide appropriate social interaction, to prepare the mind for education, and to undergird a civic society through the experience of teamwork. Folk dance was perceived to be especially useful in accomplishing these goals.

Pine Mountain's core values were stated from its earliest days. During its initial semester, the staff produced the first of many calendars illustrating its goals and accomplishments. The settlement school took its stand as mediator between tradition and modernization, grounded in progressive ideals, including the importance of recreation. Some months' pages featured illustrations that focused on the old ways and the true American ancestry of the people, while some illustrated a commitment to progressive goals. The narrative for January described William Creech's hope that the school would "arouse interest in the arts of farm and home" to counteract the effects of logging and mining, which

Figure 6.2. "Playing together is a way to learn working together." Pine Mountain calendar image, 1940s. Courtesy of Berea College Southern Appalachian Archives.

he believed undermined the traditional way of life in his home area of Harlan County. The September page bemoaned the loss of "the old arts of hackling, carding, spinning, dyeing and weaving." Another page outlined the goals of the board of trustees. Recreation was explicitly included in these goals. Along with providing health and sanitation and practical training in farming, cooking, and woodworking: "They wish the school . . . to help solve the problem of recreation by clubs, outdoor games and wholesome social diversions." Recreation was even highlighted by a page devoted only to a photo of the school playground, one of the first structures built at the fledgling institution.[10]

Correspondence and reports clarified these goals and values, and dance and recreation were often part of the narrative. Dance, formerly mentioned only in the context of drinking and violence, now was frequently mentioned in letters and reports as an innocent entertainment. A January 1914 fundraising/report letter was the first of many instances in which Pine Mountain staff spoke happily about dancing. After a long description of the introduction at the school of Christmas customs such as decorating a tree and giving gifts, the writer stated that "the young people spent the afternoon in their favorite way, running sets whose very names suggest hilarity and merriment," listing figures called Crillie Crankie, Wild Goose Chase, and Box the Gnats. The following year a letter from Clara M. Davis, a Pine Mountain teacher, about a visit to a home some miles away, reported in an almost jocular fashion: "After supper there was banjo-pickin and beatin' by the Turner boys, 'hoe downs' [what today we would call "clogging"] by Jim Huff, Sam John, and even Mr. Lloyd himself. His performance was cut short by the rattling of the vases falling from the organ and the ominous creaking of the floor joists."[11] Almost every letter or report for the next three years included at least some brief mention of young people "running sets" along with references to other recreation, such as baseball, games, or playground activities. Dancing was beginning to represent local culture and enjoyable recreation to the Pine Mountain leaders, and hence to their supporters.

Recreation and Dance for Good Health and Good Citizenship

During the last decade of the nineteenth century and the first two decades of the twentieth century, development of recreation and dance opportunities was an important endeavor for those interested in education and social uplift. Beginning in 1861, a physical culture movement took root internationally, with various exercise systems establishing their own normal schools, or teacher education programs. In the 1890s, a national recreation movement emerged in conjunction with the development of parks to provide grassy areas where urban children could play. Educators came to believe that children needed structured play to counteract the unruliness that occurred when children played freely. Clearly the workers were aware of these developments, because at a teachers' institute in Sassafras Miss McNab taught games and gave a talk on the "importance of playing with and directing the play of their pupils" and a "talk on the psychological value of play and the dangers of neglecting children at playtime." Pettit and Stone lamented the fact that children "have no playthings and know no games" of the sort they hoped to see.[12]

Whereas upper-class recreation had involved individual sports such as hunting and riding, taking advantage of their land holdings, team sports were newly encouraged as opportunities for middle- and working-class people.[13] Baseball was increasing in popularity, and in 1891 basketball was invented. Between 1885 and 1906, as many professions established organizations and institutions, several associations were formed to promote exercise and organized play, including the American Physical Education Association (1885), the Public Schools Athletic League of New York City (1903), and the Playground Association of America (1906). Physical educator Luther Halsey Gulick, Jane Addams, and other settlement workers were leaders in the Playground Association of America, and Hull House, Henry Street Settlement, and other such houses included gymnasia and offered a variety of physical activities. Education reformers banded with social reformers in the belief that recreation was crucial to developing healthy, moral individuals. Progressive education leader John Dewey had early "insisted on the beauty, the necessity, and even the utility of the play impulse." Jane Addams, founder of Chicago's Hull House, believed that "recreation is stronger than vice, and recreation alone can stifle the lust for vice." Even President Theodore Roosevelt was a passionate supporter of recreation, speaking and writing about the fundamental need for play, and accepting the honorary presidency of the Playground Association of America.[14] These efforts reached a crescendo between 1900 and 1910, while Katherine Pettit and her colleagues were clarifying their goals in settlement-school work.

Dance was part of the progressive education and recreation movements and a way of helping to achieve the goals of education and social reform. Calisthenics and social and aesthetic dance emerged during the late nineteenth century as forms of exercise and social training for middle- and upper-class women. As early as the 1860s, musical gymnastics was taught in girls' schools. By the 1880s, normal schools in exercise for women had been established, and by the turn of the century, women's colleges, many of them teacher-education institutions, routinely included training in the teaching of exercise and recreation and sometimes dance.[15] In 1894 Melvin Ballou Gilbert introduced into the gymnasium the "art of dancing." His 1903 booklet on athletics for women included an article on dance, in which he stated, "Dancing ought to form a part of the physical education of children, not only for their better health but also to counteract undesirable tendencies. Dancing is not only necessary, but almost indispensable, to those who are fond of society. The manner of presenting one's-self and of receiving others, with a graceful propriety and an easy and polite demeanor, is acquired most effectually by those who have learned to dance."[16] The Pine Mountain leaders came to believe that dance was especially suited to developing social interaction, as Gilbert had said. Dance was a regular part of teacher preparation by 1910, and professional teachers returned to Columbia University, Harvard, New York University, and the University of Chicago for summer sessions to learn new methods.[17] Ethel deLong, the co-founder of Pine Mountain Settlement School, had graduated in 1901 from Smith College, so she undoubtedly brought with her this training. Reports do not indicate that she actively used it in the teaching of the Pine Mountain children, though it may have contributed to her openness to the set running enjoyed by the youth of the area. Perhaps, because of exposure to the new folk dance movement that had begun growing in the early twentieth century, deLong and her colleagues recognized set running as a local folk dance, to be encouraged.

By the 1910s, folk dance had joined aesthetic dance and gymnastics in the curricula of settlement houses and children's after school programs. Its inclusion was believed to forge a link with immigrants' former homes and customs, to help them to become healthier, more productive workers, and to develop in them an understanding of citizenship in a democracy. Two energetic women led the early folk dance movement. Elizabeth Burchenal, a physical education teacher in New

York City, and Mary Hinman, an independent dance teacher working with Hull House in Chicago, each traveled individually to various European countries to learn folk dances. Burchenal began making her trips in 1904, and Hinman first visited Europe in 1909. Both learned dances from England, Denmark, Sweden, Russia, Italy, and Spain. Sometime between 1904 and 1908, Burchenal saw the morris dancing that Cecil Sharp was just beginning to document in England, and she continued her trips to Europe for several years thereafter, studying at Sharp's summer dance school at Stratford-upon-Avon and producing a number of folk dance manuals which were widely circulated. She began in 1905 to teach folk dance for girls through the Girls' Branch of the Public School Athletic League in New York City, and later at Columbia University. Her 1909 manual *Folk-Dances and Singing Games* included dance directions, music, and illustrations of dances from twenty-six countries, including England, Denmark, and the United States. Hinman's dance curriculum at Hull House between 1898 and 1907, and later at the University of Chicago, included, among other elements, folk dances, clogging reels, and English country dances. Burchenal soon became director of the Folk Dance Committee of the Playground Association of America; Mary Hinman was also a member of the committee. Their work reached an ever-broadening audience through their teacher workshops and published dance manuals. In 1910 Burchenal published an article called "Dance around the Maypole" in *Women's Home Companion* magazine.[18] Not only would settlement workers have been aware of such articles, involved as they were in distributing periodicals and other reading material to area residents, but their close connections with progressive education would have insured their cognizance of this trend. Their summer study may even have included courses on folk dance, because in 1914 their first May Day celebration included a Maypole dance.

Urban settlement houses provided opportunities for immigrants to enjoy the dances and other customs similar to those they had brought with them from their homelands, and they also taught other kinds of dance. In this manner, the staff hoped to smooth the newcomers' transition to mainstream modern American culture.[19] The Pine Mountain leaders' goals for dance were similar. They saw dance as a way to maintain local culture while providing a means to help with adaptation to modernization. Set running was welcome as a local custom, and by providing controlled settings, it was used to teach manners and to allow appropriate socializing. Later, English folk dance was used to connect with a theoretical ethnic heritage and to offset and mediate with contemporary dance and music trends.

Luther Gulick, a founder of major recreation associations, wrote extensively about the benefits of dancing. In his 1910 book, *The Healthful Art of Dancing*, he pointed out the effect of folk dance on circulation and respiration and identified it with the "spontaneous and instinctive play" described as so important by

G. Stanley Hall. Gulick argued folk dance's special suitability for urban children because it demanded the movement of large muscle groups and the substantial cardiovascular investment necessary for physical maturation and good health, to keep young people strong for factory labor. This was in contrast to the less-strenuous demands of aesthetic dancing enjoyed by middle- and upper-class women.[20] The same theory made sense in relation to the children of Eastern Kentucky, with regard to the hard farm work they were required to do. Reformers like John Ruskin and Jane Addams saw factory work as demoralizing, just as Pettit saw the long, strenuous hours of farm work as breaking people's spirits. Folk dance offered recuperation from both kinds of heavy labor while helping to provide the type of exercise that developed stronger hearts and stronger muscles to give workers more stamina to be better able to do the required work. Pine Mountain workers subscribed to these theories about the healthful effects of dance. A letter to a benefactor described a community Christmas party: "Of course we had to run sets again [after dinner] for you know one of the most important health rules is to exercise thoroughly after eating."[21]

Additionally, dance offered emotional and societal benefits. Gilbert believed, "We should feel it our duty—to make the most of ourselves physically as well as morally and mentally . . . dancing may be said to be to the body what reading is to the mind." He said also that "the girl who dances [socially] and who loves to dance is the girl . . . whose heart is as light as her feet."[22] Folk dancing was believed to be particularly valuable. Psychologist G. Stanley Hall, in his book *Adolesence*, proclaimed that folk dancing was "one of the best expressions of pure play," having no goal beyond the doing of it.[23] It could also contribute to the development of citizens for a democracy. Joseph Lee, who is sometimes called "The Father of the Playground Movement," referred to "Play as a School of the Citizen" in a 1907 article. In team sports he saw the "dedication of the free, self-directed individual to a common purpose" and "an identification of one's own interests and purposes with the interests and possible purpose of the whole." He believed that organized games like football were "the sheer experience of citizenship in its simplest and essential form—of the sharing in a public consciousness, of having the social organization present as a controlling ideal in your heart."[24] Pine Mountain workers shared these beliefs. Not only was a playground one of the early features of Pine Mountain, but writings also made reference to introducing and encouraging team sports like baseball at the school and its branches. A 1915 report described how a visiting theological student organized the playground in order to "teach the boys manliness in sport—how to play fair."[25] Luther Gulick applied these ideas to dance, saying that "freedom lies in the recognition and joyful acceptance of relationships."[26] The dance emphasized at Pine Mountain supported these same goals, involving groups of students working together, contributing as individuals to the success of the whole group. Organized play, including folk dance, was seen as an important route to physical and social health, and physical health was believed to be closely linked with moral health and civic responsibility.

Dance Hall Reform

In the theory of the time, only certain kinds of dance were beneficial. As science and philosophy came to support dance as a legitimate activity, the dance hall reform movement was underway, beginning in about 1910. The timing of the national movement perhaps contributed to the growing openness of the Pine Mountain directors to dancing. With increasing industrialization, courting and socializing had begun to move out of the home and into public dance halls in both urban and rural areas. Popular dances of the time included "animal dances" of African American origin, in which dancers mimicked the movements of animals in dances like the "Buzzard Lope," "Fish Tail," "Eagle Rock," and other dances like the "Fanny Bump" and the "Shimmy."[27] Some immigrant dances also appeared wild to settlement workers accustomed to nineteenth-century ballroom dances in the context of the well-chaperoned ball, just as hoedowning (clogging) and set running must have seemed wild to Pine Mountain workers.[28] Elements of classism and racism may be imagined in the philosophical opposition to contemporary dances, as well as some romanticizing about bygone days. Experts believed that a controlled dance environment and the proper kinds of dances could offset the effects of this untamed dancing. As G. Stanley Hall believed, "Right dancing can cadence the very soul, give nervous poise and control, bring harmony between . . . body and mind. It can . . . pre-dispose the heart against vice, and turn the springs of character toward virtue. That its present decadent forms . . . can be demoralizing, we know in this day too well."[29] Joseph Lee echoed this belief, expressing the perils of the new dances. "There is a danger in the use of rhythm . . . because it so easily lends itself to . . . the mob spirit. . . . [T]he corrective . . . seems to be in the selection of music, of dances . . . that require a firm hold on reality, either in the form of external objects and conditions or through a nice sense of proportion and of the more subtle demands of art."[30] Folk dancing was a form of "right dancing" that provided the "external objects and conditions" by requiring dancers to move in accord with the phrasing of the music, to execute a set series of movements, and to move in prescribed spatial patterns in relation to the other dancers. Later, the style taught along with English folk dancing required "subtle demands of art," and its lilting phrases might "cadence the soul" and lead to poise and control.

Though disapproving of the behavior at public dance venues, Jane Addams believed that "prohibiting dance halls would do more harm than good" and that young people needed "a rationalized program of regulated and municipalized recreation resources."[31] She differentiated between "the public dance halls filled with frivolous and irresponsible young people in a feverish search for pleasure" and "the old dances on the village green in which all of the older people participated." Settlement workers led the fight for dance hall reform beginning in 1910. Opposed to drinking, inappropriate dancing, and loose behavior, they offered an alternative at settlement houses, "model dance halls" which enforced "standards of etiquette, chaperonage, atmosphere, and dance styles," which hoped to replicate the conditions of the imagined village green. In such a setting, Mary Hinman said, "They lose their desire to go elsewhere for this necessary social intercourse."[32] Although the settlement workers in the Eastern Kentucky mountains were horrified by the drinking and violence that so often seemed to accompany local dancing and music making, they came to see an alternative approach to the problem. In addition to offering singing and parlor games as they had during their summer sessions, Pettit and deLong discovered that they could create a controlled dance environment at Pine Mountain, demanding that no alcohol or firearms be present on the premises, and requiring appropriate social behavior. In a report in late 1914 titled "Christmas at Pine Mountain," deLong said that because drinking was banned, the time "when girls from away yon side of the mountain run sets with sweethearts from miles away in the opposite direction, was charming revelry."[33] The rowdy neighborhood frolics must have continued, however, because even in a 1926 article, Pine Mountain staff member Evelyn Wells still needed to defend dance, saying that it was not the cause of the disorder, but that the environment in which it took place must be controlled, and appropriate dancing must be offered. Morris and sword and English country dances were among dances she deemed acceptable.[34]

Philanthropy, Recreation, and Appalachia

Events between 1910 and 1920 brought recreation theory and practice directly to settlement workers' doorsteps by way of the Conference of Southern Mountain Workers (CSMW), founded in 1912 with John C. Campbell as director. Campbell, having served as an educator and college president in Alabama, Tennessee, and Georgia, undertook the task of surveying the people of the Appalachian region under the auspices of the Russell Sage Foundation in 1908. As a result of his work he was appointed secretary of the Southern Highland Division of the foundation, and he established CSMW, with membership made up of workers at settlement schools, colleges, and missions in the central Appalachian region.[35] Katherine Pettit was one of the earliest members of the conference, and in letters to Berea College president William Goodell Frost, she reported attending meetings. For example, in 1913, Pettit went to Atlanta for the "Mountain Conference" and the Southern Sociological Conference, and the following year she attended the conference of Kentucky mountain workers at Highland College in Breathitt County.[36] The Russell Sage Foundation supported the Conference of the Southern Mountain Workers from its founding until 1949, and it surely influenced practices at the settlement schools.

The foundation had been established in 1907 with the specific goal of affecting public policy with regard to recreation. Among its founders were Jane Addams and Luther Gulick. The Laura Spelman Rockefeller Memorial Foundation and the Sage Foundation were leaders in the effort to secure government support for recreation. Their work was "dominated by discussions of morality," because they believed that "organized recreation was crucial to the public's moral as well as its physical health. Fit Americans best exemplified civic virtue."[37] As a financial supporter of the CSMW, the Russell Sage Foundation promoted its agenda through the settlement network. As they discussed the problems they encountered in the region and looked for solutions, settlement workers at regional and statewide meetings of CSMW learned the importance of recreation in achieving their goals. It was deemed so important, in fact, that it was used as an argument by Katherine Pettit for developing a road over the mountain to the vicinity of the school. In a letter to the assistant director general of the National Highways Association, she asserted that for the eight hundred children in a seven-mile radius in their area, among other issues, "the recreational problem is, of course, very serious." "Our plan is to develop a school . . . which shall be a social center as well as an educational institution."[38] The Russell Sage Foundation, through the CSMW, undoubtedly contributed to her belief in the crucial importance of recreation in educating her students, in insuring their good health, and in preparing them to be good citizens.

As the Pine Mountain workers developed the school from 1913 on, they welcomed local set running as part of the recreation they believed to be a primary means of achieving their goals. A letter from a visitor in 1914 described how connected the school was to the community, whose farmers came to sell their vegetables and "boys and girls gather of an evening to 'run sets.'"[39] Hosting social events at which area residents could enjoy set running in an orderly and sober environment was one way to address "the recreational problem" and at the same time teach appropriately regulated interaction.

Set Running and English Country Dance

The encouragement of set running as recreation was soon to have an unexpected effect on Pine Mountain Settlement School's image in the minds of its leaders. Set running was used in reports during the first years of the school as a symbol of local culture and wholesome recreation. It seized the attention of English folk dance and music collector Cecil Sharp during his 1917 visit. His

Figure 6.3. Far House, Pine Mountain Settlement School, where students demonstrated set running for Cecil Sharp. Courtesy of Berea College Southern Appalachian Archives.

interpretation of the local tradition and his introduction of English country dance at Pine Mountain inspired the teachers to further highlight dance, and to add another rationale for its inclusion in the school's program. They now had a kind of dance that they believed connected their students to their true ancestral roots in England, and could "restore a broader tradition that was rightfully theirs by ancestry."[40]

Sharp had begun collecting English folk music and dance in the early twentieth century, and he had come to the United States in 1914 to teach English country dancing, with the dream of establishing a branch of the English Folk Dance Society here. He was aided in his efforts by Elizabeth Burchenal, who began promoting his visit to her influential colleagues in 1910. A Russell Sage Foundation official saw to it that Sharp received a copy of Appalachian ballads collected by Olive Dame Campbell, wife and colleague of John C. Campbell. Sharp invited Mrs. Campbell to visit him in New York, and as a result of that meeting, the Campbells arranged his Appalachian tour for 1916–1917. The Russell Sage Foundation provided a small travel stipend, and a wealthy benefactor supported the remainder of the expenses. He associated the speech patterns and the songs he collected in the mountains with England and soon declared Appalachian people to be "just English peasant folk." He eventually determined that, since they did not have the self-consciousness of British folksingers, "they are just exactly what the English peasant was one hundred or more years ago," espousing the "contemporary ancestors" concept set forth by President Frost of Berea College and repeated by the Pine Mountain leaders.[41]

Toward the end of his trip, Sharp spent a week at Pine Mountain Settlement School. According to May Ritchie Deschamps, a student at the time, "One evening Miss deLong invited our best set running people to come to Far House to run sets for Mr. Sharp."[42] Sharp subsequently observed set running also at Hindman and Hyden Settlement Schools. At the time, he likely expressed an interpretation similar to the one he published a year later: "We realized at once that we had stumbled upon a most interesting form of the English Country-dance, which, so far as we know, had not been hitherto recorded, and a dance, moreover, of great aesthetic value." He also included his opinions about the ancestry of the dance. He decided that it was a survival of something that had existed before 1651. Because of "the forceful, emotional character of the dance," the speed, and the "unconventional way in which the dancers comport themselves . . . we are led to infer that the Running Set represents a stage in the development of the Country-dance earlier than that of the dances in *The English Dancing Master*."[43]

The Pine Mountain teachers were delighted with this interpretation and immediately adopted it. In a 1919 edition of "Notes from the Pine Mountain Settlement School" the authors described their joy in being home to an ancient dance. They said that, besides having been taught ballads by the children, "we have learned the gayest and liveliest old dance from various parts of the mountains. The pedigree of our ancient, beautiful songs we know, but of the origin of our dances we were not sure. We believed them to be old, but that they were older than any country dances collected in out-of-the-way hamlets in Mother England we did not dream, until Mr. Cecil Sharp visited us and by chance saw our young people dancing."[44] In fact, the set running he observed may have been influenced by relatively recently introduced dances. In his interviews with Letcher County dancers in 1975, Peter Rogers learned from consultants born in the 1880s that square dancing in a four couple set was first introduced in the area in the 1890s. Further, a typed transcription of an 1885 Louisville Commercial newspaper article appears among Katherine Pettit's papers. It includes a description of a cotillion danced in the street at a celebration for the founding of Knott County. It seems, then, that contemporary social dances were known and enjoyed in Eastern Kentucky, and it is known that local dance traditions were influenced by them.[45]

In 1918, Cecil Sharp published *The Country Dance Book—Part V*, with extensive description of "The Running Set," as he dubbed it, thus installing this local dance as an icon of American folk dance. He based his estimation of its antiquity on stylistic characteristics: "The fact for instance, that the movements of courtesy, which occur in almost every one of the Playford dances, are conspicuously absent from the Running Set is of itself the strongest testimony in favour for the priority of the latter." In the following pages, he glossed over nineteenth-century movement vocabulary he observed in set running, including the promenade and do-si-do, saying they did not alter his determination of the antiquity of the dance.[46] He hypothesized that courtesy movements such as honoring your partner, siding, setting, and arming were undoubtedly added when the dances of the common people were brought into the drawing room in the seventeenth century. In these movements, partners face one another and relate only to each other, instead of couples relating to other couples or to the whole group. He also identified three figures known only in children's games in England, and he asserted that all came from ancient pagan ceremonials. His assumptions were based on a volume titled *Traditional Games of England*, by Alice B. Gomme. Sharp associated the California Show Basket figure with ancient well-worship ceremonies, Wind Up the Ball Yarn with dancing around a sacred tree, and the Wild Goose Chase with magical serpentine dances. Of course, any actual occurrence or significance of these movement sequences from preliterate times can never really be proved or disproved, but Sharp's beliefs were formed in the context of European folklore theory, in which customs existing in the present were assumed to be survivals from ancient times. American folklorists took a different view. They attempted to discover unique American expression rather than to identify "holdovers from the pre-modern past."[47] However, Sharp's declaration reinforced the beliefs of the Pine Mountain leaders who had already adopted terms like "our contemporary ancestors," and it helped lay the groundwork for English country dance at Pine Mountain. His own descriptions hinted at a different truth, however.

> It [set running] was danced one evening after dark, on the porch of one of the largest houses of the Pine Mountain School, with only one dim lantern to light up the scene. But the moon streamed fitfully in, lighting up the mountain peaks in the background and, casting its mysterious light over the proceedings, seemed to exaggerate the wildness and the breakneck speed of the dancers as they whirled through the mazes of the dance. There was no music, only the stampings and clapping of the onlookers, but when one of the emotional crises of the dance was reached—and this happened several times during the performance—the air seemed literally to pulsate with the rhythm of the "patters" and the tramp of the dancers' feet, while, over and above it all, penetrating through the din, floated the even, falsetto tones of the Caller, calmly and unexcitedly reciting his directions.[48]

Some of Sharp's own observations demonstrate the influence of cultural groups other than Anglo Saxon in the dancing he saw at Pine Mountain, Hyden, and Hindman. People of many cultures inhabited the area. Indigenous people had, of course, lived in the region for centuries; European descendants arrived in the late eighteenth century, and African descendants had likely arrived about the same time. As elsewhere in the coalfields, central European immigrants and African American southerners had begun arriving for work in the timber, railroad, and mining industries around the turn of the twentieth century. All groups shared their customs.

While it is not possible to attribute any characteristic of the music or dance to a particular cultural group, the descriptions Sharp recorded point to the likelihood that the dances are of mixed cultural heritage rather than purely English. In Sharp's description of "the Running Set," some characteristics seem distinctly African American: for example, dancing to the sounds of the "patters" or clappers, the "cool" voice of the caller floating above the intense, multilayered rhythms, and the manner of calling, with "certain prescribed verbal phrases, a mixture of prose and doggerel rhyme that in the course of time has become stereotyped."[49] Sharp was looking for ancient English dance. The experience of observing an unusual dance in the dark at the foot of a seemingly isolated mountain must have been a powerful, moving experience, and one that would arouse a strong response. In his book, Sharp sets a scene he calls "mysterious," taking place after dark, with only a single lantern, and shadows cast by the moon on the mountain peaks. The dancers seemed "wild" or untamed, dancing as they did in this apparently primeval setting. This dancing, with its frequent "emotional crises," did not have the reserve he was accustomed to seeing. The air pulsated; the experience was exotic, sensual, and archaic. He felt he was seeing something deeply connected to ancient ritual. But, not just any survival, this dance was, for Sharp, his own heritage come to life—English dancing in a very old form. And so he felt he must preserve it and also include it in his efforts to reinvigorate Anglo Saxon heritage both in America and in England. So, too, Pettit and deLong hoped that "the mountains (would) make a significant contribution to America as the carrier of traditional Anglo-Saxon values."[50] They came to believe that their local dance embodied this heritage.

Sharp seemed thrilled with the abandon of the dancing, celebrating the naturalness of the local dancers and describing the practice and skill required to keep the dance going at "break-neck speed" and yet "smoothly, quietly, almost nonchalantly." However, he expressed a preference for practiced dancers, and preferred notating dances performed by the select handpicked group at Hyden. He based his description of style on the Pine Mountain dancers because "the dance was executed more perfectly and with greater finish than elsewhere."[51] His aesthetics may have corresponded to those of the Pine Mountain teachers, reinforcing their emphasis on "right dancing," and certainly influenced them in the years to come. Though he wrote enthusiastically about the naturalness of the dancing he found in Kentucky, Sharp promptly set about teaching drawing-room manners. He taught English country dances to the students and staff during his stay at Pine Mountain, as he had been doing elsewhere since his 1914 arrival in the United States. He was very interested in promoting a specific style of dance, and his 1909 book on English country dance contained eight pages of detailed description of that style. For example, he directed that "the step should fall on the ball of the foot, not on the toe, with the heel off, but close to, the ground" with the feet parallel, legs close together, and the movement should be "made by spring and not by stride." When hands are joined in a promenade hold linking right to right and left to left, they are "brought lightly together, not clenched, the four fingers of each hand resting on the palm of the other, and the thumb pressing on the knuckle of the middle finger."[52] These stylistic requirements imbued English country dance as he taught it at Pine Mountain and across the country. Similarly, he judged English tunes to be of higher quality than Appalachian ones, which he characterized as being of "melodic poverty," and included English dance tunes that he felt better suited the dance. He seemed not to realize that in set running, rhythm was more important than musical phrasing, perhaps partly as a result of African American and Native American influence on the music and dance. Though he noted that the music controlled the steps and not the figures of the dance "which may begin, or end, at any part of a musical phrase," he was definite in his preference for congruence between the phrases of the music and the dance.[53]

Figure 6.4. English country dance Gathering Peascods, from booklet *Pine Mountain Settlement School*, September 1920. Courtesy of Berea College Southern Appalachian Archives.

The English country dances Sharp taught at Pine Mountain were Gathering Peascods, Black Nag, and Rufty Tufty, the ones he usually chose for novices. All are dances dating from the late seventeenth century, published by John Playford, and reconstructed by Sharp in 1911. Each has certain similarities to the set running Sharp had observed, making them readily accessible to the Kentucky students. All are dances for male-female couples requiring teamwork and participation of the entire group to make the dance work. Rufty Tufty is a dance for two couples facing each other, as in set running, except in Rufty Tufty the sets of two couples are not part of a larger circle. Gathering Peascods is, like set running, a circle for any number of couples. Along with Black Nag, a three-couple longways dance, all are lively, energetic dances that Sharp probably imagined would be readily accepted by people accustomed to dancing at "break-neck speed." When Sharp later arranged for the recording of music for these dances, he set the tempo between 124 and 136 beats per minute, a very fast tempo, requiring a running step.[54]

Unlike set running, all of these dances are composed of phrases that match the phrases of the music, repeated in AB or ABC patterns. Set running, according to Sharp, had an introduction, followed by as many as fourteen figures and a conclusion. Each couple danced each of the figures three times, once with each of the other couples in the circle. The order of the figures was determined on the spot by the caller. For the dancer, the pleasure of English country dance is in moving repeatedly through established patterns, carried along by the lilt of the music. The pleasure of set running is in the surprise of not knowing what will come next, responding quickly to the new directions from the caller, and keeping the whole group moving seamlessly. The caller chooses when to change to a new figure based upon the readiness of the dancers, not upon the demands of the music, which provides a driving rhythm to propel the dancers. All three English dances emphasize some of the courtesy movements Sharp found missing from set running. Perhaps Pine Mountain leaders saw the courtesy movements, the reliance on the musical phrase, and the specific genteel style as ways to contribute to an orderly, controlled dance environment and to prepare their students for presenting themselves in mainstream society.

They definitely saw English country dance as a natural extension of the local dance tradition and a connection with a deeper past. Perhaps they believed, as Jane Addams did when she attempted to establish links with immigrants' traditions, that "by connecting [the immigrant] with what has gone before, [we] free him from a sense of isolation and hardship."[55] The May 1919 issue of *Notes from Pine Mountain* defended the children's performance of these new dances at their May Day celebration: "In the country where set running and such singing games as 'Skip-to-My-Lou' are the only forms of dance, there is nothing artificial about the introduction of other singing games and English country dances." Maud Karpeles, who had accompanied Sharp on his collecting trips in the mountains, similarly asserted that the English "songs and dances are not foreign importations, but a vital part of the traditional culture of America."[56] Sharp had introduced a brand new movement vocabulary with some similarities to the existing one and had helped to set Pine Mountain on a course that would influence the development of a form of recreational dance in the United States.

Cecil Sharp, it should be recalled, was not the first person to teach English dances in the United States. Both Elizabeth Burchenal and Mary Hinman had studied with Sharp in England and returned to teach English country, morris, and sword dance. Burchenal included some of what she learned in the instruction books she published, which were used in teacher-training programs in women's colleges. Summer sessions in folk dance, including English, were offered for professional teachers at many colleges. Evelyn Kendrick Wells, the Pine Mountain secretary since 1915, had been introduced to English country dance at Wellesley.[57] However, there is no record that the Pine Mountain workers introduced English dancing prior to Sharp's visit, though they believed their constituents to be of English ancestry, and they believed in restoring their traditions. The particular confluence of personalities and goals seems to have brought English dancing to the school, or perhaps the leaders needed Sharp's imprimatur to pursue this avenue. Still, the term "country dances," rather than a reference to people "running sets," appeared first in a 1914 letter from deLong. In this document, apparently a funding request, among the accomplishments listed are a hookworm clinic, a farmers' institute, summer Bible school, the first Pine Mountain Christmas, and events at the school, including "neighborhood good times . . . box suppers, bean stringings, squirrel roasts, country dances, log rollings, wool pickings, quiltings, [and] stir offs."[58] The term "country dance" had made its way into her vocabulary, seeming to indicate that the Pine Mountain teachers had exposure to the broader folk dance repertoire being taught in America at the time. Since the school's first documented direct experience with English country dancing was in 1917 with Sharp, it appears that they were applying the term to set running rather than to English country dancing.

Dance as Symbol

After Sharp's visit, Evelyn Wells became the resident dance director, continuing English dancing at Pine Mountain.[59] By 1919, she had established connections with the English Folk Dance Society of America, and surely she attended at least one of their summer sessions. Beginning in 1923, Dorothy Bolles, one of three leaders of the American Branch of the English Folk Dance Society, came to Pine Mountain Settlement School each spring for ten years to prepare the students for May Day, increasing their repertoire of country dances and teaching morris and sword dances. English dance increased in importance at Pine Mountain in the ensuing years, and it began to appear as almost emblematic of the school. Reports and letters between 1913 and 1917 frequently mentioned people running sets at events at the school. Not long after the 1918 publication of the set running description in Sharp's *Country Dance Book—Part V*, Pine Mountain Settlement School began to capitalize on their special dance and on the appearance of innocence and antiquity that English folk dance and set running promoted, as evidenced in the 1919 *Notes*, cited above. A small book titled *Pine Mountain Settlement School* published by the school in September 1920 included several photos, among which was a group of students dancing the English country dance Gathering Peascods. Only the name of the dance was given under the photo, without accompanying narrative.[60] Publications and reports during ensuing years continued to include photos of and narratives about English country dance.

Dance was used as a symbol for the simple mountain lifestyle in making a case to Pine Mountain's funders. For example, in 1929 set running, rather than English country dance, was used as a centerpiece of an ambitious fund-raising performance in New York City. Well-known actress Lucille LaVerne offered a performance of Lula Vollmer's play *Sun-Up* to benefit the school by making "most liberal terms" for the performance in her theater. The printed program included Sharp's description of seeing set running, a note about folk music collected in Eastern Kentucky, and a piece about reviving spinning and weaving. Colorful stories about students, complete with dialect, illustrated the Pine Mountain locale. In one story, a woman berated her recently married son, who held a dance to celebrate his wedding: "And have you giv' over your house to antickin', and frolickin', and tearin' down beds!" (to make room to dance). The play itself depicts killing and revenge among the cabins of 1917 Western North Carolina mountains, Vollmer's home, with the hero rejecting the old ways of violence, even against the will of his mother. This performance was apparently arranged or supported by the English Folk Dance Society of America, presumably with the aid of Evelyn Wells's connections. Copies of Sharp's book were offered for sale. Between the first and second acts of the play there was "singing of mountain ballads by Miss Evelyn K. Wells, and the dancing of the Kentucky Mountain Running Set," followed by a funding appeal by Miss LaVerne.[61] The program notes that "the set-runners have gathered for this performance at the invitation of Mr. Milton Smith," chair of the drama department at Columbia University and a leading instructor for the English Folk Dance Society of America. New York City was, along with Boston, an important center for the EFDS of America, so the dancers were undoubtedly members of that group.[62] One may question the choice of performers, but Appalachian dance and song were used as symbols for Pine Mountain, as a way to insure its future through funding.

Figure 6.5. May Day at Pine Mountain, 1920s. Courtesy of Berea College Southern Appalachian Archives.

Sharp's visit focused the Pine Mountain leaders' approach to festivals as well. Nationally, a trend for community festivals had begun in 1904 or 1905 at Henry Street Settlement in New York City, and the practice was supported in writings by Hall and Gulick. Across the country, pageants or festivals were mounted to celebrate holidays such as Thanksgiving, Christmas, and May Day, with the goal of replacing naturally occurring community festivals that had died out. Percival Chubb, a promoter of such festivals, believed that they would "arouse a natural piety in children." At his Normal Course in Festival Methods, which began in 1907, Chubb, originally from England, included morris and English country dancing published by Sharp, especially for May Day festivals.[63] During its first two years, Pine Mountain presented at least two pageants. May 1914 saw the first May Day celebration, and at Christmas 1914 a Nativity Pageant was presented. The first "May Day began very simply . . . with the chance for the children to play games together and wind the May-pole, and, most important of all, white dresses for everybody." Sharp suggested some revisions during his 1917 visit, which the leaders took to heart. He believed that May Day "should be a festival developing logically from the English ancestry of many of our children, and the fact that many of the old dances and singing games of the English countryside survive in the Mountains. This is the second year that our children have gathered on the playground to dance the ancient 'Gathering Peascods' which symbolizes the worship of the tree and the joy in returning life in nature. . . . All the old contest games, such as . . . London Bridge, which spring from the ancient idea of the contest of light and darkness with the final victory of light, the little ones play with abandon, while the older children run sets and dance 'Rufty Tufty' and 'Black Nag.'"[64] As a result of Sharp's influence, the pageant had moved from a simple celebration of spring to an embodiment of a version of history that identified Appalachian people as purely British descendants and that ascribed ancient ritual motives to dances and games. Neither of these ideas could be proved, but they added to a mystique for this seemingly isolated area that supported the leaders' ideals and coincidentally appealed to donors.

Folk Dance as an Antidote to Popular Culture

Besides linking children with their imagined English ancestry, folk dance, along with recreation in general, was identified as a mediating force between the perceived isolation of the local people and the encroaching modernity, preparing them for social intercourse. In 1917, deLong bemoaned the fact that "the evils of the outside world are filtering slowly over the mountain."[65] Seven years later, she described the role of the settlement workers, which included recreation efforts, in dealing with this infringement. They feared the coming of the coal-mining industry with corporations such as International Harvester, United States Steel Company, and many more, in the growing town of Harlan, on the other side of Pine Mountain. Perhaps they were most concerned about the cultural changes that came with the industry. They said that this phenomenon "among so isolated and ignorant a people has its dangers." Local people were becoming suspicious of outsiders, they said, and needed "the friendly daily contact of our extension workers, in sickness and at merry-makings . . . and on the playground . . . to modify prejudice and hostility."[66] Pine Mountain, it was declared in a May 1926 report, provided the "first chance to learn the ways of community living—good sportsmanship in all their affairs, respect for others' property, self- control and courtesy." People living among "miles of shut-away mountains, eighteenth century pioneer housekeeping and sanitary standards, inherited lore in ballads, folk-dances, dye recipes, and weaving patterns, [with] a medieval faith and ignorance" needed the skills of social interaction with the newcomers that recreation and folk dance could teach.[67]

During the same years that Pine Mountain intensified its involvement in dance, folk dance grew nationally as a recreational outlet and educational tool, for some of the same reasons that the settlement school valued it—developing good health, promoting teamwork, and encouraging individuals to see themselves as part of the greater whole, as members of a civic society. By the late 1920s, the message regarding the importance of recreation and especially folk music and dance had been expanded, and they were considered a way to combat a variety of social ills from mechanization to unsavory music. Harlan County's population grew along with the coal-mining industry, and it was becoming increasingly diverse. The jazz age was in full swing, and the Charleston and then the lindy hop emerged as the dance crazes of the nation, enjoyed socially at venues in the coal towns and certainly in bustling Harlan. Phonograph records were easy to acquire, necessitating a strict music policy at Pine Mountain and other settlement schools. James Greene cites deLong's musical beliefs stated in a 1926 letter: "Up here we try to have all the music . . . really superior in beauty, knowing that everything else will come their way inevitably through the stores and the railroad, and thinking that we had better take the one chance we have to fill up their minds with things that may help them to make better choices for themselves." Beliefs about race and class may have played a part in this decision. According to Greene, "Classical music and standard songs were acceptable; jazz and blues were beyond the pale, as were 'hillbilly' songs." Louise Browning, music teacher in the late 1920s, said, "We hoped they would forget" jazz, blues, and hillbilly music "if they would learn the ballads." Ballad singing, like English folk dancing, was a means of building taste, a sense of style, and a set of aesthetic principles.[68] The English Folk Dance Society of America, closely associated with Pine Mountain since 1919, also emphasized proper style in the teaching of folk dance, and this was useful in developing social graces among the students. Though Pine Mountain directors had ceased discussing the concept of "pure Anglo-Saxon stock," in fact their music and dance practices continued promoting those particular aesthetic values. Jazz and blues were strongly influenced by Jewish and African American music. "Hillbilly music" was the moniker given to the offerings of regional musicians such as the Carter Family and Jimmie Rodgers first recorded in the 1920s, and which were broadcast on shows such as the Grand Ole Opry beginning around that time. Perhaps, as Greene suggests, these kinds of music were seen by the directors as lower class or unrefined.

The Pine Mountain directors were not alone in eschewing these kinds of music, and their beliefs were supported by industrialist Henry Ford, whose publications had national influence. In 1926, Ford began his campaign to reinstate "old fashioned dances," publishing a book that included directions primarily for contra dances and quadrilles, along with extensive directions for dance style.[69] He soon hired Benjamin Lovett to lead dancing in his home area in Michigan and produced records for use in teaching folk dance. His efforts to reestablish late-nineteenth-century dances were in fact aimed at mitigating what he saw as unsavory characteristics in American music and dance. Earlier he had published a diatribe against the Jewish and African American influence in American culture in a series of articles.[70] Ford's records were used at Pine Mountain, as they were at schools across the country. Pat Napier reported that when he attended Highland School in Breathitt County (another settlement school) in the 1930s and 1940s, records were usually forbidden. Recreation leader Frank Smith brought records when he came to Highland to teach "folk games," the euphemism for folk dancing, but these records were acceptable because they were mostly Henry Ford records.[71] Both Burchenal and Sharp had produced records of folk dance music between 1910 and 1916, and they may have been used as well.[72]

There is no evidence that the Pine Mountain leaders shared Ford's overt racism, but they did share his belief in using dance from an older time to accomplish goals for the present and future. The commitment to English country dance was deeply connected to the school's mission to create healthy citizens rooted in their past, at least as the directors imagined it, and to establish a restorative for the adversity brought about by industrialization, as well as to teach teamwork and to provide positive recreation. There may have been an element of class aspiration as well. In cities, English country dance was a recreation of the elite and of established professionals. Perhaps the Pine Mountain workers hoped to prepare their students for polite society.[73]

The Pine Mountain leaders remained firm in their conviction that recreation was essential even in the depths of the Depression and in the midst of the labor strife in "Bloody Harlan County," and it could be that they believed in recreation as an antidote to the struggles surrounding them. Douglas Kennedy, director of the English Folk Dance Society, voiced this same belief in 1936, and it was reiterated later by Frank Smith: "Philosophers and sociologists are becoming aware that there is a new meaning to be found in recreation as re-creation. We become spiritually and physically sick without music and dancing . . . the machine age has resulted in increased leisure and also in a lack of creativeness in our work." He promoted reviving rural arts such as music, dance, and crafts as a way to help people through "agricultural adjustment" as they moved to off-farm employment.[74]

A 1935 brochure announcing the establishment of a fund for furtherance of English Folk Dance Society instructor Dorothy Bolles's work at the school affirms the connection between dance and the goals of the school.

> It is hard to think of any one aspect of Pine Mountain's social, cultural or physical training that has gone further in helping to realize its ideals, than has her teaching. Every spring for ten years, she came to build upon the inherited dance and folk music traditions of the children, giving them new appreciation of their own past as she added to the inheritance from her vast store of English sword and country dances. As she drew successive generations of Pine Mountain children within the exciting circle of her friendly, vigorous, enthusiastic personality, she absorbed their interest so completely that the shy forgot their awkwardness, the "nonconformists" learned team play, and children who had known nothing of physical recreation

> grew young and gay and hearty, as they should be. May Day, beginning at dawn with a group dancing from house to house, and continuing through an afternoon of garlanded processionals, the May Pole, and dancing outdoors and in, to the evening of "set-running" when neighbors joined in, left everyone feeling that they had been restored by some deep and elemental spring of well-being. For you must remember that on the far side of Pine Mountain life is full of reminders of desperate need and cruel poverty, and sources of recreation are very important.[75]

In the brochure, the Pine Mountain leaders went so far as to identify dancing as a source of personal empowerment in the face of adversity and negative influences. "Pine Mountain has thus, through the impetus and vision of Dorothy Bolles, set loose a great source of power in the lives of its boys and girls, and created a tradition in the intelligent and artistic use of folk material that brings the school great responsibility."

The Mountain Folk Festival

Pine Mountain students helped to disseminate dance among the other schools and even introduced it in at least one coal camp, even during the years of mining strife in Harlan County. "English folk dance is now (1935) a vital force in the life of the school, the great enthusiasm of all the boys and girls. Our young school teachers go out into their little mountain schools with new and fascinating games to teach their young'uns; visitors from far and near come to see the dancing and learn more about it; our groups of dancers visit other schools in the mountains and outside, or take part in folk festivals, invariably making friends for themselves and for a school that has given them such a valuable source of happiness. This last spring a worker from the school had a week in a huge nearby mining camp, teaching between three and four hundred children, because the superintendent had seen the dancing at Pine Mountain."[76]

During the 1930s several factors combined to encourage dance at Pine Mountain: the growth of folk dance nationally, the continued commitment to recreation, and the expansion of folklore collection. Folk dance was becoming ever more popular as a leisure activity, and English Folk Dance Society of America groups were increasing rapidly in numbers.[77] Recreation and folklore efforts were amplified by federal support. The Works Progress Administration established a recreation division, building parks and recreation centers and training recreation leaders whose skills included folk dance. The interest in collecting traditional music widened. The Federal Writers' Folklore Project trained individuals to document stories and songs of passing traditions and to collect accounts of social customs of various cultural and ethnic groups, including those in the Appalachian region. Most famous among these collectors was perhaps John Lomax, who recorded music in Harlan County in 1933 and continued to make trips to Eastern Kentucky until at least 1937. Alan Lomax continued his father's Kentucky work into the 1940s. Others recording in Eastern Kentucky in the 1930s and 1940s included Mary Elizabeth Barnicle, Finley Adams, and Samuel Simpson Adams.[78] Perhaps Pine Mountain's collecting efforts, begun by Katherine Pettit and continued by Elizabeth Wells and others, helped to arouse these collectors' interest in Eastern Kentucky. Some, like Richard Chase, collected, edited or rewrote, published, and performed versions of folktales, ballads, and songs. A visit to Pine Mountain Settlement School in 1925 began his lifelong quest. His published volumes of *Jack Tales* and *Grandfather Tales* have influenced perceptions of Appalachian storytelling for decades.[79] The spread of English country dance along with the attention to folk materials and the focus on recreation at the federal level contributed to a supportive atmosphere for Pine Mountain's continued interest in folk music and dance. Added to this were their solid connection with the English Folk Dance Society of America and ready access to guest instructors and teaching materials. Thus they experienced both practical and philosophical support for their ideals into the 1940s.

In this environment, in 1935 the Conference of Southern Mountain Workers established an annual folk festival, which was attended by students from Pine Mountain and other schools and colleges in the CSMW network, with Berea College as host. This event grew out of the experience of the leaders of the member schools at their annual conferences, which always included singing games, folk plays, song, and other recreational activities. In addition, many CSMW Workers had reportedly attended the recreational course at the John C. Campbell Folk School in Brasstown, North Carolina, learning and enjoying "folk games."[80]

Some recent folk festivals may have inspired them. Bascom Lamar Lunsford had established the Mountain Dance and Folk Festival in Asheville, North Carolina, in 1928, believed to be the first event called a "folk" festival. It continues in another form to the present. In 1932, the Whitetop Folk Festival was first held in Grayson County, Virginia, and continued through the 1930s. In 1934, Sarah Gertrude Knott founded the National Folk Festival, which was the first to include a broad range of cultural groups and people from various parts of the country. So the Conference of Southern Mountain Workers had some examples on which to base their concept. Another model was to be found in park fetes. These events had been held as public events in the early twentieth century, especially in large cities. Elizabeth Burchenal organized the first ones for the Girls Branch of the Public School Athletic League in 1908. Since the Russell Sage Foundation and the PSAL shared leadership, the idea of fetes likely was communicated to organizations supported by Sage. In these fetes, hundreds of girls came to a large open area such as Central Park, and, grouped in their school teams, all danced the same dances at the same time. They danced around Maypoles and performed international folk dances, including English dances like Sellenger's Round. Park fetes were not intended as public performances but were designed for the participatory experience of the girls, scheduled during the school day as they were.[81]

While the Mountain Folk Festival was similar to the festivals, it was more comparable to the park fetes. The festival involved teams of young people coming from schools that were part of the CSMW network, unlike the Asheville festival, which presented adult traditional performers or specially invited groups, and it was not a contest. Among Whitetop Festival performers were local musicians as well as morris and sword dance teams from Richmond, Virginia, trained by Richard Chase, and in 1935 boys from Pine Mountain Settlement School doing a sword dance.[82] The National Folk Festival featured among the performers those whose work had been collected by the Federal Writers' Folklore Project workers.[83] The Mountain Folk Festival included some local dance and song as learned by the students in their schools or communities, though set running was invited as a demonstration only and not as a dance for group participation. The focus was on dancing and singing together and learning new dances, songs, and games. "The [Mountain Folk] festival is primarily for the joy of sharing and passing on such folk material as each center has accumulated. . . . One of the great reasons for the occasion, however, is the joy which comes from doing games together." In this it had more in common with the park fetes than the other folk festivals, since all school teams were expected to learn certain dances in order to dance them together, though they did have the opportunity to demonstrate something especially their own. Schools were encouraged to bring folk songs and "plays of a folk character" as well as perform a demonstration dance. Pine Mountain was expected to "do English Country, Morris or Sword, as these have been their special interest."[84] The music, dance, and drama selections were kept within a particular aesthetic framework. Ballads rather than popular songs or banjo tunes were included, and group teamwork dances rather than contemporary social dances were permitted.

The organizing committee chose seventeen "games" (dances) that all participants should know before they came. Organizer Marguerite Butler, co-founder of John C. Campbell Folk School and former Pine Mountain teacher, reported that these were chosen "because of their variety, simplicity, and also because Mr. Frank Smith [John C. Campbell extension recreation leader at the time] has taught most of them to many schools and centers." The list included seven Danish dances, six English dances, and four American singing games, with an invitation for teams to perform "the set-running [*sic*]" as a demonstration. The festival had institutional support in addition to CSMW. Guest speakers included Lynn Rohrbaugh of the Church Recreational Service, Delaware, Ohio, publisher of books of folk songs, games, and recreational activities, who was expected to teach "traditional games from all over the world." And Mrs. John C. Campbell planned "to speak on the value of folk material."[85]

Berea College was a logical host for this festival because of its institutional stability and because of its history of recreation outreach. Berea Normal School had published a book entitled *Games for Rural Schools* in 1914. Recreation was part of the college's outreach program through the Opportunity School under Helen Dingman's direction and was seen as a valuable means to achieve the larger educational goals of the college, even in the difficult financial times of the Great Depression. In support of this work, Berea College president William J. Hutchins, in a 1933 letter to a New York foundation, wrote, "Faculty who had been doing extension work in the mountain area had become convinced that recreation was needed in isolated mountain schools and communities . . . that it would help improve the community spirit and create an atmosphere where formal education would have a better opportunity." In the *Mountain Life and Work* article announcing the festival, Marguerite Butler said that besides the fact that Berea was better able to care for a group than the smaller schools, "we turn to Berea as a sort of mother of mountain schools."[86] The Mountain Folk Festival was certainly an influence in further institutionalizing recreation and dance as important features of the settlement school network, and the annual syllabus of required dances helped to solidify a particular repertoire at Pine Mountain, Berea College, and other schools.

The Mountain Folk Festival led to the establishment of structures that helped to sustain dance at Pine Mountain. Folk games for mixed couples are said to have first appeared at Berea College after physical education teacher Oscar Gunkler took the John C. Campbell Folk School short course in 1933. It apparently took root quickly, with a repertoire based largely on the one shared by the Folk School and Pine Mountain. In the years immediately following the first festival, Frank Smith joined the staff of Berea College, and in 1937 the college's Recreation Extension was formally established under his direction, and recreation classes were offered in the sociology department.[87] Through his Recreation Extension work, Smith traveled to settlement schools and communities teaching morris, sword, and English country dances, along with puppetry and folk drama. In 1938, after attending the English Folk Dance and Song Society of America summer session at Pinewoods, he founded Christmas Country Dance School. During their winter break, he brought teachers from the settlement schools to Berea College for a week to learn the dances chosen for the upcoming Mountain Folk Festival so that they could teach them to their students, thus making it possible to reach more schools. The Christmas course took place under the auspices of the Council of the Southern Mountains, with May Gadd, national director of the English Folk Dance and Song Society of America, as a primary instructor. Twenty-six people participated in the weeklong workshop between

Christmas and New Year, including staff. Perhaps as a result of the partnership among the three institutions, the 1939 Folk Festival boasted twenty groups and 201 participants.[88]

The Berea College commitment to recreation grew, thanks to Smith's efforts, and Pine Mountain was a beneficiary. In a 1939 report for the Keith Fund, which had funded his recreation program for two years, Smith described his classes as the source for the "development of Berea College as the headquarters of the recreational movement in the Southern Highlands." Eventually, Berea became a co-sponsor, with the Conference of the Southern Mountain Workers, of community recreation work under his direction.[89] Smith continued to expand the network of dance teachers in the region through his college courses. By the early 1940s, Smith's Recreational Techniques class included three units: Arts, Music, and Folk Dancing and Games. The last unit was very specific as to content: American, English, and Danish country dances; sword and morris dances; and singing games for dances. Thus, working through the "mother of mountain schools," Smith extended the reach of the original Mountain Folk Festival repertoire, which was largely based on the Pine Mountain Settlement School repertoire. The Mountain Folk Festival and Christmas Country Dance School continue to the present. The repertoire of both still consists of English, Danish, and American dance, though now the balance among the three is more even, and Christmas School often includes other elements, such as Irish set dancing. The connection between Pine Mountain and Berea College was always very close, with the school's directors recommending students for admission to the college and requesting that the college send teachers. So the establishment of recreation and dance at Berea nourished those efforts at Pine Mountain, just as the Pine Mountain vision for dance influenced the program at Berea, and through it the development of English country dance nationally.[90]

During these years, Pine Mountain continued its commitment to dance as training for citizenship and as a manifestation of folk culture. In the 1938 Silver Jubilee Edition of *Notes from Pine Mountain*, the lead article mentioned, in tandem, that students were given every opportunity for "assuming responsibility in a democracy" and that Pine Mountain "has given much attention to the folklore of the Highlands and has consistently fostered . . . the appreciation of this cultural heritage. Songs and folk dances are a natural and delightful part of the daily life; at the school the country dances and the running set are the popular recreation."[91] The reader will note that the leaders had, by this time, adopted Sharp's term for their local dance, perhaps thinking it more recognizable to their supporters.

An article by May Gadd followed in this publication, giving a brief history of English and American folk dances. While some information was factual, she perpetuated the notion that "all folk dances have their origin in rituals designed to ensure the continuance of Life" and attributed set running figures to ceremonial sword dance moves. She alluded to the mutual benefit enjoyed by the English Folk Dance and Song Society of America and Pine Mountain, saying, "Pine Mountain School, and the English Folk Dance and Song Society of America, are both interested in preserving their common heritage of dance and song, and in making it known to the present generation. Just as Pine Mountain provides its students with opportunities for dancing and singing the English as well as the native variants, so the Society has introduced many people to the mountain songs, and fun of dancing the Running Set."[92] The length and prominence of this article, appearing on the second page of the publication, demonstrate that dance, and especially English dance, continued to be a central feature of Pine Mountain's image and philosophy. However, Gadd's reference to broader enjoyment of "the Running Set" may not have been carried out in practice. According to Bicky McLain, in early Christmas Country Dance School sessions only English country dance, Danish folk dance, morris, and sword dances were taught. American dances were "rather looked down upon . . . you didn't dare do it," with the exception of play parties or singing games. She said that Frank Smith was of the opinion that American square dances would be unacceptable in rural communities, and so he did not teach them.[93] Settlement-school teachers seem to have been opposed to their students dancing, other than the folk games as taught by Frank Smith and others in sanctioned settings. Pat Napier, a 1949 Berea College alumnus and longtime staff member at Christmas Country Dance School, told a humorous story about his experience at Highland School. He and the other students entertained themselves in their dormitory by doing square dances from home, without benefit of music. According to Napier, when the teacher discovered them doing this, the first reaction was negative. However, after watching the students dance awhile, the teacher determined that, when dancing, the students were too busy to get into trouble, and after that approved of their square dancing. By the 1940s, American dance had begun to be incorporated into the CCDS curriculum.[94]

Danish Dancing in the Mountains

Not only was English dance promoted above local dance, but Danish dance also took precedence. As has been noted earlier, at the first Mountain Folk Festival in 1935, seven of the dances were Danish. In fact, the photo accompanying the article appears to be a Danish dance. Two couples stand side by side, hands on hips, looking in the partner's eyes. The women tilt slightly forward from the hip, one leg outstretched with the heel of the flexed foot touching the ground. Philosophically, the Pine Mountain leaders had justified the inclusion of English dance as being a natural extension of the local dances because of the students' presumed ancestry. The inclusion of Danish dance cannot be explained in the same way.

Danish dance was added to the settlement school repertoire in the 1920s. This unlikely addition had roots in Pine Mountain's extension work, which was led by Marguerite Butler. Within a few years after its founding, the Pine Mountain directors established branches with Harlan County Schools in order to contribute to the education of the children, to encourage recreation, and to improve the health of the communities. Each school was provided with a teacher, a public health nurse, and an individual worker. Butler's responsibilities as an extension worker included supervising county teachers and establishing classes for the schools in "canning, cooking, sewing, playground, and Sunday School." Workers at the branches helped to upgrade schools by providing curtains for windows, gathering school supplies, repairing windows, and also by treating trachoma, a chronic conjunctivitis that can lead to blindness. Along with all this, they organized Saturday baseball games on the school playgrounds.[95]

Because such a partnership between a settlement school and the local school system was so unusual, Butler was asked to present a talk at the 1919 Conference of Southern Mountain Workers about her newly established extension work. At the conference, John C. Campbell admired her work and noted its similarity to the Danish Folk School system. He had been introduced to the concept in 1908 by Tennessee educator and United States Commissioner of Education Philander P. Claxton, who had first learned about Danish education practice during his studies in Europe in the 1880s, continuing his interest during the next two decades.[96] Campbell was inspired to plan a visit to Denmark with his wife, Olive Dame Campbell, in 1914, but the trip was canceled with the onset of World War I. After John Campbell's death, Olive Dame Campbell and her sister, along with Marquerite Butler, followed through on the plans. In 1922 they traveled to Denmark to study folk schools and the educational system, and there they were first introduced to Danish folk dance and singing games. Butler had an interest in folk music and dance because of her association with Pine Mountain, and in fact she had been present when the students demonstrated set running for Cecil Sharp in 1917. They concluded their travels in 1923 by attending, along with Evelyn Wells, the Vacation School hosted by the English Folk Dance Society at Stratford-upon-Avon. Butler and Campbell returned to found the John C. Campbell Folk School in Brasstown, North Carolina, in 1925, basing it on the noncompetitive education they had observed in Denmark. Perhaps during their stay in Denmark they had met Georg Bidstrup. The following year, he arrived in North Carolina to become director of the farms and teacher of gymnastics and Danish folk dance at their new school.[97]

Bidstrup taught widely throughout the region and beyond for more than four decades. His influence on the settlement schools was secured by his teaching

Figure 6.6. "Kentucky Running Set" at Pine Mountain, May Day, 1943. Courtesy of Berea College Southern Appalachian Archives.

of the short course at the folk school and the publication of his book *Singing Games Old and New*. Although Denmark did not figure in the heritage of the students of the region, Danish cooperative recreation philosophy fit well with the education philosophy of certain of the settlement schools. No record exists of when Danish dance first entered the Pine Mountain repertoire, but it appears that the students were prepared to perform the seven Danish dances at the 1935 Mountain Folk Festival. Since Butler had close ties with Pine Mountain, she likely introduced Bidstrup and his dances to them soon after his arrival. Danish dance was probably readily accepted because it fit the criteria for "right dancing," unlike contemporary popular dances. Danish folk dances encouraged sociability and teamwork, with each individual having an integral role to play in the successful functioning of the group. The dances were robust, energetic, and good natured, and therefore they were believed suitable for hardworking, rural people. Though the Danish repertoire continues to be taught in connection with the Mountain Folk Festival and at Christmas Country Dance School, the dances have not established themselves as a popular recreation nationally as English country dance has.

A Return to Local Tradition

The Pine Mountain dance emphasis began with the recognition of a local dance tradition, but it soon focused almost exclusively on English dancing. In the late 1940s, a self-awareness had developed among the Southern Mountain Worker leadership regarding the need for a greater emphasis on American dance and on regional dance in particular. In the summer 1949 issue of *Mountain Life and Work*, Napier's full description of "Old Side Door: A Kentucky Mountain Square Dance" appeared, along with a description of the setting in the home, and a list of tunes commonly used for the dancing. The periodical's editors introduced the description by saying, "One of the difficulties we face in strengthening the American part of our three-fold dance tradition—American, Danish, and English—in the Southern Highlands is the lack of published material describing native dance. In the hope of stimulating people in other parts of the region to set down local dances and share them with us, the Recreation Editor asked Patrick E. Napier, a student at Berea College whose home is in Perry County, Kentucky, to describe one more or less typical dance along with a description of the social and cultural setting in which it was used."[98]

The editors seem not to have been aware of Ida Levin's little book *Kentucky Square Dances*, published in 1928 by the Recreation Council of Louisville, Kentucky. Collections of dances from New England and the western United States had appeared in the late 1930s, so this CSMW effort was overdue.[99] Their interest led to the publication of two books. For a term paper in 1945 at Berea College, Napier had documented square dance figures as he had known them growing up, and in 1960 he published them as a booklet called *Kentucky Mountain Square Dancing*. In 1955, Frank Smith had published his book *The Appalachian Square Dance*, which included a number of similar figures.[100] He did this with the help of Mary Rogers of Pine Mountain Settlement School, who created woodcuts for the illustrations. The Conference of Southern Mountain Workers had provided the impetus for inclusion of Appalachian dance, returning full circle to the beginnings of dance at Pine Mountain, when set running was first allowed at the school. Pine Mountain's support of local dance was later carried forward via two avenues of folk dance training that had begun in the early twentieth century: the folk dance recreation movement and the English Folk Dance and Song Society of America. Each had a role in disseminating traditional dance of Eastern Kentucky. Sharp's book introduced set running to English country dance enthusiasts, and teachers' manuals promoted by education and recreation organizations introduced square dancing to schoolteachers and youth-group leaders.

In 1949, with school consolidation, Pine Mountain was no longer a boarding school but continued as one of the consolidated schools. Their well-respected dance team was suspended, but folk dancing was one of the special activities that could be chosen on certain afternoons. Others included singing, recorder, weaving, woodworking, crafts, cooking, sewing, dramatics, nature, conservation, and even judo.[101] The school continued its commitment to traditional arts while it adapted to a new situation. Weekly community dances were still held at Laurel House, and school secretary Dorothy Nace became the dance leader in the 1950s, followed by Millie Mahoney. In 1956, Charlie and Joyce Whitaker joined the Pine Mountain staff and took over dance leadership, with a folk dance, rather than a local dance, repertoire. Peter Rogers, who attended Pine Mountain during this time, recalled that his brother, a Country Dancer at Berea College, learned to call set running. Though it was not taught at Pine Mountain, Rogers was determined to call set running for the dance team, briefly touching back to the initial impetus for dance there. The school was closed completely in the late 1960s but has continued as an environmental education center to the present day. According to Peter Rogers, as recently as 1980 community dance parties were still popular at Pine Mountain.[102] Today, Appalachian square dancing is included as a recreational offering at the school for participants in environmental education courses and for groups of visitors.

Establishing Tradition

The Pine Mountain leaders' view of dance was multilayered. It included the acceptance of a local expression and its presentation as emblematic of the school; the use of dance to achieve educational goals and its function as a vehicle to promote the school to funders; the encouragement of local culture and the creation of an imagined history. Recreation—including dance—was at the heart of the Pine Mountain mission—to build strong, moral citizens, to promote good health and the joy of participatory work, and to counteract the effects of industrialization and its accompanying social changes. From early days, they believed what dance scholars have come to understand in recent decades: that not only does movement reflect culture, but it can also shape culture. By choosing particular dance structures and styles, and promoting them in controlled environments, they hoped to change the students' lives in fundamental ways. The dances they chose emphasized individuals working together as part of a larger whole for a common goal. Their decisions were based on contemporary thought and practice at the time of the school's founding and continued to be central to the school's mission for decades, supported in part by the Russell Sage Foundation's recreation focus. Paired with this ideal was a belief in preserving and promoting local cultural expression, encouraged by early folklore efforts and later by the work of the Works Progress Administration folklore and recreation projects. Their beliefs led them to interpret local culture as essentially of British origin, and so, with the help of the English Folk Dance Society of America, they introduced English dance to restore the students' heritage as they believed it to have been. Today we may believe their choices in this regard to be misguided. However, the dedication and determination of the leaders cannot be denied, nor can the longlasting effects of their labors.

Georg Bidstrup said of English and Danish dances: "While these were brought in mainly to serve as a bridge to the traditions of the people . . . [t]hey have become . . . traditions in their own right; and they are on their way to being incorporated into the Southern Mountain dance form."[103] Pine Mountain's dance program did have an effect locally, and perhaps the founders would be satisfied with the result, though it is not the one Bidstrup anticipated. Though they thought that English country dance would become a local tradition, this was not to be. Instead, the CSMW network, building upon dance at Pine Mountain, provided the inspiration for the continuation of two local dance venues: the Carcassonne Community Center and Hoedown Island at Natural Bridge State Resort Park. Few venues exist in Eastern Kentucky for traditional Appalachian square dancing on a regular basis. Both Carcassonne and Hoedown Island came into being in the 1960s and continue to the present in an unbroken thread. In each case a principal dance leader received his inspiration and some of his training at settlement schools. Though the repertoire at each place does not duplicate Pine Mountain's, some similar dances are continued, and central to both is the ideal of regular, participatory recreational dance events.

The dance program at Pine Mountain contributed substantially to the growth of English sword, morris, and country dance nationally. Because of its focus on recreation as a means to develop citizens for the democracy, with dance as a principal method, Pine Mountain Settlement School was pivotal in introducing these dance forms, along with Danish dance, to Kentucky and to the region. One version of local dance was supported and encouraged, and because of this, it became the primary dance associated with Kentucky and the region in many people's minds. Through workshops, demonstrations, and participation in the Conference of the Southern Mountain Workers' Mountain Folk Festival, the school led by example. Its vibrant dance program fed into the goals of the English Folk Dance Society of America, which both supported it and was supported by it. The Pine Mountain repertoire served as the basis for that of the Berea College country dance programs. Berea College continues to be one of several centers for Anglo-American folk dance, attracting hundreds of people from around the nation and the world to Christmas Country Dance School each year. Today, English country dance, morris, and sword dance are popular recreations nationally and internationally, taught at dance camps and enjoyed by community groups in towns large and small. These types of dancing have taken root as living tradition, with families participating in three or four and even five generations and choreographers writing new dances in these forms. Pine Mountain Settlement School's dance initiatives can be seen as one of the sources for this widespread interest. Institutional support and powerful, persistent individuals, buttressed by accepted philosophy and theory, contributed to the establishment of a new tradition.

7. "Rise and Shine"

Dancing for Community Development at Hoedown Island

At Natural Bridge State Resort Park in Powell County, Kentucky, freestyle clogging and old time square dancing were the centerpieces of weekly summer gatherings for more than four decades, and dancing continues to the present.[1] To regular participants and one-time visitors, these kinds of dancing came to symbolize local heritage and all that is good about local culture. The vision of one dedicated individual, Richard Jett, is responsible for this. He led the dancing for forty-four years, believing that dancing and singing were vital to individual growth and community development. The park used this symbolism as part of its publicity campaign to draw tourists. Their brochure beckoned, "Mosey on down to Hoedown Island where knee-slappin', toe-tappin', and swingin' your partner is a barrel of fun!" Jett's own promotional flier always concluded with his standard, "A Good Time Will Be Had By All." My college folk dance group and I loved to go to Hoedown Island to perform and to enjoy the evening's dancing. Over the years, beginning in 1999, some of my students and I have interviewed the dancers and documented the evening's dancing.[2]

Natural Bridge State Resort Park

Powell County, Kentucky, is the site of stunning natural environments. The Red River Gorge attracts thousands of people annually from all over the world to hike, climb, boat, and fish, and part of the Daniel Boone National Forest is within the boundaries of the county. Natural Bridge State Resort Park adjoins the Red River Gorge and is popular as well for camping, hiking, and now a skylift and zipline. It was one of the first state parks in Kentucky, established in 1926 when the land was donated to the newly formed Kentucky State Park Commission by the Louisville and Nashville Railroad. During the 1930s, the

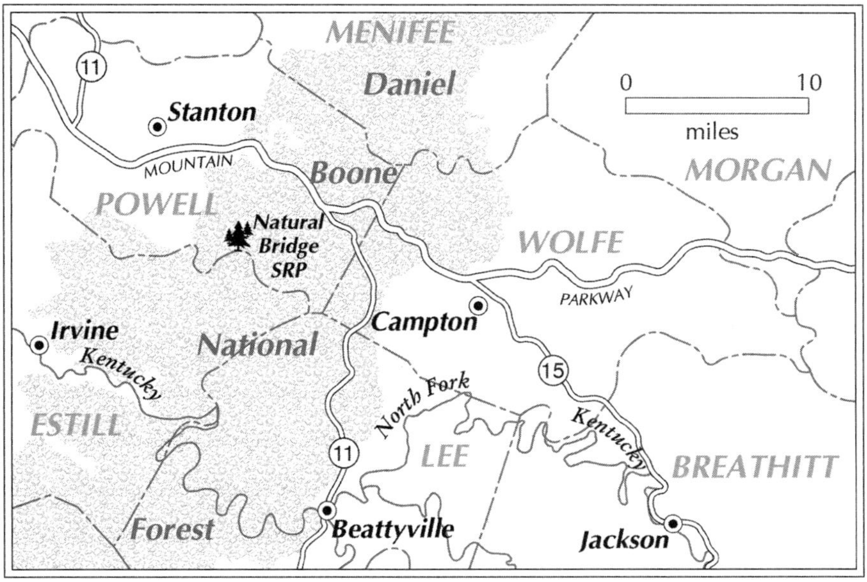

Map 6. Area surrounding Natural Bridge State Park and Hoedown Island. Cartography by Dick Gilbreath, Director, Gyula Pauer Center for Cartography and GIS, University of Kentucky.

Civilian Conservation Corps built lodging, trails, and picnic areas at Natural Bridge and other new state parks.[3] Its history as a tourist destination predates its establishment as a state park, however.

The area has attracted visitors since the late 1800s. In the 1890s the Lexington and Eastern Railroad completed a line into the rugged Cumberland Plateau, connecting Lexington and Jackson, Kentucky. In 1900, the railroad published a promotional booklet about its accomplishment, titled *Natural Bridge in the Kentucky Mountains*, demonstrating their interest in promoting tourism to the area as a secondary source of income. Their primary goal was to facilitate the transport of timber and coal from the ridges farther to the east, Jackson and beyond. "The valuable timber, rich mineral deposits and fertile soil of Eastern Kentucky offer exceptional opportunities for safe and profitable investment of capital, while its substantial and progressive cities and towns afford every advantage for manufacturing and mercantile pursuits."[4] The Red River is a tributary of the Kentucky River, so it is likely that before the coming of the railroad Powell County farmers and merchants enjoyed commerce similar to that in other mountain counties.

In describing the route of the railway, the booklet pointed out Clay City and Stanton, two of Powell County's largest towns. Stanton was said to be "an important point for shipment of lumber and forest products." Clay City was described as "one of the largest hardwood saw-mills in the country. Red River and numerous small creeks bring down from the mountains quantities of logs, which supply the mills at Clay City with material for the manufacture of staves for all kinds of barrels, flooring and siding, interior finish and piece stock." It went on to say that in the early 1800s, Clay City was home to the Red River Iron Works, where high quality nails, stoves, and cooking pots were made, along with cannon balls used in the Civil War. Another nearby town was described as having "one of the oldest flour and grist mills in the state." Beyond Natural Bridge, continuing to Jackson, the landscape was peppered with sawmills that processed logs delivered via the South Fork of the Kentucky River. Coal is emphatically suggested as a crucial resource to the industrial future of that area.[5]

By contrast, the description of the area of Powell County and Wolfe County between Natural Bridge and Torrent focused entirely on tourist pursuits, and dancing was part of that, even in the 1890s. The booklet claimed that in the summer of 1899 alone, more than twenty-five thousand people visited Natural Bridge, where there was a well-stocked lake with boat docks and bathing houses. "Bowling alleys, dancing pavilions, café, lunch pavilion and gardener's cottage face the lake." Summer camping, a new recreation at the time, was encouraged. The train schedule was deliberately arranged so that visitors could leave Lexington or Winchester in the morning, enjoy a day of exploring the woods or dancing and lunching, and return home the same evening. The summer resort town of Torrent, five miles away, boasted a luxury hotel centered around a large dance hall. Its staff, African Americans all, were hired not only for their ability to do the required work of the resort but also to play musical instruments for the dancing each night. Nearby Swango Springs provided mineral water said to have healing properties, and hay-fever symptoms were believed to disappear immediately upon arriving in Torrent. In 1915, a dance pavilion was added at a large rock ledge uphill from the hotel. Such rock ledges are like huge notches in the hillside, open on one side to the valley below. Their flat surfaces can be thirty feet deep and are protected from the weather by a rock overhang. Musicians played there for dances throughout the summer. Richard Jett recalled that these dances were still going on in his youth in the 1930s and that people traveled from Cincinnati and Louisville to attend.[6] Ballroom dancing and popular dances like Charleston and lindy were likely the styles offered, since orchestras are mentioned.

Though World War II brought an end to these dances, in some ways the Hoedown Island dances rekindled the attraction of dancing under a star-filled sky, with a different kind of dance. Of the seven Powell County special events listed in "Kentucky Facts" in 1987, three were dance festivals held at Hoedown Island, and the others were outdoor events like wildflower walks and canoe races. The economy of the county relied heavily on tourism and on timber in the late nineteenth and early twentieth century. Even at the end of the twentieth

Figure 7.1. Big Set at National Mountain Square Dance and Clogging Festival at Hoedown Island, 1970s. Note the different costumes worn by various teams. Courtesy of Berea College Southern Appalachian Archives.

century, commercial forests constituted the only major resource, and almost half of the employed residents of Powell County worked in *other* counties. Civic leaders like Richard Jett devoted considerable attention to ways of making life better for Powell, Wolfe, and other nearby counties.

Dancing in the Mountain Air

From 1962 until he passed away in 2006, on weekend nights from May to October, Richard Jett conducted entertainment structured almost as a ritual designed to crystallize experiences of the past, to bring them into the present, in order to influence the future. His goal was to transform both individuals and the region by instilling traditional regional values, by developing self-confident individuals who would contribute to their communities, and by cultivating tourism and regional pride.

Hoedown Island is a pavilion surrounded by Mill Creek Lake in Natural Bridge State Resort Park, built on the site of the former train platform near the foot of the original trail up Natural Bridge. In the 1940s the tracks were removed and replaced by a swimming pool, bathhouse, and gift shop.[7] A wooden dance pavilion was built, but it did not long survive the elements and was replaced by concrete. High above the dance floor stands the magnificent Natural Bridge, "like a sentinel," as Richard Jett said. It is a sandstone arch sixty-five feet high and seventy-eight feet across. A stage covered by a roof is at one end of the dance pavilion. From this vantage point, Richard Jett directed the progress of the evening, spinning records, CDs, and tapes like a disc jockey, keeping up a friendly patter, acknowledging various individuals and groups, and promoting local events and businesses. Jeffrey Driggs, editor of the *Doubletoe Times*, remembered "as a brand new clogger coming to the Island with fellow West Virginians and being amazed at the social ease of the place and the skill that Richard had of getting total strangers up on a dance floor under the Kentucky stars on a Saturday night." Jett regularly hosted local or nationally known singers, musicians, and cloggers, and he "always sat back and beamed whenever he laid down the mic and let a performer take the spotlight."[8]

A typical evening in the 1990s and through 2006 began with a "Warm-up" at 6:30, with a variety of dances including line dancing, mixers, freestyle clogging, partner dances like Cotton-Eyed Joe, the waltz and the polka, and even children's dances like the Hokey Pokey or the limbo. Though the evening was advertised to begin at 7:30, Jett knew that the sound of music would draw visitors down from the Hemlock Lodge on the hill above the dance pavilion. "See those people up there?" asked regular Sarah Gross in 1999, pointing toward the lodge. "In a few minutes they'll all be down here." She spoke from experience, having been drawn by the music her first time.[9] The regulars began arriving at 6:30, staking out their usual territories on the bleachers lining three sides of the pavilion. At 7:30, the evening officially commenced with the singing of a hymn by a local singer, one of Jett's many protégés. The mix of dances continued, highlighting square dancing and clogging, with short performances by one or more clogging teams and solo freestyle clogging exhibitions. The climax of the evening was always a performance by the Hoedown Island Cloggers at around 9:45, with the full attention of the audience. After their performance, people begin to drift away, until, by the 10:30 conclusion of the evening, the audience was substantially diminished. To close the evening, Jett chose a farewell song, like Porter Wagoner's "A Good Time Was Had by All," finally bidding the crowd, "Have a good night and drive careful and do something good for someone every day." Richard Jett configured the evening to offer something for everyone, to insure that people kept coming back to participate in the local values embodied in Appalachian square dancing, individual freestyle clogging, and the performance of the Hoedown Island Cloggers.

Natural Bridge, like other Kentucky state parks, had a pavilion especially for dancing for many years, but in 1962, when Carl M. Clark retired as director of the dance events, Richard Jett determined to have that position.[10] Clark, a University of Kentucky professor, formed a teenage dance group, the Pioneer Buckskin Dancers, in the 1950s, and in 1958 he asked a college student to teach the group Scottish Country Dancing. From this early group grew the Kentucky Heritage Dancers, a group established to "portray the history of dance in the United States." The group performed widely, including appearances at International Folk Festivals at Wolf Trap Farm in Washington, D.C., at national square-dance conventions, and as part of a 1976 tour of Poland. The group became a branch of the international Royal Scottish Country Dance Society in 1976 and continues to offer classes and dance events in Lexington, Kentucky.[11] In the late 1970s, Clark still taught, led square dancing, and wrote a book citing some of Jett's materials, along with other sources. The Kentucky Heritage Dancers performed at Hoedown Island, and Clark maintained a presence at Natural Bridge into the 1980s. In his 1986 news release, "History of Hoedown Island," Jett praised Clark as "the Dean of Kentucky Square Dance Calling." His work perhaps contributed to Jett's vision for dance, including performing and touring. He quoted Jett's belief that "square dancing offers great opportunity for achieving individual and community unity and happiness."[12] Prior to Clark, Clarence Henson, a well-known United States Forest Service Ranger, had led dancing at Natural Bridge.

Jett had been a teacher in nearby Morgan County Schools for only five years when the dance opportunity at Natural Bridge presented itself, but he had seen how the dancing he led at his school drew the community together. He had begun to form a vision for using dance as a means to develop stronger bonds within the community, to build self-esteem and self-confidence in the young people of the area, and to draw tourists with a representation of local culture. Jett held the position throughout his tenure as teacher, principal, superintendent of Wolfe County Schools, and Mayor of Campton in Wolfe County. Over the years, as a result of his leadership, a multigenerational community formed around the dancing, and young people have grown into successful adults, having been nurtured in the dance teams or singing groups Jett established. Dancers have gone on to professional careers at places like Branson, Missouri, and singers have become regular performers at Renfro Valley, Kentucky, but most important, young people have developed the self-esteem that has made them successful in school and work.

People from all over the country have been introduced to Appalachian culture as represented here, and many return frequently to Natural Bridge, bringing tourist dollars to a region with little industry and no coal mining. As a community leader, Richard Jett had community development foremost in his thoughts, and dancing at Hoedown Island was part of his mission. Believing that pride in one's heritage was crucial to individual and community betterment, he helped to establish the Wolfe County Historical Society, donated books to schools, and organized community events and cleanup campaigns, personally picking up trash on the streets of Campton. He saw dancing as a way to draw people to the area as visitors and as residents, postulating the notion of these counties becoming bedroom communities for nearby cities like Lexington and Winchester, in order to establish a stronger tax base. He also saw dancing as a way toward development of the individual, which, to him, was inextricably linked to development of the community. He saw dance as a good source of exercise, a way to enhance academic achievement, a means of "therapy" to relieve stress, and an antidote to crime. "Anyone who is on a dance floor, swinging his pardner and listening to the caller and the music is not going to have time to think up what folks in the hills still call devilment." But most of all, as early as the 1960s he set forth his beliefs that dance, besides being a positive pastime, could enhance academic ability and build self-confidence, preparing a student for college or for a career, which in turn would result in the improvement of the community.[13]

Community and Cooperation

In the 1960s and 1970s, Appalachian square dancing and clogging were the primary kinds of dancing at Hoedown Island. In the 1990s and the early years of this century, they were featured during an evening filled with variety. At least once or twice during an evening, Richard Jett called a traditional Appalachian square dance for any number of couples in a circle. When he announced this dance, a huge circle formed, entirely encompassing the pavilion. In this dance, as in Northeast Tennessee, the circle repeatedly divides into sets of two couples who dance together. After one figure is completed, one couple of each set moves on to dance with the next couple. Cooperation is essential. Everyone gets a chance to interact with many others, taking hands and smiling at new friends. More experienced dancers guide less experienced ones through the figures. Before calling the dance, Jett always emphasized the place of this dance in Appalachian heritage, saying something like, "this is the old mountain square dance like we used to do years ago," sometimes adding a little more specific information, talking about dancing after workings or mentioning specific facts of area history. He deliberately connected the interactive dance form with the home-based cooperative history as he experienced it. As a result, local residents had reason to feel proud of their heritage, and newcomers learned that they were participating in an expression of regional culture. This story illustrates what the dancing meant to him:

> My first experience in mountain dancing was in the home of Carrie McIntosh near the mouth of Puncheon Creek, Breathitt County, Kentucky when I was a boy. The neighbors and young folks of that area would get together in her home once or twice each week and enjoy the fun of dancing such old-time figures as the Wild Goose Chase, Old Side Door or Grapevine Twist. We had three sources of music: French Johnson's guitar, the radio, and the clapping of hands. I remember one dance especially at the McIntosh home. It was my first experience in this type of game. Mrs. McIntosh, a widow, was sparking Park Lawson, who was crippled and unable to dance. Carrie, who later married Mr. Lawson, grabbed me by the arm

> and pulled and pushed me through my first dance. After that night I was "on my own" in mountain dancing and have enjoyed it ever since.[14]

With this story, he demonstrated his belief in the importance of an intergenerational community, a spirit of cooperation, the hospitality and welcoming atmosphere of the home, and the nonverbal transmission of tradition from one generation to the next, all regional traditions that informed his youth.

The regulars at Hoedown Island did not talk about tradition or history, but they expressed verbally, as well as kinesthetically, the values Jett tried to instill through dance. When I asked dancers whether they thought about keeping a tradition alive, the answer was often "It's just fun!" It is so much fun, in fact, that one spring night I noticed a girl who arrived in a long gown and high heels. She had left her high school prom early because she thought she would have a better time at Hoedown Island. Dancers' comments are peppered with references to "family." The sentiment that "this is what it's all about—family, being together" was echoed and re-echoed. Many families come each week in three or four generations. A dancer in his twenties when I met him in 1999, said, "My grandmother forced me to start dancing when I was five. She literally had to drag me out of the car." On the night my students and I spoke with him, his grandmother, mother and aunts, sister, and two-year-old nephew were all on the dance floor. Jane Bolen's two children, son Chris, and daughter Sarah, have literally grown up at Hoedown Island. Richard Jett had a photo of Jane holding newborn Chris in her arms as she waltzed, and both children have attended almost every week, except when they were away for military service.[15]

The multigenerational community is not limited to blood relations. Lewis Arnett said he called Irene Walters "Granny," because when he came as a child, he would always sit on her lap. Until she passed away, they were both present every Saturday night, and he always asked her to dance at least once or twice during each evening. One retired teacher gestured toward the pavilion full of dancers aged 20 to 45, and said, "I knew almost all of them as kids in school." Richard Jett embodied the family spirit himself. When Lewis Arnett's father passed away, Jett, then mayor of Campton, canceled the city council meeting so that he could attend the funeral. Arnett said, "He's one of a kind, honey. A good friend, too. He cares about people." Jett received the same care in return. When he had a heart attack, Hoedown Islanders visited him in the hospital and sent him cards and flowers.[16] Naomi and Virgil McIntosh from Booneville in Owsley County, Kentucky, became regulars in 1992, never missing a Friday or Saturday night. If they missed a week or two, Jett would send a personal note—by mail, never having taken to email—saying they were missed, and hoping for their return. Naomi McIntosh was known to bring chicken and dumplings, banana pudding, and corn on the cob for pre-dance picnics with some of the other regulars. She said, "If you asked everybody in this place, most of them would tell you that it's one of the greatest places on earth to be entertained and have fun. Everybody around here is like brothers and sisters." Jett reflected, "It's a togetherness, a oneness, that's kind of rare."[17]

This feeling of family extended to people who traveled monthly from places like Columbus, Ohio, a four-hour drive, to spend an evening at Hoedown Island. They were drawn to the close-knit atmosphere and got to know the others who regularly attended. Richard Jett encouraged the feeling of family. He pointed out visitors from various states and countries and asked for applause for them. He joked with groups who always staked out their particular territory on the bleachers, like the flock from Owsley County he named "the Owl's Nest," the group he called "the Beattyville Bunch," or the cluster he dubbed "the Briar Patch." Each week he invited one or more clogging teams from elsewhere in Kentucky and from North Carolina, Ohio, Tennessee, or Virginia to perform, and he sang their praises, telling how long they had been dancing and where they had performed, saying how pleased he was to have them there. The "Shack Shakin' Cloggers" from Franklin and Scott Counties, Kentucky, led by Sue Tackett, performed in September 2002, but many of the team's members came regularly to dance at Hoedown Island, even when they were not performing. This was true of most of the guest performers who lived within driving distance.

The spirit of cooperation was evidenced in many ways. One dancer said, "You never have to worry about your kids. Whoever is beside you, it's like they're theirs. They look after them."[18] Irene Walters and her husband in years gone by would arrive an hour early and set up the sound system and sweep the dance floor. Once Mr. Walters passed away, these jobs fell to others, but Mrs. Walters continued to bring a little cooler with soft drinks in it for Richard Jett. On a Saturday night in 2004, I watched as Jane Bolen used the big push broom to clear fallen leaves and twigs from the dance floor. Within a few minutes, someone else had taken it from her to continue the job. The broom changed hands again, and the next time I looked, the music had started, and the broom had become someone's partner for the Electric Slide, before being returned to its storage place behind the stage. At the end of each evening's dancing, several people routinely flocked to the stage, efficiently putting away the sound equipment in a matter of minutes. They then strolled leisurely to the parking area, chatting with Jett as they went, lingering by the cars under the canopy of trees for a few last words. On the night I videotaped for the Smithsonian Institution, they completed their tasks while I was still dismantling my camera equipment, and before I knew it, they had my things packed up and ready to go. The principle of cooperation that Richard Jett associated with traditional square dancing had taken root in the Hoedown Island community.

Figure 7.2. Richard Jett calling a square dance at Hoedown Island, 1999. Courtesy of Lexington Herald-Leader.

Each dance evening, Jett called at least two Appalachian square dances, or "big sets," and he had Irvine, Kentucky caller I. D. Ball call a "Kentucky Running Set." When he announced a square dance, Jett left the stage and stood in the middle of the pavilion, which was completely encircled by couples. Lewis Arnett and Jane Bolen positioned themselves directly in front of the stage, serving as role models for the dance. Once the circle was assembled, Jett would have the whole group circle left and then right before giving instruction. He had every other couple step into the circle and face the couple to their right and walked everyone through a few figures before calling them. This was essential, since every evening there were so many people new to the dancing. One night in 2002, he chose to call "Take a Little Peek," "Chase the Rabbit," "Birdie in the Cage," "Do paso," "Right Hands Across," and "Four Hands Across" (basket). For each figure the inside couple moved along to dance with the next couple after a neighbor swing and partner swing. The music he almost always used was a medley from the album *Dances from Appalachia*, produced by Berea College and featuring Donna and Lewis Lamb and the McLain Family Band.[19] He wore out several editions of this record over the years because the track was long enough for a whole square dance and was composed of old time tunes Jett loved.

Once the dance got going, he inserted joking patter here and there in his calls. For example, in "Chase the Rabbit," the woman led her partner around the woman in the neighbor couple, and then her partner led her around the neighbor gent. Jett began his call in the usual way, and then threw in a word or two for a laugh. "Chase that rabbit, chase that squirrel, chase that pretty girl around the world. Chase the possum, chase the coon, chase ol' Sidewinder around the moon." The neighbor and partner swing that usually punctuated each figure was distinctive to Hoedown Island. He had described this particular swing in the dance called "Jitter Square" in his 1971 book. Perhaps dancers liked it so well that he decided to keep it for other dances. Partners did a quick once-around walking swing, then stepped backward away from each other, holding hands, man's left to woman's right. They pulled toward each other for another swing, rebounded away as before, and returned for one more swing. Typically, Jett coached this swing using calls similar to the ones in his book: "Swing your partner . . . step right back and watch her smile . . . step right up and swing awhile . . . step right back and watch her grin . . . step right up and swing again."[20] The square dance ended with an inward-spiraling windup, led by Arnett. As the long line of dancers holding hands wound tighter and tighter, Jett quipped, "Hope they don't get smothered in there!" After the windup, Jett coached the final brief promenade off the floor, telling how to hold hands. Though Jett said he remembered square dances in the home running as long as three hours without a break, this dance lasted only about ten minutes, even with so many figures.

Besides the square dance, the evening included a number of group dances designed to encourage interaction with friends and strangers. Some mixers like the Patty Cake Polka included a large circle of dancers changing partners after each completion of the sequence. Others, like the Ninepin Reel, were for smaller groups. In Ninepin Reel as called at Natural Bridge, one man stood in the center of a square of four couples. After swinging each woman in turn, he joined the other men to circle together in the center until Jett called "Swing!" and four of the men retrieved partners, leaving one to be in the center alone again. As some other callers have been known to do, Jett would keep a running stream of chatter going so that as dancers we never knew when the magic word would be spoken. Such dances may not have been traditional Appalachian square dance, but they contained some of the same values Jett believed in—cooperation, interaction with neighbors, and most of all, enjoyment of each other's company.

Individual Expression

While the community was important at Hoedown Island, participants were more than just members of a group. During much of the evening, individual expression was encouraged with freestyle clogging. Individuals took the floor, creating rhythmic patterns with their feet in response to the music. Often the music was bluegrass, country, or old time music, chosen by Jett from his extensive collection of tapes, records, and compact discs. Each person danced alone, though many were dancing at the same time. Sometimes one dancer moved closer to another dancer and a little dialogue in rhythm ensued, along with smiles and perhaps laughter, but it rarely became a partner dance. Richard Jett sometimes pointed out a particular person by name, calling attention to the fancy footwork, and noting his or her hometown and honors achieved. Once during each evening, it was usual for Jett to call a few freestyle cloggers to the pavilion in front of the stage to freestyle simultaneously, then one by one, to show their particular style of clogging. The styles varied widely. On an evening in 1999, James Pieratt, who had been on Jett's first clogging team in 1958, danced in a flatfoot style, feet close to the floor, Wayne Mattingly scooted smoothly sideways between quick rhythmic riffs, and Vince Redmon mixed Irish and French Canadian steps with local clogging moves. They danced first with music, and then without, so that the sounds of their feet could be heard clearly. On another evening, Jane Bolen was in the line, along with her then-eight-year-old daughter. On still another evening, Jett beckoned Lori Beth Rogers and Colin Ditty to the front of the stage.

The pair stepped through a short unison routine, and then each took solo improvisational turns, first with and then without music. Jett "bragged on" them, describing Lori Beth's multitude of clogging trophies displayed in the window of her father's insurance agency. "I thought her Dad had gone into the trophy business," he quipped. Lori Beth went on to be chosen for the Clogging Champions of America All-Pro team in 2000 and 2001, and attended Georgetown College. Jett announced that Colin Ditty had won World Championships in clogging and had earned a clogging scholarship to Mars Hill College in North Carolina, home of the Bailey Mountain Cloggers, and one of the few colleges to offer scholarships for skill in traditional dance. Colin was a particularly strong role model for local youth because his attendance at a college in the region was made possible by his ability to do something expressive of the region.

Hoedown Island was not the only place where individual expression in clogging was valued. In her 1983 in-depth study of clogging in Western North Carolina, folklorist Gail Matthews discovered through interviews that freestyle clogging was preferred there over precision clogging because it allowed for freedom of expression by the individual. The idea of everyone doing the same step at the same time seemed alien to their lifestyle, in which a tight-knit community supported the free expression of the individual, even within the framework of a square dance. Matthews likened the improvisational footwork within a set square dance structure to jazz music performances, with improvisation within a musical structure.[21] At Hoedown Island, people expressed a preference for the old-style clogging but made no such value judgments. They liked the idea that everyone had personal signature moves and an individual style, and they also appreciated the crisp, synchronized performances by visiting precision clogging teams in which everyone did the same step at the same time. Both precision cloggers and freestyle cloggers also enjoyed doing clogging line dances like Little Red Riding Hood.

Richard Jett believed that each person had special gifts, and freestyle clogging was one representation of that. He used other tactics to make everyone feel noticed. During the practice for the Hokey Pokey, he asked various participants, from toddlers to elders, to demonstrate their own special way of shaking an arm or a leg, freely distributing bits of candy to reward extravagant performances. As he talked through a particular mixer, he called on individuals to demonstrate their own personal versions of the four backward chugging steps, and everyone applauded as people threw in silly moves. In this way he seemed to thank the regulars for helping to make the evening a success, and he encouraged everyone to make a personal movement statement. One individual had a special comedic role. At a certain point in each dance evening, Jett called out "the old man from the mountain," Jim Savage, who drove more than an hour each Friday and Saturday night from Nicholasville, Kentucky, to join in the fun. Savage was an accomplished dancer and regularly participated in English country dances and other community folk dances in Central Kentucky. But as "the old man from the mountain," he hopped from his seat wearing a crumpled hat and a big grin, and scooted around the perimeter of the dance floor, hunched over, doing eccentric movements of his arms and legs, joking and teasing with people in their seats and evoking giggles and guffaws. Learning, too, was individualistic, as Charlie Rogers explained. "The way we do here, when somebody wants to learn how to dance, they get in front of somebody and watch them. That's how they pick it up."[22] Jane Bolen, a regular dancer and the lead woman in the Hoedown Island Cloggers, taught clogging lessons in town, but at Hoedown Island, oral and kinesthetic tradition was—and continues to be—the way that dancing is passed on.

Even the name of the pavilion at Natural Bridge proclaimed the importance of individual expression within the local aesthetic. Hoedowning is the Eastern Kentucky name for the footwork dancing known elsewhere as clogging, flatfooting, jigdancing, or buck dancing. In announcing the first National Mountain Square Dance and Clogging Festival and Competition he organized at Natural Bridge in 1967, Jett realized he needed to include the name of a place in the publicity. In casting about for a name for the pavilion, Jett chose "Hoedown Island" to represent the dance of the region. He had entertained other possibilities, including, for example, Shindig Island, after dance groups he directed early in his career. Shindig is a name for a dance event, so it would have been appropriate. But the name of the Island had to be about clogging, hoedowning, the individual expressing himself or herself in traditional dance "language." "I thought the old hoedown will be here forever, so I gave it the name Hoedown Island, and it stuck."[23] The name seemed to summarize how, in Richard Jett's vision, development of the region was dependent on development of the individual. His belief in the importance of fostering each person's talents and of cultivating a spirit of cooperation rather than competition resulted in an important decision in 1977: the elimination of the competitive aspect of the National Mountain Square Dance and Clogging Festival. He said, "You would see these kids crying when they'd get beat . . . so I thought I'm gonna quit that

. . . just have a festival and have them all and I could brag on them, where they'd been and where they'd danced and everything. Otherwise, if you had a contest you couldn't say anything cause you don't want to influence the judges."[24]

Eventually, the single festival became three: the Shindig in the Mountains in May, beginning in 1970; the National Mountain Style Square Dancing and Clogging Festival in June; and the Western Style Square Dance Festival in September, beginning in the mid-1970s. The June festival was the highlight of the season, with dance groups from many states attending year after year, to reconnect with people from other teams they had come to think of as family. One dancer from Maryland told me it was "like coming home," since he had become fast friends with dancers from Powell County and several states through these annual gatherings. The festival continued until 2002, teams performing for each other and for the large audience, and leading dancing for the several hundred in attendance. The teams rolled into the Natural Bridge campground in campers, setting up near each other so that they could socialize before and after dancing. Performances during the day included precision clogging teams, freestyle clogging teams, and individual cloggers. Workshops were offered in clogging, square dancing, and "fun dances" like the novelty dances and mixers enjoyed at Hoedown Island every week.[25] During the nightly dance, the circling, spinning, and weaving in and out of the brightly colored costumes of all the different teams created a spectacle to behold. In 1999 a concluding Grand March for one of the square dances filled nearly every inch of the pavilion. Even when the festival was no longer scheduled, some of the dance teams continued to return to Natural Bridge the last weekend in June, just as they had for almost four decades. Through the members of these teams, the values of individual excellence within the framework of a cooperative, multigenerational community instilled at Hoedown Island rippled outward to their far-flung homes.

A Dream for Dance

Richard Jett's beliefs in the power of dance had roots in his youth. Besides his experiences of dancing in the home as a child, he was a member of a folk dance team at Highland Institute (high school), in Guerrant, Breathitt County, a sister institution to Stuart Robinson school in Blackey, Kentucky, in the network of settlement schools established in the early 1900s. Cooperative recreation was an important element of the progressive education theories that informed the teachers at these schools, and at some schools folk dance was seen as a valuable tool to promote health, citizenship, social interaction, and personal presentation. Highland was one of the schools that valued folk dance, and teachers came to lead English country dancing, morris dancing, and play parties. In the 1930s, the Council of Southern Mountain Workers established the Spring Mountain

Figure 7.3. The Ralph Case Square Dancers at Hoedown Island, 2002. Courtesy of Warren F. Case.

Folk Festival for dance groups from schools in Kentucky and elsewhere in the Appalachian region.[26] Though Jett himself never attended the festival, he danced with the Highland group, learning the value of working together in a team to perfect a dance for performance and experiencing the attendant development of interpersonal skills and self-confidence. His high school education was formative in another way. Among his teachers in 1949–1950 was Pat Napier, a graduate of Highland Institute and of Berea College who had grown up square dancing in Perry County, Kentucky. Napier had compiled a collection of square dance figures from his youth and had taught square dancing to Jett and the other students, along with English country dances, morris dances, Danish dances, and play parties for the Mountain Folk Festival. Jett credited Napier with helping to get him started on the road to dance teaching.[27]

During the Korean War in the early 1950s, Jett was stationed at Fort Belvoir Army base in Fairfax County, Virginia, about thirty miles south of Washington, D.C. During and immediately following the Second World War, square dancing underwent a national revival.[28] Four-couple modern western square dancing had evolved from traditional square dance forms and was a common form of recreation promoted for people in the military. But Jett met Ralph Case, who taught square dancing similar to the kind he remembered from home: a circle of any number of couples breaking into squares of two couples. Ralph Case (b. 1910) was from Western North Carolina, where traditional square dancing had been invigorated by Bascom Lamar Lunsford's Mountain Dance and Folk Festival in Asheville, North Carolina. Lunsford founded his festival in 1928 to present authentic Appalachian music and dance. In his youth, Case had danced on a team that had won awards at the festival. His Upper Marlborough, Maryland, troupe performed at war-bond shows and USO centers, and later at the inaugurations of Presidents Nixon, Carter, and Reagan. He "was known for a clear and energetic style of calling, and he attracted an enthusiastic following." His team danced to live music similar to that Jett had known at home. Among Case's musicians was banjoist Roy Clark, later of Grand Ole Opry fame.[29] As Jett told it, "It wasn't long until the charm of his band's mountain music had me dancing with his groups about four nights a week." This took some resolve, because traveling from Fort Belvoir, Virginia, to Upper Marlboro, Maryland, would have required a trip of forty-five minutes or more each way, each time he attended. When he returned home to Kentucky after his service, he was determined to revitalize, or even to reintroduce, square dancing to his home area, since "no one else seemed interested in leading them anymore." "I started teaching these dances that Ralph Case had taught me and he was teaching me the same dances that we had danced back in those hills down through the years, but evidently it had kinda died out, but I had to go to Washington, D.C., to learn it, brought it back home."[30]

Returning from the army in 1957, Jett became a vocational agriculture teacher at Ezel High School in Morgan County, Kentucky. He must have begun looking for, and trying to create, dancing opportunities from the moment he arrived. He found teachers Cassie Morton and James Prince at Lees Junior College in Jackson, Kentucky, leading folk dance, and he promptly instituted a "folk games (folk dancing) club" at his school. "The kids were wanting something to do and it was a small school, and they didn't have a band, they didn't have a football team—but I started leading some of these dances and boy, the community went wild over that, they just loved it."[31] Older people familiar with this kind of dancing noticed what he was doing and began to join him in calling the dances. Before long, the dance classes grew into weekly events for the community, and crowds grew. On June 2, 1958, Jett and local farmer Fred Mays called what may have been the first Ezel community dance after Jett's return. They seem to have continued their calling partnership for a time. An undated news clip, seemingly from the late 1950s, reported that the annual West Liberty, Morgan County, July Fourth street dance called by Jett and Mays attracted thirty-five hundred to four thousand people and went on until midnight. He apparently began immediately to promote talent of all kinds, establishing the "Ezel Opry" as a community talent show. In August of 1958, just one year after arriving at Ezel, he took a clogging team from the school to the Kentucky State Fair, dubbing them "The Mountain Shufflers," the first of the dozens of creatively named clogging teams and singing groups he would groom. "The Shindiggers" followed soon thereafter.[32] His path as a promoter of local talent was clearly established from the outset, and he pursued it with a passion for the next five decades.

In his days teaching at Ezel High School, Jett already displayed not only his boundless energy for dance and for his community, but also his far-reaching curiosity. He began his collection of dance manuals, including Frank Smith's and Patrick Napier's recently published works on Appalachian dance, Henry Ford's book on American set dance, books on modern western square dancing, and a whole series of booklets published by the Cooperative Recreation Service. He also began adding dances to a small black binder, which, within a few decades, was stuffed with directions to dances of all sorts. His curiosity did not stop at learning new dances, however. He evidently wrote to someone at the Encyclopedia Britannica for information on square dance history, because in 1960 he received from them several typewritten pages of material from S. Foster Damon's 1952 presentation to the Antiquarian Society. Damon's book, still respected, was published in 1957, but it was perhaps not available to Jett at the time of his letter to the Britannica.[33] Given his interest, energy, and promotional skills, leading the dances at Natural Bridge was an obvious next step in expanding the popularity and influence of local dance traditions. He took over the Natural Bridge dances just five years after returning to his home area, and in 1963 he hosted ten weekend nights. By 1984, his programs took place on fifty-seven nights.

Once Jett began leading the dance evenings at Natural Bridge, he quickly looked for ways to attract attention to the programs and to promote the talents of those who participated. He established the National Mountain-Style Square Dance and Clogging Contest in 1967 and developed clogging teams associated with Natural Bridge. Charlie Rogers, who danced regularly at Hoedown Island, was on the Kentucky Mountain Hoedowners, one of Jett's teams that began that year. It included four other members of Charlie's family, among them his brother Darrell, creator of the Hoedown Island Cloggers' signature dance. Teams from outside the immediate area had begun coming to Jett's dances by the second year, and the contest drew many more. The Pisgah View Ranch Dancers from Candler, North Carolina, were the first to come, followed in the ensuing years by groups from Boone and Canton, North Carolina, from every state surrounding Kentucky, and from the East Coast and the Midwest. Well-known performers were attracted to the contest. The wife of bluegrass musician Lester Flatt was among those who competed in the individual clogging competition in 1970, placing third.[34]

Hoedown Island and the many clogging teams and singing groups born there rode the wave of the national folk revival and the interest it engendered in the music and dance of the central Appalachian region. Photos from Hoedown Island during this period are striking for the number of young people, teenagers and young adults, enthusiastically dancing, singing, and playing in their own string bands. Jett's goal of promoting the region and its talents intersected perfectly with the national interest in Appalachian culture. In the early 1970s, Jett formed his youngest team yet, composed of elementary-aged children, and named them "Ralph's Ramblers" for the manager of the park's lodge. Hoedown

Island's reputation spread. In 1973, the Kentucky Mountain Hoedowners performed at the National Folk Festival, danced with the Tom T. Hall Show in Gatlinburg, and appeared twice on the Grand Ole Opry, having their photo taken with Grandpa Jones in 1976. They were National Champions in 1973 and 1974, and World Champions in 1972, 1973, and 1974. Charlie Rogers himself won national and state freestyle championships. "I've lived and breathed clogging, you know. I grew up on it, and my whole family are musicians and singers, and so it was kind of bred in me, more or less, the dance and singing."[35] Rogers was one of perhaps hundreds of dancers aged 6 to 60 who pointed with pride to their experience on one of Jett's teams. Their skill, in turn, demonstrated the talents of the people of the region to residents and visitors alike, as well as nationally, through the festivals, television shows, and competitions. Richard Jett's goal was always individual achievement and community enhancement through local tradition and values, and he took advantage of every opportunity to promote both individual and community.

Hoedown Island flourished during the 1960s, 1970s, and 1980s, and Richard Jett expanded his promotional efforts in several directions. He brought well-known performers like the Osborne Brothers to Natural Bridge, drawing increased attendance. He graduated from a western square dance course in Lexington, Kentucky, in 1975, and around that time he established a western square dance festival at Hoedown Island. His creativity took a different turn in establishing "Richard Jett Tours and Mountain Music Productions." As a school principal, he dealt with tour bus companies for various teams and class excursions. After a number of years, as he said, "I thought, I can do this" in order to design tours tailored specifically for people from his area. A 1984 press release that he must have sent outside the region demonstrated how he combined his promotional activities. That year, he scheduled bus tours to Nashville, Daytona Beach, New Orleans, and Williamsburg, Virginia. To the press release, he attached a list of the dates he would be in each town and offered his services as caller. "Richard Jett, tour broker and mountain style square dance caller from the Eastern Kentucky hill country, will be in the areas listed below and will be happy to conduct an old-fashioned Kentucky mountain square dance frolic for clog clubs." He brought Kentuckians and Kentucky culture to cities outside the region and endeavored to entice new visitors to what he had begun calling "Kentucky's Clog Dance Capital."[36]

He expanded his promotion of local talent as organizer of the clogging presentations at the Renfro Valley Barn Dance in Rockcastle County, Kentucky. The Barn Dance had been established in 1939 by Rockcastle native John Lair, formerly of the WLS National Barn Dance. In the 1950s, the broadcasts ceased, but the live shows continue to the present, featuring big-name country artists and offering exposure to local artists.[37] In scheduling clogging and singing groups there and at festivals and other events, Jett simultaneously promoted local culture and provided an outlet for some of his groups. He was proud of each of his dancers and singers, and especially proud when they went on to contribute to their communities. His tireless efforts did not go unnoticed, and in 1982 he was honored at Hoedown Island in a special ceremony involving Professor Carl Clark, square dance leaders Ralph and Frances Case, dancers Darrell Rogers and Jimmy Loveless, and Professor Steve Smith, whom Jett dubbed a "top clogging instructor" from Georgetown, Kentucky.

A 1987 press release claimed that nearly one thousand dancers attended on Saturday evenings, and that sixty different groups had performed the previous year, including some from Madison, Wisconsin; Bulls Gap, Tennessee; Ocala, Florida; Boone, North Carolina; and Upper Marlborough, Maryland. The following year eighteen teams had registered for the twenty-second annual National Mountain Square Dance and Clogging Festival.[38] Lewis Arnett and others remembered the 1980s as a special time at Hoedown Island. According to Arnett, there were "more regulars then, more the kind of regular neighborhood people. Like going to a family reunion, really. Everybody hugged you. You'd spend 30 minutes hugging people as they'd go."[39]

Hoedown Island's fame endured through the 1990s and beyond, and Jett continued to inspire youngsters and to organize teams. On the Powell County radio station throughout the 1990s and for a few years longer, I regularly heard announcements for the Richard Jett Singers or the Hoedown Island Cloggers appearing at Meadowgreen Park Music Hall in Clay City or at one of the many annual festivals in several counties. The informal group known as the Hoedown Island Cloggers performed each Saturday night at Natural Bridge. As leader Lewis Arnett said, "We dance here, and if Richard wants us to, we dance with him wherever he wants us to." Community festivals and special occasions were usual venues, but in 2000 and 2001 they were televised on the Kentucky Educational Television program, "In Performance at the Governor's Mansion," sharing the bill with the Lexington Singers and the River City Drum Corps, a Louisville, Kentucky, youth steel drum group. Rather than wearing commercially produced costumes, the group represented a home-based tradition. The men wore blue shirts and jeans and the women wore simple short white skirts and blue tops. All wore white clogging shoes.[40]

Continuing a Legacy

In 1999, Richard Jett, then sixty-six years old, spoke about the future of Hoedown Island as he considered the possibility of retiring. He had thought about various successors, hoping for someone who would keep the dance evenings fun for everyone and who would maintain the tradition of festivals rather than competitions. He compared his festival with Bascom Lamar Lunsford's Mountain Dance and Folk Festival in Asheville, North Carolina, noting the longevity of that festival, begun in 1928. Jett said, "Mine is the second longest. Who knows, it may have a ninety-ninth or one-hundredth edition one of these days."[41] In contemplating the future of Hoedown Island, dancers said that the place is unusual, in that not many like it exist for this kind of dancing. Several said they were glad that I was documenting the activities. "This is a good thing that you're doing. Things like this need to be remembered." Charlie Rogers said, "The old traditional mountain clog is something I would like to see continue on some way, somehow." I. D. Ball wished Jett would offer a callers' workshop for young people, fearing that otherwise the skill would be lost.

When asked about the prospect of Richard Jett's eventual retirement, Lewis Arnett shook his head. "Honey, I don't know. It's a sad time to think about." Other dancers agreed. "No, you wouldn't want to think about it. He's such a unique man." Arnett responded, "There's not but one Richard Jett, and that's him. I've got the highest respect for the man."[42] Charlie Rogers expressed gratitude. "Richard Jett has done so much for us here in these mountains, for us cloggers, dancers, singers." In his remembrance of Jett in 2006, clogger Jeffrey Driggs summarized the feelings of many: "You see, the key to Richard Jett's wonderful success in clogging and in life was not the great things that he did (and he certainly did many) but the fact that none of his efforts were done for his own edification. Everything Richard did was for the dancers and singers he admired and the audiences he adored sharing them with. He gave back to the schools that he was so dedicated to and gave back to the community that he was a part of, because he truly had a heart for others."[43] The singing group he founded in 1990, the Appalachian Troubadours, now with some new members, still performs at festivals, state parks, health care centers, banquets, and benefits. They feel themselves part of his legacy, inviting guest performers via their website: "In keeping with Richard Jett's traditions, [we] are always looking for opportunities to promote talent." His dream not only came to fruition, but it lives into the future.

Richard Jett saw himself paralleling the efforts of Bascom Lamar Lunsford in maintaining and presenting what is special to Appalachian culture. He often referred to him and his work, and Jett shared his love for mountain culture. Jett resembled Lunsford in his beliefs, background, and skills. Jett, like Lunsford, believed "that there was a connection between the cultural riches of the Appalachian region and 'the fine honor of our people.'" Also like Lunsford his effectiveness was enhanced by his "doubleness of vision." He was a local resident who had traveled and gained master's degrees in vocational agriculture and educational administration, and he could see Powell, Wolfe, Lee, and other nearby counties as part of the state and national economy. Jett and Lunsford were both talented promoters, and each saw his efforts to promote local musicians and dancers as his "work as a citizen." Each became a "symbol of mountain culture" for "the audience within and beyond the mountains."[44] As Richard Jett saw it, his work existed in a lineage from Lunsford through Case to himself, and he maintained that connection in living terms. Not only had he danced with Case in the 1950s, but Case regularly brought his team to Jett's National Mountain-Style Square Dance Festival. The team seemed to be the highlight of the festival, advertised on fliers and leading the huge square dances during the evening dances. In 1999, Case's son Warren was the leader of the group, and he spoke proudly of his father's team having won competitions at Lunsford's Mountain Dance and Folk Festival. He said that his father drew his inspiration from Sam Queen, the legendary leader of the Haywood County, North Carolina, Soco Gap Dance Team, winners of Lunsford's first festival in 1928 and many thereafter. They even performed for Franklin Roosevelt and for the Queen of England.[45] Both Jett and Case projected a sense of mission, a sense of continuing a legacy that was begun in 1928.

Though Jett declared that the dances Case taught were "the same" as the ones he had learned growing up, in fact there were likely differences, since Case's dances had come originally from North Carolina, and he had lived for some time in the rapidly developing Washington, D.C., area. Case matured as a dancer in the framework of Lunsford's Mountain Dance and Folk Festival. The festival had contributed to changes in the dancing through the effect of the competition, though Lunsford's intent was to celebrate local culture as it was. Both American Studies scholar David Whisnant and dance ethnologist Gail Matthews deNatale have proven that the style of the dancing and the style of presentation changed at least in part as a result of the festival. Prior to 1928, square dances for any number of couples were purely social, invitational events in the home. For the first festival groups of family members and neighbors gathered a few times to practice, but there were no actual teams. Square dancing was done with a smooth step in some communities and with a clogging step in others. According to Whisnant's interviews, "they got to playing music faster" as a result of the festival, and this was accompanied by a "heightened sense of theatricality." Within a few years, all square dance teams practiced for months for the festival. They were separated into distinct classifications as "smooth dancers" and "clogging teams."

Whisnant compared photos of the 1930 and the 1933 teams from Candler, North Carolina. The men on the earlier team wore suits and ties and the women wore dresses of different styles and colors, and for the later team, men all wore white, open-collared shirts and the women all wore light-colored dresses of a more formal cut. Matthews learned that taps were added to shoes when music became louder due to amplification, and that footwork became faster to maximize the effect of the taps. Ralph Case may have been on an early team that experienced these changes. By the 1950s, steps were more complex and costumes were typically jeans, cowboy shirts, and hankies for men and crinolined gingham dresses for women—the style of costume still worn by the Ralph Case Dancers in 2002.[46] The costuming and style differed, but Jett recognized the structure and many of the figures as being similar to those he remembered from his youth in Breathitt County. Banjoist Lee Sexton played for dancing at Hoedown Island in the days when Jett used live music for the dances. He saw some contrasts between the dancing in Letcher County, his home, and what he saw at Natural Bridge. "They do the hoedown (footwork) as a square dance down there at Natural Bridge. . . . Way back they used to move their feet during square dances around [the community of] Ulvah [Kentucky]," but no longer. He was surprised to see, in the 1960s, the Boone, North Carolina, team called "The Daniel Boone Dancers" performing with "toe plates and heel irons." Sexton also described Jett's calling as "modern square dances" as opposed to the "old style" from Letcher County—perhaps they were faster paced or more complex than those he knew.[47] Still, to Richard Jett, though he himself was influenced by mid-twentieth-century American culture in his teaching, the essence of the dance was the same as the dancing with which he had grown up. The values and aesthetics of Eastern Kentucky, reawakened by his experience with Ralph Case, had set him on his mission.

It is important to make the point that Richard Jett did not indulge in nostalgia for the old days. He attempted to distill the best of traditional culture and to bring it into the present to influence the future in a positive way. During the first years of his directorship of dancing at Natural Bridge, his evenings were almost exclusively square dancing and clogging to live music, provided by Letcher County banjoist Lee Sexton, Madison County fiddler Lewis Lamb, and others.[48] Over the years, he adjusted the events to include other kinds of dances and shifted to recorded music so that he could better control the flow of the evening. His 1971 book of dance instructions gave a glimpse of the ways he began to expand the repertoire of his dance evenings. It included sections on "Kentucky Running Set and Big Set Figures," "Appalachian Mountain Dances," and "Easy Western Square Dances" with singing calls, as well as a section of "Miscellaneous Dances." Included in this last are line dances like "Blame It On the Bossa Nova," "Settin' the Woods on Fire" (a line dance with clogging steps), and specialty dances like the "Salty Dog Rag," in which couples do a set sequence of steps as they travel around a circle. Many of the dances described in his book remain popular at Hoedown Island today. Among the "Appalachian Mountain Dances" are old time square dance figures as well as dances from the folk dance recreation movement like Kentucky Circle (mixer), Nine Pin Reel, and the Virginia Reel.[49] The book does not happen to include the folk dance recreation Circle Waltz mixer that Jett always called to the old Eddy Arnold recording of "Cattle Call."

He continued to expand the repertoire more and more, welcoming dances introduced by participants, such as the "Cha-cha Slide." His aim was to include something for everybody, in order to keep the crowds coming back to experience the qualities of local culture valued in the Hoedown Island evenings and to participate in the local traditions spotlighted among the variety of fun dances. His strategy worked. The dance floor was never empty, and news articles reported regular crowds of up to eight hundred from toddlers through retirement age. Richard Jett attributed the success of the program to "the drawing power of friendship."[50]

The Hoedown Island Cloggers

The climax of the evening was the performance by the Hoedown Island Cloggers, the quintessential statement of Hoedown Island ideals, and of Richard Jett's vision for community. Around 9:00 each Saturday evening, Leader Lewis Arnett quietly gathered the dancers for the night's performance: usually four to six couples, but sometimes as many as eight, who represented a range of ages, and some of whom were visitors. He would catch Jett's eye and gesture to the back of the performing area, where he took the group to run through the figures of the dance. When they were ready, Jett noticed their return to the bleachers near the stage and soon announced their performance, saying they do "the real old-style clog dance." All others took their seats, riveting their attention on the dancers.

To the tune "Arkansas Traveler" they performed a dance that was set in the 1970s by Darrell Rogers of the Kentucky Mountain Hoedowners and that has choreographic similarities to North Carolina team clogging routines. Lewis learned it from Darrell Rogers and said that he tried to preserve it unchanged. Though he had tried other tunes, he believed "Arkansas Traveler" allowed for different styles of footwork. The dance involved multiple rearrangements of the group in stars, figure eights, and lines, with the performers doing their own

Figure 7.4. The Hoedown Island Cloggers, "In Performance at the Governor's Mansion," 2000. Lewis Arnett and Jane Bolen are front left. Courtesy of Berea College Southern Appalachian Archives.

freestyle footwork throughout the dance. The many different configurations seemed to represent the variety and stability of the group, and perhaps of the ideal community.

As the music began, the couples, lined up on the pavilion to the right of the stage, started their own energetic clogging steps, and never paused until the end of the dance. Arnett made an almost ceremonial entrance from the rear of the line by dancing under arches created by the raised arms of the other couples, leading his partner, Jane Bolen, who took the hand of the next man, pulling the whole group through in a line. Each individual was linked to the community, and the progress of one resulted in the progress of all. They formed a circle, a single cohesive group in which each person could see and acknowledge everyone else. The women formed a star in the center of the circle while the men kept their freestyle footwork going in place on the periphery, and then the men had a turn, each group being the center of attention for a moment. The circle re-formed, and the dancers greeted each other with a grand right and left. Returning to their partners, the men joined right hands in the center and traveled clockwise around the circle, and then reversed direction to join left hands, drawing their partners to them by wrapping right arms around their waists, traveling counterclockwise around the circle. The couples wheeled around so that the women joined hands in the center, still connected to their partners. All the couples were connected, first through the men and then through the women. In the figure-eight pattern that followed, the men and women snaked into separate circles revolving side by side in opposite directions, the men counterclockwise and the women clockwise. For one full revolution, they stayed in their own realms, each giving the partner a "high-five" hand slap when passing close to him or her. In a move that has the visual effect of a magic trick, the men and women filtered into each other's circles until they had reversed positions. The move required simultaneous awareness of space and time and of oneself and of the others in the group in order to accomplish the exchange without the slightest hesitation. Once again forming the circle, partners joined for an energetic swing.

The climax of the dance has sometimes been called "rise and shine." The circle split into two lines of couples facing each other, perpendicular to the stage, and watched appreciatively as each couple danced down the center with their own fancy footwork. Taking the microphone from Richard Jett, Lewis Arnett announced the names of each couple as they stepped into the open space at the top of the set near the stage and danced toward the bottom. With the exception of Arnett and Bolen, who usually danced last, couples rarely attempted to synchronize their steps. This was a moment for personal display. Each couple received a hearty round of applause as they completed their performance. Once every couple had had a turn, the group circled up again and promenaded in a line of couples toward the end of the pavilion farthest from the stage. Arnett and Bolen turned, raising their joined hands to form an arch over the oncoming dancers, followed successively by each couple. Reaching the end of the line, they turned and bowed under the other dancers. The line of couples folded back and forth over and under the other dancers twice. It appeared as if they honored each couple, giving them an archway through which to process. Arnett signaled the conclusion by continuing to promenade toward the far end of the pavilion. There was no bow or punctuated closure, as if to indicate that they had been dancing for themselves and their own enjoyment, and that our presence as an audience was incidental to their dancing. It seemed to say that the dance could go on forever, and so would the community it represented.

The dance, like the community created at Hoedown Island, celebrated individual achievement, stable partnerships, and community collaboration. Soon after the performance of the Hoedown Island Cloggers, some audience members began to pack up their things, bidding farewell to friends and acquaintances, and stopping to have conversations along the way. Though other groups performed earlier in the evening, the Hoedown Island Cloggers were the main attraction, and almost everyone made a point of staying to watch their performance. After they performed, it seemed, people felt they could leave the pavilion, satisfied with the completion of the evening's celebration.

As I talked with the group right after they performed one night in 2002, someone brought up the fear of making mistakes. Lewis Arnett referred to a youngster from another team, whom he had invited to dance with them on that night. "That little girl tonight said 'I messed up,' and I asked her, 'Did you have fun?' She said, 'Yeah,' I said, 'Don't worry about it. That's all that matters. It don't hurt nobody.'" On another occasion, Charlie Rogers said, "Even us guys who've done it so many years, you'd think we never goof up, but you goof up sometimes. And you laugh about it and have a good time about it."[51] It was not the case that there were no norms or standards in this dancing. "Messing up" or making mistakes was possible. But what was important was how the dancer dealt with it: just letting it go and enjoying the rest of the dance with friends.

Perpetuating Customs

The Hoedown Island Cloggers' demonstration embodied the values contained in the entire event. They coupled the pursuit of excellence in dancing with the acceptance of mistakes. They combined performance and participation. That is, as they performed for the audience, they appeared to be dancing simply for their own enjoyment. They participated in the entire evening's dancing and in no way stood out until their special moment arrived. But when it did, they put themselves forward, seeming to say, "This is what we do here!" By displaying

Figure 7.5. Richard Jett receiving the 2005 Sarah Gertrude Knott Award, in recognition of lifetime achievement and excellence in the traditional arts, from the Kentucky Folklife Program. Courtesy of the Kentucky Folklife Program Archives, Western Kentucky University.

their talents, they invited others to do the same. Their dance demonstrated the regional values Richard Jett held dear. Kaleidoscopically shifting formations required cooperation and awareness of the others in the group, while at the same time each individual expressed himself or herself with rhythmic footwork. During "rise and shine," each pair had a moment to show off their skill under the watchful gaze of their fellow dancers and the audience. People selected to dance ranged in age from early teens to retirement years, representing the traditional multigenerational community.

Richard Jett understood the power of dance to transform individuals, to cohere groups, and to communicate ideals. He used the wide variety of dances to attract people and to keep them coming back, in order that they might experience the traditional dances and their associated values. On summer weekends, Jett compressed a whole constellation of beliefs and values into a series of experiences in a single night, and he repeated this over and over again for decades. It couldn't have happened without him, but it also couldn't have happened without the many regular participants who contributed their particular energy and talents to make each evening a success so that the dance kept going year after year. In 1971, Jett stated the purpose of his book, which seemed to reflect the purpose of the Hoedown Island evenings: "To help preserve and perpetuate the square dancing customs and traditions of yesteryear and to permit today's generation to learn and enjoy some of the dances and games." He transformed people who came to Hoedown Island, and perhaps the region, through the medium of "the mountain dancing with its atmosphere of friendliness, excitement, and gaiety."[52]

Richard Jett passed away in September 2006. His dedication was so great that, "even as he was stricken during the start of his dance program, [at Hoedown Island] his concern was that someone would keep playing the music," as Jeffrey

Driggs recalled.[53] The very next night, protégés Jane Bolen and Lewis Arnett directed the dance in his stead, using the same repertoire and format. In the ensuing years, clogging line dances have come to predominate, but still an old-time square dance is called each evening, as are some mixers, the Virginia Reel, Cotton-Eyed Joe and the Hokey-Pokey. Lewis Arnett retired the Hoedown Island Cloggers dance in 2009 due to his health, and he passed away in the spring of 2010. Jane Bolen continues in her devotion to Richard Jett's commitment that, on every Friday and Saturday night during the summer, "A Good Time Will Be Had By All."[54]

8. The Carcassonne Square Dance

A True Revival

High on a mountaintop in Letcher County, Kentucky, individuals and families stroll into the small, white school building on Square Dance Road, greeted by conversation and the sound of banjos and fiddles playing an old time tune. Dale Johnson and Jon Henrikson have a genial hello for each person at the door, while Beverley Caudill Johnson and Loretta Fugate Henrikson and her sister Von Hill prepare hot dogs and chili in the kitchen. The atmosphere is warm and friendly, almost like a welcoming family's home. Indeed, the long history of this dance began in the home of Clifton and Ruby Caudill in the 1930s, when they held a square dance to celebrate their new log house, built with the help of their neighbors.

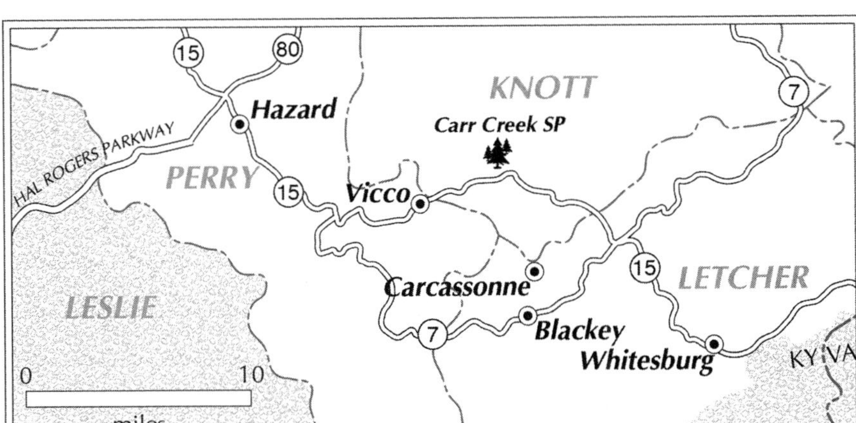

Map 7. Area surrounding Carcassonne, Kentucky. Cartography by Dick Gilbreath, Director, Gyula Pauer Center for Cartography and GIS, University of Kentucky.

In October 2011 the dance had a distinctly youthful feel, with driving old time music provided by teenagers who studied traditional music at Cowan Creek Mountain Music School, their friends joining in the dances called by Randy Wilson. The reputation of the Carcassonne square dance extends far and wide. Visitors come from many states and even other countries. Mission work groups regularly attend the dance and are quickly drawn into the dancing. Still, this is a community event, and much more than a dance. It frames an overall opportunity to visit, to exchange news, and to discuss politics. Young children often join in the dancing and otherwise play together in the audience area or on the playground outside. The dance of 2011 maintained features of the dance of a decade earlier and incorporated new elements as well. In 1999 most in attendance were middle aged or older, though many brought their families. Lee Sexton's band played the music, and Charlie Whitaker called the dances, while Clifton and Ruby Caudill greeted everyone warmly at the door.

The Carcassonne square dance has not existed in unbroken continuity since 1934, having been interrupted by World War II and urban migration, but it reveals a continuity of spirit, maintained by key committed individuals, always welcoming and providing a homey atmosphere. The history of the dance is defined by a fruitful partnership between local culture and "outside" involvement. Though seemingly remote, the Carcassonne community has intentionally welcomed and sometimes sought outside participation within the framework of local culture. They have cultivated awareness of and a relationship with the wider world of thought and action. Important to the social fabric are regular gatherings to exchange news and ideas and to plan for the well-being of the community. Such socializing forms the context for the dance, as it did for the school and its activities. Community leaders and dance organizers are dedicated and determined to insure the future of the dance and, thereby, the community. The Carcassonne square dance at the turn of the twenty-first century reflected the century-old history of square dancing in Letcher County, as well as its own four-decade history, and it prepared the way for its own 2010 renewal. To study

Figure 8.1. The Carcassonne square dance, 2009. Caller Charlie Whitaker is in the center. Randy Wilson, back right, brimmed hat, plays music for the dance. Photo by Suzanne W. Madden, courtesy of Joyce Whitaker.

the dance at Carcassonne and the surrounding area is to trace the continuous evolution of a tradition.

The dance in its current incarnation began spontaneously in 1967, soon after the establishment of the Carcassonne Community Center, through joint efforts of community members and the Appalachian Volunteers and VISTA workers. This was neither the first nor the last time that influences from beyond the community had had an influence on dancing in this apparently secluded area. Formerly the center was the Carcassonne School, a boarding school founded by Clifton Caudill's father, Hendricks D. Caudill. Philanthropists from the North supported the school from its founding in 1924, introducing classroom music and bringing radios. Instructors taught folk dancing at a school in nearby Blackey, Kentucky, in the 1940s and 1950s, taking student groups to the Mountain Folk Festival at Berea College. Some of those same students became teachers in Carcassonne and surrounding communities, sharing the dances and songs they had learned. Folklorists like Alan Lomax, John Jacob Niles, John Cohen, Anne Romaine, and Mike Seeger visited Letcher and neighboring counties, not only documenting local traditions but also introducing others.[1] The people who dance at Carcassonne have been involved in an outdoor drama, have been featured in films, and have demonstrated square dancing at the Kentucky Folklife Festival and at the Festival of American Folklife. The "outside" attention has helped to promote the continuity of the dance without disrupting its role as a community event. At the opening of the Carcassonne School in the 1920s, a local woman was quoted as saying, "In a few years' time, learning will be all wove into the pattern us mountain folks lives by. But the old time ways will keep on making the main figure of the pattern."[2] In some ways the dance provides a pattern into which all else is woven. Inspired by the commitment of the founders and dedicated volunteers, many who have experienced the dance mirror their determination to keep it going in the face of social and economic odds. I have danced at Carcassonne whenever I could since 1998, and I enjoy talking with dancers, musicians, and organizers. I always wish I lived closer so that I could attend more often. Clifton Caudill's books about the area have been invaluable in presenting a picture of life in the area throughout the twentieth century and the context in which the Carcassonne dance takes place, as have dancer and dance historian Peter Rogers's 1975 interviews with area square dance callers, and folklorist Dale Johnson's 1998 interviews with Ruby and Clifton Caudill.

Carcassonne School

Carcassonne School was founded in 1923 for children in the area surrounding the community and post office of Gander. H. D. Caudill's vision from the start included national and global connections with the local community. He had read a poem about the city of Carcassonne in France, with a picture of a village on a mountaintop plateau surrounded by cliffs. He felt that his home area had a similar appearance, so he named the school after the French town. He took advantage of the growing coal industry by salvaging lumber to build the school as local people cleared timber to make way for electric lines to power coal mines. Though the electricity did not serve the school or homes until later, a teacher brought a gas-powered generator in 1925, providing lights for nighttime study hall for boarding students and amazing pupils and community members by showing movies. In planning and developing the school, Caudill sought the help of Alice Lloyd, the New England philanthropist and educator who had founded a college, which now bears her name, on Caney Creek, in Knott County, Kentucky. Carcassonne School's first teachers came from Caney College. Lloyd advised the school's founders and attracted donors to help support it since it was not supported by a religious denomination. Besides making direct financial contributions, people in big cities like Philadelphia, New York, Detroit, and Boston donated clothing items for the Carcassonne rag sale. Local people bought them for pennies, getting clothes for themselves and contributing financially to the school.[3] Caudill even made use of the Works Progress Administration, whose workers completed the last bit of road to the school and built a wall for the basketball court. Ideally located at the headwaters of several creeks, including Elk, Bull, Montgomery, and Defeated, the school allowed an additional few hundred day students to walk up the creeks during the school year. Students worked two hours a day at the school and paid $7.50 a month for room and board, many bringing home-grown produce to barter for the fee. Carcassonne opened as both a high school and an elementary school in 1924. At its peak the school had twenty buildings, including dormitories for eighty students, a gymnasium, a library, and a dining hall. In a 1937 article for the *Mountain Eagle* newspaper in Whitesburg, Kentucky, founder H. D. Caudill described the school:

> The modern white school is in shining contrast to the rustic houses which make up the [Gander] community center. Sprawling over the hillside and connected with a pattern of fragrant mossy paths, are logged and boarded buildings, a church, a community kitchen, a half-dozen odd cabins, a workshop and a comfortable two-story frame with spreading porches housing the post office and store.[4]

The school produced "many lawyers, doctors, politicians, and ministers," according to Clifton Caudill. The high school closed in 1948, "a victim of consolidation," and the elementary school continued in various forms until 1974.[5]

Music had a place in the school from its beginning, both directly and indirectly. Musicians were among those who built the school, including Dow Hamilton, a "master banjo player and dancer" who always won first prize at fairs and other programs held at the school. Classroom music and traditional music met at the school. The staff always included music teachers like Dorothy

Chandler and her mother from Detroit, who likely taught singing and music appreciation according to the current practice supported by the Music Educators National Conference,[6] and music and dance took place informally outside of class as well. Clifton Caudill remembered that students would "assemble at about dusk dark on Saturday [at one of the buildings] and clap our hands as Kelly Combs picked his five string banjo and sang 'Ida Red, Ida Blue, I'm plumb fool about Ida too,' all the while patting his bare feet on the rough puncheon floor." Though dance was not taught at the school, square dances and dance contests were part of the fairs and other school fundraisers like pie suppers. Folklorist, musician, and composer John Jacob Niles was among the guests who stayed at the school's Friendship Lodge, as did benefactors and a University of Kentucky president. According to H. D. Caudill, Niles was "just Johnny to the mountain folk [and had] endeared himself to these people." Other regional traditions were valued at the school as well. Among the early teachers was Marie Campbell, who collected "European" and local tales from storytellers around Carcassonne and Letcher and Knott Counties, publishing several volumes.[7]

Like those at other settlement schools, Carcassonne teachers hoped to introduce students to modern ways and to broaden their understanding. Not long after the school's opening, one teacher brought a battery-operated radio. According to Caudill, "we listened and came to realize that there was a larger world and other people beyond our hills . . . and because of Carcassonne we were to have the opportunity to exchange ideas and culture." In 1933, the University of Kentucky organized twenty-six radio listening centers at various locations in order to make educational broadcasts available to rural communities. A National Youth Administration supervisor attended each of the listening sessions to answer questions or to send them to the University of Kentucky for replies. Gander was one of those sites, and Corsia Whitaker, a young local woman, was the supervisor there and at several other communities. Caudill believed that "the community radio has been the germ for community organization. In each group of listeners is found a nucleus of progress." More than three hundred area residents attended a conference held at Carcassonne School in 1937 to provide feedback to the university regarding the content and success of the project. The many tiny schools throughout the mountains served as hubs for their communities, and Carcassonne intentionally developed that role by hosting such conferences and community fairs and by housing the local post office. According to an article by H. D. Caudill in the *Mountain Eagle*, people who participated in the listening groups reported liking the news, weather, and agricultural broadcasts best, and chose "old mountain ballads and symphonies" over jazz music. He described a special series of music prepared by John Jacob Niles "designed to impress the mountain people with the purity and value of their culture" and to "give them added joy in their Gregorian [*sic*] songs which had been handed down to them as their natural heritage."[8] The Radio Project conveyed particular images of local culture, encouraged a certain kind of progress, and allowed for discussion of new ideas. Residents of Carcassonne seem to have taken from these experiences what was meaningful to them, placing it in the context of their existing culture. They valued both the focused attention of folklorists like Niles and the opportunity to exchange ideas with those from elsewhere. This pattern continues to the present and helped to shape the Carcassonne dance.

Farms and Coal Mines

The Caudill family is deeply embedded in their community and the surrounding area, having arrived from Virginia in the late 1790s as a result of a Revolutionary War era land grant. By the time Clifton Caudill published his books of local history in the 1990s, the sixth generation lived on the two-hundred-acre Caudill farm in Letcher County. Born in 1913, Caudill remembered walking to school on wooded mountain paths, when farming was the primary source of income. As coal mining increased in the area, his family sold melons at the coal camps nearby, including Blackey, Ulvah, and Cornettsville.[9]

In 1912, the first trains arrived in Hazard, Kentucky, eighteen miles from Carcassonne, and in Blackey, Kentucky, just five miles from Carcassonne. Once coal mining began in earnest, "short dog" lines ran up many hollows in the area to reach the coal mines. Passenger trains ran certain schedules on these lines, with an engine and two cars carrying workers to the various mines and rural residents to the towns. From 1913 to 1929, surrounded by seven coal camps, Blackey was a booming coal town, with a mayor, a bank, "auto dealerships, two hotels—one for whites, one for 'colored' guests—four restaurants, and a theater." Because of the trains, people in outlying areas had access to all of these modern experiences. Floods and fires in 1927 and 1928, followed by the Great Depression, brought an end to Blackey's prosperity, though other coal camps continued operation into the 1930s. The C. B. Caudill Store remained a hub of activity for the area after Blackey's decline. In 1966, Joe and Gaynell Caudill Begley took over the store from Gaynell's parents. It closed as a store in 1997 after sixty-four years of operation and is maintained as a cultural center and museum of local history.[10]

Clifton and Ruby Caudill believed that during the Depression, people in their area had much more food on average than anywhere in the whole country because everyone cultivated their own food, including fruits and vegetables, corn, hogs, chickens, and cows, even raising sheep for wool to make clothing. Later in the twentieth century, deep mining was replaced by strip mining and then mountaintop removal, dramatically changing the landscape. Residents tell stories about homes cracked by blasting and wells destroyed. In 1996, Clifton

Caudill wrote poetically about the damage, but also expressed his concern for the needs of local people, placing them in the dual contexts of national advances and local tradition.

> The Buzzard Hollow as we knew it no longer exists. The bulldozers, graders, trucks, drills, and thousands of pounds of explosives have come and gone, taking the coal and leaving the timber, water, flowers, wildlife and even the earth in total destruction. . . . These destructive forces are creeping ever nearer to us here on Bull Creek. We hear the great machines of destruction growl and rumble as they disembowel the earth as God created it. The house, pots and pans therein shake and rattle as the explosives rip apart even more of our beautiful mountains. What can be done? . . . Admittedly we need the coal, the jobs and wages, but at what price? It seems that a nation that can put a man on the moon . . . could come up with some substitute for coal and leave the land as god intended—for our enjoyment and to produce food for our survival.[11]

He thought broadly about his community and treasured his homeplace but understood people's need to earn a livelihood. The same kind of thinking informed his approach to the Carcassonne square dance.

Square Dancing in Letcher County

Square dancing has been a longstanding passion for residents of Letcher County since they first experienced it in the 1890s. In 1975, Peter Rogers interviewed square dance callers in Eastern Kentucky, providing a sketch of its evolution over a period of three-quarters of a century or more.[12] According to Hiram Brashear (b. 1872), square dancing was a novelty introduced in Letcher County when he was a young man. Prior to that time, he said, people had "shindigs and hoedowns." "They'd go around the ring, give one another a hand [perhaps grand right and left], and when you meet your partner [the couples] danced. Then they'd march through and go back." He said they had a "song they'd sing while they was swinging around and also have someone making music." He or his sister often held shindigs in their homes. As in Northeast Tennessee, the earlier dances seem to have been simpler, for any number of couples in a circle, and they sometimes involved singing, like play parties. The first four-couple square dance Brashear remembered took place in about 1890, introduced by Mart Ackman from Breathitt County, Kentucky, who was followed soon thereafter by a man named Kip Benton, a timber company employee from Virginia. Veldon and A. O. Fields likewise identified Virginia as the source of square dancing, saying that their great-grandparents migrated from that state in the late 1800s, bringing it with them. According to Brashear, as more people came in with the companies, they also taught people to square dance. Soon the dance had become so popular that there were several local callers. Brashear held a square dance and hoedown at his place to send his son off to World War I, and he remembered frequent square dances in his area. He recalled there being many more calls for square dance figures in his day than in 1975. During his lifetime, he square danced not only in his hometown of Viper but also in other communities like Cornettsville and Big Branch. By the turn of the twentieth century, square dancing seems to have supplanted the earlier, simpler dances in some communities. Caller Grover Sizemore (b. 1894), almost a generation younger than Brashear, knew only of square dancing, rather than any other form of dance. As a boy, he would dance all night in four couple sets to a banjo or fiddle.[13]

Clifton Caudill began square dancing as a teenager in the 1920s in a neighbor's home. His wife Ruby danced as a girl in her home in a community down Bull Creek, three miles away. She said they "worked hard all week and [on the weekend] have a play [a party] and run sets." She described workings like all-day corn hoeings or grubbings, with women quilting and preparing food, followed by dances. Music was provided by two or three people on banjo, and "lots of people could call" square dances. For each dance, one couple would visit each of the other couples all the way around the ring, "until everybody gets so tired that they drop." Clifton and Ruby Caudill married in 1933, and they held a square dance in their new home as soon as the floor was laid, before windows were even installed. His father, an Old Regular Baptist preacher, lectured him about it afterward, but the Caudills were not deterred, and soon their home became a regular gathering place for musicians, especially on Saturday night. According to Caudill, more and more people came, "so everyone agreed we might as well do some square dancing." Ruby Caudill remembered an all-night dance when people "got hungry, so we killed a chicken and made chicken and dumplings." From that time until the early years of World War II there was a square dance at their house or a neighbor's house every Saturday night. The square dance grew spontaneously out of a gathering of neighbors, just as the dance at the Carcassonne Community Center would three decades later. Writing in 1996, Caudill saw workings and dancing as key to community. "With the passing of workings, stir-offs, bean stringing, corn husking and square dances, our sense of being neighbors and a close knit community has been almost lost." Like today's dance at the Carcassonne Community Center, working and the ensuing square dance were "a social event, a get together to swap news."[14]

From the beginning, music and dancing connected the Caudills and other area residents with communities beyond their own and drew others to them. A band grew out of the gatherings at the Caudills' home, and Clifton Caudill and the other musicians played for pie suppers and other programs in all the one-room schoolhouses in the area. The reputation of Caudill's band spread beyond the community, and they played on the Whitesburg, Kentucky, radio station. In the late 1930s, the band played on Lowell Blanchard's "Mid-Day Merry-Go-Round" program on WNOX in Knoxville, Tennessee. According to Caudill, they were asked to be regulars on the show, but they did not want to be away from home. He habitually listened to such programs, having purchased his first radio in 1934, enjoying a station from Bluefield, West Virginia, and "listening to the Grand Ole Opry until midnight every Saturday night." Others in the area did the same. Carcassonne caller Bill Bates invited his neighbors and extended family to hear the Saturday Night Barn Dance and Li'l Abner on the radio he got in 1935, and he listened to Jimmie Rodgers and Riley Puckett records on his Victrola.[15]

Banjo player Lee Sexton (b. 1928) reminisced about frolics following workings all around his neighborhood in Linefork. Beginning when he was a child in the early 1930s, he joined in playing for the square dances, always with the same tune, "Hook and Line," over and over. He said one banjo player would play until he got tired, and then another would take over. If a string on the instrument broke, the dancers would pat with a steady beat and keep dancing, "clapping and stomping." Like others, he recalled no fighting or trouble connected with dances. Other old dance tunes he played were Black-eyed Susie, Sourwood Mountain, Old Hen Cackle, Buck Creek, and Cumberland Gap, which, he said, was especially good for hoedowning (flatfooting). Sometimes the dancing would go on for two hours before stopping for a break, and the musicians would just "play until [they felt] like quitting." Even in the 1930s, people had opportunities to dance beyond their own communities. Sexton reported that at that time, before the advent of good roads, people readily traveled many miles to a square dance, thanks to the coal companies' railroad tracks. Besides riding horses and mules, and the occasional car, over the muddy roads, people could take the train to Blackey or Whitesburg or Mason's Creek and then walk three or four miles from the train stop to the home or school where the dance was held. According to Charlie Whitaker, who grew up at the same time, word of mouth was the source of news about the locations of the upcoming dances, and news was often spread by the traveling doctor, as he made his circuit from one community to the next.[16]

Side by side with this vigorous square dancing and music tradition in Eastern Kentucky, two contrasting phenomena existed: jazz music and dance, and settlement school interpretations of traditional music and dance. Undoubtedly the booming coal town of Blackey offered opportunities for hearing jazz music and enjoying jazz dances in the 1920s, and it was not difficult for people from Carcassonne and other communities to attend. Jazz music could be heard on the radios and Victrolas that arrived in the community in the 1930s, bringing it into people's homes. For some, at least, it was a passing phase. The Caudills recalled that the Charleston was popular around Carcassonne during the 1920s but that it didn't really last or influence local styles. They agreed that "hoedown was here a long time before Charleston," and that "hoedown covers all kinds of individual dancing," including a kind no longer seen in the area, called buck dance. To them, the definition of hoedown was "each person's way of keeping the time and the rhythm." Jazz music and dance influenced Lee Sexton in his youth, however. He learned to play swing music right along with old time music in the 1930s and 1940s, and moved on to rock and roll as a teen, returning to old time music as an adult. Other local musicians likely did the same.[17]

The folk dance recreation movement of the first third of the century influenced the dancing of a segment of the population. The network of settlement schools encouraged folk dancing as part of a recreation program for good health and good citizenship, along with other progressive education methods. Pine Mountain in Harlan County and certain others hosted dances for area residents, including both local dance traditions and folk dances from the recreation movement. Some local dancers' backgrounds thus included both local dance traditions and folk dance repertoire. Caller Charlie Whitaker (b. 1929) had experience with both in school. He attended Carcassonne School during his elementary years in the late 1930s and early 1940s before going on to high school at Blackey's Stuart Robinson Settlement School. No dancing was taught in school at Carcassonne, but pie suppers and box suppers were hosted, followed by square dances, to raise money. Folk dance, including English country dance, was taught at Stuart Robinson Settlement School, which had been established by the Presbyterian Church in 1913. He claimed that he did not dance much as a boy in part because he was reluctant and in part because his father was opposed to dancing for religious reasons. However, he said that some religious people participated in "play parties," accompanied only by singing and not by instrumental music. According to Whitaker, the moves were the same, but it was not a dance "unless you had fiddles." People knew which houses offered square dancing and which offered play parties, and they chose to go accordingly. At some homes, in fact, play parties took place between the square dances, while the musicians rested. However, some dancers, like Willis Fields, reported dancing during the day on Sunday.[18] Apparently in some families or communities, no conflict between religion and dancing was discerned.

Dancing Interrupted and Restored: From World War II to the OEO

Letcher County had a lively square dance and old time music culture during the first half of the twentieth century, with dancing on a regular basis in many communities. Bill Bates listed several callers, saying that "most every community had a caller": Dennis Dixon on Elk Creek, May Ison at Upper Brighton, Carol Whitaker at Carcassonne, George Wooten at Middle Branch. "Dennis Dixon in my community was a major part of my dancing . . . and we would migrate [to] Cobbler's Branch, Bull Creek, Carbon Glow, Blackey, Middle Branch," walking five or ten miles.[19]

In Carcassonne and some other communities there seems to have been a break in the practice in the 1940s and 1950s. World War II was a contributing factor, with people leaving to serve in the armed forces and to work in factories to produce equipment and materials for the war. Some were drawn to Detroit and other large cities by the high wages and abundant overtime, which "seemed to be the opportunity of a lifetime." Ruby Caudill believed that half of Letcher County went to Detroit during the war. She and Clifton spent the years from 1944 to 1946 there, and their apartment was a social center and gathering place, just as their home had been in Carcassonne. Grazia Combs said that the war scattered people, and that those who remained in the area were too busy with children to have dances. Fifteen miles away on King's Creek, Willis Fields blamed school consolidation for the downturn in square dancing opportunities. He remembered dancing in his 1940s childhood and youth in "every one of these [one-room] schools up through here." Three small schools existed in close proximity to his home, but in the late 1940s, the small schools were consolidated, and children were bussed to Whitesburg or Kingdom Come. Without the need for pie suppers to raise funds for the small schools, square dancing opportunities diminished. Clifton Caudill also cited television as a cause for waning interest in square dancing. "When television first came to this country, people parked in front of it and pretty well stayed there" until the late 1960s.[20]

The folk revival and the Office of Economic Opportunity in conjunction with the Council of the Southern Mountains contributed directly to the renewal of square dancing in Carcassonne after its near demise. The Appalachian Volunteers and their VISTA (Volunteers in Service to America) colleagues had a hand in the new beginning of the dance at Carcassonne, as did Anne Romaine and the Southern Folk Cultural Revival Project. The Caudills and their counterparts in Blackey, C. B. Caudill Store owners Joe and Gaynell Begley, knew "that the effort to maintain a rich and enduring public life in the . . . area requires preserving and strengthening not only the physical community but the shared sense of common history, cultural identity and overlapping social relationships that is the essence of community."[21] Believing this, they sought out and took advantage of opportunities afforded by regional and national programs that would support both the physical community and their cultural identity.

They were well positioned to do so. Ruby Caudill had become Carcassonne postmaster in 1955, maintaining that position until her retirement in 1980, when the local post office was closed. The rural community post office, like the general store, was a center of the community. It often served not just as a place to receive mail but as a place to meet friends and neighbors and to pass the time of day, to share news and information, and to discuss community events. Ruby Caudill was a natural for the central position of postmaster, her home having served as a sort of community center and gathering place since her marriage. In addition, the Caudills exercised community leadership. For instance, once the Carcassonne high school had closed in 1948, its students were faced with a dilemma. The closest high school was Stuart Robinson in Blackey. Traveling the five steep, winding miles was a long process even with a car, and few people had vehicles. The Caudills sent their son away to high school at the Berea Foundation School for a year and at Hellier High School in Pike County for a year. Realizing the inequity of services for the children of their area, they approached the Letcher County Board of Education in 1951 and gained bus transportation to Stuart Robinson for all the high school students in and around Carcassonne. They remarked on the growing numbers of students completing high school, once this arrangement had been made.[22] Fifteen years later they were in the forefront when the occasion arose for community improvement via the Council of the Southern Mountains.

When the Appalachian Volunteers (AVs) arrived in Carcassonne in 1966, the community welcomed them. The Council of the Southern Mountains had a focus on Eastern Kentucky in the early 1960s and launched a "crash program" in 1963–64, recruiting hundreds of students from nineteen Eastern Kentucky colleges. The practical goal was to winterize schools with new windows, patched floors, and a fresh coat of paint. It was hoped that regional colleges and communities would have a closer relationship, that community members would gather to "plan and carry out physical improvements for their schools and communities . . . combining their skills with the boundless energy of college students." Three hundred college students spent Christmas break of 1963 in Eastern Kentucky communities. Within the first three years, the Appalachian Volunteers, which had partnered with VISTA, had sent one thousand college students to renovate one-, two-, and three-room schools in forty-three Eastern Kentucky communities.[23] The program grew to encompass adult education and preschool programs to foster an "interest in education" in adults and to "stimulate the learning desire in children" in Blackey and other communities. The two main programs in Letcher County were a woodworking cooperative in Carcassonne and a low-cost housing project in Blackey. Carcassonne, grounded in the desire for learning since 1923, became a volunteer outpost for Letcher County.[24]

In 1966, a dozen students arrived from Earlham College in Indiana to spend the summer working in Carcassonne. Supervised by John Laborietz, a VISTA volunteer assigned to the AVs, they "were to help communities organize and work together." As the result of meetings, council elections, and drafting of by-laws, "renovation of the abandoned Carcassonne School building [which was missing a roof, windows, and doors] was made a first priority." They stayed with local families, who, in a true partnership, refused their offer of money for room and board, using the funds instead to buy roofing for the building. Ruby and Clifton Caudill kept two boys, enjoying having them and the "many long and interesting conversations with them." Laborietz stayed on another six months, and Jon Henrikson arrived later that year as an AV staff member, after VISTA's Nancy Grigorski Brown. When Henrikson arrived, the school became an Outpost Education Center focused on nursery school and dropout education. A one-room school occupied the Northeast corner, but the rest was "pretty junked up." During ensuing months, a garage mechanic shop, a woodshop, and a kitchen were established, and the big open room now used for dances was repaired.[25] Programs grew to include a sewing club and quilting group, recreation, and crafts lessons, all of which continued decades into the future. When asked in 1999 who taught or led these programs, Ruby Caudill said "we all do." The school had once again become a true center of the community, and the building was used for weddings, family reunions, birthday parties, and monthly square dances.

Local unemployment had become an issue for the Appalachian Volunteers, who worked with the Appalachian Committee for Full Employment and the Appalachian Group to Save the Land and People. Joe Begley was active in the latter group. A mid-1960s federal program provided wages for people to work on needed projects in their communities. In Eastern Kentucky, participants in this program were known as the "Happy Pappies," some of whom earned money by helping with maintenance and upkeep of the newly renovated Carcassonne School building. Elsewhere in the region the work of the AVs was fraught with controversy as they became involved in political action, challenging local power structures, community action agencies, and the coal companies, and as time went on, protesting the Vietnam war. Some, like Joe Mulloy, tried for sedition in Pike County, Kentucky, were fired as the Office of Economic Opportunity issued directives specifically aimed at preventing such political engagement. Such controversy seems not to have surrounded the work of the AVs in Carcassonne. Not only are they remembered fondly, but Jon Henrikson, after his time as an AV, remained in the community as a school teacher at Carcassonne, Blackey, Whitesburg, and Letcher, and married Carcassonne resident Loretta Fugate.[26]

Besides the efforts of the Appalachian Volunteers, the folk revival movement directly fueled the rebirth of the Carcassonne dance. In fact, it was partly Jon Henrikson's interest in folklore and folk music that led him to Carcassonne, after reading Jean Ritchie's *Singing Family of the Cumberlands.* Interest in the traditional culture of Eastern Kentucky, and in musicians in particular, had begun at the turn of the twentieth century, assisted by the collecting efforts of the settlement school workers and British folk music collector Cecil Sharp. The interest had heightened in the 1930s, with John Lomax, followed in the 1940s by his son Alan, and by Artus Moser. In 1959, as the national folk revival was gaining momentum, John Cohen documented Letcher County musicians, including Roscoe Halcomb, who resided near Blackey.

Local residents in both Blackey and Carcassonne encouraged this interest. Joe Begley was widely known as a dancer and could often be found hoedowning on his store's front porch or joining in the regular dance at the old Carcassonne School. The Begleys, like the Caudills, valued local culture, and they worked both to maintain it and to pass it on. They believed that cultural expression, social interaction, and planning for community betterment all went hand in hand. They helped to plan square dances and concerts at the Blackey Community Center and were instrumental in bringing Anne Romaine's Southern Folk Cultural Revival Project to Blackey. Hazel Dickens, Sarah Ogan Gunning, and Nimrod Workman were among those who performed there.[27]

The Southern Folk Cultural Revival Project (SFCRP) had a specific role in the renewal of square dancing in Carcassonne. Anne Romaine was a musician, historian, writer, and civil rights activist who, with Bernice Johnson Reagon, founded the SFCRP. It included a roster of more than 160 touring folk musicians and presented joint performances by black and white musicians throughout the South from 1966 to the 1980s. Musician and organizer Guy Carawan, of Highlander Research and Education Center, said that "while a lot of people talked about it, Anne Romaine actually collected together the South's musical heritage and directly gave it back to thousands of Southerners through the folk tour and later through festivals."[28] Among the stops on one of the SFCRP tours was a 1967 concert at the newly renovated Carcassonne School/Community Center. Romaine herself performed that night with African American blues guitar player Babe Stovall, from Mississippi, and Bessie Jones and her grandchildren, of the Georgia Sea Island Singers. After the performance by Romaine, Stovall, and Jones, the music continued, and Clifton Caudill suggested a square dance. All of these performers would have had some experience with dancing. Ann Romaine played old time country guitar and Bessie Jones grew up with African American singing games. Stovall may have played for "frolics" in his youth in Mississippi, as had other black musicians throughout the South and the Appalachian region. So many enjoyed the dance and expressed interest in having more that it was brought before a community meeting. It received strong support, despite the fact that a number of the community belonged to the Old Regular Baptist Church, whose members do not participate in dancing. It was seen as a way to provide recreation for people in the area and as a source of economic support for the Carcassonne Community Center.[29] As a result a new Carcassonne square dance sprang to life—"a true revival," as Jon Henrikson said, of the dances once held in the Caudill's home.

Henrikson saw the dance fitting into OEO goals to maximize participation of local people and to encourage pride in themselves and their community. Soon it became a monthly event, with people even coming "with tire chains and jeeps" in the winter, so determined were they to attend the dance. At one point, when they tried to suspend the dance, people asked for it. Ruby Caudill believed it was so popular because "it's a family thing they can enjoy together as a family group."[30] After three years of operation, the Carcassonne Community Center supported itself with proceeds from the dance and other activities. As of 1975, the dance paid for the electricity used, and dance musicians received half the door receipts. Enough funds were raised by the center's activities that they could give everyone treats at Christmas, hold an Easter Egg hunt, and host community dinners, according to Ruby Caudill. Besides square dancing, other cultural traditions were encouraged by the Appalachian Volunteers. A Native American craftsperson and herbalist from the East Tennessee mountains came to teach old remedies, for example, and in June 1967 an "Oldtime Festival" was held at Carcassonne Community Center to celebrate Kentucky's 175th year of statehood. The festival included an "old fashioned house raising, quilting, bean stringing, home cooked supper," and an "Old Time Country Fair." A photo in Caudill's *Eastern Kentucky Memories* shows Jon Henrikson and another Appalachian Volunteer surrounded by a group of children in front of the newly raised playhouse.[31]

Other Letcher County communities held square dances during the 1970s in conjunction with special events like family reunions and town celebrations, but none seemed to have established regular monthly dances as Carcassonne did. Peter Rogers looked for others during that period but was unable to locate one. Those who loved to square dance took advantage of the individual dance events whenever they occurred. In their 1975 interview, the Caudills declared, "We go to dances anywhere we can, when we hear where they are." Willis Fields said there were lots of good square dancers in the area, and his relatives A. O. and Veldon Fields were calling dances in several communities, including Kingdom Come and Linefork, and at "big parties" like the fourth of July "hoedown" in Whitesburg.

The Carcassonne Square Dance after Three Decades

By 1999, the monthly Carcassonne square dance had become an institution, and every month saw a gathering of old friends and new visitors. On a warm June evening, cars pulled into the small parking lot at the end of Square Dance Road on the top of a mountain southwest of Hazard. Families and individuals gathered at the small, white building where Ruby and Clifton Caudill sat by the door, greeting each person warmly and collecting the two-dollar admission fee. Neighbors chatted with each other and welcomed newcomers with friendly conversation. Among the visitors were students in an herb class at Hindman Settlement School, members of a Mennonite work group, and three Berea College students who accompanied me.

Figure 8.2. The Carcassonne square dance, 1999. Photo by Layla Thomas. Courtesy of Susan Spalding.

At one end of the big open room, musicians tuned up, Beverly May on fiddle and others on bass, guitar, and two banjos, as caller Charlie Whitaker prepared his wireless microphone headset. At the other end of the room, next to the big pot-bellied stove, chairs were lined up in rows facing the stage, leaving plenty of space for dancers on the hardwood floor between them and the stage. Groups of family and friends settled into seats here and there, sharing news. In the kitchen through the door at the rear of the room, Loretta Henrikson and other women prepared hot dogs and chili, serving soft drinks and visiting. People sat at the long tables in the kitchen trading news and intently talking about local current events.

A few minutes after 7:00, Whitaker announced a square dance, and couples moved unhurriedly to the dance floor.[32] Some subtle organizing took place as the circle gathered, Whitaker placing experienced dancers between less experienced ones, and Beverley Caudill Johnson partnering newcomers with regulars in a gentle and friendly way. Whitaker taught the figures he planned to include in the dance so that the newer dancers would be prepared for his calls. After the first square dance, the evening proceeded with a Virginia Reel, another square dance, a cakewalk, and a final square dance, with breaks of approximately fifteen minutes between each one. No one hoedowned between dances, but there was lots of conversation. The dance floor was packed for most of the dances, but by the third square dance only twelve couples participated, others choosing to watch and visit or to step outside for air on this warm night. By mid-evening, almost all visitors had become accustomed to the lively, centered dance style. Though the dancing was performed with a smooth running step, the pace of the figures seemed leisurely, with plenty of time for everyone. My attention was called to this at a callers' workshop led by Charlie Whitaker at Carcassonne in 2002. During my turn to call, Charlie and Joyce Whitaker quietly corrected me, saying I should leave more time between calling the parts of the figures so that no one felt rushed.

The third and last square dance of the evening typified a Carcassonne square dance called by Charlie Whitaker. After the teaching and organization were completed, Whitaker, joining the circle, chanted, "All hands up and circle left . . . Hey hey back the other way . . . swing your partner and promenade . . . and circle left." To start off a figure, he called to one couple who were regulars at the dance: "Bird in the cage three hands round . . . Bird hop out and crow hop in . . . Circle four and gone again."[33] Leading smoothly into the chorus, Whitaker accented the first syllable of "DO-sa-do your partner . . . SWING the opposite lady . . . EVERYBODY swing and promenade . . . Circle left." Directing the second couple to dance the figure with the third couple, he emphasized "NEXT couple out" and repeated the calls for the figure. After they completed the figure and chorus, the third couple moved on to dance with the fourth couple.

All the while that two couples were doing a figure, everyone else in the circle clapped their hands and sometimes let out a whoop, moving energetically into the "Everybody swing." Once a few couples had had a turn leading the first figure, Whitaker directed another couple across the circle to begin the same figure, so that two sets of two couples were doing it simultaneously. After five repetitions of Cage the Bird, Whitaker directed the next couples to "Take a little peek."[34] Again, another two couples picked it up once it got started. After five repetitions of that figure, Whitaker explained the ending figure for the dance and asked Peter Rogers to lead it off. Rogers swung his partner, leaving her to the right of the man on his own right. He took that man's partner for a swing, placing her beside the third man in the circle, and so forth, keeping the last woman for his new partner. Once he was home, Whitaker called the usual chorus followed by "NEXT man out." The next man and each one thereafter repeated the process, for a total of about ten minutes for the twelve men to swing each of the twelve women, and no one was rushed, the music carrying everyone on. Everyone clapped throughout, people interacted with their current partners, and frequent whoops burst from the dancers. To conclude, Whitaker said emphatically, "*Swing your partner* and promenade . . . Anywhere, I don't care, Take her to an easy chair." Couples concluded a brief promenade and strolled off the floor individually and together, as the music played on for a while. Some went forward to talk with the band, some stopped and chatted with others on the dance floor, and others headed back to the chairs to talk with friends. No one was in a hurry to leave, though the evening was coming to an end.

The system of progression and the chorus figure described above had been used in the area for at least four decades, and their background is discussed later, along with some of the other regular Carcassonne practices. The do-si-do (pronounced do-sa-do by Charlie Whitaker) is unlike those taught in schools and most folk dance groups. Callers have described it at least as far back as the 1940s. In it, the man leads his partner in a small circle around him, his right hand joined to her left. He does not turn. Completing the circle, she walks into the arms of her neighbor, the other man in the "square" of two couples, for a swing in a social or casual ballroom hold. At the same time, her partner swings his neighbor's partner. Finally they return to swing their own partners, the caller directing all couples to swing their own and promenade. After the promenade, everyone circles left to "get everyone straight," according to Willis Fields. Finding your place in the circle is important, so that everyone has a turn leading a figure. After the partner swing, each couple makes sure to be next to the same couples, in the same order. This happens smoothly and seamlessly, and almost unnoticeably. Willis Fields made a point of saying, "When you accommodate [promenade], you fall right back in line, right back where you started from."[35]

The other dances on that night in 1999 included two or three figures each, among them Four Leaf Clover, Mountaineer Loop, Lady 'Round the Lady, and Dive for the Oyster, each led by one couple and then the next, as usual. Many people, clearly regulars, seemed at ease with the dancing and fell right into the figures when their turns came, using an easy, lilting, walking step. By the second square dance of the evening, newcomers had incorporated the movement vocabulary and were becoming comfortable with the easygoing style. Most often the regular dancers chose to dance with their spouses or other family members, but they willingly invited visitors to dance and happily helped them through the moves. When a foursome got tangled up or confused, Whitaker stepped over and gently guided them with a touch of his hand. When they successfully completed a difficult move, the whole circle cheered.

The cakewalk that took place halfway through the evening was designed to raise money to support the Community Center. It was a cooperative affair. Numbered paper plates were brought from the kitchen, and several hands reached to take a stack to put them in a large circle surrounding the dance floor. The area was entirely encircled with people of all ages who paid fifty cents to take a chance on a cake. Several delicious-looking homemade cakes were carried to the stage, including some made by Ella Mae Fugate, Loretta Henrikson's mother. Music played and people stepped from plate to plate until the music stopped. Jon Henrikson pulled a number from a bowl, and the lucky winner ran to the stage to choose a cake. When the last cake had been claimed, everyone stooped to pick up their own plates and handed them to others who took them to the kitchen for use at the next month's dance.

Charlie Whitaker reported that he began calling at Carcassonne in about 1980, and he continued to call there until he passed away in October 2009. Among the dancers during his time were his children and grandchildren, who danced so energetically that my students remarked in 1999, "When they swing you, you really know you've been swung!" Both Charlie Whitaker and his wife Joyce attended Carcassonne school from 1935 to 1943 and later returned there as teachers for a short time. He had seen square dancing at Carcassonne as a child, but his father did not allow him to participate. As a student at Stuart Robinson in the mid-1940s, Whitaker experienced folk dancing as taught through the Council of Southern Mountains recreation program. Lee Cooper came to the school from Whitesburg to teach English Country Dance. Whitaker took a folk dance course as a student at Peabody College, but dancing really took hold in his life when he and Joyce were teachers at Pine Mountain Settlement School from 1956 to 1965. Charlie assumed the folk dance teaching responsibilities not long after arriving at the school. At Pine Mountain, Whitaker broadened the repertoire by teaching international folk dances such as Mayim that he had learned at Peabody. Dance was a regular recreational activity that Pine Mountain students could choose, and by 1960 Whitaker took students from his class, including Peter Rogers, to perform in Harlan and elsewhere in the area. In 1965 the Whitakers moved on to teach at Alice Lloyd College in Knott County. Charlie not only taught folk dance there, but he also took students each year to the Mountain Folk Festival and participated in the monthly leadership-training sessions followed by potlucks and dances held at Hindman, Berea, Pine Mountain, Somerset, and other schools and colleges in Eastern Kentucky. At these events he learned more dances to share with his students. When the Whitakers returned to Letcher County in 1980, Charlie called square dances at Carcassonne and taught folk dance classes in Letcher, Knott, Leslie, and Perry Counties. Whitaker was a practitioner of other traditional skills as well. He was a woodworker, making dulcimers and small woodcraft items like flowers, and he and Joyce kept a big garden and preserved its produce.[36]

Charlie Whitaker worked hard to increase the number of dance opportunities in his area, building upon the success of the Carcassonne dance. He taught square dance classes at Cowan Creek Mountain Music School, called at Appalshop events, and in 1999 was trying to establish a cycle of weekly dances, including Cowan, Seco, Campbell's Branch, and Linefork Fire Department. Beverly May, a local nurse practitioner as well as a fiddler and supporter of local music and dance, also contributed to this effort. The cycle of dances did not materialize, but square dancing continued to be popular at Cowan Creek Mountain Music School, and growing numbers of young and old alike have attended the school since its founding in 2000. Its popularity there undoubtedly contributed to the numbers of young people now attending and providing music for the Carcassonne dance. Whitaker served as a consultant for *All Join Hands*, the 2005 compact disc of square dance music produced by faculty at Cowan Creek Music School.[37]

As a square dance caller, Whitaker integrated elements of his folk dance background. He introduced a buzz step swing to Carcassonne and really encouraged its use, sometimes saying "Buzz!" when he called for a swing or the basket-like figure called Hug 'em Up. In 1975, he himself, as well as others, had noted that typically a walking swing was used locally. He also introduced the Virginia Reel, now a regular part of each dance evening. He often added a galopede as an ending to the Virginia Reel.[38] Over the years he tried to introduce other folk dances, but it seems that many people preferred the type of square dancing that had been done in the area for decades. Jon Henrikson said that he personally liked to do the same dances every time rather than to try the new dances. He liked the "big circle dances" because they were simple and not strenuous, and it didn't matter if people made mistakes. Henrikson wondered aloud how traditional Whitaker's calling was, considering his folk dance recreation background, but he immediately followed his own question with the belief that authenticity was really not as important as "that people keep dancing, and keep the tradition of Carcassonne going."[39]

The dance at Carcassonne maintained its own integrity as a social institution, welcoming newcomers and accepting some changes introduced by callers. It seemed to have a life of its own that encompassed much more than the dance. The conversations at the tables in the kitchen, on the front porch of the community center, and around the edges of the room seemed to be more than small talk, as family, community and county issues were intently discussed. Some came expressly for this exchange, never choosing to dance. Each element of the evening—the square dances, the cakewalk, and the Virginia Reel—was separated from the others by a break of about a quarter hour. The breaks and the interaction during them and before and after the dance seemed as important as the dancing. The theme of community interaction has been an important aspect here since the founding of the school. Clifton Caudill described all the neighbors who came when the first Carcassonne School teachers arrived, "to welcome the teachers and visit with each other and maybe hear a bit of news." In 1975, Ruby Caudill described a scene that was still repeated more than two decades later at the dance: they'd "be sitting around and talking like neighbors will, about their crops and their health and the weather and stuff like that."[40] At the Community Center, dancing was a way to draw people together, but socializing and sharing news was just as important as dancing. The square dance was only one factor knitting the community together, as it had been for decades.

According to Henrikson, crowds of about fifty to seventy-five people attended the dance in the early years of the twenty-first century. A core group attended almost every time; a number came just to watch and socialize. Few teens participated. Ruby Caudill said at the time that only about four or five families came from the area immediately surrounding Carcassonne because many, for religious reasons, did not believe in dancing. However, people traveled to the dance from elsewhere in the county, as well as from farther away. Henrikson believed that people wanted to come to Carcassonne because of the smallness, the friendliness, and the live music. He said the dance was "blessed with good musicians" like Ray Slone and Kentucky Governor's Award in the Arts recipient and master musician Lee Sexton.[41] It was important to Ruby and Clifton Caudill that visitors came from elsewhere. Not only were they welcome, but they made an important contribution to the dance. By their presence they seemed to testify to the significance of the dance and its role in bringing together local tradition and a broad worldview.

The Dance Evolves

In some ways the dancing and the dance event in 1999 were similar to those of twenty-five years earlier, and in some ways they were different. The organization of the evening and the length of each square dance had changed, as had the preferred structure of the sets and the style of calling. Hoedowning, once common between and sometimes during the square dances, had all but disappeared. Some sequences for the whole set had disappeared from the repertoire and new ones had been added, while many two-couple figures remained the same. The characteristic visiting couple pattern and do-si-do established in the early days of the dance continued, along with a variation on the informal relationship with the music.

At a 1975 dance evening at Carcassonne and in the surrounding area, each square dance lasted twenty-five or thirty minutes, much shorter than the hour-long dances of the early- to mid-twentieth century, but a little longer than more recent ones, which were typically eighteen minutes or less.[42] The 1975 evening consisted of square dancing, hoedowning, and waltzing. By the late 1990s, waltzes never appeared and very few people hoedowned at the Carcassonne dance. Hoedowning often started off the evening in 1975, as the band played before the first square dance. Ruby Caudill laughed and said, "They'd play a tune or two and everybody got the foot patting over with." Phil Jamison observed this also in 1991, along with individual styles of hoedowning. In 1975

Figure 8.3. The Carcassonne square dance, 1970s. Note the two circles, one in the foreground and one close to the band. Courtesy of Dale Johnson.

Figure 8.4. Ruby Caudill (white dress) and Clifton Caudill welcoming people to the Carcassonne dance, 1970s. Courtesy of the Kentucky Folklife Program Archives, Western Kentucky University.

Clifton Caudill said, "Each person has a different way of expressing his rhythm and his step to the music." He and his wife identified characteristic styles of some of the dancers and named three who they claimed danced "the original hoedown." According to callers Veldon and A. O. Fields, footwork was part of the dance as people circled left and right in the square dance. "You're doing a regular hoedown as you go . . . and when you stop, you don't quit, you just keep making music with your feet and hands . . . the music can quit. You don't need the music. You all got the music in your hands and feet when you're dancing." Hoedowning still took place as a solo dance in the 1980s, and Willis Fields demonstrated it in Mike Seeger's 1987 documentary *Talking Feet.* In the late 1990s, though hoedowning rarely occurred, people still "made music with their feet and hands" by clapping and tapping their feet while other couples danced the figures, just as they had twenty-five years earlier. Veldon Fields said, "When you ain't dancing, you're standing there patting your feet and clapping your hands and hollering. . . . When you ain't in motion, you're in tune."[43]

In the 1970s, the Carcassonne square dance was structured somewhat differently from the way it has been since the 1990s, according to Peter Rogers, who has danced there frequently for almost forty years. In the earlier years, the band set up at the end of the room near the kitchen, and chairs were placed around the edges of the room so that the entire big room could be used for dancing. Usually, two circles of dancers formed. One circle was near the band, and the other was at the far end of the room. Willis Fields regularly called for the circle near the band, dancing with them. Various callers led the other set, and no effort was made to coordinate the two sets. The set near the band tended to be a little smaller to allow room for the band, with six to ten couples, while more couples could join the other set. According to Rogers, Lee Sexton was the primary musician in the 1970s, bringing others with him, and he controlled the sequence of the evening. After playing a tune or two to begin the evening, Sexton would say, "Let's square dance." Upon conclusion of that dance, he would announce, "Let's hoedown," and "all sorts of people got up—oldtimers, kids, women, men," often including Joe Begley. Next, Sexton and the band would play a tune or sing a song and couples might dance a waltz or a slow dance. He rotated among the three kinds of dances, with a break halfway through the evening.[44]

The method of progression now in use was developed during the 1970s. During the first half of the twentieth century, Letcher County square dances were usually performed with one couple visiting each of the other couples around the set, doing the same figure with each. After a chorus figure, the next couple would do the same. In a large set of eight couples or more, it could take a long time for the first couple to make the entire circuit, whereas in a set of four couples, the process would be much shorter. Some callers expressed a preference for smaller sets. Both Willis Fields and Harding Ison explained in 1975 that you could do more figures with an "eight-handed reel [four-couple set] than you can with a "sixteen-handed reel [eight-couple set]." You "can't call a lot of complicated things when there are a lot of people in the square dance, but if you just got an eight-handed reel you can do it all."[45] Bill Bates and Clifton Caudill took exception to this, however. Bates enjoyed sets that involved as many as ten couples, with an even or odd number. Caudill much preferred having more than four couples in each square dance. He said that "six to eight couples really make a good square dance. Everybody gets to participate in one like that," especially when two couples on opposite sides of the ring start the dance.[46]

At Carcassonne, a solution has been in place since the 1970s to accommodate the larger number of couples and to keep everyone involved. At the direction of the caller, one couple leads out and dances with the couple to their right, and then everyone dances the chorus. After the figure and the chorus are completed, the second couple becomes active, moving to their right to dance the same figure with the third couple, and so on around the set. The dance flows leisurely on, each couple rippling out in turn to dance with the next. In this way, each couple dances the figure twice, "once as a receiving couple and once as a leading couple." Sometimes the caller designates another couple on the other side of the set to do the same figure, so that four couples are dancing at the same time, while the rest of the circle pats and watches and waits their own turns. Ruby Caudill said that method was developed "when we have so many in and it's so hot and that way people don't get so tired." She said, "We've done it that way ever since we started up in 1967." According to Bill Bates, Willis Fields was the first one to use this characteristic progression. Callers at Carcassonne in recent years have used the same system. Peter Rogers remembered that in the 1970s, the circle nearest the band, called by Willis Fields, progressed in this way, but the other circle, with its own caller, often used a different method. The caller would lead out to the couple on his right, dance with them, and then move on to the next couple to the right. Sometimes another couple would start out once the leader had moved on a bit, and sometimes a third couple would join in. Rogers said that it occasionally happened that each foursome would do different figures as they went. Caller Harding Ison, while using the original single visiting couple all the way around the set in 1975, chose to have each visiting couple do a different figure, so that "it didn't get boring."[47] By the 1990s, twenty or more couples joined the ring for each square dance during the evening, and the progression introduced by Fields allowed for inclusion of newcomers and experienced dancers alike.

Willis Fields was a regular caller at Carcassonne in 1975, though others called as well, including Clifton Caudill and his son Randall, Bill Bates, Dudley Halcomb, Dennis Dixon, and Maynard Watts.[48] Clifton and Ruby Caudill agreed that the caller is very important to the dance, though Fields reported that in the 1940s and 1950s, the caller didn't call much. According to him, everybody could call a set, so special callers were not necessary, and even in 1975, Veldon and A. O. Fields said that once a figure was started, there was no need to say more. Because many people could call, Clifton Caudill articulated a point of etiquette. If more than one caller was present, only one would call a particular set, dancing as he did. It would be rude for another caller to interrupt. "It makes for a better dance to have a designated caller."[49] Perhaps this is one factor that led to the practice of having one regular caller at Carcassonne. In the late 1990s and for years after, Charlie Whitaker was the primary caller at Carcassonne, and dance organizers felt dependent on him for the continuity and success of the dance.[50]

Calling Conventions

Veldon Fields mixed patter with straightforward directions in his calling in the 1970s. "Wave that ocean, wave that sea, wave that pretty girl back to me. Four square [two couples join hands in a foursome—note the use of four square or four in a square, rather than "circle up four"], you get mine, I'll get yours, everybody swing, accommodate [promenade] home. Move children move. . . . Stop at home and watch me."[51] Willis Fields and Harding Ison used some patter that was simply poetic rather than directive: "Red bird's eye and a pigeon wing, everybody get a left hand swing" or "Call a ship, call a ring, everybody get a right hand swing."[52] In 2002, Charlie Whitaker's style was clear, simple, and directive. He chanted the calls, accenting the first syllable in an attention-getting device, but he added little patter between the calls. Once he had called a figure for the first and second pair of couples, he usually did not call it again, preferring instead to step in and physically assist those who needed it, or to quietly coach them through the moves. He did call the chorus each time, however, getting everyone in the circle moving together before the figure moved on to the next two couples.

Whitaker inserted the same chorus after each pair of couples danced through a figure: do-si-so your partner (described earlier), swing your opposite, swing your own, promenade, circle left. In 1975, Willis Fields used right hands across as an alternate to the do-si-do in the chorus. He said, "Anytime you start a play [figure], you circle left . . . to get your people started and get their minds on the call." Grazia Combs remembered that when she was dancing in the 1920s and 1930s, the caller used "different things between the calls." The caller might direct a promenade or rights and lefts all the way around, or circle left. She said the fun was in never knowing what was coming next. Grover Sizemore, dancing in the decade after 1910, clearly recalled a chorus figure almost exactly like the one used by Charlie Whitaker in 2002, but it was danced only after one couple had visited all three of the other couples in the set with a figure, instead of after each foursome danced together. All agreed that the chorus figure was "not a dance [figure]" but "just something to complete and smooth off a thing that you have started."[53]

Carcassonne and Letcher County have a long tradition of informal conclusions to square dances. Though a caller directed the action of the dancers, in the 1940s Letcher County square dances ended when the dancers or the musicians were tired, rather than at the caller's direction. Musician Lee Sexton said in 1975 that he took his tempo from the dancers, and musicians would "play until you feel like quitting," noting that he had sometimes played for two hours before there was a break in the dancing. When Phil Jamison attended a Carcassonne dance called by Harmie Griffie in 1991, he remarked that the band ended the tune "without regard to the progress of the dance figures." Ruby Caudill said they would "dance 'til you drop" in the 1930s.[54] When Charlie Whitaker was the regular caller in the 1990s and later, he directed the conclusion of the dance, but it often ended casually, with the band continuing to play after the dance concluded, the dancers walking leisurely off the dance floor or stopping to visit with others as they went. There was often a big finish to a dance—"into the middle with a great big shout," which everyone did with great gusto—but the community had a casual attitude about the ending, as if the dance were just part of the ongoing conversation.

Previously, some callers had used certain figures to end a square dance, but apparently musicians stopped playing when they were tired, whether these figures had been concluded or not. Bill Bates said that Dennis Dixon always ended with Winding Up the Maple. Figures used by Willis, Veldon, and A. O. Fields included the Grapevine Twist and Wind Up the Maple. This last is a spiraling line of the circle of dancers inward and then outward. Veldon Fields said it was called "wind up" because it was the ending of the dance, and, in answer to a question from Peter Rogers, insisted it was always called Wind Up the Maple, and never Maypole. In the Grapevine Twist, the lead man dropped the hand of the woman to his left and led the line of dancers under the arch made by the joined hands of that woman and her partner. Once all had passed through, her partner had his right arm around his own neck with his right hand still joined to her left. The leader went through successive arches until all were linked in a single-file circle, right arms around their own necks. To conclude, arms were raised and the circle was re-formed. Grapevine Twist had previously existed as a dance or play party in its own right, with nonsense verses sung to accompany it, various chants and moves used in different communities.[55]

Other figures sometimes used in 1975 to conclude square dances had also formerly existed as separate dances. Willis Fields and Harding Ison both mentioned Gents Back to Back, or, as Bill Bates chanted, "Ladies in the center and the gents sail around; Gents in the center and ladies sail around." All men in the set made a small circle facing outward while the women moved around them counterclockwise. Each woman passed her own partner and swung the next man in the circle, promenading the ring with him. The process was repeated until all were home with their own partners.[56] Willis Fields also described one figure still used to conclude a square dance by Charlie Whitaker at the turn of the twenty-first century, Swing the One that Stole the Bone. Whitaker called this same figure, described earlier in this chapter, sometimes by explaining it and then appointing one man to lead off or by saying to one man, "Bill, change 'em over." Originally a dance in and of itself, the lead man swung his partner and placed her to the right of the next man in the circle, going counterclockwise. He swung that man's partner and placed her to the right of the third man, and so forth around the circle. Each man took a turn swinging each woman, so the dance could "run you to death." Willis Fields chanted, "You swing the one that stole the bone and the one you call your own. Then the one you love the best and the one you put to rest."[57] The figure was used at the turn of the twenty-first century, but without the call.

One dance appears to have continued as separate from, but related to, the square dance. Speaking in 1975, Clifton Caudill said that "before they quit dancing, they call for a Tucker." In it, a ring of couples surrounds a solo man who hoedowns in the center as the couples circle around him. The odd man steals someone's partner, leaving another man to hoedown in the center. "Old Dan Tucker" was a pre–Civil War minstrel song that came to be used as accompaniment for a dancing game in various places around the country. It was documented in several states, including Missouri and Michigan, in the 1880s. It was accompanied there, as in Kentucky, by singing. In 1917, Cecil Sharp documented "Tucker" as a customary ending to a square dance, and Alonzo Turner remembered doing it around that same period. "Tucker" seems to have been commonplace at dances in the 1970s, according to both Clifton Caudill and Willis Fields. Mike Seeger, in his 1987 film *Talking Feet*, included footage of "Give the Old Tucker a Chance" at Carcassonne. I never experienced it at Carcassonne in the 1990s or thereafter, but Randy Wilson reintroduced it in 2011.[58]

Many figures from the Carcassonne dance of the 1970s were still performed there at the turn of the twenty-first century and sound familiar to old time square dancers today. In 1975, Willis Fields listed Right Hands Cross, Ladies Change and Gents the Same, and Take a Little Peek. Veldon Fields demonstrated Lady Round the Lady, Wave the Ocean, and Dive for the Oyster. Charlie Whitaker named Little Back Door and Chase the Possum, Chase the Squirrel. Clifton and Ruby Caudill listed some of these plus Cage the Bird and one that sounds like a figure eight: "Out to the right (to the next couple), left around that lady, back to the right, around that gent."[59] Some they mentioned, like Shoot the Owl, are less commonly known today, though some appeared in Pat Napier's *Kentucky Mountain Square Dancing*, a book describing figures from Perry County in the 1930s and 1940s, as well as in Ida Levin's 1928 *Kentucky Square Dances*. Hug 'em Up is a figure mentioned by Willis Fields that I have not met by that name elsewhere, and it was still being danced at Carcassonne in the at the turn of this century, with the same name. In it, two couples join together with their arms around each other and turn their tight little circle clockwise to their left until they are told to break from it. Square dancers will recognize the similarity between this and the basket, but at Carcassonne it was truly a hug, rather than being formed by ladies' joined hands and men's joined hands around their partners' backs. Willis Fields described a figure I have never experienced at Carcassonne since 1999: Waltz the Hall or Waltz Right Up. One couple danced toward the center of the set and home again. The lady then went to her left, the gent to his right, and "cut off" (passed around) two, three or more people, before going home to swing and repeat at the caller's direction.[60]

Growing Attention and Concerns for the Future

Once the dance had been established in 1967, its reputation rapidly spread, attracting media attention locally and nationally. Appalshop, a media collective founded in Whitesburg, Kentucky, in 1969 to document and preserve Appalachian culture and traditions, included the Carcassonne square dance in a short 1973 film entitled "Tomorrow's People," so named in order to correct the assumption that Appalachian residents are "yesterday's people," a term coined in the early 1900s. *Little Shepherd of Kingdom Come*, the outdoor drama based on the novel by John Fox Jr., was staged at an amphitheater in Van, Kentucky, from 1971 until 1980, with Frances Amburgey directing the folk dancing. Clifton and Ruby Caudill, along with their son Randall and three of their grandchildren, participated in the drama for nine years, dancing, acting, and providing support services. Ruby Caudill told Peter Rogers in 1975 that she and Clifton were in charge of the dancing for the drama for a time.[61] The Caudills themselves came to be sought out and seemed to represent to many the deeply held cultural beliefs and practices of the region. Articles have appeared about them in newspapers in Lexington, Kentucky, and in Virginia. In 1979 they appeared in the film *Coal Miner's Daughter* in a scene depicting a pie supper, and several years later they were filmed at Lee Sexton's homeplace for the video version of Karen Tobin's song "Carolina Smokey Moon." The Caudill family also danced and played roles in a local history drama in Hazard, about a prominent nineteenth century citizen, William Wellington Baker. Other dancers included John Cleveland, Artie Ann Bates, Beverley Caudill, and Randall Caudill. Music was provided by the band Bluegrass Uprising, with Ray Slone and others. The Carcassonne Square Dance and the Carcassonne Community Center were represented at the Kentucky Folklife Festival in Frankfort in 1999, 2000, 2003, and 2005.[62] Charlie Whitaker called square dances for visiting school children, and quilters and woodcarvers set up a booth on the capitol grounds. In 2003 they danced at the Festival of American Folklife in Washington, D.C. Rather than simply performing, they created "Carcassonne in Washington," as Charlie Whitaker said, inviting the audience to join in with them from the first dance of each session.

As well as garnering institutional and media attention, the Carcassonne dance continued to attract regional and international visitors individually and in groups. Work groups make a Carcassonne visit a regular part of their week, as do students in classes at area institutions. Visitors from elsewhere have not simply been welcomed in the course of the four decades of the dance. They have always been an integral part of the dance, in the vision of Clifton and Ruby Caudill and the other dance organizers. Carcassonne leaders regularly recount that people have come from almost every state in the union to dance, and that exchange students have come from many countries, including Japan, France, and England.[63] They point with pride to the involvement of Appalshop, the Kentucky Arts Council, and the interest of Folklife Festivals. This level of media and institutional interest has undoubtedly contributed to the longevity of the dance, and the actual participation of such individuals has been significant to the experience of dancing at Carcassonne. Almost every month the community dance has included both local residents and visitors from miles and even continents away. This has been central to the life of the dance, just as similar involvement was crucial to the success of Carcassonne school. At the same time, the dance remains first and foremost a community dance, and the feeling is unmistakable as soon as one enters the door.

The Carcassonne square dance continued in 2011 with renewed vigor. In 1975, the dance was only eight years old, self-supporting and full of energy. The future was bright, though Clifton and Ruby Caudill were a little troubled that the responsibility fell to just a few people. Clifton Caudill believed that "young people now are . . . interested in what's gone by in the past and they're wanting to do some of it, too. It's been there all along and I'm glad to see the young people, because they can carry it on." By 1991, they had begun to express concerns about the future of the Carcassonne dance after their generation was gone. Jon Henrikson continued to express these concerns in 1999 and 2002, because of the diminishing numbers and increasing age of the local population. He wondered if people would step forward to run the dance and how they could afford to pay the musicians the going rate. He believed that the continuation of the dance would depend on a younger generation, who at that time he saw as more interested in hunting, fishing, and car racing.[64] Around that time, too, Letcher County was experiencing a growing punk and hip hop culture. Lee Sexton's granddaughter Stacie preferred to play in the local punk band If I Die Tonight, and the Letcher County hip hop group Kuntry Killaz had posts on YouTube.[65] Youth had both recreational and musical interests that took them away from old time music and dance. However, even then three generations of Whitakers regularly attended the Carcassonne dance, as did four generations of Caudills. Henrikson hypothesized that the dance might be handed down within these families, but he worried what would happen with the passing of Clifton and Ruby Caudill and Charlie and Joyce Whitaker. Ruby Caudill saw the dance at that time as part and parcel of the community center, saying that she would like to see it all go on as it was at that time, with a stronger educational component, so that young people could learn how to work to support their community.[66]

Locally, new initiatives contributed both directly and indirectly to the ongoing success of the dance. In the mid-1990s, an old time jam session was begun in Whitesburg by volunteers, and young people began to learn the music. The Cowan Creek Mountain Music School (CCMMS) was founded in 2000 in Letcher County by the Cowan Community Action Group, and it continues to the present, growing every year, teaching local traditional music to people of all ages. Besides an annual weeklong workshop, CCMMS offers an after-school program known as "Passing the Pick & Bow," with the collaboration of the Letcher County School System and Appalshop and support from the Kentucky Arts Council. In 2004 Lee Sexton said that, though "it was just about forgot about at one time . . . there's a heck of a lot of younger people taking that old time up. Man, they just eat it up, buddy, they can't get enough."[67] Youth attending the Music School and Cowan community dances learned to square dance from

Figure 8.5. Charlie Whitaker with his calling apprentice Erin Cokenaugher, sponsored by the Kentucky Folklife Master/Apprentice Progam. Courtesy of the Kentucky Folklife Program Archives, Western Kentucky University.

Charlie Whitaker. One young participant, Erin Cokenaugher (now Stidham), immediately picked up Whitaker's calling and eventually became his apprentice through the Kentucky Folk Arts Master-Apprentice Grant Program. Proactive as always, the community center applied for and received Folk Arts Project grants from the Kentucky Arts Council to help pay musicians at the monthly square dances in 2004, 2005, 2006, 2007, 2009, and 2010. Beverly May helped to promote the dance through her work with Appalshop and played for the dances herself as a volunteer. When praised for her involvement in 2002, she said, "I am just proud to be part of the tradition."[68]

While it was true that the passing of Clifton Caudill in 1999 and of Charlie Whitaker in 2009 took a toll on the dance, others stepped in to insure its continuity. Beverley Caudill Johnson and her husband Dale have taken up her grandparents' mission. Together with Jon and Loretta Henrikson, they work tirelessly to insure the success of the monthly dance, preparing the hall, purchasing and preparing food, gathering cakes for the cakewalk, and greeting

Figure 8.6. Young musicians at Carcassonne, 2009. Photo by Bev Futrell.

people who come to dance. Randy Wilson and Erin Cokenaugher Stidham have become regular callers. In 2011 Wilson's son Gabe played for the dances along with a group of middle and high schoolers who learned to play old time music at Cowan Creek Mountain Music School. This critical mass of young people attracted their friends to the dance floor. Jon Henrikson was correct that the future of the dance depended on the involvement of young people. Forty-five years after its inception, the dance showed new life and energy. It still attracts visitors from many states and countries, and work or study groups come for recreation after a busy week in Eastern Kentucky. However, as with most nonprofit groups, finances are always difficult. In August 2013 Mountain Comprehensive Healthcare sponsored a fundraiser at the community center, drawing hundreds of newcomers, many of whom stayed for that night's dance.

Community through Square Dancing

The Carcassonne dance embodies traditions reaching back more than one hundred years in Letcher County, more than eighty years in the community, and more than forty years at the Carcassonne Community Center. Its longevity can be attributed to the deeply rooted value placed on local tradition by its founders, and to their intentional seeking of connections with "other people beyond our hills [and] the opportunity to exchange ideas."[69] It has been as important to the dance that individuals and institutions from elsewhere witness local traditions as it has been for the organizers to learn from them. The presence and participation of visitors is as necessary as the true community-centered feeling of the dance. The welcoming spirit of the first dance in the Caudills' home in the 1930s continues to pervade the dance event, and the dancing provides a context for community gathering and sharing. Not least valuable is the dedication of the volunteers who have been committed to the success of the dance for more than four decades.

Clifton and Ruby Caudill were key to the dance until Clifton passed away in December 1999, and the dance maintains the spirit instilled by them since the beginning, a spirit that continues to renew itself and to reenergize the dance. The dance experience at Carcassonne is just as welcoming and homey as it was in 1967. In 1975 Ruby Caudill exclaimed, "I just enjoy doing it. It's good exercise. It's good clean fun." And most of all, she says, "It's something the whole family can participate in. There's nothing like having fun with your children and your grandchildren. And that's what we do at Carcassonne." Mrs. Bates was warm: "I think Carcassonne is probably about the most spontaneous place . . . the atmosphere, the setting, everything is right." My student LaVon Rice described her experience of being at the dance in 1999. She was drawn to the "expression of local values where people matter as much as time, where change is present and evident but slow like country creeks rather than the swirling eddies of cities."[70] Dale Johnson, in his dual role as folklorist and member of the community, describes the dance as having a feeling of "timelessness—a connection to earlier generations and younger selves. When you are dancing, it could be 1890, 1934, or the future." He says the dance is "related to community identity and sense of self within the community." Clifton Caudill expressed a broad philosophical understanding of the square dance event and hinted at its underlying social import and why deep conversations take place on the porch and in the kitchen at Carcassonne: "There's more to it than just doing the figures and all. . . . It seems that when the music starts and everybody starts circling the dance, everybody feels closer together or they're tied together. . . . They're thinking about the same thing, it just seems to pull people together. . . . Something about it just makes everybody feel closer to the other people that are doing it. You love everybody at that time. [laughing] . . . That carries over after today, tomorrow, next week, when you see somebody that was [at the dance]. We have a special feeling for them. . . . It's community through square dancing, I guess."[71]

Afterword

As I come to closure on this book, I find it hard to draft a true "conclusion" or to put a "period" at the end of this work. So this chapter is called an "afterword," because it is not so much an ending as an invitation to the reader to take this work further. Each story is intended to stand on its own, and I hope the reader will find in each one something that piques interest or raises questions, and that all six stories taken together will perhaps stimulate thinking and exploration.

It has been a great privilege to have had the opportunity over the course of the last twenty-five years to dance with, talk with, and get to know so many wonderful people—and a privilege as well to experience once again each community in my kinesthetic memory as I wrote its story. As I have "listened" again to interviews, either recorded or in print, I have heard each person's voice and particular inflections and emphases, and I have "seen" in my mind's eye their movements as they spoke, danced, called dances, or made music. I have again experienced each person's lively engagement with the dancing and the sense of it as an integral part of the fabric of life. Each one was clearly a contributor to his or her community's living, evolving tradition: both by participation and by expression or enactment of preferences regarding music, kinds of dancing, particular movement patterns, or the structure of dance events. In telling these stories, I have tried to focus on what has given life and meaning to old time dancing in communities where it has thrived in the late twentieth and early twenty-first centuries.

I could have chosen to do an in-depth, book-length study of just one community, and surely each community merits such attention. It would be beneficial to look at this dancing more thoroughly in the context of other dancing in the community, other movement expressions, other traditions, and community structure and interaction. However, placing these six communities side by side, it is possible to see similarities and differences and to get a more nuanced picture of the culture, or cultures, of the Appalachian region.

The dance conventions are specific to each community, while having drawn on larger pools of custom and popular culture over the course of a century or more. Perhaps the reader has been aware of the way that some people, places, and events appear in more than one story, to different effect. The evolution of dance traditions can be compared to a tapestry with interwoven threads. Communities develop distinct traditions but are not truly isolated from each other, though they may be separated by distances. The similarities and differences have their roots in historical, geographical, and societal factors, dating from the earliest non-indigenous arrivals.[1] Though each community's dancing bears witness to elements of its own history, tradition is dynamic, never static, constantly changing over time.

The particular blending of elements in each place has resulted in dissimilar conventions. The structure of one community may have been disrupted by industrialization more than that of another, opening the way for new customs to take root more readily. The local music and dance of one area may have been more extensively represented in the media, validating a resurgence in interest. Institutions may have sustained and influenced dance customs in one area, opportunities for participating in popular dance and music may have been more accessible in another, and another may have had more direct experience with the folk revival. But any of these circumstances was not in itself responsible for the appearance of the dancing in the late twentieth century. Rather, a variety of circumstances came together over the course of time. Residents of each community experienced and responded to these circumstances within their own frame of reference.

I believe that the participants' creative responses to societal change, rather than simply the change itself, shaped the dancing. For example, industrialization took different forms in each place, and some residents used old time dancing as a way to react to it, based upon their own community's history, expectations, and aesthetics: by maintaining old ways, by reviving old ways, by incorporating new ways, or by attempting to stave them off. Changes in musical taste resulted in movement changes in response to new music, and elements of popular dance forms were incorporated into various local dances. Certain specific individuals have guided each community in one direction or another, but every participant had a role.

The dancing as it appeared in each place at the time described in this book was the result of continual such decisions made by individuals and groups. Besides the mutual influence of traditional and popular culture, various other kinds of cultural exchange affected decision making: interaction among urban and rural practices, among national trends and local customs, between northern and southern approaches, and among customs of African Americans, European Americans, Native Americans, and recent immigrants to the United States. Other factors were deliberate interventions by the government or philanthropic institutions, the focus of collectors, or the response of media. No community was a passive recipient of any influence; rather, each was a creative participant in the evolution of its own expression. Old time dancing, where it continues to exist, still unfolds as a result of cultural exchange and creative decisions: at a particular Saturday night dance a few years ago, one young freestyle clogger ripped off an improvised routine with a style blending the angularity, sharpness, and isolated arm, leg, and head movements of hip hop with the complicated foot rhythms of contemporary clogging.

Having emphasized the particularity of each community, I must also recognize that some commonalites do exist. All of the communities I have described in this book seem to share, to a greater or lesser degree, the theme of family and community centeredness—this, in spite of the fact that most of the dance events are or were held in venues separate from the home.[2] In almost all of these cases a multigenerational experience was valued, though it was more apparent in some than in others. Even descriptions of the nights out at places like Mr. Perry's Sweet Shop sounded more like those of community-centered old time dancing events than they resembled Katrina Hazzard-Gordon's accounts of the juke joints of the time. Still, individuality has been valued in many of the groups, within the local aesthetic and within the supportive framework of the community. Luther Gulick's statement that "freedom lies in the recognition and joyful acceptance of relationships" seems to ring true in the context of these particular community dances. Many of the dance events involved an element of contribution to the community, either through fundraising or through the development of the individual or the community through the dance experience. At each place, dancers seemed to express, with their regular attendance and sometimes with their words, a sense of responsibility for the success of the event. Declarations of gratitude for the organizers were frequent, and some participants stated their concern for the continued future of the dance.

Related to the paired issues of community and individuality is another seeming dichotomy: performance dance and participation dance. Much dance scholarship is focused on performance forms like ballet or modern, in which highly skilled and trained individuals express a choreographer's ideas, concepts, or feelings. Among the communities represented here, some did value personal demonstration of skill. It seems to me that even when such displays took place, they were within the context of cooperation rather than competition. Soloists or small groups who took the limelight were supported by the surrounding circle; by local accounts, their excellence helped to lift everyone up. In less obvious ways, improvisation within the aesthetic framework in the communities also helped to energize the whole group. The questions arose for me: When is performance actually participation? When does competition serve a cooperative function? Even in the most flamboyant examples of performance described in these chapters, the individual had to be communicating with the group—or, at the very least, with the partner—in order to be in keeping with local custom. I wonder about other dance forms such as hip hop and Capoeria. In my brief contact with these dances, it somehow seems that although an individual may be spotlighted, communication and group cohesiveness is still important.

Break and Revival

During the twentieth century, old time dancing experienced cycles of decline and revival in the mountains of Northeast Tennessee, Southwest Virginia, and Eastern Kentucky. It is important to recall that old time dancing was in fact popular culture in the beginning of that century, being supplanted or altered in some places by jazz dances like the Charleston and lindy in the second quarter. With World War II, old time dancing almost disappeared in many of these places, only to reemerge in conjunction with the folk revival of the 1960s and succeeding decades, and then to fade again by the turn of the twenty-first century.

Seemingly, those who returned to the tradition felt "restored by some deep . . . spring of well-being."[3] A large number of consultants looked back to an earlier time when talking about traditional square dancing or footwork dancing. Of course, many of us look to our youth and young adulthood as a happy time, but most of these accounts seemed deeper than that, including discussion of mutual support, tenacity, and ingenuity. Though the circumstances differed in each community, dance seemed to link them to experiences or values from decades earlier. But these were not mere reenactments or exercises in nostalgia: the dancing very clearly brought these experiences and values into the present.

Currently, old time square dancing may be undergoing another revival, coinciding with a broader folk revival and a growing interest in both black and white string band music. However, it is taking place in localities and among populations very different from the ones in which it had originally emerged. A lively old time movement exists on the West Coast, with callers traveling to other areas. A former settlement school has had a national influence as well. In 2011, John C. Campbell Folk School hosted a weekend called Dare to be Square, bringing together well-known modern western, traditional western, New England, and Appalachian square dance callers, and sixty participants from as far away as California, Vermont, and New Mexico. A syllabus was subsequently published and similar weekends were held in Virginia in 2012 and in West Virginia in 2013. Several such weekends are planned for 2014 from Tennessee to Los Angeles. In

Louisville, Kentucky, a caller formerly from Washington State leads a monthly old time square dance, frequented by an intergenerational community, many of whom did not grow up with the tradition and are unfamiliar with the culture out of which it grew. Yet old time square dance draws them month after month. What is its meaning for them? And, more broadly, what is its place in twenty-first-century urban culture? Dance ethnologist Deidre Sklar believes that dance embodies large questions: "Where do I belong? How do human beings behave? Where do I come from and with whom do I go through life? What do I value?"[4] Perhaps these questions hold a key to the interest of these new old time dancers. One may wonder, too, if this new interest will lead to a reawakening of the traditions in mountain localities, as the last folk revival did, and if local and regional styles and repertoires will develop. It may be worth considering why these kinds of dance seem to keep reemerging, sometimes seemingly from grassroots sources and sometimes as a result of deliberate intervention.

Change, Continuity, and the Power of Tradition

Change is a thread that runs through this volume, and in fact at one point the word had a place in the working title. On the other side of the same coin is continuity. These accounts make clear that the Appalachian region keeps changing and that cultural expression takes shape with it.

In the first chapter, I cited Theresa Buckland's contention that "traces of the past may be discovered in the ways in which people execute particular movements and use their bodies."[5] In almost every one of these communities, it is possible to trace certain elements that have roots in older traditions in that community. However, even within periods of a decade or less, these elements have undergone formal, stylistic, or contextual changes. Dances that once existed as singing games in their own right became endings to square dances, footwork was separated from or added to square dancing, methods of progression changed, or recorded music was substituted for live music to open the way for a broader repertoire, for example. In one case, a completely new form replaced the old one while maintaining some stylistic and contextual elements; in another, efforts were made to introduce entirely new kinds of dance, yet local tradition prevailed.

I have come to wonder which constitutes the thread of continuity that binds a tradition within a community: the beliefs or the physical enactment. I have emphasized the effect of individual and group creativity in shaping dance traditions. A question arises as to how far individual creativity can push before a tradition completely develops into something new or is dropped altogether. To state this issue another way: How much change can a community absorb before its structure and affect are transformed? On the other end of the spectrum is the problem of what happens when a tradition is maintained unchanged, despite rapid social transformation surrounding it.

Both change and continuity are evidence to me of the power of local tradition. I have seen how local traditions have the flexibility and resilience to absorb new elements and still retain integrity as an expression of the community. Even with the dramatic change in style in Dante, Virginia, the dancing still drew the community together as it once had. Eastern Kentucky residents report thoroughly enjoying the English folk dance offered at settlement schools, but for regular recreation, a number returned to the local traditional dancing. The new kinds of dance did not take root as a community expression, but the remembered enjoyment of them influenced local dance events. Carcassonne, in Kentucky, both maintained its local repertoire and retained its integrity as a community event even with substantial numbers of guests almost every month. Richard Jett believed that local traditional dance had the power to transform individuals and society. Many who danced at Hoedown Island credited that experience with giving their lives new direction. What is it about the dynamic between continuity and change that has kept these kinds of dance going into the twenty-first century in some communities while in so many they have disappeared entirely?

Local Appalachian cultures continue to evolve. Many kinds of dance are found in various community settings in the Appalachian region, including such styles as hip hop, stepping, and salsa. In response to my brief study of Appalachian hip hop, my colleague Chad Berry posed a problem: "You have established that hip hop is *in* Appalachia, but what makes it *of* Appalachia?" Similar inquiries may be made about such present-day dance trends as Argentine tango and contemporary swing dancing, around which communities coalesce in various places in the Appalachian region. Do their manifestations here have similarities to the older local kinds of dance, in structure, affect, or context, or do they reflect some other aspects of local culture? Or are they entirely distinct from other local expressions, containing the same meanings and values they do in, for example, New York City?

Dance as a Way of Being

I mentioned in chapter 1 a number of studies of vernacular dance that had influenced my thinking. They are among a small but growing body of literature on the subject. Of these, only a few discussed social dance, and only a few more studied dance in North America. Add to those some insightful cultural studies of United States social dance that focus on hip hop, salsa, underground house dancing, krumping, Cajun and zydeco dance, polka, DanceSport, and ballroom dancing.[6] This list of studies of popular dancing seems long, but it by no means covers the territory of all kinds of dance in the United States. While the number of such ethnographies is increasing, they are few compared with historical studies of related forms or with critical analyses of theatrical dance, and infinitesimal when compared, for example, with the number of works of literary criticism. We will understand and appreciate any one kind of social dance much more when it has been the subject of multiple studies by different individuals, and when more comparisons among dance forms become possible. As a result, we may come to deeper understanding of the particular society which forms the context for the dancing.

The sparseness of research in this field may be due in part to the fact that movement style is "so ubiquitous, so 'naturalized' as to be nearly unnoticed as a symbolic system, . . . complex, [and] continuously changing."[7] However, anyone who has danced can discuss the meanings his or her chosen form holds. A colleague of mine typically asks classes of beginning dancers to consider what values and beliefs their own popular social dances express, and she reports that when she does this, the class discussion is always lively and insightful. I hope that the present volume encourages the reader to ask these same questions of his or her own dance experiences. It will become clear that dance is expressive of the dancer, of his or her relationship with the other dancers, of the group's aesthetic preferences, and of their cultural background. Dance grows out of a community and a culture, expresses what is important to it, helps to navigate through periods of change, and can sometimes contribute to change. No dance takes place in a vacuum but rather "exists in a complex network of relationships to other dances and other nondance ways of using the body" and within the framework of the particular society and the many elements of its history.[8] The very ubiquity, naturalness, complexity, and malleability of dance and its relationship to other ways of moving and engaging in society is what makes it an ideal object of study.

It is worth considering various modes of expression in relation to one another: popular dance forms, language, dress, foodways and social gatherings, even the arrangement of our homes and towns. All are connected by aspects of the elements of space, time, weight, and flow. A recent article in the New York Times caught my attention in relation to the ebb and flow of old time square dancing. It examined, using data from an extensive Google analysis, the change in frequency in the use of certain words. Political and cultural commentator David Brooks observed that since 1960, "words and phrases like 'personalized,' 'self,' 'unique,' 'I come first' and 'I can do it myself' were used more frequently. Communal words and phrases like 'community,' 'collective,' 'tribe,' 'share,' 'united,' 'band together' and 'common good' receded." He suggested that these "shifts in language reflect . . . shifts in culture" demonstrating less interest in "community bonds and obligations because they are less central to our lives."[9] One might ponder the connection between such a shift and the decline in popularity of old time square dancing during the last half century, and one might look for clues in the language choices of those involved in the contemporary old time dance revival. Whether this link is factual or imagined, it opens the door to studies that bring together linguistics and dance ethnology. Further, if we approach dance as "a way of being,"[10] rather than as a recreational activity, then the distinction between community economic and political studies and studies in cultural expression may come to seem entirely arbitrary, beckoning to new scholarly partnerships in these areas.

At the beginning of this volume, I made the point that I have offered just one of many possible ways to tell the stories of these six communities. I hope that I may have brought this dancing to life for the reader in some measure. I trust that the stories of other communities will be told—Native American, African American, Latin American, Asian American, European American, and more—both in the Appalachian region and elsewhere. These stories represent not a conclusion but a process, building on the work of previous researchers. More can be said, more can be understood, and these and other American dance traditions can be studied in new ways. It is my desire that others will find this work useful as a step toward future such projects.

Notes

Chapter 1. Dynamic Traditions

1. Farnell, "It Goes without Saying," 148.
2. Hobsbawm and Ranger, *Invention of Tradition*, 2.
3. Novack, *Sharing the Dance*, 8.
4. Sklar, "Remembering Kinesthesia," 92.
5. Grau, "Fieldwork, Politics, and Power," 165.
6. Griswold, "A Methodological Framework," 1–5.
7. See, for example, Sally Ann Ness, *Body, Movement, and Culture: Kinesthetic and Visual Symbolism in a Philippine Community* (1992); Yvonne Daniels, *Rumba: Dance and Social Change in Contemporary Cuba* (1995) and *Embodied Wisdom in Haitian Vodou, Cuban Yoruba, and Bahian Candomblé* (2005); Barbara Browning, *Infectious Rhythm: Metaphors of Contagion and the Spread of African Culture* (1998); Deidre Sklar, *Dancing with the Virgin: Body and Faith in the Fiesta of Tortugas, New Mexico* (2001); Elizabeth Fine, *Soulstepping: African American Step Shows* (2007); Anthony Barrand, *Six Fools and a Dancer* (1991).
8. See, for example, Mary McNab Dart, *Contra Dance Choreography: A Reflection of Social Change* (1995); Daniel J. Walkowitz, *City Folk* (2010); John Bealle, *Old-Time Music and Dance: Community and Folk Revival* (2005).
9. See Friedland, "Traditional Folkdance in Kentucky," 5–19; Feintuch, "Dancing to the Music," 49–68; Dalsemer, *West Virginia Square Dances*; Matthews, "Cutting a Dido"; Matthews-DeNatale, "Wild and Yet Really Subdued," 111–26.
10. Hall, "Madness and Recall," 127.
11. Buckland, *Dance in the Field*, 205.
12. Ness, "Being a Body," 123.
13. Farnell, "It Goes without Saying," 148; Buckland, *Dancing from Past to Present*, 13.
14. Desmond, "Embodying Difference," 31.
15. Buckland, *Dancing from Past to Present*, 12.

16. Ward, "Dancing around Meaning," 18.
17. Desmond, "Embodying Difference," 31.
18. Sklar, "Remembering Kinesthesia," 91.
19. Sklar, "Five Premises," 1.
20. Bull "Sense, Meaning, and Perception," 282, 279, 281, 275.
21. Sklar, "Embodying Difference," 99.
22. Ness, "Understanding Cultural Performance," 39–50.
23. Grau, "Fieldwork, Politics, and Power," 165.
24. Buckland, *Dancing from Past to Present*, 8.

Chapter 2. Lively Dance Currents

1. Dunaway, *First American Frontier*, 1–2.
2. Batteau, *Invention of Appalachia*, 1.
3. Dunaway, *First American Frontier*, 14; Billings and Blee, *Road to Poverty*, 34.
4. Lewis, "Beyond Isolation and Homogeneity," 22–23; Noe, *Southwest Virginia's Railroad*, 13–14.
5. Noe, *Southwest Virginia's Railroad*, 36–37.
6. Carson, *Theatre on the Frontier*, 64.
7. Dunaway, *First American Frontier*, 125–27.
8. Noe, *Southwest Virginia's Railroad*, 13.
9. Billings and Blee, *Road to Poverty*, 28.
10. Noe, *Southwest Virginia's Railroad*, 32.
11. Lewis, "Beyond Isolation and Homogeneity," 23–24.
12. Noe, *Southwest Virginia's Railroad*, 54.
13. Lewis, "Beyond Isolation and Homogeneity," 22–23.
14. Dunaway, *First American Frontier*, 131.
15. Noe, *Southwest Virginia's Railroad*, 111.
16. Lewis, "Beyond Isolation and Homogeneity," 28, 31, 24.
17. Hsiung, *Two Worlds*, 187.
18. Lewis, "Beyond Isolation and Homogeneity," 31–32.
19. Lewis, "Beyond Isolation and Homogeneity," 32–33; Caudill, *Eastern Kentucky Mountain Memories*, 126; Sexton, interview, 1975.
20. Lewis, "Beyond Isolation and Homogeneity," 34; Lee, *Tennessee-Virginia Tri-Cities*, 106.
21. Lewis, "Beyond Isolation and Homogeneity," 35, 38.
22. Mrs. John C. Campbell, "Flame of a New Future," 9.
23. Desmond, "Embodying Difference," 31.
24. See Benson, "Itinerant Dancing."
25. Sobel, *World They Made Together*, 5, 8.
26. Needham, *I See America Dancing*, 62.
27. Eslinger, *Citizens of Zion*, 55.
28. Smith, "Horace Holley," 2.
29. Aldrich, "Nineteenth Century Social Dance."
30. Wolfe, "Davy Crockett's Dance," 36–38.

31. Szwed and Marks, "Afro-American Transformation," 36–38.

32. Jamison, "Square Dance Calling," 387–98; Roger D. Abrahams, *Singing the Master*, 127–30.

33. See Wolfe, "Rural Black String Band Music," 32–35; and Wolfe, "Lost Tradition."

34. Meyen, *Ball Room Guide*, 17.

35. Aldrich, "Nineteenth Century Social Dance"; KP series V, box 1 folder 8.

36. Spurgeon, *Waltz the Hall*, 202, 203; Jones and Hawes, *Step It Down*, 94.

37. Aldrich, "Nineteenth Century Social Dance;" Condee, *Coal and Culture*, 27.

38. Sharp, *Country Dance Book, Part V*.

39. Calhoun, presentation, 1989; Cunningham, interview; Powell, interview; Kincaid, interview; Kent, "Frolics," 9–11, 15.

40. Carson, *Theatre on the Frontier*, 2–4; 64.

41. Brooks, "John Durang."

42. Robinson, *Old Wagon Show Days*, 22, 28.

43. Swift, *Belles and Beaus*, 42–33, 63.

44. Swift, *Belles and Beaus*, 221–22, 187.

45. Needham, *I See America Dancing*, 158.

46. Condee, *Coal and Culture*, 99; Winans, "Black Instrumental Music Traditions," 52; see also Kyriakoudes, "Grand Ole Opry."

47. Swift, *Belles and Beaus*, 81–83.

48. New National Theatre, *New National Theatre*.

49. Condee, *Coal and Culture*, 103, 145, 131, 140, 65.

50. Condee, *Coal and Culture*, 103, 48.

51. Condee, *Coal and Culture*, 59, 151, 122.

52. Condee, *Coal and Culture*, 28; Francois Delsarte (1811–1871) developed methods and principles for improving "vocal and dramatic expression [and] aesthetics. . . . American Delsartism featured training methods for physical and vocal expression, exercises for physical conditioning, and performance forms (statue-posing, pantomime, drills and even dance)." American modern dance pioneers Isadora Duncan and Ruth St. Denis were among those influenced by American Delsartism. See Ruyter, "Delsarte Heritage," 62.

53. "Denishawn Dance Company Tour 1922–23."

54. Hardinge, conversation.

55. See Delamont and Duffin, *Nineteenth Century Woman*; and Gilbert, "Dancing," 283–87.

56. See Tomko, *Dancing Class*.

57. "Records and Memorabilia," UTK.

58. Dunn, "To Be a Dancer," 1–2.

Chapter 3. Old Time Dancing in Northeast Tennessee: Traditional Values in an Industrial Region

1. Johnson and Spalding, *All Join Hands*. Video documentary and footage of dancing and interviews at Beechwood and of Old Time Dance Conferences are housed in the Archives of Appalachia, a unit of the Center for Appalachian Studies and Services, East Tennessee State University.

2. Lee, *Tennessee-Virginia Tri-Cities*, 241.

3. Wolfe, *Tennessee Strings*, 47.

4. Lee, *Tennessee-Virginia Tri-Cities*, 7, 6.

5. Miller, interview, July 21, 1987.

6. Hsiung, "How Isolated Was Appalachia," 345.

7. Winders, *History of Kingsport*, 19.

8. Hsiung, "How Isolated Was Appalachia," 345.

9. Jamison, "Square Dance Calling," 387–88.

10. Lee, *Tennessee-Virginia Tri-Cities*, 45–50; 91–95.

11. Wolfe, *Tennessee Strings*, 15, 17.

12. Malone, *Singing Cowboys*, 73.

13. Malone, *Singing Cowboys*, 64; Wolfe, *Tennessee Strings*, 30, 21.

14. Wolfe, *Tennessee Strings*, 21, 23. After his terms as governor, Robert Love Taylor traveled a speaking and performing circuit in which he included stories of music and dancing, and a story about a dance following a quilting bee, called by "Old Uncle Ephraim, a black man" dressed in his master's finery (Wolfe, *Tennessee Strings*, 25).

15. Lee, *Tennessee-Virginia Tri-Cities*, 79.

16. Lee, *Tennessee-Virginia Tri-Cities*, 106, 108; 180, 162.

17. Crawford, interview.

18. Lee, *Tennessee-Virginia Tri-Cities*, 158.

19. Baines, interview.

20. Baines, interview; Cassell, interview; Warren, interview.

21. Wolfe, "Davy Crockett's Dance," 35.

22. Cassell, interview; Baines, interview.

23. Taylor, interview; Zwigoff, "Black Country String Bands," 50–51.

24. Wolfe, *Tennessee Strings*, 41, 28, 46.

25. Malone, *Singing Cowboys*, 71, 79.

26. Kyriakoudes, "Grand Ole Opry," 68; Berry, *Hayloft Gang*, 92.

27. See Cox, *Fiddlin' Charlie Bowman*.

28. Malone, *Singing Cowboys*, 65, 67.

29. Wolfe, *Tennessee Strings*, 61; Kyriakoudes, "Grand Ole Opry," 71, 69.

30. Buckland, *Dancing from Past to Present*, 17.

31. Lee, *Tennessee-Virginia Tri-Cities*, 185, 190–91; 242.

32. Brown, *Dimensions of Change*, 24–27.

33. Rowland, interview; Cassell, interview.

34. Cox, *Fiddlin' Charlie Bowman*, 149.

35. According to square dance historian LeeEllen Friedland, traditional western square dancing had earlier developed from a blending of features from square dances from the Northeast, Southeast, and Midwest. Four-couple sets are the norm in western square dancing. In the 1930s, Lloyd Shaw promoted Western square dance through educational materials, demonstration teams, and seminars for teachers. By the 1950s, the teaching became standardized into modern western square dancing and the clubs became more formalized and hierarchical. Dress was formalized as well, with western shirts for men and frilly, crinolined skirts for women. Professional callers increased the repertoire of calls,

and in order to participate, one had to enroll in a series of standardized classes of increasing difficulty. Hundreds of modern western square dance clubs were formed all over the world, including in countries as various as the United Arab Emirates, China, New Zealand, and the Czech Republic. For further information on other forms of square dancing see LeeEllen Friedland, "Square Dancing," in *The International Encyclopedia of Dance*, edited by Selma Jean Cohen, vol. 5, 689. See also Damon, *History of Square Dancing*.

36. Malone, *Singing Cowboys*, 100.

37. See Rollins and O'Connor, *Hollywood's West*.

38. Malone, *Singing Cowboys*, 90–91.

39. Brooks, *Behind the Scenes*, 7, 9.

40. Thompson, *Wagon Train*, 148.

41. Baines, interview.

42. Miller, interview, August 4, 1987; Baines, interview. The connection between square dancing and wagon training is not unique to Northeast Tennessee. The Fancy Gap, Virginia, dance grew out of wagon training in the 1970s and continued for at least twenty-five years. The dance that the Fancy Gap Elementary School Parent Teachers' Association held for the wagon train each year was so successful that organizers decided to make the dance a weekly event to benefit the school, separate from the wagon train. See Spalding, "Frolics."

43. Malone, *Singing Cowboys*, 105, 107.

44. Jamison, "Green Grass Cloggers," 169–70.

45. Malone, *Singing Cowboys*, 114.

46. Sloan, interview.

47. Sundell, "Rural Square Dances," 62; Miller, interview, August 4, 1987.

48. Netherland, "Carter Family Fold."

49. Leland, "At Home With/The Carter Family."

50. Baker, interview.

51. Sturgill, interview.

52. The two-step style performed at Beechwood and at other old time dance venues in the Tri-Cities area was a variation of the fox trot. Male and female partners held each other in a casual ballroom style and progressed sideways to the man's left around the room in a counterclockwise direction. The step pattern was a six-count phrase, performed against duple meter music. The man's step pattern was: Left—together, Left—together, Right–together. (1 and, 2 and, 3 and).

53. Beechwood dancers did not use the term "figures" to refer to movement sequences. Two couple moves were called "circle fours" or sometimes "dances." Large group moves were called only by specific names, like London Bridge or Grapevine Swing.

54. At the Chilhowie (Virginia) Lions' Club, an hour's drive north of Beechwood, the square dances had much the same choreographic form: large group circles and figures begin and end the dance, with circle fours separated by a promenade in the middle portion. However, in Chilhowie dancers coupled up four with the same couple each time, rather than finding a new couple with whom to dance, so the dancing was more about socializing among couples than about interaction among all dancers. People there also tended to dress up a bit more, so the feeling of the evening was more like a couple's

night out. A number of dancers from both Beechwood and he Chilhowie Lions' Club attended the dance at the other venue, accommodating to local custom.

55. Some communities use footwork during a square dance, and some do not; this has been true historically in North Carolina, Tennessee, Virginia, and Kentucky. James Kesterson is credited with popularizing precision clogging in the 1950s. In it, everyone does the same step at the same time, often organized in line formations, but sometimes dancing square dance figures.

56. For more on Hugh Miller's calling style, see Sundell, "Rural Square Dances," 62–63.

57. Miller, interview, July 21, 1987.

58. Miller, interview, August 4, 1987; Sundell, "Rural Square Dances," 63; for more on Robert Dotson, see Jamison, "Robert and Myrtle Dotson."

59. All material on effective calling comes from Miller, "You Have to Watch Your People," 31–34.

60. Miller, interview, August 4, 1987.

61. Crawford, interview; Miller, interview, July 21, 1987; Baines, interview; Rowland interview. Miller interview.

62. Baines, interview; Miller, interview, July 21, 1987.

63. Kirby, interview.

64. Jamison, "Robert and Myrtle Dotson," 17.

65. Cassell, interview.

Chapter 4. Blue Ridge Breakdown: Stability and Tradition in an African American Community

1. See Lornell, *Virginia Traditions*; Wolfe, "Lost Tradition"; Wolfe, "Rural Black String Band Music"; and Conway, *African Banjo Echoes*.

2. Calhoun, presentation; Powell, interview; Wolfe, "Rural Black String Band Music," 32–35. Mathews, "Eight Hands Up!" 12–15.

3. Holloway, "Origins of Afro-American Culture," 16; Musser, "Economic and Social Aspects," 58; Lewis and O'Donnell, eds., *Ivanhoe, Virginia*, 13, 27; See Sobel, *World They Made Together*.

4. Cunningham, interview; Kent, "Frolics," 9–11; Zwigoff, "Black Country String Bands," 50–52; Cabbell, interview.

5. Reece, "Selected Folksongs," 35–40.

6. Powell, interview.

7. Lewis and O'Donnell, *Ivanhoe, Virginia*, 101.

8. Kent, "Frolics," 10; Zwigoff, "Black Country String Bands," 51; Carter and Trent, interview; Iva Turk, interview with author; Earl and Eleanor Kincaid, interview.

9. Cabbell, interview; Arnow, "A Part and Apart," 10; Powell, interview.

10. Bowles and Cook, interview; Lornell, *Virginia Traditions*, 12.

11. Data from United States Census Bureau.

12. Arnow, "A Part and Apart," 9.

13. Siler, *Fayette Street*, 50; Chittum, "Draped in Prosperity"; Packer, "Ghost Town"; *The Economist*, "Unemployment and the Mid-terms."

14. Virginia African American Heritage Program, "The Block."

15. Bowles, interview, July 23, 1992; Virginia African American Heritage Program, "Dr. Dana Baldwin"; Siler, *Fayette Street*, 34, 59.

16. Siler, *Fayette Street*, 66, 59, 46; Lornell, *Virginia Traditions*, 4.

17. Bowles, interview, July 23, 1992; Siler, *Fayette Street*, 53–54; Bowles and Cook, interview.

18. Old Fiddler's Convention: History; Siler, *Fayette Street*, 54, 59; Lornell, *Virginia Traditions*, 4.

19. North Carolina Office of Archives & History, "Way We Lived."

20. Siler, *Fayette Street*, 31, 54–59; Virginia African American Heritage Program, "What Is a JGB?" and "Going to the Ball."

21. Siler, *Fayette Street*, 26, 19, 21, 66, 45, 72, 79.

22. *History of the American Negro*, 290–91, quoted in Siler, *Fayette Street*, 23.

23. Lewis and O'Donnell, *Ivanhoe, Virginia*, 68–69; Debose, interview; Carter and Trent, interview; Powell, interview.

24. Brooks, interview; Bowles, interview, July 23, 1992.

25. Bowles, interview, July 23, 1992; Brooks, interview.

26. Bowles, interview; Brooks, interview; Raitz and Ulack, *Appalachia, A Regional Geography*, 117, 121; Bowles, interview, July 23, 1992.

27. Siler, *Fayette Street*, 104–5; Lewis and O'Donnell, *Ivanhoe, Virginia*, 108, 95, 140; Conway, *African Banjo Echoes*, 149–50.

28. Brooks, interview; Bowles, interview, July 23, 1992; Bowles, interview, February 28, 1977; Kent, "Frolics," 9; Lornell, *Virginia Traditions*, 9; Zwigoff, "Black Country String Bands," 50–51; Conway, *African Banjo Echoes*, 10, 69, 150; Bowles, interview.

29. Brooks, interview; Bowles, interview, July 23, 1992; Bowles, interview, February 28, 1977.

30. Bowles, interview, February 28, 1977.

31. Kent, "Frolics," 10.

32. Szwed and Marks, "Afro-American Transformation," 31; Winans, "Black Instrumental Music Traditions," 50–51, 53; Conway, *African Banjo Echoes*, 141–51.

33. Kent, "Frolics," 10; Martin, "Joe and Odell Thompson," 4; Bowles, interview, July 23, 1992.

34. Bowles, interview, February 28, 1977.

35. Brooks, interview; Bowles, interview, July 23, 1992; Hazzard-Gordon, *Jookin'*, 96–97, 111–16.

36. Martin, "Joe and Odell Thompson," 5; Kent, "Frolics," 9–10; Bowles, interview, February 28, 1977.

37. Bowles, interview, July 23, 1992; Brooks, interview.

38. Martin, "Joe and Odell Thompson," 6; Bowles and Cook, interview; Bowles, interview, February 28, 1977; Bowles, interview, July 23, 1992; Brooks, interview.

39. All description and analysis is based upon video documentation of the Martinsville dancers by Kip Lornell. See Blue Ridge Institute, *Way Out West*.

40. Bowles, interview, July 23, 1992; in European American communities in the Blue Ridge, flatfooting was a solo dance, but many people did it at the same time, aware of each other, but not purposely dancing with someone. No one took the limelight. For

further discussion of African and African American traditions of dancing solo in the center of the circle, see Abrahams, *Singing the Master*; Emery, *Black Dance*; Epstein, *Sinful Tunes and Spirituals*; and Jones and Hawes, *Step it Down*.

41. Brooks, interview (Leonard Bowles was present and inserted his comment); Kent, "Frolics," 11.

42. By contrast, in nearby European American communities, the swing is a fluid, one-circle walk-around clockwise, usually in ballroom position, the man and woman seeming to step beside each other's right feet, rather than facing each other directly. For further analysis and comparison of African American and European American old time dance, see Spalding, "Aesthetic Standards."

43. Epstein, *Sinful Tunes and Spirituals*, 159; For discussion of Old Dan Tucker in Eastern Kentucky, see chapter 8.

44. Williams, *Cotton Needs Pickin'*, 12–14; Szwed and Marks, "Afro-American Transformation," 33; Kent, "Frolics," 11.

45. Bowles, interview, July 23, 1992. In the similar figure, Georgia Alabam, as it was performed in Fancy Gap, Calvin Cole said that the dancers "catch hands and go around," emphasizing the fluid circular motion rather than the exchange of partners.

46. Brooks, interview; Bowles, interview, July 23, 1992.

47. Bowles, interview, July 23, 1992.

48. Kent, "Frolics," 11.

49. Bowles, interview, July 23, 1992; Jones and Hawes, *Step it Down*, 20, 90; Bowles, interview. In some European American square dance communities, people clap while others dance in the center of the circle. See chapter 8 for an example.

50. Some people in European American old time dance communities have also called my attention to the similarity between local footwork dancing and the dancing in certain churches.

51. Brooks, interview.

52. Bowles, interview, July 23, 1992.

53. Cunningham, interview; Powell, interview; Kent, "Frolics," 11.

54. Siler, *Fayette Street*, 66, 72–73, 65, 92, 79, 92–93.

55. Siler, *Fayette Street*, 92, 106.

56. Gates, *Colored People*, 184; Powell, interview.

57. Siler, *Fayette Street*, 98; Bowles, interview, July 23, 1992.

58. Siler, *Fayette Street*, 86.

59. Arnow, "A Part and Apart," 10.

60. Bowles, interview, July 23, 1992.

61. Cantwell, *Bluegrass Breakdown*, 51–52. Bowles, interview, July 23, 1992; Brooks, interview.

62. Wolfe, "Rural Black String Band Music," 33.

63. Winans, "Black Instrumental Music Traditions," 50–51; 53, 52.

64. Lornell, *Virginia Traditions*, 10.

65. Wolfe, "Rural Black String Band Music," 32–34; Wolfe, "Lost Tradition," 1–2; Jamison, "Square Dance Calling," 395; Mathews, "Eight Hands Up!" 12–15; Jones, "DeFord Bailey," 30.

66. Whisnant, *All That Is Native and Fine*, 244–45, 321.

67. Wolfe, "Rural Black String Band Music," 32.
68. Wolfe, "Lost Tradition," 2.
69. Bowles, interview, February 28, 1977.
70. Cantwell, *Bluegrass Breakdown*, 74.
71. Siler, *Fayette Street*, 101, 107.
72. Bowles, interview, July 23, 1992.
73. Bowles and Cook, interview; Leonard and Naomi Bowles, interview.

Chapter 5. Mr. Perry's Sweet Shop and a New Old Time Dance

1. Kincaid, interview.
2. See Johnson and Spalding, *Step Back Cindy*, for footage of old time dancing at the Dante Fire Hall and elsewhere in Southwest Virginia. Footage of dancing and interviews is housed in the Smithsonian Center for Folklife and Cultural Heritage and at the Berea College Hutchins Library Department of Special Collections and Archives.
3. Debose, interview.
4. For descriptions of African American dance style see Hazzard-Gordon, *Jookin'*; Thompson, "Kongo Influences"; and Dixon-Gottschild, *Digging the Africanist Presence.*
5. Crow, *Do, Die, or Get Along*, 4, 11, 8.
6. Shearer, *Memories from Dante*, 428; Kincaid, interview; Hoffman, "Appalachian African American Cultural Center," 1; Taylor, interview.
7. Crow, *Do, Die, or Get Along*, 14, 17, 18–21.
8. Corbin, "Class over Caste," 93.
9. See Swidler, "Culture in Action: Symbols and Strategies," 273–86; and Hobsbawm and Ranger, *Invention of Tradition.*
10. Rosa Powell, interview; Kincaid, interview; Cabbell, interview; Deel, interview; Cassell, interview.
11. Zwigoff, "Black Country String Bands," 50–51; Kincaid, interview.
12. Deel, interview.
13. Taylor, interview.
14. Quentin "Fris" Holloway (now deceased) and John "Dee" Holman are National Heritage Fellows. Their performance and interview were videotaped at the 1989 Traditional Dance Conference sponsored by the Center for Appalachian Studies and Services at East Tennessee State University. Footage is housed in the Archives of Appalachia, a Unit of the Center for Appalachian Studies and Services, East Tennessee State University.
15. Kincaid, interview.
16. Deel, interview; Kincaid, interview.
17. Crow, *Do, Die, or Get Along*, 24–25.
18. Shearer, *Memories from Dante*, 293–94; Kincaid, interview; Deel, interview; Crow, *Do, Die, or Get Along*, 26.
19. Avery, interview.
20. Thompson, "Kongo Influences," 148–49.
21. Crow, *Do, Die, or Get Along*, 49, 62, 61.
22. Crow, *Do, Die, or Get Along*, 63.

23. Laing, "Negro Miner in West Virginia," 74.
24. Corbin, "Class over Caste," 107.
25. Crow, *Do, Die, or Get Along*, 47–50; Kincaid, interview; Deel, interview; Lonesome Pine Office on Youth, *Life in the Coal Camps*, 157–60.
26. Crow, *Do, Die, or Get Along*, 50–52.
27. Kincaid, interview; Crow, *Do, Die, or Get Along*, 49.
28. Corbin, "Class over Caste," 98.
29. Taylor, interview.
30. Crow, *Do, Die, or Get Along*, 51.
31. Gilmore, interview; Carter and Trent, interview; Cunningham, interview; Taylor, interview; Kincaid, interview. It is interesting to note that no consultant referred to any of the gathering places as "jook joints" and when asked, responded emphatically that these places were not jooks, but sweet shops or tea rooms.
32. Kincaid, interview.
33. Kincaid, interview; Hurston, *Sanctified Church*, 60.
34. Kincaid, interview; Stearns, *Jazz Dance*, 326; Jones and Hawes, *Step It Down*, xv.
35. Hazzard-Gordon, *Jookin'*, 80.
36. Gilmore, interview; Kincaid, interview.
37. Taylor, interview; Debose, interview; Cabbell, interview; Powell, interview; Deel, interview. Jazz bands were not unique to this area of the mountains. See Archer, "Jazz in the Mountains?"
38. Stearns, *Jazz Dance*, 112; Hurston *Sanctified Church*, 63; Abrahams, *Singing the Master*, 7. For discussion of probable African origins of the Charleston, see Robinson, "Africanisms and the Study of Folklore," and Thompson, "Kongo Influences."
39. Stearns, *Jazz Dance*, 323–26.
40. Kincaid, interview; Taylor, interview.
41. Hazzard-Gordon, *Jookin'*, 93.
42. Shearer, *Memories from Dante*, 284.
43. Stearns, *Jazz Dance*, 326.
44. Shearer, *Memories from Dante*, 178–85; Avery, interview.
45. Shearer, *Memories from Dante*, 289.
46. Kirby Smith, interviews.
47. Shearer, *Memories from Dante*, 353.
48. Kirby, discussion.
49. Mabel Hardison Parker Smith, interview.
50. Deel, interview; Cole, interview.
51. Deel, interview; Crow, *Do, Die, or Get Along*, 119–20, 79.
52. Johnson and Spalding, *Step Back Cindy*.
53. Sklar, "Five Premises," 1; Bull, "Sense, Meaning, and Perception," 269–88.
54. Jones and Hawes, *Step It Down*, 124.
55. Hazzard-Gordon, *Jookin'*, 81.
56. Corbin, "Class over Caste," 97.
57. Abrahams, *Singing the Master*, 94.
58. Johnson and Spalding, *Step Back Cindy*.

59. Turner, "Demography of Black Appalachia," 242.
60. Deel, interview; Powell, interview; Kincaid, interview.
61. Taylor, interview; Kincaid, interview; Hazzard-Gordon, keynote address.
62. Asante, "Commonalities in African Dance," 80.
63. Taylor, interview; Crow, *Do, Die, or Get Along*, 163.

Chapter 6. Dance at Pine Mountain Settlement School: Ideals and Institutions

1. Delamont and Duffin, *Nineteenth Century Woman*, 185.
2. Batteau, *Invention of Appalachia*, 63, 78.
3. Lucy Furman, "Katherine Pettit"; KP series V, box 1, folder 2.
4. KP series V, box 1, folder 10, Summer Program Reports Camp Cedar Grove, Hazard, Kentucky Summer 1899.
5. KP series V, box 1, folders 12–13, Summer Program Reports Camp Industrial June–August 1900, 32–45 and 46–74.
6. KP series V, box 2, folders 1, 3, 6, Summer Program Reports Sassafras 1901.
7. KP series V, box 2, folder 2, Sassafras, 29.
8. KP series V, box 2 folder 3, 4, Sassafras, 30, 36, 71.
9. KP series V, box 2, folder 3, 2–6, Sassafras, 157.
10. PM pt. I series V, box 2, folders 9–10, Calendars 1914–1971.
11. PM pt. I series II, box 1 folder 6, Progress Reports 1915. The Turner family mentioned in this passage has been identified by dancer and dance historian Peter Rogers as a well-known family of dancers and dance callers, two of whom called dances at Pine Mountain. Members of the family continued to lead dances at Pine Mountain at least as recently as 1997 (Rogers, letter).
12. KP SAA 11 series V, box 2, folder 3, Sassafras, 57.
13. Delamont and Duffin, *Nineteenth Century Woman*, 93.
14. H'Doubler, "Educational Possibilities of Dance," 62–63; Addams, *Spirit of Youth*, 20; Walkowitz, *City Folk*, 27.
15. Delamont and Duffin, *Nineteenth Century Woman*, 93.
16. Gilbert, "Dancing," 287.
17. Tomko, *Dancing Class*, 17, 155.
18. Tomko, *Dancing Class*, xii, 147, 153, 191, 196; See Walkowitz, *City Folk*, for more on Burchenal and her relationship with Cecil Sharp.
19. Tomko, *Dancing Class*, 84.
20. Tomko, *Dancing Class*, 171; Walkowitz, *City Folk*, 27–28.
21. PM pt. I, series II, box 1, folder 6, Progress Reports 1915.
22. Gilbert, "Dancing," 284, 287.
23. Hall, *Adolescence*, I:213.
24. Lee, "Play as a School," 67, 70, 72.
25. PM pt. I, series II, box 1, folder 6, Progress Reports 1915.
26. Tomko, *Dancing Class*, 199.
27. Stearns, *Jazz Dance*, 24.
28. Aldrich, *From the Ballroom to Hell*, xvii.

29. Hall, *Adolescence*, I:213–14.
30. Lee, "Play as a School," 76.
31. Bergman and Bernardi, *Our Sisters' Keepers*, 233; Addams, *Spirit of Youth*, 13.
32. Tomko, *Dancing Class*, 143–144, 148.
33. PM pt. I, series II, box 1, folder 5, Progress Reports 1914 August–December.
34. PM pt. I, series II, box 1, folder 3, Progress Reports 1926–29.
35. Campbell, *Southern Highlander*, preface.
36. PM pt. I, series II, box 1, folder 11, Progress Reports 1923.
37. Sealander, *Private Wealth and Public Life*, 189.
38. PM pt. I, series II, box 1, folder 8, Progress Reports 1917.
39. PM pt. I, series II, box 1, folder 5, Progress Reports 1914 August–December. The report of December 23, 1914 excerpts a letter from Miss Margaret McCutcheon.
40. Greene, "Progressives," 180.
41. Walkowitz, *City Folk*, 100, 119; Whisnant, *All That Is Native and Fine*, 116; Scherman, "Man Who Mined," 188; PM pt. I, series I, box 1, folder 1, Letter from Frost to Pettit.
42. Deschamps, letter to Peter Rogers, August 3, 1975.
43. Sharp, *Country Dance Book—Part V*, 7, 10–13.
44. "Notes from the Pine Mountain Settlement School," 1.
45. KP series IV, box 1, folder 8; Eastern Kentucky Folk Dancing Oral History Project. See especially Hiram Brashear and Veldon and A. O. Fields interviews with Peter Rogers; KP series V, box 1, folder 12. For description of cotillions, see Aldrich, *From the Ballroom to Hell.*
46. Sharp, *Country Dance Book—Part V*, 10–13. For descriptions of the courtesy movements, see Sharp, *Country Dance Book—Parts I and II.* For descriptions of the set running figures that follow, see Napier, *Kentucky Mountain Square Dancing.*
47. Abrahams, "Foundations," 259.
48. Sharp, *Country Dance Book—Part V*, 14–15. It should be noted that typically the music of a banjo or fiddle accompanied set running, as Sharp observed at both Hindman and Hyden Settlement Schools.
49. Sharp, *Country Dance Book—Part V*, 14–15; 19. For further information about African American cultural influence see Abrahams, *Singing the Master*; Conway, *African Banjo Echoes in Appalachia*; and Jamison, "Square Dance Calling."
50. Greene, "Progressives," 178, 180.
51. Sharp, *Country Dance Book—Part V*, 8, 20. Sharp made other aesthetic judgments in his presentation of Appalachian dance. He reported seeing people "hoe-down" (clog or flatfoot), but he did not describe it, though he had documented solo jigs in English morris dancing. There are a few mentions of hoedowning in some Pine Mountain letters, but it never became part of the Pine Mountain repertoire.
52. Sharp, *Country Dance Book—Parts I and II*, 21, 26.
53. Sharp, *Country Dance Book—Part V*, 18.
54. Walkowitz, *City Folk*, 47, 150.
55. Addams, *Spirit of Youth*, 101.
56. "Notes from the Pine Mountain Settlement School," 1; Walkowitz, *City Folk*, 117.
57. Walkowitz, *City Folk*, 136; Greene, "Progressives," 180;.

58. PM pt. I, series II, box 4, folder 5, Progress Reports 1914, August–December.

59. Wells had begun collecting folk songs in 1916. She later became internationally known as a collector of English and American folk songs. *The Ballad Tree* is her best-known publication.

60. PM pt. I, series II, box 1, folder 10, Progress Reports 1920–21.

61. *Sun-Up* for Pine Mountain theater program January 7, 1929, PM pt. I, series VIII, box 5. In this production, two southern women used their talents to support Pine Mountain. LaVerne was from Nashville, and Vollmer, who was from Western North Carolina, regularly contributed proceeds from her play to Appalachian communities. *Sun-Up* had previously been produced in Chicago in 1923 to benefit Hindman Settlement School. (Whisnant, *All That Is Native and Fine*, 84.)

62. Walkowitz, *City Folk*, 142–144.

63. Tomko, Linda, *Dancing Class*, 98, 102.

64. "Notes from the Pine Mountain Settlement School," 4. Gathering Peascods, in John Playford's 1651 manual, is a circle dance, with slipping steps around the circle, and steps into center with claps. It does suggest a celebratory feeling, but no documentation exists to associate it with tree worship.

65. PM pt. I, series II, box 1, folder 8, Progress Reports 1917.

66. PM pt. I, series II, box 1, folder 12, Progress Reports 1924.

67. PM pt. I, series II, box 1, folder 13, Progress Reports 1926–29.

68. Greene, "Progressives," 185.

69. Ford, *Good Morning*.

70. Ford, "Jewish Jazz" and "Jewish Jazz Trust."

71. Napier interview; discussion at Christmas Country Dance School 1973.

72. Walkowitz, *City Folk*, 147.

73. Walkowitz, *City Folk*, 135.

74. Frank Smith, "Recreation," CSM box 205, folder 10, 3–4.

75. "In Memory of Dorothy F. Bolles . . . The Pine Mountain Dance Fund." CSM, Commission Records, box 179, Schools and Community Centers. Evelyn Wells of Wellesley, Massachusetts, is listed among the Dance Fund Committee.

76. "In Memory of Dorothy F. Bolles."

77. Walkowitz, *City Folk*, 133.

78. See for example AFC 1935/002 John Lomax Southern States Collection, AFC 1938/009 Mary Elizabeth Barnicle Kentucky Collection, AFC 1948/003 Artus Moser Collection, AFC 1948/023 Margot Mayo Collection, AFC 1939/012 Alan Lomax Recordings of Aunt Molly Jackson, in "Kentucky Collections in the Archive of Folk Culture."

79. Richard Chase Collection, AOA.

80. "Folk Festival Plans," 5.

81. Tomko, *Dancing Class*, 189, 185.

82. Whisnant, *All That Is Native and Fine*, 201.

83. See Williams, *Staging Tradition*.

84. "Folk Festival Plans," 5.

85. "Folk Festival Plans," 5. *Singing Games Old and New*, by Georg Bidstrup, published by John C. Campbell Folk School, was given as the source for the Danish dances included

in the first Mountain Folk Festival (Weaving, Shoemaker, Gustaf's Toast, the Meadow Is Mowed, the Crested Hen, Trallen, and the Danish March). English dances (Bonnets so Blue, Sellenger's Round, Rufty Tufty, Brighton Camp, and Gallopede) came from *The English Country Dance-Graded Series* by Cecil Sharp, and the American dances (Sandy Land, the Paw Paw Patch, the Old Brass Wagon, and Jennie Crack Corn) were "Published by Church Recreation Service, Delaware, Ohio."

86. Berea Normal School, *Games for Rural Schools*; REC RG 5.45; "Folk Festival Plans," 5.

87. Gunkler, *May I Say a Few Words?* 74–75; Recreation Extension Programs/Courses (1937–1958) REC RG 5.45.

88. Frank Smith, Report to Hutchins for Keith Fund, 1939, Recreation Extension Programs/Courses (1937–1958) REC, box 2, RG 5.45; Discussion at Christmas Country Dance School 1973.

89. Recreation Extension Programs/Courses (1937–1958), and Recreation Extension Games/Reports REC, box 2, RG 5.45.

90. KP series I, box 1, folders 1–2.

91. 1938 Silver Jubilee Edition of *Notes from the Pine Mountain Settlement School*. PM pt. I, series VIII, box 3, Miscellany 1923–1949.

92. 1938 Silver Jubilee Edition of *Notes from the Pine Mountain Settlement School.*

93. Discussion at Christmas Country Dance School 1973.

94. Napier, interview; Discussion at Christmas Country Dance School 1973.

95. PM pt. I, series II, box 1, Progress Reports 1920–21 and Progress Reports 1923.

96. Whisnant, *All That Is Native and Fine*, 128

97. PM pt. I, series II, box 1, Progress Reports 1923; "Craft Revival."

98. *Mountain Life and Work* 25, no. 2 (Summer 1949): 23, CSM, series VIII: Mountain Life and Work 1925–1970.

99. Page and Tolman, *Country Dance Book*; Shaw, *Cowboy Dances*.

100. Of the twenty figures for two couples included in Smith's book, seventeen match those in Napier's book. Smith included ten figures for large circles, of which only three are in Napier's book.

101. *Pine Mountain Settlement School*, 19–21.

102. Rogers, interview; Rogers, presentation.

103. Whisnant, *All That Is Native and Fine*, 168.

Chapter 7. "Rise and Shine": Dancing for Community Development at Hoedown Island

1. Dances are typically held every Saturday from the last weekend in April through the last weekend in October, and every Friday from the last weekend in May through the first Friday in September.

2. In the summer of 1999, through a Berea College Undergraduate Research Grant, three students accompanied me, documenting dancing and interviewing dancers at Hoedown Island: LaVon Rice, Layla Thomas, and Dana Mason. Videotapes from 1999 and 2002 are housed in the Berea College Department of Special Collections and Archives SAA 158 and the Smithsonian Center for Folklife and Cultural Heritage.

3. Landrum, *Histories*, 57–59.

4. Lexington and Eastern Railroad, *Natural Bridge*, 1.

5. Lexington and Eastern Railroad, *Natural Bridge*, 13, 29; Lee, *Brief History*, 499.

6. Lexington and Eastern Railroad, *Natural Bridge*, 13, 17, 33, 56–58; Jett, interview, June 12, 1999.

7. Jett and Staley, *Square Dancing*, 14.

8. Driggs, "Keep the Music Playing," 2.

9. Isaacs, "Hoedown Happiness," 2.

10. Woodford, "Hoedowning in Kentucky."

11. Royal Scottish Dance Society.

12. Jett, "History of Hoedown Island"; Clark and Longstreet, "Mountain Square Dancing."

13. Jett, interview, June 12 and July 8, 1999; Jett and Staley, *Square Dancing*, 11–12.

14. Jett and Staley, *Square Dancing*, 2.

15. Photo, n.d., RJ, box 1.

16. Arnett, interview.

17. Isaacs, "Hoedown Happiness," 2.

18. Hoedown Island Cloggers, discussion.

19. McLain and Berea College Christmas Country Dance School, *Dances from Appalachia*. Tunes in this medley are Sally Goodin, Boil Them Cabbage Down, Bill Cheatham, Ragtime Annie, and Devil in Georgia.

20. Jett and Staley, *Square Dancing*, 40.

21. Matthews-DeNatale, "Wild and Yet Really Subdued," 117; See also Matthews, "Cutting a Dido," and Hall, "Improvisation."

22. Rogers, interview.

23. Jett, interview, September 7, 2002; Jett, "History of Hoedown Island."

24. Jett, interview, July 8, 1999 and September 7, 2002.

25. National Mountain Style Square Dancing and Clogging Festival fliers, 1984, 1985, RJ.

26. See chapter 6 for further discussion of settlement schools and the folk dance recreation movement.

27. Jett, interview, July 8, 1999; See also Napier, *Kentucky Mountain Square Dancing*.

28. For a summary of the phenomenon of the square dance revival, see LeeEllen Friedland, "Square Dancing," in Selma Jeanne Cohen, ed., *International Encyclopedia of Dance* Vol. 5. New York: Oxford University Press, 1998: 685–90.

29. "Ralph Case."

30. Jett and Staley, "Square Dancing," 3. Jett, interview, June 12, 1999.

31. Jett, "Square Dancing in Eastern Kentucky," RJ; Jett, interview, 2002.

32. Jett, interview, June 12, 1999; News clipping, no title, n.d., RJ; Jett, interview, 2002.

33. Smith, *Appalachian Square Dance*; Napier, *Kentucky Mountain Square Dancing*; Cooperative Recreation Service, Delaware, Ohio; Damon, *History of Square Dancing*; RJ.

34. News clipping, no title, n.d., RJ.

35. Reed, "It's Dough-si-Dough for Wolfe Schools," RJ, box 1; Rogers, interview.

36. RJ, box 1; Jett, interview, July 8, 1999; Jett, "Hoedown Island—Kentucky's Clog Dance Capital."

37. John Lair Papers, Introduction, SAA 66.

38. RJ, box 1; Richard Jett, "Traditional Square Dancing."

39. Arnett, interview.

40. Arnett, interview; "In Performance at the Governor's Mansion."

41. Jett, interview, July 8, 1999.

42. Rogers, interview; Ball, interview; Arnett, interview.

43. Rogers, interview; Driggs, "Keep the Music Playing," 2.

44. Whisnant, "Finding the Way," 97–100. Jett also followed in Lunsford's footsteps as the dance director for Renfro Valley.

45. Case, interview; See also Matthews, "Cutting a Dido."

46. Whisnant, "Finding the Way," 100–102; Matthews, "Wild and Yet Really Subdued," 120.

47. Sexton, interview.

48. Jett, interview, 2002; Ball, interview; Sexton, interview; Lamb, interview.

49. Jett and Staley, "Square Dancing."

50. Jett, interview, June 12, 1999.

51. Arnett, interview; Rogers, interview.

52. Jett and Staley, "Square Dancing," 2.

53. Driggs, "Keep the Music Playing," 2.

54. Jett and Staley, "Square Dancing," 2; Hoedown Island annual schedule fliers.

Chapter 8. The Carcassonne Square Dance: A True Revival

1. See Alan Lomax and Elizabeth Lomax Kentucky Collection AFC 1937/001; Southern Folk Cultural Revival Project Collection SFC 20004; and Scott Matthews, "John Cohen in Eastern Kentucky."

2. Campbell, *Tales*, 13.

3. Caudill, *Carcassonne*, 33; 43–44; 36, 45; Caudill, *Eastern Kentucky Memories*, 99, 125.

4. Caudill, *Carcassonne*, 46, 171–72; Caudill, *Eastern Kentucky Memories*, 99. The post office had been moved to the school from the community of Gander in 1937.

5. Caudill, *Carcassonne*, 44, 148, 34.

6. Mark and Gary, *History of American Music Education*, 271–75.

7. Caudill, *Carcassonne*, 39–40, 188, 191, 173; Whitaker, interview, June 27, 1975, 10–11. John Jacob Niles was a classically trained singer and composer who collected folk songs and created new songs based on the ones he had learned. Perhaps his best-known song is "I Wonder as I Wander." During a brief period in the 1930s he was music director at John C. Campbell Folk School. For further discussion of John Jacob Niles, see Ron Pen, *I Wonder as I Wander.*

8. Caudill, *Carcassonne*, 46, 170–73; Newborg, "Educational Radio's First Rural Radio Station."

9. Caudill, *Eastern Kentucky Memories*, 1–3.

10. Caudill, *Eastern Kentucky Memories*, 126, 128, 122; "C. B. Caudill Store and History Center."

11. Caudill, interview, June 29, 1975, 10; Caudill, *Eastern Kentucky Memories*, 49.

12. Eastern Kentucky Folk Dance Oral History Transcripts SAA 116, Berea College Hutchins Library Department of Special Collections and Archives. "Thirty-one audio

cassette recordings and transcripts of interviews that document the development of traditional square and related dance activity in southeastern Kentucky. The interviews were with mostly elderly residents of Harlan, Letcher, and Leslie Counties and were recorded by Peter Rogers in 1975."

13. Hiram Brashear, interview, 2; Veldon and A. O. Fields, interview, 23; Grover Sizemore, interview, 11. Note that almost no consultant used the term "figure." A movement sequence was usually referred to as "a call," "a thing," or "a play." When asked, Veldon Fields said there were no names for calls. You "just holler them out." (interview, 6).

14. Caudill, *Carcassonne*, 79, 78, 60–61; Caudill, interview, 1975, 22; Ruby Caudill, interview.

15. Caudill, *Carcassonne*, 80, 84; Bates, interviews. For more on the influential WNOX, see Ed Hooper, *Knoxville's WNOX*.

16. Lee Sexton, interview, 1975, 7; Whitaker, interview, 1975, 5.

17. Caudill, interview, 1975, 19; Lee Sexton, oral history interview.

18. Whitaker, interview 1999; Whitaker, interview, 1975, 5–7; Willis Fields, interview, 5.

19. Bates, interview, 3.

20. Caudill, *Eastern Kentucky Memories*, 156; Caudill, interview, 2002; Hayes, Combs, and Brashear, interview; Willis Fields, interview, 14; Caudill, interview, 1975, 28.

21. "C. B. Caudill Store and History Museum."

22. Caudill, *Eastern Kentucky Memories*, 129–130.

23. Kiffmeyer, *Reformers to Radicals*, 37–38, 40; "The Appalachian Volunteers." AV SAA 2, series XII, box 17, folder 4, 2.

24. Kiffmeyer, *Reformers to Radicals*, 53; Henrikson, interview.

25. Caudill, *Eastern Kentucky Memories*, 171; Henrikson, interview.

26. Whisnant, *Modernizing the Mountaineer*, 204–5; Henrikson, interview.

27. Henrikson, interview; Kentucky Collections AFC; Matthews, "John Cohen;" "C. B. Caudill Store and History Center."

28. Anne Romaine Papers SFC 20304; Southern Folk Cultural Revival Project SFC 20004; Guerrero, "Anne Romaine," 16. Guy and Candie Carawan were good friends of the Begleys and were frequent visitors to Letcher County, according to Jon Henrikson.

29. Caudill, interview, 1975, 5, 6.

30. Henrikson, interview; Caudill, interview, 1975, 6.

31. Caudill, *Eastern Kentucky Memories*, 172, 174, 175; Caudill, interview, 1975, 6. Interestingly, in his chapter on the Appalachian Volunteers in *Eastern Kentucky Memories*, Caudill segued directly into a discussion of dancing.

32. Video documentation of Carcassonne dances from 1999 and 2002 are housed in the Susan Spalding Appalachian Traditional Dance Video Collection SAA 158 and at the Smithsonian Center for Folklife and Cultural Heritage.

33. In Bird in the Cage, two couples circle left; one woman steps into the middle of the circle made by the joined hands of her partner and the other couple, dancing until the call to hop out. Her partner then steps into the center of the circle of three and dances until the call to "circle four."

34. In Take a Little Peek, two couples circle left; the active couple faces toward the outside of the big circle, releases hands, separates to go around the other couple and peeks at each other, while the inactive couple takes a few steps forward between them.

Both couples take steps backward to place. The active couple swings and repeats the "peek." When both couples return the second time, they join hands and circle left.

35. Willis Fields, interview, 4.

36. Whitaker, "Biography;" Whitaker, interview, 1975; Rogers, interview; Whitaker, interview, 1999.

37. Whitaker, interview, 1999; Henrikson, interview.

38. Apparently the Virginia Reel was not altogether unknown in the area prior to Whitaker's introduction of it at Carcassonne. Bill Bates said that in the 1930s, "sometimes we would have kind of sophisticated people around, and we would want to do [the Virginia Reel]." (Bates, interview, 21.)

39. Whitaker, "Biography;" Whitaker, interview, 1999; Henrikson, interview.

40. Caudill, *Carcassonne*, 37; Caudill, interview, 1975, 17.

41. Henrikson, interview.

42. Whitaker, interview, 1975, 22; Sexton, interview, 1975, 18.

43. Caudill, interview, 1975, 17, 20; Veldon and A. O. Fields, interview, 19; Willis Fields, interview, 8, 18–19; See Seeger and Pershing, *Talking Feet.*

44. Rogers, interview.

45. Willis Fields, interview, 3; Ison, interview, 8.

46. Bates, interview, 27; Caudill, interview, 1975, 12.

47. Rogers, email; Caudill, interview, 1975, 23; Jamison, "Square Dance at Carcassonne Kentucky," 6; Rogers, interview; Ison, interview, 9.

48. Caudill, interview, 1975, 13, 26.

49. Willis Fields, interview, 31; Veldon and A. O. Fields, interview, 17; Caudill, interview, 1975, 25.

50. Henrikson, interview.

51. Veldon and A. O. Fields, interview, 2.

52. Willis Fields, interview, 8–9; Ison, interview, 16.

53. Willis Fields, interview, 22, 7; Hayes, Combs, Brashear, interview, 32; Sizemore, interview, 1.

54. Sexton, interview, 1975, 17; Jamison, "Square Dance at Carcassonne Kentucky," 8; Caudill, interview, 2002.

55. Willis Fields, interview, 27–28; Veldon and A. O. Fields, interview, 2, 10.

56. Willis Fields, interview, 16; Ison, interview, 2; Bates, interview, 11; See also Levin, *Kentucky Square Dances*, 14–15, for her description of Ladies in the Center Back to Back. A version of Ladies Back to Back appears as one of the many figures of "the German" or "Parlor Cotillion" in Howe, *American Dancing Master*, 159.

57. Willis Fields, interview, 6.

58. Casey, *Dance across Texas*, 41; Gardner, "Some Play-Party Games in Michigan," 116–17; Spurgeon, *Waltz the Hall*, 13, 15; Willis Fields, interview, 23–24; Caudill, interview, 1975, 24. Sharp, *Country Dance Book—Part V*, 35; Turner, interview. "Tucker" has similarities to some of the flirtatious game-like figures of the nineteenth century "German" or "Parlor Cotillion." See Howe, *American Dancing Master.*

59. Willis Fields, interview, 2; Veldon and A. O. Fields, interview, 2; Whitaker, interview, 1975, 17; Caudill, interview, 1975, 14.

60. Willis Fields, interview, 19–20; Spurgeon, *Waltz the Hall*, 54, 198–99. Spurgeon

describes a very different dance called Waltz the Hall collected by Vance Randolph in the Ozarks in the 1920s along with other play parties. Levin, *Kentucky Square Dances*, 23, has a description that is somewhat similar to the Waltz Swing in Cecil Sharp, *Country Dance Book—Part V*, 41. The Carcassonne Waltz the Hall sounds more like Cutting Off Three, Two, and One, in Sharp, *Country Dance Book—Part V*, 42.

61. *Little Shepherd of Kingdom Come* Outdoor Drama; Caudill, *Carcassonne*, 136; Caudill, interview, 1975, 2; Caudill, interview, 2002.

62. Caudill, interview, 2002; Caudill, interview, 1975, 2; Caudill, Carcassonne, 136; Brown, email.

63. Caudill, interview, 1975, 5; Caudill, *Carcassonne*, 193; Henrikson, interview.

64. Caudill, interview, 1975, 28; Jamison, "Square Dance at Carcassonne," 8; Henrikson, interview.

65. Brookes, "What Do You Get When You Cross a Banjo Picker and a Punk Rocker?"; Berkes, "Hick-Hop: Hip-Hop Meets the Hollow."

66. Whitaker, interview, 1999; Caudill, *Eastern Kentucky Memories*, 173; Henrikson, interview, 2002; Caudill, interview, 2002.

67. Brookes, "What Do You Get?"; Cowan Creek Mountain Music School; Sexton, oral history interview.

68. Brown, email; May, conversation.

69. Caudill, *Carcassonne*, 46.

70. Bates, interview, 46; Rice, Appalachian Studies Association, 2000.

71. Johnson, note; Caudill, interview, 1975, 29–30.

Afterword

1. The stylistic and contextual similarities among traditions in African American and European American communities suggest that, as Mechal Sobel asserts, a new American—or Southern American—culture had been created by the two groups, beginning with their earliest arrival to this continent in colonial times. See *The World They Made Together.*

2. Not all old time dance communities in these three states evidenced this same family-centered atmosphere. The Lions' Club dance in Chilhowie, Virginia, for example, while suitable for all ages, attracted primarily middle-aged couples out for a night of fun together.

3. "In Memory of Dorothy F. Bolles . . . The Pine Mountain Dance Fund." CSM Commission Records, box 179, Schools and Community Centers.

4. Sklar, "Five Premises," 1.

5. Buckland, *Dancing from Past to Present*, 12.

6. See Bosse, "Exotica, Ethnicity and Embodiment"; Desmond, *Staging Tourism*; Keil, *Polka Happiness*; Malnig, *Ballroom, Boogie, Shim-Sham, Shake*; Mayo, *Step by Step*; Perkins, *Droppin' Science*; and Picart, *From Ballroom to DanceSport.*

7. Desmond, "Embodying Difference," 31.

8. Desmond, "Embodying Difference," 31.

9. David Brooks, "What Our Words Tell Us."

10. Ward, "Dancing around Meaning," 18.

Works Cited

Archival Collections Consulted

AFC Archive of Folk Culture, American Folklife Center, Archive Collections and Services, Library of Congress

AOA Archives of Appalachia, Center for Appalachian Studies and Services, East Tennessee State University

BCA Berea College Archives, Hutchins Library Department of Special Collections and Archives

CSM Council of the Southern Mountains Collection, Southern Appalachian Archives 1, Berea College Hutchins Library Department of Special Collections and Archives

EKFD Eastern Kentucky Folk Dancing Oral History Project, Southern Appalachian Archives 116, Berea College Hutchins Library Department of Special Collections and Archives

KP Katherine Pettit Collection, Southern Appalachian Archives 11, Berea College Hutchins Library Department of Special Collections and Archives

LOC Library of Congress Music Division

PM Pine Mountain Settlement School Collection, Southern Appalachian Archives 10, Berea College Hutchins Library Department of Special Collections and Archives

REC Recreation Extension Collection, Berea College Archives, Administrative Divisions, Berea College Hutchins Library Department of Special Collections and Archives

RJ Richard Jett Collection, Southern Appalachian Archives 911, Berea College Hutchins Library Department of Special Collections and Archives

SAA Southern Appalachian Archives, Berea College Hutchins Library Department of Special Collections and Archives

SFC The Southern Folklife Collection at the Louis Round Wilson Special Collections Library, University of North Carolina Library Archives

UTK University of Tennessee at Knoxville John C. Hodges Library Special Collections

WCU Western Carolina Hunter University Special Collections

Interviews, Presentations, and Personal Communications Cited

Lewis Arnett, interview with the author, Slade, Kentucky, September 7, 2002.

Columbus Avery, interview with Elizabeth Barrett, Williamson, West Virginia, September 16, 1982.

Bob and Nellie Baines, interview with the author, Locust Mount, Tennessee, August 11, 1987.

Helen Baker, interview with the author, Fall Branch, Tennessee, July 29, 1987.

I. D. Ball, interview with the author, Irvine, Kentucky, September 18, 2002.

Mr. and Mrs. Bill Bates, interview with Peter Rogers, Blackey, Kentucky, August 3, 1975, EKFD SC-CT-852–019.

Leonard Bowles and Irvin Cook, interview with Kip Lornell, Henry County, Virginia, October 10, 1976. Blue Ridge Institute Archives, Ferrum College. Available at http://www.blueridgeinstitute.org/heritage.htm (accessed July 12, 2011).

Leonard Bowles, interview with Kip Lornell, Henry County, Virginia, February 28, 1977. Blue Ridge Institute Heritage Archives. Ferrum, Virginia: Ferrum College. Available at http://www.blueridgeinstitute.org/heritage.htm (accessed July 12, 2011).

Leonard and Naomi Bowles, interview with author, Martinsville, Virginia, July 23, 1992.

Verlyn Brady, interview with the author, Hillsville, Virginia, July 30, 1989.

Hiram Brashear, interview with Peter Rogers, Viper, Kentucky, n.d., EKFD SC-CT-852-023.

Ernest Brooks, interview with the author, Martinsville, Virginia, August 12, 1992.

Mark Brown, Folklife Specialist with the Kentucky Folklife Program, an interagency program of the Kentucky Historical Society and the Kentucky Arts Council, email, November 29, 2011.

Edward J. Cabbell, telephone interview with the author, November 22, 2002.

Walker Calhoun, presentation at Old Time Dancing Conference, East Tennessee State University, Johnson City, Tennessee, April 29, 1989.

Walker Calhoun, presentation at Southern Dance Traditions Conference, East Tennessee State University, Johnson City, Tennessee, March 3, 1990.

Ellen Carter and Sue Trent, interview with the author, Abingdon, Virginia, August 7, 1992.

Warren Case, interview with the author, Slade, Kentucky, June 25, 1999.

Emmett and Pauline Cassell, interview with the author, Nickelsville, Virginia, July 28, 1987.

Clifton Caudill with Ruby Caudill, interview with Peter Rogers, Carcassonne, Kentucky, June 29, 1975, EKFD SC-CT-852-003.

Ruby and Clifton Caudill, interview with Dale Johnson, Carcassonne, Kentucky, June 12, 1998.

Ruby Caudill, interview with the author, Carcassonne, Kentucky, September 14, 2002.

Calvin Cole, interview with the author, Hillsville, Virginia, June 30, 1989.

Melvin and Opal Crawford, interview with the author, Fall Branch, Tennessee, July 15, 1987.

Ross and Geneva Cunningham, interview with the author, New Market, Tennessee, August 15, 1992.

David B. Debose, interview with the author, Abingdon, Virginia, July 15, 1992.

Nova Deel, interview with the author, Dante, Virginia, July 5, 1989.

May Ritchie Deschamps, excerpt from letter to Peter Rogers, August 3, 1975, excerpted in Peter Rogers, letter to Robin Lambert, director of Pine Mountain Settlement School, September 21, 1997.

Discussion at Christmas Country Dance School 1973 (audio cassette tapes). John Ramsay leading discussion among Ethel Capps, Bicky McLain, Leila Smith, and others; BCA SC-CT-441–9, 10.

Veldon and A. O. Fields, interview with Peter Rogers at Kings Creek, Kentucky, August 2, 1975, EKFD SC-CT-852–018.

Willis Fields, interview with Peter Rogers, Kings Creek, Kentucky, August 2, 1975, EKFD SC-CT-852–016.

Earl Gilmore, interview with Andrew Garrison, Clinchco, Virginia, October 31, 1988.

Constance Hardinge, conversation with the author, Bristol, Virginia, August 21, 1987.

Bill and Fern Hayes, Grazia Combs, and Ruby Brashear, interview with Peter Rogers at Viper, Kentucky, July 15, 1975, EKFD SC-CT-852-008.

Katrina Hazzard-Gordon, keynote address, "A Moving Community: Dance in a Center of Culture and Power," Regional Conference of the Congress on Research in Dance at the University of Maryland—College Park, June 26, 1992.

Jon Henrikson, interview with the author, Carcassonne, Kentucky, September 14, 2002.

Hoedown Island Cloggers, discussion with the author, Slade, Kentucky, September 7, 2002.

Harding Ison, interview with Peter Rogers, August 2, 1975, EKFD SC-CT-852-017.

Richard Jett, interview with the author, Slade, Kentucky, June 12, 1999.

Richard Jett, interview with the author, Campton, Kentucky, July 8, 1999.

Richard Jett, interview with the author, Slade, Kentucky, September 7, 2002.

Dale Johnson, note to the author, October 13, 2012.

Earl and Eleanor Kincaid, interview with the author, Dante, Virginia, July 30, 1992.

Rich Kirby, discussion with the author, March 31, 1995.

Rich Kirby, telephone interview with the author, September 23, 1987.

Donna and Lewis Lamb, interview with the author, Paint Lick, Kentucky, October 15, 1996.

Beverly May, conversation with the author, Carcassonne, Kentucky, September 9, 2002.

Veronia Miller, interview with the author, Bristol, Tennessee, August 4, 1987.

Veronia Miller, interview with Jane Woodside and the author, Bristol, Tennessee, July 21, 1987.

Pat and Irene Napier, interview with Harry Rice, Berea, Kentucky, December 30, 1996, on audio cassette tape, BCA AC-CT-011–010.

Rosa Powell, interview with the author, Abingdon, Virginia, August 14, 1992.

Charlie Rogers, interview with Layla Thomas, Slade, Kentucky, June 26, 1999.

Peter Rogers, interview with the author, Lexington, Kentucky, December 8, 2011.

Peter Rogers, letter to Robin Lambert, Director of Pine Mountain Settlement School, September 21, 1997.

Peter Rogers, presentation at "Symposium on Settlements in the Southern Mountains," June 7–10, 2000, Pine Mountain, Kentucky.

Elva Rowland, interview with the author, Fall Branch, Tennessee, July 29, 1987.

Lee Sexton, interview with Peter Rogers, Ulvah, Kentucky, July 19, 1975, EKFD SC-CT-852-009.

Lee Sexton, oral history interview, Hindman, Kentucky, June 14, 2005, Front Porch Project. Appalshop, Inc. Available at http://appalshop.org/frontporch/artists/lsexton.htm (accessed September 15, 2011).

Grover Sizemore, interview with Peter Rogers at Dry Hill, Kentucky, July 26, 1975, EKFD SC-CT-852-011.

Floyd Sloan, interview with the author, Duffield, Virginia, September 19, 2002.

Kirby Smith, interview with the author, Abingdon, Virginia, August 21, 1989.

Kirby Smith, interview with the author, Abingdon, Virginia, October 11, 2002.

Mabel Hardison Parker Smith, interview with the author, Big Stone Gap, Virginia, August 13, 1992.

Susan Spalding, LaVon Rice, Layla Thomas, and Dana Mason. "The Drawing Power of Friendship: Dance Builds Community in Eastern Kentucky," presentation, Appalachian Studies Association, 2000.

Susan Spalding, Marcus Leslie, Joshua Gampfer, Shekina Huffman, and Casey Lambdin. "Appalachian Hip Hop?" presentation, Appalachian Studies Association, 2009.

Evelyn Sturgill, interview with the author, Chilhowie, Virginia, August 3, 1989.

Shirley Taylor, interview with Maxine Kenny, Pennington Gap, Virginia, July 22, 1992.

Iva Turk, interview with the author, New Market, Tennessee, August 15, 1992.

Alonzo Turner, interview with Peter Rogers, 1975, EKFD SC-CT-852-012.

Fern Simpson Warren, interview with the author, Fall Branch, Tennessee, August 3, 1987.

Charlie Whitaker, interview with Peter Rogers at Alice Lloyd College, Pippa Passes, Kentucky, June 27, 1975, EKFD SC-CT-852-002.

Charlie and Joyce Whitaker, interview with Susan Spalding, Layla Thomas, LaVon Rice, and Dana Mason, Blackey, Kentucky, July 7, 1999.

Printed Sources and Dissertations

Abrahams, Roger D. "The Foundations of American Public Folklore." In *Public Folklore*, edited by Robert Baron and Nicholas R. Spitzer, 245–62. Washington: Smithsonian Institution Press, 1992.

———. *Singing the Master: The Emergence of African American Culture in the Plantation South*. New York: Pantheon, 1992.

Addams, Jane. *The Spirit of Youth and the City Streets*. New York: Macmillan, 1909.

Aldrich, Elizabeth. *From the Ballroom to Hell: Grace and Folly in Nineteenth-Century Dance*. Evanston, Ill.: Northwestern University Press, 1991.

Archer, William. "Jazz in the Mountains? One Town's Amazing Story." *Appalachian Heritage* 19, no. 4 (1991): 44–50.

Arnow, Pat. "A Part and Apart." *Now and Then* 3, no. 1 (1986): 9–11.

Asante, Kariamu Welsh. "Commonalities in African Dance: An Aesthetic Foundation." In *African Culture: The Rhythms of Unity*, edited by Molefi Kete Asante and Kariamu Welsh Asante, 71–82. Trenton, N.J.: Africa World, 1990.

Batteau, Alan. *The Invention of Appalachia*. Tucson: University of Arizona Press, 1990.

Benson, Norman Arthur. "The Itinerant Dancing and Music Masters of Eighteenth Century America." PhD diss., University of Minnesota, 1963.

Berea Normal School. *Games for Rural Schools*. Berea, Ky.: Berea Normal School, 1914.

Bergman, Jill, and Debra Bernardi, eds. *Our Sisters' Keepers: Nineteenth Century Benevolence Literature by American Women*. Tuscaloosa: University of Alabama Press, 2005.

Berry, Chad. *The Hayloft Gang: The Story of the National Barn Dance*. Urbana: University of Illinois Press, 2008.

Billings, Dwight B., ed. *Back Talk from Appalachia: Confronting Stereotypes*. Lexington: University Press of Kentucky, 1999.

Billings, Dwight B., and Kathleen M. Blee. *The Road to Poverty: The Making of Wealth and Hardship in Appalachia*. Cambridge: Cambridge University Press, 2000.

Bosse, Joanna. "Exotica, Ethnicity and Embodiment: An Ethnography of Latin Dance in U.S. Popular Culture." PhD diss., University of Illinois at Urbana-Champaign, 2004.

Brooks, Cynthia, from the files of Charles Hall. *Behind the Scenes: Wagon Train and the Cherohala Skyway: A Thirty-Eight-Year History*. Tellico Plains, Tenn.: Tellico, 1996.

Brooks, David. "What Our Words Tell Us." *New York Times*, May 20, 2013.

Brooks, Lynn Matluck. "Dancing Masters in Eighteenth Century Philadelphia." *Dance: Current Selected Research* 2 (1990): 1–21.

Brown, Louie A. *Dimensions of Change in East Tennessee, Tennessee, the South, and the Nation: A Comparative Analysis*. Monograph 2, July 1966. Johnson City: East Tennessee State University Institute of Regional Studies, 1966.

Buckland, Theresa J., ed. *Dance in the Field: Theory, Methods and Issues in Dance Ethnography*. London: Macmillan, 1999.

———. *Dancing from Past to Present: Nation, Culture, Identities*. Madison: University of Wisconsin Press, 2006.

———. "[Re]Constructing Meanings: The Dance Ethnographer as Keeper of the Truth" in *Dance in the Field: Theory, Methods and Issues in Dance Ethnography*, edited by Theresa J. Buckland, 196–207. London: Macmillan, 1999.

Bull, Cynthia Jean Cohen. "Sense, Meaning, and Perception in Three Dance Cultures." In *Meaning in Motion: New Cultural Studies of Dance*, edited by Jane C. Desmond, 269–88. Durham, N.C.: Duke University Press, 1997.

Burchenal, Elizabeth. *Folk-Dances and Singing Games*. New York: Schirmer, 1909.

Campbell, John C. *The Southern Highlander and His Homeland*. 1921. Lexington: University Press of Kentucky, 1969.

Campbell, Marie. *Tales from the Cloud Walking Country*. 1958. Westport, Conn.: Greenwood, 1976.

Campbell, Mrs. John C. "Flame of a New Future for the Highlands," *Mountain Life and Work* 1 (1925): 9.

Cantwell, Robert. *Bluegrass Breakdown: The Making of the Old Southern Sound*. Urbana: University of Illinois Press, 1984.

Carson, William G. B. *The Theatre on the Frontier: The Early Years of the St. Louis Stage*. 1932. New York: Benjamin Blom, 1965.

Casey, Betty. *Dance across Texas*. Austin: University of Texas Press, 1985.

Caudill, Clifton. *Carcassonne: People, Places, and Events*. 1994. Self-published, 1998.

——. *Eastern Kentucky Mountain Memories.* Self-published, 1996.

Clark, Carl M., and Teresa Longstreet. "Mountain Square Dancing." Self-published, n.d., RJ.

Condee, William Faricy. *Coal and Culture: Opera Houses in Appalachia.* Athens: Ohio University Press, 2005.

Conway, Cecelia. *African Banjo Echoes in Appalachia: A Study of Folk Traditions.* Knoxville: University of Tennessee Press, 1995.

Cooperative Recreation Service. Delaware, Ohio. (Now called World around Songs.) Celo, N.C.

Corbin, David A. "Class over Caste: Interracial Solidarity in the Company Town." In *Blacks in Appalachia*, edited by William H. Turner and Edward J. Cabbell, 93–113. Lexington: University of Kentucky Press, 1985.

Cox, Bob L. *Fiddlin' Charlie Bowman.* Knoxville: University of Tennessee Press, 2007.

Crow, Peter. *Do, Die, or Get Along: A Tale of Two Appalachian Towns.* Athens: University of Georgia Press, 2007.

Dalsemer, Robert G. *West Virginia Square Dances.* Haydenville, Mass.: Country Dance and Song Society, 1982.

Damon, S. Foster. *The History of Square Dancing.* Barre, Mass.: Barre Gazette, 1957.

Delamont, Sara, and Lorna Duffin, eds. *The Nineteenth Century Woman: Her Cultural and Physical World.* New York: Harper and Row, 1978.

Desmond, Jane C. "Embodying Difference: Issues in Dance and Cultural Studies." In *Meaning in Motion: New Cultural Studies of Dance*, edited by Jane C. Desmond, 29–54. Durham, N.C.: Duke University Press, 1997.

——, ed. *Meaning in Motion: New Cultural Studies of Dance.* Durham, N.C.: Duke University Press, 1997.

——. *Staging Tourism: Bodies on Display from Waikiki to Sea World.* Chicago: University of Chicago Press, 1999.

Dixon-Gottschild, Brenda. *Digging the Africanist Presence in American Performance: Dance and Other Contexts.* Westport, Conn.: Praeger, 1998.

Driggs, Jeffrey. "Keep the Music Playing." *Doubletoe Times* (October 2006): 2.

Dunaway, Wilma. *The First American Frontier: Transition to Capitalism in Southern Appalachia, 1700–1860.* Chapel Hill: University of North Carolina Press, 1996.

Emery, Lynn Fauley. *Black Dance from 1619 to Today.* 1972. Princeton, N.J.: Princeton Book Co., 1988.

Epstein, Dena. *Sinful Tunes and Spirituals: Black Folk Music to the Civil War.* Urbana: University of Illinois Press, 1977.

Eslinger, Ellen. *Citizens of Zion: the Social Origins of Camp Meeting Revivalism.* Knoxville: University of Tennessee Press, 1999.

Farnell, Brenda. "It Goes without Saying—But Not Always." In *Dance in the Field: Theory, Methods and Issues in Dance Ethnography*, edited by Theresa J. Buckland, 145–60. London: Macmillan, 1999.

Feintuch, Burt. "Dancing to the Music: Domestic Square Dances and Community in Southcentral Kentucky (1880–1940)." *Journal of the Folklore Institute* 18 (1981): 49–68.

"Folk Festival Plans." Conference of the Southern Mountains. *Mountain Life and Work* (January 1935) 5–7, 23. CSM Series VIII: Mountain Life and Work 1925–1970.

Ford, Henry. *The International Jew*, vol. 3: "Jewish Influence in American Life." 1920. York, S.C.: Liberty Bell, 2004.

———. "Jewish Jazz Becomes Our National Music" and "How the Jewish Jazz Trust Makes You Sing." In *The International Jew*, vol. 3: "Jewish Influence in American Life." 1920. York, S.C.: Liberty Bell, 2004, chapters 47 and 48.

Ford, Henry, and Mrs. Henry Ford. *Good Morning—After a Sleep of Twenty-five Years, Old-fashioned Dancing Is Being Revived by Mr. and Mrs. Henry Ford.* Dearborn, Mich.: Dearborn Publishing, 1926.

Friedland, LeeEllen. "Traditional Folkdance in Kentucky." *Country Dance and Song* 10 (1979): 5–19.

Frost, Helen. *Clog and Character Dances.* New York: Barnes, 1924.

Furman, Lucy. "Katherine Pettit: A Pioneer Mountain Worker." *Mountain Life and Work* (October 1936). KP series V, box 1 folder 2.

Gardner, Emelyn E. "Some Play-Party Games in Michigan." *Journal of American Folklore* 33 (1920): 116–17.

Gates, Henry Louis, Jr. *Colored People: A Memoir.* New York: Vintage, 1995.

Gilbert, Melvin Ballou. "Dancing: Aesthetic and Social." *Athletics for Women: A Series of Articles on Exercising for Health and the Perfection of Physical Development* 12 (1903): 283–87.

Grau, Andree. "Fieldwork, Politics, and Power." In *Dance in the Field: Theory, Methods and Issues in Dance Ethnography*, edited by Theresa J. Buckland, 163–74. London: Macmillan, 1999.

Greene, James S. III. "Progressives in the Kentucky Mountains: The Formative Years of Pine Mountain Settlement School, 1913–1930." PhD diss., Ohio State University, 1982.

Griswold, Wendy. "A Methodological Framework for the Sociology of Culture." *Sociological Methodology* 17 (1987): 1–35.

Guerrero, Gene. "Anne Romaine." *Southern Changes: Journal of the Southern Regional Council 1978–2003* 17, no. 3–4 (1995): 15–17.

Gulick, Luther Halsey. *The Healthful Art of Dancing.* New York: Doubleday.

Hall, Frank. "Improvisation and Fixed Composition in Clogging." *Journal for the Anthropological Study of Human Movement at New York University* 3 (1984–85): 200–217.

———. "Madness and Recall: Storied Data on Irish Dancing." In *Dance in the Field: Theory, Methods and Issues in Dance Ethnography*, edited by Theresa J. Buckland, 123–33. London: Macmillan, 1999.

Hall, G. Stanley. *Adolescence.* New York: Appleton, 1904.

Hazzard-Gordon, Katrina. *Jookin': The Rise of Social Dance Formations in African-American Culture.* Philadelphia: Temple University Press, 1990.

H'Doubler, Margaret. "Educational Possibilities of the Dance." *Journal of Physical Education and Recreation* 5, no. 4 (April 1934): 62–63.

Hobsbawm, E. J., and Terrence Ranger, eds. *The Invention of Tradition.* New York: Cambridge University Press, 1983.

Holloway, Joseph E., ed. *Africanisms in American Culture.* Bloomington: Indiana University Press, 1990.

———. "The Origins of Afro-American Culture." In *Africanisms in American Culture*, edited by Joseph E. Holloway, 2–18. Bloomington: Indiana University Press, 1990.

Hooper, Ed. *Knoxville's WNOX*. Charleston, South Carolina: Arcadia, 2009.
Howe, Elias. *American Dancing Master and Ballroom Prompter*. Boston: Elias Howe, 1862.
Hsiung, David C. "How Isolated Was Appalachia: Upper East Tennessee, 1780–1835. *Appalachian Journal*, Summer 1989: 336–49.
———. *Two Worlds in the Tennessee Mountains: Exploring the Origins of Appalachian Stereotypes*. Lexington: University of Kentucky Press, 1997.
Hurston, Zora Neale. *The Sanctified Church*. Berkeley: Turtle Island, 1981.
Isaacs, Barbara. "Hoedown Happiness." *Lexington Herald-Leader*, section J, August 22, 1999, 1–2, RJ.
Jamison, Phil. "Barn Dance with Calls:" Old-Time Southern Square-Dance Calls on 78s: 1920s–early 1930s." *Old Time Herald* 7, no. 8 (May 2001): 14–16.
———. "The Green Grass Cloggers: The Appalachian Spirit Goes International." In *Communities in Motion: Dance Community, and Tradition in America's Southeast and Beyond*, edited by Susan Spalding and Jane Woodside, 169–74. Westport Conn.: Greenwood, 1995.
———. "Robert and Myrtle Dotson." *Old Time Herald*, Summer 1994: 16–17.
———. "The Square Dance at Carcassonne Kentucky." *Old Time Herald*, February 1991: 6–8, 50.
———. "Square Dance Calling: The African-American Connection," *Journal of Appalachian Studies* 9, no. 2 (Fall 2003): 387–98.
Jett, Richard. "History of Hoedown Island," 1986, RJ.
———. "Hoedown Island—Kentucky's Clog Dance Capitol," 1984, RJ.
———. "Square Dancing in Eastern Kentucky in the 1950–60 Era, As Enjoyed by Richard Jett," RJ.
———. "Traditional Square Dancing—A Major Recreational Activity at Natural Bridge State Resort Park," RJ.
Jett, Richard, and Helen Price Staley. *Square Dancing in the Mountains of Eastern Kentucky: Instructions for Beginners*. West Liberty, Ky.: Mountain Dance, 1971.
Jones, Bessie, and Bess Lomax Hawes. *Step It Down: Games, Plays, Songs, and Stories from the Afro-American Heritage*. Athens: University of Georgia Press, 1972.
Jones, Jessica Janice. "DeFord Bailey." *Black Music Research Journal* 10, no. 1 (Spring 1990): 29–31.
Keil, Charles, and Angelika V. Keil. *Polka Happiness*. Philadelphia: Temple University Press, 1992.
Kent, Dot. "Frolics: African American House Dance Traditions of the North Carolina Piedmont." *Old Time Herald* 5, no. 7 (Spring, 1997): 9–11, 15.
Kiffmeyer, Thomas. *Reformers to Radicals: The Appalachian Volunteers and the War on Poverty*. Lexington: University Press of Kentucky, 2008.
Kyriakoudes, Louis M. "The Grand Ole Opry and the Urban South." *Southern Cultures*, Spring 2004: 67–84.
Laing, James T. "The Negro Miner in West Virginia." In *Blacks in Appalachia*, edited by William H. Turner and Edward J. Cabbell, 71–78. Lexington: University of Kentucky Press, 1985.
Landrum, Ney C. *Histories of the Southeastern State Park Systems*. Association of Southeastern State Park Directors, 1992.

Lee, Joseph. "Play as a School of the Citizen." *Kindergarten Review* 18, no. 2 (October 1907): 65–78.

Lee, Lloyd B. *A Brief History of Kentucky and its Counties.* Berea, Ky.: Kentucky Imprints, 1981.

Lee, Tom. *Tennessee-Virginia Tri-Cities: Urbanization in Appalachia 1900–1950.* Knoxville: University of Tennessee Press, 2005.

Levin, Ida. *Kentucky Square Dances.* Louisville, Kentucky: Recreation Council, 1928.

Lewis, Helen M., and Suzanna O'Donnell, eds. *Ivanhoe, Virginia: Telling Our Stories, Sharing Our Lives.* Ivanhoe, Va.: Ivanhoe Civic League, 1990.

Lewis, Ronald L. "Beyond Isolation and Homogeneity: Diversity and the History of Appalachia." In *Back Talk from Appalachia: Confronting Stereotypes,* edited by Dwight B. Billings, 21–38. Lexington: University Press of Kentucky, 1999.

Lexington and Eastern Railroad. *Natural Bridge in the Kentucky Mountains on the Line of the Lexington and Eastern Railway.* Published by the Passenger Department, 1900.

Lonesome Pine Office on Youth. *Life in the Coal Camps of Wise County: In Honor of Wise County's Sesquicentennial.* Wise County, Va.: Lonesome Pine Office on Youth and the Virginia Foundation for the Humanities, 2006.

Lornell, Kip. Essay and Notes, *Virginia Traditions: Non-Blues Secular Black Music.* BRI-001. Recording and book. Ferrum, Va.: Blue Ridge Institute, Ferrum College, 1978.

Malnig, Julie. *Ballroom, Boogie, Shim-Sham, Shake.* Urbana: University of Illinois Press, 2009.

Malone, Bill C. *Singing Cowboys and Musical Mountaineers.* Athens: University of Georgia Press, 1993.

Mark, Michael L., and Charles L. Gary. *A History of American Music Education.* New York: Rowman and Littlefield, 2007.

Martin, Wayne. "Joe and Odell Thompson." *Old Time Herald* 1 no. 8 (1989): 5–7.

Mathews, Burgin. "Eight Hands Up! Square Dance Calls by Black Musicians on 78 Records." *Old Time Herald,* Spring 2005: 12–15.

Matthews, Gail. "Cutting a Dido: A Dancer's Eye View of Mountain Dance in Haywood County, North Carolina." Master's thesis, Indiana University, 1983.

Matthews-DeNatale, Gail. "Wild and Yet Really Subdued: Cultural Change, Stylistic Diversification, and Personal Choice in Traditional Appalachian Dance." In *Communities in Motion: Dance, Community, and Tradition in America's Southeast and Beyond,* edited by Susan Eike Spalding and Jane Harris Woodside, 111–26. Westport, Conn.: Greenwood, 1995.

Mayo, Jim. *Step by Step through Western Square Dance History.* Bloomington, Ind.: 1st Books Library, 2004.

Miller, Veronia. "You Have to Watch Your People: Calling Old Time Appalachian Square Dance." In *Communities in Motion: Dance, Community and Tradition in America's Southeast and Beyond,* edited by Susan Eike Spalding and Jane Harris Woodside, 31–34. Westport, Conn.: Greenwood, 1995.

Musser, Carl Wilson. "Economic and Social Aspects of Negro Slavery in Wythe County, Virginia, 1790–1869." Master's thesis, Columbia College, George Washington University, 1958.

Napier, Patrick. *Kentucky Mountain Square Dancing.* Berea, Ky.: Berea College, 1960.

Needham, Maureen. *I See America Dancing: Selected Readings 1685–2000*. Urbana: University of Illinois Press, 2002.

Ness, Sally Ann. "Being a Body in a Cultural Way: Understanding the Cultural in the Embodiment of Dance." In *Cultural Bodies: Ethnography and Theory*, edited by Helen Thomas and Jamilah Ahmed, 123–44. Oxford: Blackwell, 2004.

———. "Understanding Cultural Performance: Trobriand Cricket." In *Anthropology, Sport, and Culture*, edited by Robert R. Sands, 39–50. Westport, Conn.: Bergin and Garvey, 1999.

Netherland, Tom. "The Carter Family Fold," *Richmond Times Dispatch*, July 22, 2002.

New National Theatre (Cincinnati, Ohio), Zoe Gilbert, Phillipe Martinetti and Blondin. 1858. *New National Theatre . . . Wednesday evening, April 21, third night of the Martinetti and Blondin Troupe!* Cincinnati, Ohio: Daily Commercial Steam Job Press. Historic New Orleans Collection, John A. Pentz Collection of Nineteenth Century Playbills, no. 30.

Noe, Kenneth W. *Southwest Virginia's Railroad: Modernization and the Sectional Crisis*. Urbana Chicago: University of Illinois Press, 1994.

Noland, Carrie, and Sally Ann Ness, eds. *Migrations of Gesture*. Minneapolis: University of Minnesota Press, 2008.

"Notes from the Pine Mountain Settlement School, Pine Mountain, Harlan County, Kentucky" vol. 1, no. 2 (1919).

Novack, Cynthia. *Sharing the Dance: Contact Improvisation and American Culture*. New Directions in Anthropological Writing. Madison: University of Wisconsin Press, 1990.

Page, Ralph, and Beth Tolman, *The Country Dance Book*. Guilford, Vt.: Countryman, 1937.

Pen, Ron. *I Wonder as I Wander: The Life of John Jacob Niles*. Lexington: University of Kentucky Press, 2010.

Perkins, William Eric. *Droppin' Science: Critical Essays on Rap Music and Hip Hop Culture*. Philadelphia: Temple University Press, 1996.

Picart, Caroline Joan. *From Ballroom to DanceSport*. Albany: State University of New York Press, 2006.

Pine Mountain Settlement School, Inc. *The Pine Mountain Story 1913–1980*. Viper, Ky.: Graphic Artss, 1980.

Raitz, Karl B., and Richard Ulack. *Appalachia: A Regional Geography; Land, People, and Development*. Boulder, Colo.: Westview, 1984.

Reece, Cortez Donald. "A Study of Selected Folksongs Collected Mainly in Southern West Virginia." PhD diss., University of Southern California, 1955.

Reed, Billy. "It's Dough-si-Dough for Wolfe Schools." *Louisville Courier-Journal* (1976), RJ.

Robinson, Beverly J. "Africanisms and the Study of Folklore." In *Africanisms in American Culture*, edited by Joseph E. Holloway, 211–23. Bloomington: Indiana University Press, 1990.

Robinson, Gil. *Old Wagon Show Days*. Cincinnati: Brockwell, 1925.

Rollins, Peter C., and John E. O'Connor, eds. *Hollywood's West: The American Frontier in Film, Television, and History*. Lexington: University Press of Kentucky, 2005.

Ruyter, Nancy Lee Chalfa. "The Delsarte Heritage." *Dance Research* 14, no.1 (Summer 1996): 62–74.

Sands, Robert R. *Anthropology, Sport, and Culture.* Westport, Conn.: Bergin and Garvey. 1999.

Scherman, Tony. "A Man Who Mined Gold in the Southern Hills." *Smithsonian Magazine*, April 1985: 173–195.

Sealander, Judith. *Private Wealth and Public Life: Foundation Philanthropy and the Reshaping of American Social Policy from the Progressive Era to the New Deal.* Baltimore: Johns Hopkins University Press, 1997.

Sharp, Cecil J. *The Country Dance Book—Parts I and II.* London: EP Publishing, 1972 (Novello, 1909).

———. *The Country Dance Book—Part V.* London: Novello, 1918.

Shaw, Lloyd. *Cowboy Dances.* Caldwell, Id.: Caxton, 1939.

Shearer, Katharine C., ed. *Memories from Dante: The Life of a Coal Town.* Abingdon, Virginia: People Incorporated of Southwest Virginia, 2001.

Siler, Jeanne Nicholson. *Fayette Street: A Hundred-Year History of African American Life in Martinsville, Virginia, 1900–2005.* Produced by the partnership between Fayette Area Historical Initiative and Virginia Foundation for the Humanities, 2007.

Sklar, Deidre. "Five Premises for a Culturally Sensitive Approach to Dance." *Dance Critics Association News* (Summer 1991).

———. "Remembering Kinesthesia: An Inquiry into Embodied Cultural Knowledge." In *Migrations of Gesture*, edited by Carrie Noland and Sally Ann Ness, 85–112. Minneapolis: University of Minnesota Press, 2008.

Smith, Frank H. *The Appalachian Square Dance.* Berea, Ky.: Berea College, 1955.

———. "Recreation as An Academic Subject at Berea College," CSM, box 205, folder 10, 3–4.

Sobel, Mechal. *The World They Made Together: Black and White Values in Eighteenth Century Virginia.* Princeton, N.J.: Princeton University Press, 1989.

Spalding, Susan Eike. "Aesthetic Standards in Old Time Dancing in Southwest Virginia: African American and European American Threads." Ed.D. diss., Temple University, 1993.

———. "Frolics, Hoedowns, and Four-Handed Reels." In *Communities in Motion: Dance, Community, and Tradition in America's Southeast and Beyond*, edited by Susan Eike Spalding and Jane Harris Woodside, 11–29. Westport, Conn.: Greenwood, 1995.

Spalding, Susan Eike, and Jane Harris Woodside. *Communities in Motion: Dance, Community and Tradition in America's Southeast and Beyond.* Westport, Conn.: Greenwood. 1995.

Spurgeon, Alan L. *Waltz the Hall: The American Play Party.* Jackson: University Press of Mississippi, 2005.

Stearns, Marshall, and Jean Stearns. *Jazz Dance: The Story of American Vernacular Dance.* New York: MacMillan, 1968.

Sundell, Jon. "Rural Square Dances in East Tennessee." *Country Dance and Song*, Magazine of the Country Dance and Song Society of America 11/12 (1981): 53–64.

Swidler, Ann. "Culture in Action: Symbols and Strategies." *American Sociological Review* 51 (April 1986): 273–86.

Swift, Mary Grace. *Belles and Beaus on Their Toes: Dancing Stars in Young America.* Washington, D.C.: University Press of America, 1980.

Szwed, John F., and Morton Marks. "The Afro-American Transformation of European Set Dances and Dance Suites." *Dance Research Journal* 20 no. 1 (Summer 1988): 29–36.

Thomas, Helen, ed. *Dance in the City/The City in Dance.* New York: St. Martin's, 1997.

Thomas, Helen, and Jamilah Ahmed, eds. *Cultural Bodies: Ethnography and Theory.* Oxford: Blackwell, 2004.

Thompson, Jim. *Wagon Train: Thirty Years across the Far Blue Mountains.* Tellico Plains, Tenn.: Tellico, 1988.

Thompson, Robert Farris. "Kongo Influences on African-American Artistic Culture." In *Africanisms in American Culture*, edited by Joseph E. Holloway, 148–83. Bloomington: Indiana University Press, 1990.

Tomko, Linda. *Dancing Class: Gender, Ethnicity, and Social Divides in American Dance, 1890–1920.* Bloomington: Indiana University Press, 1999.

Turner, William H. "The Demography of Black Appalachia: Past and Present." In *Blacks in Appalachia*, edited by William H. Turner and Edward J. Cabbell, 237–61. Lexington: University of Kentucky Press, 1985.

Turner, William H., and Edward J. Cabbell, eds. *Blacks in Appalachia.* Lexington: University of Kentucky Press, 1985.

Walkowitz, Daniel J. *City Folk: English Country Dance and the Politics of the Folk in Modern America.* New York: New York University Press, 2010.

Ward, Andrew. "Dancing around Meaning (and The Meaning around Dance)." In *Dance in the City/The City in Dance*, edited by Helen Thomas, 3–20. New York: St. Martin's, 1997.

Warner, L. A. *Traditional Dances of Tennessee.* (No publisher, no date.)

Whisnant, David E. *All That Is Native and Fine: The Politics of Culture in an American Region.* Chapel Hill: University of North Carolina Press, 2009 (1983).

———. "Finding the Way Between the Old and the New: The Mountain Dance and Folk Festival and Bascom Lamar Lunsford's Work as a Citizen." *Appalachian Journal* 7, no. 1–2 (Autumn–Winter 1979–80). Reprinted in *Communities in Motion: Dance, Community, and Tradition in America's Southeast and Beyond*, edited by Susan Eike Spalding and Jane Harris Woodside, 91–109. Westport, Conn.: Greenwood, 1995.

———. *Modernizing the Mountaineer: People, Power, and Planning in Appalachia.* Knoxville: University of Tennessee Press, 1994.

Whitaker, Charlie. "Biography" for Kentucky Folklife Festival, September 15–17, 2005.

Williams, Charles H. *Cotton Needs Pickin': Characteristic Negro Folk Dances.* Norfolk, Virginia: Guide, 1928.

Williams, Michael Ann. *Staging Tradition: John Lair and Sarah Gertrude Knott.* Urbana: University of Illinois Press, 2006.

Winans, Robert B. "Black Instrumental Music Traditions in the Ex-Slave Narratives." *Black Music Research Journal* 10, no. 1 (Spring 1990): 43–53.

Winders, W. F. *The History of Kingsport: "Up the Years from the Boat Yard."* Presentation to the Rotary Club of Kingsport, April 16, 1986. Hard copy given to author, 1987.

Wolfe, Charles K. "Davy Crockett's Dance and Old Hickory's Fandango." *Devil's Box* 16, no. 3 (September 1, 1982): 34–41.

———. "Rural Black String Band Music." *Black Music Research Journal* 10, no. 1. (Spring 1990): 32–35.

———. *Tennessee Strings: The Story of Country Music in Tennessee.* Knoxville: University of Tennessee Press, 1996 (1977).

Woodford, Rex. "Hoedowning in Kentucky." *Charleston Daily Mail*, n.d., RJ.

Zwigoff, Terry. "Black Country String Bands." *American Visions* (February 1991): 50–52.

Electronic Resources Cited

Aldrich, Elizabeth. "An American Ballroom Companion: Dance Instruction Manuals ca. 1490–1920." 1988 LOC. Available at http://memory.loc.gov/ammem/dihtml/dihome.html (accessed September 23, 2011).

Aldrich, Elizabeth. "Nineteenth Century Social Dance." In "Western Social Dance." 1988 LOC. Available at http://memory.loc.gov/ammem/dihtml/diessay6.html (accessed September 23, 2011).

Berkes, Howard. "Hick-Hop: Hip-Hop Meets the Hollow. Kickin' It in Rural Kentucky with the Rap Group Kuntry Killaz." *All Things Considered*, March 27, 2004. National Public Radio. Available at http://www.npr.org/search/index.php?searchinput=kuntry+killaz (accessed September 20, 2011).

Brookes, Tim. "What Do You Get When You Cross a Banjo Picker and a Punk Rocker? A Kentucky Town That Moves to Its Own Beat." *National Geographic*, May 2004. Available at http://ngm.nationalgeographic.com/ngm/0405/feature8/index.html (accessed September 20, 2011).

Brooks, Lynn Matluck. "John Durang: Forming America Onstage." York County Heritage Trust, 2009. Available at http://johndurang.yorkheritage.org (accessed February 16, 2012).

"C. B. Caudill Store History Center." Available at http://appalshop.org/cbcaudill/index.html (accessed August 27, 2011).

Chittum, Matt. "Draped in Prosperity." *Roanoke Times*, August 17, 2002. Available at http://www.roanoke.com/roatimes/henry/henry1.html (accessed August 10, 2011).

Cowan Creek Mountain Music School. Available at http://www.cowancreekmusic.org (accessed September 7, 2011).

"Craft Revival: Shaping Western North Carolina Past and Present." Virtual Collection, WCU. Available at http://www.wcu.edu/craftrevival/people (accessed September 19, 2011). Material transcribed from Pat McNelly, *The First Forty Years: John C. Campbell Folk School*. Atlanta: McNelly-Rudd, 1966.

"Denishawn Dance Company Tour 1922–23" from the Louise Brooks Society. Available at http://www.pandorasbox.com/dance/denishawn-appearances1.html (accessed February 9, 2012).

Dunn, Donna. "To Be a Dancer: Helen McGehee's Journey from Lynchburg to Martha Graham, Julliard and Back." *Lynchburg Living*, July/August 2012. Available at http://www.lynchburgliving.com/2012/05/to-be-a-dancer-helen-mcgehees-journey-from-lynchburg-to-martha-graham-julliard-and-back (accessed August 7, 2012).

Economist, The. "Unemployment and the Mid-terms: To Help or Not to Help. The Parties Wrestle over Whether America Can Afford to Create More Jobs." Martinsville, Virginia, August 26, 2010. Available at http://www.economist.com/node/16888903 (accessed August 10, 2011).

History of Broadcasting in Kentucky Oral History Project: Radio Listening Project. Available at http://kentuckyoralhistory.org/collections/history-broadcasting-kentucky-oral-history-collection (accessed September 8, 2011).

Hoffman, Carl. "The Appalachian African American Cultural Center: Building on the Past." Appalachian Regional Commission, 2005. Available at http://www.arc.gov/magazine/articles (accessed September 12, 2012).

"In Performance at the Governor's Mansion: On the Road at the Mountain Arts Center, Prestonsburg." Kentucky Educational Television (KET). Broadcast October 1, 2000, and August 18, 2001. Available at http://www.ket.org/cgi-local (accessed August 3, 2012).

Leland, John. "At Home With/The Carter Family; High on a Hilltop with Music All Around." *New York Times*, August 8, 2002. Available at http://www.nytimes.com/2002/08/08/garden/at-home-with-the-carter-family-high-on-a-hilltop-with-music-all-around (accessed August 7, 2012).

Little Shepherd of Kingdom Come Outdoor Drama. Available at http://www.littleshepherddrama.com/press/dramawillreturn.htm (accessed September 12, 2011).

Matthews, Scott. "John Cohen in Eastern Kentucky: Documentary Expression and the Image of Roscoe Halcomb During the Folk Revival." *Southern Changes: An Interdisciplinary Journal about Regions, Places, and Cultures of the U.S. South and their Global Connections* (Emory University Libraries, August 6, 2008). Available at http://www.southernspaces.org/2008/john-cohen-eastern-kentucky-documentary-expression-and-image-roscoe-halcomb-during-folk-revival (accessed August 7, 2011).

Meyen, H. *The Ball Room Guide, Being a Compendium of the Theory, Practice, and Etiquette of Dancing*. New York: Magnus, 1852. In "An American Ballroom Companion: Dance Instruction Manuals ca. 1490–1920." Elizabeth Aldrich, 1988 LOC. Available at http://memory.loc.gov/ammem/dihtml/dihome.html (accessed June 18, 2012).

Newborg, Ruth Foxx. "Educational Radio's First Rural Radio Station: A poignant account of the WBKY experiment, 1940–41, reconstructed from the original programming materials and filed-away memories of the station's program director." *Public Telecommunication Review*, Sept.–Oct., 1979. In *History of American Broadcasting* by Jeff Miller. Available at http://jeff560.tripod.com/wbky.html (accessed September 30, 2011).

North Carolina Office of Archives and History, in association with the University of North Carolina Press. "The Way We Lived in North Carolina." Available at http://www.waywelivednc.com/gallery/1920–2001/dance.htm (accessed August 6, 2011).

Old Fiddler's Convention, Galax, Virginia: History. Available at http://oldfiddlersconvention.com/history.htm (accessed July 29, 2011).

Packer, George. "Ghost Town." *New Yorker Online* (March 15, 2010). Available at http://www.newyorker.com/online/multimedia/2010/03/15/100315 (accessed August 10, 2011).

"Ralph Case: Popular Square Dance Caller." Obituary. *Los Angeles Times*, January 12, 2001. Available at http://articles.latimes.com/2001/jan/12/local/me-11449 (accessed July 31, 2012).

"Records and Memorabilia Regarding Student Organizations and Activities 1838–1985." AR.0017 series 1, box 2, folder 109, University of Tennessee Knoxville John C. Hodges Library Special Collections. Available at http://dlc.lib.utk.edu/spc (accessed June 17, 2012).

Richard Chase Collection, AOA. Available at http://www.etsu.edu/cass/Archives/Collections (accessed September 15, 2011).

Royal Scottish Country Dance Society. Available at http://www.centralkentucky-rscds.org/History.htm (accessed August 17, 2012)

Smith, Cook T. "Horace Holley." Paper presented to the Innominate Society of Louisville, 1928. Available at http://innominatesociety.com/Articles (accessed July 12, 2012).

United States Census Bureau. Available at http://quickfacts.census.gov/qfd/states/51/5118352.html (accessed August 5, 2011).

Virginia African American Heritage Program of the Virginia Foundation for the Humanities. Available at http://www.aaheritageva.org/aahv@virginia.edu (accessed July 20, 2011).

Wolfe, Charles K. "The Lost Tradition of Black String Bands." *No Depression* 38 (March–April 2002). Available at http://nodepression.com/2002/03 (accessed August 13, 2011).

Video and Audio Resources Cited

Blue Ridge Institute. *Virginia Traditions: Non-Blues Secular Black Music.* BRI-001. Recording and Book. Ferrum, Va.: Ferrum College, 1978.

Blue Ridge Institute. *Way Out West: Video Documentary of Black Virginia String Players.* Ferrum, Va.: Ferrum College, 1978.

Cowan Creek Mountain Music School. *All Join Hands! Traditional Music for Square Dancing.* Whitesburg, Ky.: June Appal, 2005.

Fayette Area Historical Initiative. Available at http://www.visitmartinsville.com/venues/attractions/ID/42709/Fayette/Area/Historical/Initiative/African/American/Museum (accessed January 13, 2014)

Johnson, Anne Lewis, and Susan Spalding. *Step Back Cindy: Old Time Dancing in Southwest Virginia.* Video documentary. Whitesburg, Ky.: Appalshop, 1990.

McLain, Raymond, and Berea College Christmas Country Dance School. *Dances from Appalachia.* Whitesburg, Ky.: June Appal, 1976.

Seeger, Mike, and Ruth Pershing, *Talking Feet: Solo Southern Dance; Flatfoot, Buck, and Tap.* Smithsonian Center for Folklife and Cultural Heritage: Smithsonian Folkways, 1987.

Spalding, Susan Eike, and Anne Lewis Johnson. *All Join Hands: Dancing at Beechwood.* Video documentary. Produced by Appalshop for East Tennessee State University Center for Appalachian Studies and Services, 1987.

Index

SUSAN EIKE SPALDING has been dancing in the Appalachian region for almost three decades and has served as a consultant for the Smithsonian Festival of American Folklife and the Kentucky Folklife Festival. She coedited the book *Communities in Motion: Dance, Tradition, and Community*, edited the dance entries for the *Encyclopedia of Appalachia*, and coproduced two Appalshop video documentaries on old time dance. Her work has long focused on intercultural exchange and other societal factors that have helped shape Appalachian dance.

The University of Illinois Press
is a founding member of the
Association of American University Presses.

Composed in 10.5/13 Adobe Minion Pro
with ITC Usherwood display
by Lisa Connery
at the University of Illinois Press
Manufactured by Sheridan Books, Inc.

University of Illinois Press
1325 South Oak Street
Champaign, IL 61820-6903
www.press.uillinois.edu